Food and Place

A Critical Exploration

EDITED BY
Pascale Joassart-Marcelli
San Diego State University

Fernando J. Bosco
San Diego State University

ROWMAN & LITTLEFIELD
Lanham • Boulder • New York • London

Executive Editor: Susan McEachern
Assistant Editor: Rebeccah Shumaker
Senior Marketing Manager: Kim Lyons

Credits and acknowledgments for material borrowed from other sources, and reproduced with permission, appear on the appropriate page within the text.

Published by Rowman & Littlefield
A wholly owned subsidiary of The Rowman & Littlefield Publishing Group, Inc.
4501 Forbes Boulevard, Suite 200, Lanham, Maryland 20706
www.rowman.com

Unit A, Whitacre Mews, 26-34 Stannary Street, London SE11 4AB, United Kingdom

British Library Cataloguing in Publication Information Available

Library of Congress Cataloging-in-Publication Data Available

ISBN 978-1-4422-6650-6 (cloth : alk. paper)
ISBN 978-1-4422-6651-3 (pbk. : alk. paper)
ISBN 978-1-4422-6652-0 (electronic)

∞™ The paper used in this publication meets the minimum requirements of American National Standard for Information Sciences—Permanence of Paper for Printed Library Materials, ANSI/NISO Z39.48-1992.

Printed in the United States of America

Brief Contents

Contents

Textboxes and Figures

Textboxes

Figures

INTRODUCTION

CHAPTER 1

Food and Place

AN INTRODUCTION

Pascale Joassart-Marcelli and Fernando J. Bosco

Food provides some of our deepest and most multifaceted connections to place and to each other. For Yi-Fu Tuan (1977), **place** is humanized space—a blank canvas made colorful by human interactions and emotional investments. And few things are more colorful than food. This volume shows how place influences food—its taste, availability, diversity, and meaning—and food practices—the ways it is produced, distributed, and consumed. It also emphasizes how food creates place by contributing to cultural identity, economic opportunity, and social structure, suggesting a co-constitutive and dynamic relationship. Indeed, growing, cooking, and eating food are primal and vital ways in which people all over the world invest in space and give it meaning. Scraping a few dollars together to put food on the table, turning an empty lot into a garden, making a traditional cheese (see textbox 1.1), running an ethnic market in an immigrant community, patronizing a trendy restaurant that transforms an old neighborhood, waiting in line for food rations, hosting a housewarming party to celebrate a new beginning, and heating up a bowl of soup to comfort a sick child are just a few illustrations of this dynamic process of **place-making**.

Textbox 1.1. Place-Making via Cheese-Making

Place-making involves both physical and sociocultural components. It typically entails the creation, transformation, or valuation of a physical place. At the same time, it requires a collective vision and shared understanding of the meaning of that place, which manifests itself through everyday social life. Food works on both fronts simultaneously. On the one hand, farms, food-processing plants, restaurants, and food shops are important landmarks that distinguish one place from another. For instance, a farm has the potential of transforming a place by altering its natural, economic, and social environments. On the other hand, everyday food practices, including the way people grow, shop for, and eat food, also shape place and give it meaning. A significant aspect of place-making also relates to the way the physical and cultural landscape of food is understood and described by various stakeholders, including inhabitants, policymakers, and actors who may potentially benefit from particular representations.

(continued)

Textbox 1.1. *Continued*

Reblochon cheese provides a useful example to illustrate the relationship between food and place-making. Farmers in the northern French Alps region of Haute-Savoie have been making this soft, raw-milk, washed-rind cheese for centuries. In 1958, the cheese was granted "AOC" status (i.e., controlled designation of origin) by the French government, which eventually became "AOP" (i.e., protected designation of origin) under European regulations. Such status recognizes the significance of place and tradition in the manufacturing of Reblochon, and presumably strengthens the livelihood of local farming communities. Today, 520 dairy farms raise Abondance, Montbéliarde, or Tarine cows—the only breeds allowed to produce milk for Reblochon. This milk is collected and industrially processed into Reblochon "laitier" by one of twenty-two local cheese cooperatives (Syndicat Interprofessionel du Reblochon 2017). In addition, Reblochon "fermier" is still crafted traditionally on more than one hundred small farms where cheese is molded twice a day, right after the farmer milks his herd of cows. These molded cheeses are then drained, pressed, washed in a salted bath, marked with a green edible patch, and dried for a minimum of two weeks on spruce planks, requiring daily attention before being sold to residents, tourists, and cheesemongers. It is a much more labor-intensive product than the "laitier" version that is produced in an increasingly mechanized fashion.

In the summer, as the snow melts, farmers bring their herds to graze on wildflowers and grasses in high-altitude alpine pastures for a minimum of 150 days, protecting the area from wildfires and avalanches while contributing to the unique and slightly nutty flavor of the cheese. This process—in which the natural environment is embodied into the flavor and quality of the food—is described as *terroir*, a term frequently used in descriptions of cheese and wine. The social, economic, and cultural significance of Reblochon for these remote mountain communities is noticeable in the multiple celebrations and rituals marking the farming seasons.

The AOC has raised the profile of Reblochon nationally and internationally. However, increased popularity has led to changes in the Aravis and Borne valleys, where Reblochon originated and represents a major source of income. While large producers and restaurateurs are able to capitalize on the cheese's notoriety, small farmers are struggling to remain profitable. Families making Reblochon "fermier" earn between €15,000 and €20,000 per year—

Figure 1.1. Reblochon
Farmers, working with milk from a single herd of cows, mold approximately 150 cheeses per day.

a meager income for 365 long days of work (Noury and Paymal 2011). Indeed, the proportion of Reblochon "fermier"—produced on the farm according to traditional methods—has declined to less than 15 percent of total production, which is now dominated by the industrialized Reblochon "laitier." Tourism has benefited from Reblochon's notoriety, as witnessed in the popularity of farm tours, cheese festivals, and a continuously expanding array of "traditional" recipes, such as *tartiflette*, *reblochonnade*, and *croziflette* on local restaurant menus. This has been important in sustaining year-round tourism in an area where visitors traditionally came for winter sports.

Initiatives by the Reblochon industry board and local tourism agencies can also be interpreted as place-making to the extent that they create a new commodified sense of place, with both physical and sociocultural aspects, in which Reblochon is a key element. Representations of mountain villages as pristine and natural places and depictions of everyday life as traditional and simple help to market Reblochon to outsiders, but likely contrast with the experiences of farmers and other local residents, hinting at the contentious politics of place-making via food.

Figure 1.1. Reblochon (*continued*)
Despite the economic hardship experienced by small farmers, Reblochon has been used to brand the valley (top) and encourage food-based tourism, as witnessed in this new steel sculpture (bottom), erected at the entrance of the Aravis Valley to honor the *reblochon fermier*.

Source: (top) Serge Laurent: https://commons.wikimedia.org/wiki/File:Cenise2.jpg.
(bottom) Guilhem Vellut: www.flickr.com/photos/o_0/8960401000.

Food and Place in a Global World

The increasing **globalization** of food production and consumption has raised concerns over a presumed homogenization of food practices and a related eradication of place. In this volume, we seek to show that place remains extremely important in understanding our relationship to food. Globalization has transformed—and in some ways heightened—the significance of place, requiring new theoretical perspectives. As Doreen Massey (1994) and others have argued, places are defined by their interconnections with other places. In other words, places are relational; their particularities emerge and evolve out of networks of relations that stretch over space and time. So it is with food; instead of having a fixed identity, its meaning continues to change along with the social relations that underscore its production and consumption. Indeed, the globalization of food is a geographically uneven and differentiated process, producing different outcomes in different places. A relational perspective allows us to see how food connects us to others "in place" (see textbox 1.2), providing an interdisciplinary framework to explore how processes unfolding at various geographic scales—from the body to the global—create unique food experiences for people living in different

---

Textbox 1.2.   Our Breakfast Connects Us to the Rest of the World

A seemingly simple breakfast of coffee and toast with butter and fruit jam connects us to global and distant places, from the mountains of Colombia to the plains of the American Midwest, the sugarcane fields of Haiti, and the orchards of California (see figure 1.2). Our fair trade coffee presumably creates unique connections with peasants in the tropical Andes. The mass-produced butter melting on our toast draws us into the unsustainable activities of large corporate dairy farms. The industrial sugar that sweetens our cup of joe engages us in asymmetrical international trade relations shaped by colonialism. Flour, the main ingredient for our bread, is the object of complex food politics involving state intervention and corporate lobbying in Washington, DC.

Closer to home, the organic strawberry jam purchased at the neighborhood's farmers' market includes us in a growing local economy of small farmers, producers, and foodies. In many places, coffee shops and bakeries carry a special and personal meaning in the everyday life of their customers and are important cultural and symbolic elements of neighborhoods and communities. Yet, while these foods connect us to some people, they also distinguish us from others who cannot afford to participate or feel that they don't belong in this specialized segment of our local food system.

Our breakfast, which is relatively common in much of the Western world, not only connects us to place economically and politically, it also does so in intimate and intensely emotional ways. The rich aroma of coffee and the smell of toasted bread are linked to real and imagined ideas of home and feelings of comfort and belonging. The simple ritual of drinking coffee in the morning is an embodied experience that may bring up a wide range of emotions, including good or bad memories of previous experiences and lived places. Pouring a cup of coffee for a loved one also symbolizes the everyday practices of social reproduction and care that take place in homes. The connections between food and place are therefore more complex than can be shown on a map.

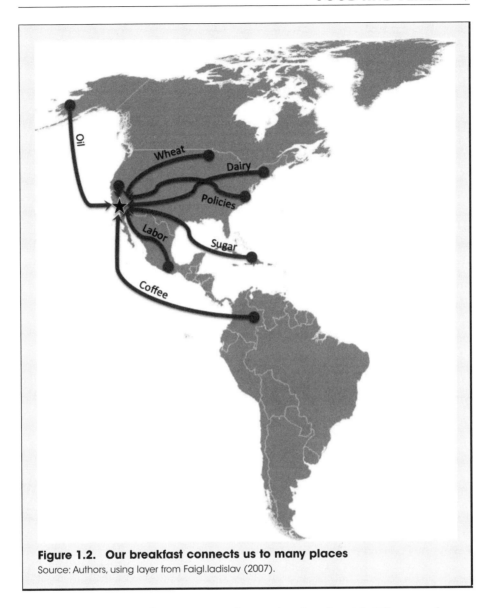

Figure 1.2.   Our breakfast connects us to many places
Source: Authors, using layer from Faigl.ladislav (2007).

places. This diversity of experiences reflects cultural and social differences that are articulated into the *body*, but is also the product of political and economic forces that shape local *food landscapes* and global *food regimes*—three important concepts developed further in chapter 2, and used to organize this volume.

A Critical Perspective

Our goal of "placing" food comes at a time when food has become a growing source of anxiety and a symbol of numerous societal problems. Approaching the study of food from a place perspective allows us to contextualize emerging concerns regarding the safety, health, equity, and sustainability of our food. Although food may contribute to place-making in rewarding, pleasurable, and sustaining ways, too often it is a major source of struggles and anxieties as witnessed in the prevalence of hunger, malnutrition, eating disorders, food scares, labor exploitation, animal abuse, and environmental degradation. These persisting concerns prompt us to adopt a **critical perspective** throughout this volume.

In the social sciences, taking a critical stand usually implies generating knowledge that informs theoretical understandings of various forms of oppression and inequality. This includes questioning the numerous biases that shape the assumptions, objects and scales of inquiry, and methods of analysis. For many, a critical approach also involves participation in efforts to challenge and resist the deleterious effects of food on bodies, subjectivities, communities, economies, and environments, as exemplified in participatory research and activist scholarship. We contend that focusing on the connections between food and places is a promising way to frame the sort of contextualized, interdisciplinary, reflexive, and transformative inquiries required to understand and challenge the current food system and to promote food *access*, *justice*, and *sovereignty*—three foundational concepts we review in chapter 2.

Food as a Geographic Fact

Many before us have argued that food is a *social fact*—a "marvelously plastic kind of collective representation" (Appadurai 1981, 494). In this book, we hope to show that food is also a *geographic fact*. While meals shape family interactions, forge relationships, reveal identities, and produce differences, they do so by connecting us to the places where the food is grown, processed, appropriated, sold, prepared, served, consumed, and discarded. Lisa Law comments that "food acquires its meaning through the place it is assembled and eaten" (2001, 275). Places like homes, neighborhoods, restaurants, grocery stores, schools, gardens, and farms profoundly influence our food experiences and practices. At the same time, our food habits impact and transform many places, often with negative consequences for society and the environment. Indeed, our meals are embedded in cultural, economic, political, social, and physical geographies that shape what, how, and where we eat. Authors in this volume view food as a *process* that differentiates people by locating them in particular places both physically/materially and culturally/discursively, as reflected in the adage "we are where we eat" (Bell and Valentine 1997). However, we also think about food as a dynamic and negotiated *project* that involves power struggles over place and everyday forms of resistance.

Structure of the Book

The primary goal of this book is to investigate how food practices—including production, distribution, preparation, and consumption—are spatially shaped, and at the same time contribute to the production of place. The following overarching questions guide the volume and individual chapters:

- How does place (constituted by its natural resources and climate, political-economy, history, culture, and social relations) influence food practices (including the way food is grown, exchanged, prepared, and eaten)?
- How do everyday food practices structure our lives and create places?
- How does food activism and resistance transform places?

We begin with a theoretical chapter that introduces key concepts and provides a framework for a rigorous and critical exploration of the complex relationships between food and place (**chapter 2**). Going from the global to the intimate, we present the concepts of food regime, food landscape, and the body, which we in turn use to organize the remaining chapters, structuring the book in three related sections.

The food regime section draws attention to the political and economic forces influencing uneven geographic patterns of food production and consumption. In **chapter 3**, Cantor, Emel, and Neo investigate global networks of production and resistance in the meat and dairy industries. Their research highlights the global spread of concentrated animal feeding operations (CAFOs) and situates their impact within global supply chains. Through case studies, they show how particular places are shaped by these global meat networks and identify opportunities and constraints related to animal rights activism. In **chapter 4**, Fitting shows how genetically modified crops have become an important technology of the global food regime and have remade Latin America's food landscape. She compares the impact of genetically modified crops on food sovereignty in Argentina, Mexico, and Colombia, and explains how place and culture influence social movements that challenge this technology. In **chapter 5**, Nelson's research connects the marginalization of immigrant farmworkers in Oregon to the contemporary global food regime and the ongoing displacement of rural livelihoods in Mexico. She shows how these global processes interact with race and unfold locally, paying particular attention to the social reproduction of racialized farmworkers in a white place. In **chapter 6**, Evans and Joassart-Marcelli investigate ethical consumerism in the context of global supply chains. Through a case study of rum labeled as sustainable, they show how ethical consumerism creates narratives that commoditize food and place and hides structural inequalities inherent to capitalist food regimes. In **chapter 7**, Ervin, Tuholske, and López-Carr situate hunger and the global food crisis in a set of political and economic relations where certain populations have become particularly vulnerable to environmental and economic shocks. They argue that hunger and malnutrition are part of the same process structured by the global food regime.

The second section focuses on foodscapes as the material and discursive environments where food acquires meaning. **Chapter 8** focuses on the role of food in transforming urban neighborhoods and relies heavily on the concept of foodscape. Joassart-Marcelli and Bosco use a number of case studies to illustrate how food and place interact to produce difference. They pay particular attention to gentrification, a process in which food plays an increasingly important role in urban change, often causing displacement and social exclusion. In **chapter 9**, Guthman takes on the obesogenic environment thesis, which claims that food landscapes cause obesity. She criticizes the major assumptions underlying this approach, arguing the need for a better understanding of the complex ways in which place influences health, including exposure to toxic chemicals that alter human metabolism and genetic expression. She also rejects narrow perspectives on the food landscape that fail to acknowledge that it is shaped by race and class relations and may impact health in ways that are not readily observable. In **chapter 10**, Warshawsky describes the rising role of food banks in providing food assistance globally and shows how this relates to neoliberal forms of urban governance. Through case studies of food banking in Chicago and Johannesburg, he illustrates the evolution of the food assistance landscape and highlights the role of the state, corporations, and civil society. In **chapter 11**, Bosco and Joassart-Marcelli focus on alternative food landscapes. Their comparative study of community gardens and farmers' markets highlights the ambivalent role of local food organizations in creating a just food system. They describe the local scale as a political-economic project that embodies contradictory goals.

In the third section, on the body, we shift our attention to the intimate and visceral qualities of food and their embodiment. This section emphasizes the ways our food choices and eating practices reflect and influence identities and subjectivities. We show how eating behaviors and attitudes toward food are shaped by spatially defined categories such as gender, class, race, and ethnicity. In **chapter 12**, Joassart-Marcelli, Salim, and Vu reject static notions of national and ethnic cuisines that reify place and difference. Instead, they acknowledge that the relationship between food, identity, and place is always in the making. While food may promote social encounters and create a sense of belonging, it may also reproduce difference as power relations shape food representations and culinary appropriation. In **chapter 13**, Hayes-Conroy and Hayes-Conroy provide a critical perspective on nutrition by showing how the material/visceral body comes to matter in the complex processes of bodily nourishment. They argue for the need to "do nutrition differently"—in ways that recognize diversity and hierarchy in claims to healthy eating and contextualize nourishment within the body, community, economic networks, and cultural landscape where it happens.

The body is a central theoretical concept in **chapter 14**, where Dempsey and Gibson describe the child's body as a scale of political intervention. They show how, in the context of fears about obesity, the child's body is increasingly subject to biopolitical modes of surveillance and control. The National School Lunch Program provides a poignant illustration. In **chapter 15**, Joassart-Marcelli and Marcelli focus on cooking as an embodied manifestation of domesticity. They show how food-preparation activities are influenced by gender roles and social expectations that are negotiated in the kitchen. They explore the tensions between cooking as a chore and a form of leisure, intersecting gender with class and race. Finally, in **chapter 16**, O'Neal and Joassart-Marcelli focus on celebrity chefs and their role in shaping attitudes toward food. They question the ability of chefs to promote a just food system by situating their activism in a broader political, social, and cultural context.

As you will discover, each chapter is centered around one or more well-defined theoretical concepts, illustrated through textboxes or case studies. Definitions of these key terms are provided in the glossary at the end of the book. Learning objectives are clearly delineated at the beginning of each chapter, and additional resources, including references to readings, websites, and films, are provided at the end. In addition, we provide "food for thought" between chapters, allowing you to "digest" the material through reflection, activities, and recipes. These are meant to get you in the community or in the kitchen to engage with food materially, not just intellectually.

Key Terms

critical perspective
food
globalization
place
place-making

References

Appadurai, Arjun. 1981. "Gastro-Politics in Hindu South Asia." *American Ethnologist* 8(3): 494–511.

Bell, David, and Gill Valentine. 1997. *Consuming Geographies: We Are Where We Eat.* New York: Routledge.

Law, Lisa. 2001. "Home Cooking: Filipino Women and Geographies of the Senses in Hong Kong." *Cultural Geographies* 8(3): 264–83.

Massey, Doreen. 1994. *Space, Place, and Gender.* Minneapolis: University of Minnesota Press.

Noury, Jean-Michel, and Carline Paymal. 2011. "Résultats Économiques des Exploitations Laitières des Alpes du Nord." Suaci Aples du Nord et CER France. www.suaci-alpes.fr/IMG/pdf/Resultats_eco_exp_laitieres__POLEM_2010_synthese_vd.pdf.

Syndicat Interprofessionnel du Reblochon. 2017. "Reblochon de Savoie." www.reblochon.fr/aop-reblochon/.

Tuan, Yi-Fu. 1977. *Space and Place: The Perspective of Experience.* Minneapolis: University of Minnesota Press.

Does Food Create Place?

What is a popular dish or common ingredient where you live? How did this dish/food become popular? What does it say about the history and identity of the place? Are there political and economic actors involved in marketing this food? To what end? Does the dish help brand the place?

We live in San Diego, where several ingredients are strongly associated with a collective sense of place, including avocados, citrus, craft beer, and sea urchin. The so-called California burrito is a dish unique to San Diego and representative of its culture; it is casual—popular with surfers and late-night crowds alike—and brings together culinary influences from both sides of the US–Mexico border that has a profound imprint on our region. Rolled in a large flour tortilla, the California burrito is distinguishable from other burritos, such as those found in San Francisco's famed Mission District or national fast-food chains, by the inclusion of french fries, which absorb the flavors of carne asada, melted cheese, and salsa. The best versions are arguably found in the many small twenty-four-hour taco shops sprinkled throughout the region, with names such as Roberto's, Rigoberto's, Filiberto's, and Alberto's. For many locals, the California burrito is a quintessential San Diegan experience, which generates pride and a sense of being home.

California Burrito

Ingredients

½ cup chopped *carne asada* meat (seasoned, thin-cut flap beef steak, grilled)
handful of french fries (preferably medium-cut)
1 large flour tortilla
3 tablespoons cheddar or Mexican cheese blend
2 tablespoons pico de gallo or fresh salsa
1 tablespoon sour cream
2 tablespoons guacamole or half avocado, sliced (optional)

Preparation

Place the hot meat and french fries at the center of a warm tortilla, top with cheese, salsa, sour cream, and avocado. Fold left and right sides, then roll tortilla tightly.

CHAPTER 2

A Place Perspective on Food
KEY CONCEPTS AND
THEORETICAL FOUNDATIONS

Pascale Joassart-Marcelli and Fernando J. Bosco

Textbox 2.1. Learning Objectives

- Consider the many ways in which food connects people and places.
- Introduce key concepts and theoretical perspectives related to place.
- Develop a framework to approach the study of food from a critical and place-based perspective.
- Draw attention to the main themes and objectives of the book.

Our primary goal in this volume is to ground the study of food in place. In recent years, as food became a growing source of social anxiety, there has been an explosion of academic and popular work on this topic. Writers like Michael Pollan, Eric Schlosser, and Barbara Kingsolver have sold millions of copies of books that describe to the general public the problems of our global industrial food system and praise the simplicity, sustainability, and fairness of earlier food practices. The success of documentaries such as *Food, Inc.*, *King Corn*, *Super Size Me*, and *Food Matters* underscores the prominence of food issues in popular culture. Meanwhile, scholars have been solidifying the relatively new field of food studies, asking a wide range of questions and developing theoretical concepts to think about food in systemic, analytically rigorous, and critical ways. Their research refines—and often challenges—popular arguments by emphasizing the particular historic, political, economic, and sociocultural contexts that shape our relationship to food and underlie food injustices. This book is inspired by this growing field of critical food studies and adopts a **place** perspective to draw attention to the embeddedness of food in its physical and social contexts. Food, we argue, must be studied "in place"—within the physical environment, social relations, economic structures, cultural practices, and political institutions that give it meaning.

This chapter provides an introduction to the theoretical concepts that inspire this volume. We begin by presenting key ideas on place, including recent work that emphasizes its relational qualities. We then turn our attention to the vast interdisciplinary body of work on food to provide an overview of important concepts and questions guiding this book, and to highlight ways in which a place perspective can contribute to a critical understanding of food in society. Moving from the global to the intimate, we focus on **food regimes**, **food landscapes**, and **bodies**—three inherently geographic concepts that help to structure this volume. In the final section, we discuss theories of **resistance** to food-related oppression and social movements associated with food justice and sovereignty.

Place

The meaning and significance of place has long been debated both in geography, where it is a foundational concept, and in other social sciences, where it competes with time as a central organizing feature of society. As geographers like to say, "Everything happens somewhere," and where things take place matters. This is certainly true of food, which must be grown, sold, prepared, and consumed in particular places, simultaneously giving food flavor and place significance. There are numerous old and new concepts linking food and place, including foodshed, food landscape, terroir, farm-to-table, food environments, community-supported agriculture, locavorism, regional cuisine, and local food systems, among others. Yet, place and food are so intimately related in popular culture that we often take this relationship for granted, and rarely explore it critically.

The relevance of place as a framework of inquiry has been threatened by the perception that **globalization** and information technologies have created a "placeless world" (Friedman 2005). Rising global mobility and interconnectedness have seemingly erased the unique characteristics of place, replacing them with homogeneity and sameness. The worldwide expansion of fast-food chains and the concomitant decline of regional cuisine provide a poignant illustration of this trend. After two decades of research on globalization, however, it has become clear that place remains relevant, although scholars recognize that the role and meaning of place in the everyday lives of people have changed and continue to evolve. This renewed attention to place owes much to the "cultural turn," which has influenced the social sciences since the early 1990s by emphasizing **difference** in people's everyday experiences as opposed to making universal and abstract claims.

Indeed, broad, global political and economic forces manifest themselves and are experienced differently across places, exacerbating geographic disparities and reinforcing the importance of place. This tension between the global and the local has animated much of the social research on food, including work on local food systems, international supply chains, alternative food networks, global food insecurity, and political ecologies of food. According to Cook et al. (2013), "Food is often researched precisely because it can help to vividly animate tensions between the small and intimate realms of embodiment, domesticity and 'ordinary affect' (Stewart 2007), and the more sweeping terrain of global political economy, sustainability, and the vitality of 'nature.'" As a theoretical concept, place allows us to contextualize the object of inquiry—in this case, food—in these interrelated local and global processes.

But what is place? According to John Agnew (1987), a geographer who has written extensively on this topic, place holds three different meanings or interrelated dimensions: location, locale, and sense of place. First, as a *location*, place is the geographic area (e.g., city, region, nation) where political and economic processes originating at larger scales unfold. This perspective is common in urban and economic studies, where researchers try to understand why certain phenomena take place in particular locations. For instance, one could ask why organic farming became an important industry in California, why GMOs are widely used in Argentina, or why certain neighborhoods lack access to supermarkets.

Second, as a *locale*, place represents the setting of everyday activities, or "the geographical context for the mediation of physical, social or economic processes" (Agnew 2011, 317). Rather than a bounded unit, place is fluid and heterogeneous. Farms, homes, grocery stores, restaurants, and neighborhoods illustrate this second type of place. This understanding dominates social and humanistic perspectives that focus on how place is constructed through social practice and how it influences social interactions. For example, scholars could investigate how community gardens promote the creation of social capital, how gendered social relations are produced in the kitchen, or how new restaurants transform urban neighborhoods.

Third, as a *sense of place*, place refers to the local structure of feeling. This meaning of place is influential in anthropology, psychology, and cultural studies, where researchers are interested in questions of identity, belonging, and emotional well-being. This third perspective also emphasizes the differences in the ways people experience place. For example, researchers could explore how refugees use food to construct a feeling of home, how farmers' markets reproduce white privilege, how school cafeterias control children's bodies, or how representations of cooking on television reinforce particular norms about gender, class, and health.

Place can be understood as existing at different **scales**, from the global to the microscopic. Scale refers to the spatial extent or reach of a process or phenomenon. While most people think of place as cities, towns, villages, or neighborhoods, a seat at the kitchen table is also a place—like Tuan's "old rocking chair by the fireplace" (1974, 245). The concept of place as a particular configuration of relations embodies multi-scalar processes (e.g., global forces and local factors). Critical perspectives on scale consider interactions between scales, do not privilege particular scales, and acknowledge that scales are social and discursive constructs devised to make sense of the world (Marston, Jones, and Woodward 2005). This is illustrated by recent work on the body—a particularly relevant scale to investigate multiple issues associated with food—in which scholars explore how capitalism, neoliberalism, and social relations of race, class, and gender become inscribed onto bodies through food. Here again, the importance of relationships and networks in constituting and shaping a particular scale stands out and begs for a relational perspective.

This volume relies on all three meanings of place, and brings together political-economic perspectives and sociocultural approaches in order to offer an interdisciplinary and comprehensive framework to analyze contemporary food issues at various scales.

Studying Food from a Place Perspective

In the past two decades, food has emerged as a serious, interdisciplinary, and respected field of study within a growing number of academic programs and publications

(Belasco 2008). The popularity of food as an academic subject is partly explained by the mounting evidence regarding the limitations of our contemporary food systems and the accompanying recognition that these shortcomings cannot be understood and addressed in disciplinary silos. Food is no longer the limited domain of housewives or the credentialed expertise of engineers, agronomists, economists, or nutritionists, who never made very good bedfellows. Instead, as Belasco (2008) explains, scholars increasingly approach food from an interdisciplinary and critical perspective, asking inconvenient and provocative questions about the food system and its impacts, including hunger, malnutrition, obesity, animal abuse, poverty, imperialism, environmental degradation, biotechnology, etc.

At a time when food was seen as trivial in the academe, the work of anthropologists and archaeologists like Mead (1943), Barthes (1961), Lévi-Strauss (1966), and Douglas (1972) was very influential in showing that food is much more than sustenance. Although there are significant differences in their arguments, generally, these scholars understood **foodways** as reflecting "attitudes" linked to cultural norms, protocols, and taboos that extend beyond the realm of food. In that sense, food is conceptualized as being structured like a system of communication or language that signifies cultural differences and social hierarchies. In other words, it is a form of cultural **representation**.

This perspective, which privileges the semantic or symbolic aspects of food, has been criticized for assuming the existence of an independent and relatively stable culture—a set of values and beliefs that are shared and internalized by members of particular groups, and reflected in their food preferences and practices. Rejecting such a static conceptualization of culture, many have argued that food production and consumption are influenced by ecological, demographic, technological, and political-economic factors, which shape food habits (Harris 1987). Therefore, foodways cannot be attributed to a rigid culture defined as inherited beliefs and values. Instead, they are constitutive of a culture conceptualized more dynamically as ways of seeing and being in the world.

This distinction illustrates a significant and larger debate about the meaning of **culture** that has had a profound impact on the way we conceptualize place and think about food. Since the late 1990s, scholars have argued against the idea that culture is "represented" in text, art, landscape, or behavior, and instead have advocated for a nonrepresentational perspective, which emphasizes practices, experiences, and feelings. This theoretical approach changes how we think about place, primarily because of the way it stresses affective relationships between humans and things (Thrift 2008). Similarly, it has important ramifications for the study of foodways, because it challenges the idea that food represents a priori social structures, values, and/or identities. If we are to take the criticism of representational perspectives seriously, we ought to consider how food does more than reveal or express identities and differences; rather, it produces and transforms them through performances of ordinary acts like picking fruits, shopping at the market, frying fish, or serving a loved one. Place becomes a central element in shaping and therefore understanding foodways. Place is no longer just a "container" where food-related human and nonhuman interactions occur; it is constitutive of and shaped by these ordinary acts.

For example, geographers have studied how gardens and urban green spaces provide the setting for everyday encounters between plants, trees, and people. These affective experiences of seeing, but also touching, smelling, and hearing, give these places particular meaning. In their study of urban foraging, Poe, LeCompte, McLain, and Hurley (2014) show how urban nature areas are "always places in the making, where identities, histories, struggles, and hopes of human and more-than-human converge." This view aligns with relational understandings of place that were introduced in the previous section and inform this volume.

Thinking about food and place relationally requires that we think about food in a systemic way that attends to its historic, political, economic, sociocultural, and scientific aspects. The idea of a **food system** has become a particularly salient framework with which to approach the study of food (Belasco 2008). LaBianca (1991, 222) defines a food system as "a dynamic and complex unity consisting of all the purposive, patterned (institutionalized), and interdependent symbolic and instrumental activities carried out by people in order to procure, process, distribute, store, prepare, consume, metabolize, and waste food." Although useful in highlighting the multiple components of food-provisioning activities and their interconnectedness, this framework tends to be under-theorized and lacks spatial specificity. For instance, it is popular among food industry experts who use it to describe the transformation of specific inputs into particular food outputs in a rather mechanical way, without consideration of the political, cultural, and social factors shaping it.

Within the broad field of critical food studies, food is typically understood as a political and economic system of production and consumption, as well as a cultural symbol and an everyday experience. These themes reflect different theoretical approaches to food that parallel distinctions in the ways geographers, humanists, and social scientists have approached place. While political economy has had a profound influence on how we think about food production and place, attention to culture has generated richer and more-nuanced perspectives.

Below, we introduce three concepts that have become important in critical food studies and reflect different orientations toward food and place. Borrowing the scalar structure of Bell and Valentine's (1987) influential book on geographies of food consumption, we introduce these concepts by beginning at the global scale, with food regime, moving to the regional and local, with food landscapes, and concluding with bodies. These three concepts help to organize this volume into three broad parts.

FOOD REGIME

The social organization of food production and distribution has evolved over time and across **space**. Hunter-gatherers acquired food in very different ways than people do today in a highly globalized world economy. The concept of food regime is useful in understanding these differences by drawing attention to the social, political, and economic arrangements that underlie the production and distribution of food on a world scale (McMichael 2009).

Harriet Friedmann (1982) began writing about food regimes in the 1980s at a time when the world economy seemed to be undergoing rapid globalization and restructuring. She argued that the corporate and global food regime emerging at that time needed to be understood as a product of historical processes of capital accumulation and state regulation. Scholars (Friedmann 1993; Friedmann and McMichael 1989; McMichael 2009) typically distinguish between three global food regimes: the colonial food regime (1870–1930s), the developmentalist food regime (1950s–1970s), and the corporate neoliberal food regime (1980s–today). These regimes evolve in a cyclical and nonlinear fashion as a result of inherent crises and contradictions that prompt expansion into new regions, change in the organization of production, and realignment of hegemonic power.

The *colonial food regime* was based on a plantation model in which European colonial powers imposed the monoculture of exotic commodities like sugar, cocoa, and tea in their territories in Asia, Africa, Latin America, and the Caribbean (see figure 2.1). European food staples like flour and preserved food were traded in exchange for these

Figure 2.1. Colonial food regime
In most colonies, plantation-style farms were established to produce exotic food commodities to be exported. This picture of a pineapple plantation was taken in 1895 in Malvern, in the British colony of Natal, which today remains one of the most important fruit-producing regions in South Africa.
Source: Forsyth, J. 1895. *The Colony of Natal: An Official Illustrated Handbook and Railway Guide.* London: Causton and Sons.

crops, creating a relation of dependency in which colonized regions compromised their local food system and ecological resources to support the growing demand for exotic commodities in the metropoles. Sugar and similar crops generated large profit for the trading companies and played a key role in promoting industrialization in England and Northern Europe, where refineries and factories were built to process these commodities with the capital accumulated through trade (Mintz 1986).

As countries began gaining independence, this model was replaced by the *developmentalist food regime* in which the United States became the leading power controlling food production in postcolonial nations. Friedmann (1993) attributes this post–World War II realignment to two related US initiatives: agricultural subsidies and food aid. In the 1930s, during the Great Depression, the US government established a farm-subsidy program that led to the accumulation of grain surplus in an effort to support farmers and keep prices high. That surplus eventually became the basis of a massive food aid program distributed to war-devastated European nations via the Marshall Plan and to newly independent countries of the Global South via the "Food for Peace" program. In that context, food became a geopolitical weapon to control allies in the Cold War and create markets for US food and agricultural technology. Although this rested on a developmentalist logic in which poor countries would eventually industrialize, it led to the formation of a new agricultural division of labor organized along international supply chains. Despite the end of colonialism, the postcolonial food regime continued to be shaped by imperialism, albeit in less-formal and transparent ways.

The *corporate and neoliberal food regime* emerged out of the deep recession and related oil and debt crisis of the 1970s and 1980s. Faced with rising oil and wheat prices, Third World countries began defaulting on the loans they had received from the International Monetary Fund and other international organizations. A new set of policies was put in place as conditions for restructuring debt reimbursement. This became known as the Washington Consensus because it reflected the dominant ideology of **neoliberalism** that was shared by major actors based in the US capital, including the International Monetary Fund, the World Bank, and the US Treasury Department. The primary purpose of these policies was to expand the role of markets in indebted countries by forcing them to privatize national assets, liberalize trade, eliminate subsidies, reduce government spending, deregulate the economy, and devaluate their currency. As a result, Global South economies expanded their agricultural exports to maximize cash revenues, while inviting transnational corporations to purchase devalued and privatized assets and flood local markets with foreign goods. These neoliberal policies had devastating effects on local and subsistence food. For example, in Mexico, rural livelihoods have been decimated by a series of structural adjustment programs linked to the 1980s debt crisis and the North American Free Trade Agreement (NAFTA). Corporate export-oriented agriculture has led to the displacement of peasants, who have lost access to communal lands and joined the flow of migrants engaged in casual labor at the periphery of large cities or further north to the United States (Echánove 2005; Pechlaner and Otero 2010).

It is in this historical context of increased transnational integration of agro-food capital and commodity markets that we must situate the current global food system and the immense resentment it has generated. Today, food regime theory remains powerful despite warranted criticism that its metanarrative fails to acknowledge the diversity of local arrangements, by emphasizing the global scale, privileging production over consumption, and attending to political-economic factors over sociocultural ones. Indeed, recent studies have broadened their focus beyond regime theory to consider a variety of so-called agrarian questions related to the differentiated and contested process of food globalization, including the emergence of global supermarkets and retailers, the ecological impacts of food production, the global nutritional crisis, and mounting efforts to challenge the world food order and reclaim food sovereignty (Goodman and Watts 1997; McMichael 2009; Inglis and Gimlin 2009). Focusing on particular places within food regimes provides a promising approach to build on this framework and connect global and local processes.

FOOD LANDSCAPE

The idea of food landscape (or **foodscape**) has emerged as another critical concept in studying food in society. It draws attention to the places where people grow food, purchase food, prepare food, discuss food, or gather information about food (Johnston and Baumann 2009; MacKendrick 2014). The concept of **landscape** is closely related to place. Often associated with art and depictions of natural topography and built environment, the idea of landscape emphasizes the way we see and represent the world. Literally interpreted as "shaped land," it draws attention to the dynamic relationships between human activity and natural environment. Geographers have long been fascinated by rural as well as urban landscapes, which have been transformed by cultural practices and relations of production, including those associated with food production, distribution, and consumption. As Cresswell (2015, 17) points out, landscape is a visual concept that implies a viewer who is looking from the outside. In contrast, places are lived and sensed from the inside. This distinction stresses the ways places are interpreted and represented in landscapes. Perspective and interpretation are crucial aspects of landscapes; they do not look the same from every angle of vision (Appadurai 1990; Cosgrove 1998). Similarly, the concept of food landscape is mindful of the ways in which food is represented and experienced spatially. In other words, a food landscape is both material and discursive; it includes stores, restaurants, farms, and kitchens, but also advertising, cookbooks, magazines, television shows, and other media—the multiple places where food acquires meaning. Like a text or a map, a foodscape can be read or interpreted to discern cultural meaning and social form.

The concept of food landscape has been particularly useful in understanding both rural and urban food environments and their relationship to consumption culture, class, and difference (see figure 2.2). For some, the term foodscape describes the spatial distribution of food in particular settings (Cummins and Macintyre 2002; Lake, Burgoine, Greenhalgh, Stamp, and Tyrrell 2010). This type of research draws attention to spatial differences in access to healthy, fresh, affordable, and culturally appropriate food as an explanation for health disparities. In particular, the food desert metaphor has been used extensively (and often problematically) to describe food landscapes where healthy food is lacking.

Figure 2.2. Urban foodscape
Street markets, like this one in Tel Aviv, Israel, are among the most common urban
foodscapes around the world. In some countries, street markets are places where
low-income people shop for food, but in other countries, like in the United States,
street markets are increasingly sites of entertainment where elite consumers browse
through gourmet and exotic food.
Source: Jorge Láscar (2012), Camel Market. Flickr: www.flickr.com/photos/jlascar/9870050066.

For others, including several authors represented in this volume, food landscape
is a broader concept describing the "social construction that captures and constitutes
cultural ideals of how food relates to specific places, people and food systems" (Johnston, Biro, and MacKendrick 2009, 512). For example, the marketing of organic
food often employs romanticized place-based images of community, nature, farming,
family, and rural life. Similarly, alternative food movements like Slow Food also rely
on these discursive constructs linking good food to particular places (Gaytán 2004;
Wilk 2006). In urban contexts, the idea of food landscape has been used to study the
cultural economy of food and its relationship to urban change (Long 2010; Zukin
2010). Here, too, food is deeply intertwined with place. For instance, food plays a
particularly important role in branding sites of consumption, defining ethnic neighborhoods, stigmatizing poor communities, gentrifying formerly neglected areas, and
promoting tourism to new destinations. These **geographical imaginaries** of rural or
urban food landscapes—the unconscious or unreflective images we have of specific
places—fetishize both food and the places where it is produced and consumed, thereby
obfuscating ecological imprints, corporate relations, and sociocultural hierarchies.

Unlike food regimes, which focus on the global political and economic structure
of production, foodscapes tend to emphasize food consumption and its embeddedness in localized social and cultural relations. Yet, both concepts are related. For many

observers, the corporate global food regime discussed above has eroded the intimate food-place connection underlying the concept of foodscape. This argument is illustrated in the term "placeless foodscape" (Morgan et al. 2006), which reflects the flat ontology of the global, industrial, capitalist, and neoliberal food regime discussed above. For instance, chicken is no longer a rare treat purchased from a specialty shop or a local farm for a special Sunday roast. Instead, it comes packaged in cellophane from an abstract and decontextualized factory "somewhere" in the Global South where more than 500,000 chickens are processed every day (Coles 2016). Under these conditions, as we discuss in the next section, reconnecting food production to specific places becomes a way to challenge agro-capitalism.

BODIES

During the past decade, the body has emerged as a powerful analytical category to study food. After all, it is the place—or perhaps, more accurately, the scale—where food is ingested and metabolized. Unlike medical experts and nutritionists who study the physiological impacts of food in the body, scholars in critical food studies have begun considering the body as materially and discursively shaped by place. The concept of **embodiment** specifically draws attention to the ways in which food and place are inscribed onto bodies. And if we agree that place is relational, then we must acknowledge the multiple social and emotional relations that produce different bodies.

There are two broad areas of research where critical thinking about the body has been very fruitful. The first relates to the emotional geographies of eating. Several authors have used the term **visceral** to describe the affective relationships between food, place, and bodies (Hayes-Conroy and Hayes-Conroy 2013; Longhurst and Johnston 2012). These scholars often build on work by Probyn (2000) that shows how bodies and spatiality are intertwined through emotions like greed, pleasure, disgust, fear, and shame. Eating connects our bodies to others in immediate, elemental, and visceral ways. These relations are experienced most intensely at the "gut level." For Probyn (2000, 14),

> "Food goes in, and then, broken down, it comes out of the body, and every time this happens our bodies are affected. While in this usual course of things we may not dwell upon this process, that basic ingestion forces to think of our bodies as complex assemblages connected to a wide range of other assemblages. In eating, the diverse nature of where and how different parts of our selves attach to different aspects of the social comes to the fore and becomes the stuff of reflection."

For example, Longhurst, Johnston, and Ho (2009) show that for migrant women in Hamilton (New Zealand), cooking is a form of "sensory engagement with the material and discursive environments" (334) in which they may feel like outsiders. These mundane activities work viscerally to create a sense of belonging while staying connected to home. Hayes-Conroy and Martin (2009) suggest that these bodily sensations also form the basis of food activism and mobilization in food movements.

Figure 2.3. Foodways and difference
The durian is considered a delicacy in most of Southeast Asia (this photo was taken in Davao, Philippines), where it is sold by street vendors and prepared in a variety of dishes. Yet many Westerners describe the fruit's smell as pungent and repulsive, suggesting that taste is socially constructed, playing a role in revealing and creating difference.
Source: Shankar, S. (2013). Flickr: www.flickr.com/photos/shankaronline/ 9103752509.

However, while food may help us express who we are, and who we want to be, it may also discriminate and marginalize. Certain ingredients, cuisines, and food practices may be associated with particular groups and used to portray them as different and inferior. There is a large literature emphasizing this process of **othering** in relation to ethnic and exotic food. The disgust and affective reactions that certain "foreign" tastes and smells may inspire are part of this process of othering. For example, from a Westerner's perspective, the pungent smell of spices, dried fish, and exotic fruits like durian (see figure 2.3) serve to essentialize and racialize people from South and Southeast Asia by devaluing their foodways (Lai 2008).

This observation brings us to the second relevant area of research involving food and the body, which relates to **body politics**, especially as it surrounds issues of **race** and difference, as well as fatness and corpulence. Guthman's work has been particularly influential in showing that biological differences in bodies are caused by structural inequalities, including classism and racism, which are embedded in public policies driven by **capitalism** and neoliberalism (Guthman 2011). In that sense, she brings food regime theory into research on the body. She describes a multidirectional process in which fat bodies are stigmatized and devalued in ways that reproduce and exacerbate class and race difference, while at the same time these differences underlie variations in exposure to endocrine-disrupting chemicals that ultimately transform the ecologies of bodies and increase the risk of death (Guthman 2012, 2014). In other words, class and race are simultaneously inscribed discursively *on* bodies and incorporated materially *in* those same bodies. This type of research provides a corrective to traditional understanding of obesity and food-related illnesses that attribute those to individual behavior, and "fail to appreciate that bodies cannot be plucked from the spaces that constitute them" (Longhurst 2005, 247).

Taken together, the concepts of food regime, food landscape, and the body provide a theoretical framework in which to critically explore the multi-scalar relationships between food and place while attending to consumption and production, the local and the global, the political-economic and the cultural, and the material and the symbolic.

Spatial Justice, Food Resistance, and Activism

In addition to generating a better understanding of the social structures and processes underlying the production, consumption, and distribution of food, recent scholarship has focused on changing the food system and resisting its various forms of oppression and inequality. For many influential scholars such as Lefebvre (1972), Harvey (1973), and Soja (2010), space and place are intimately related to social justice and injustice since they influence who is included, who belongs, who has access to resources, and who benefits from these opportunities. As Soja (2009, 4) argues, "combining the terms spatial and justice opens up a range of new possibilities for social and political action." **Spatial justice** requires a reorganization and reenvisioning of space to promote equal access to opportunities, foster participation in decision-making, and encourage different ways of being in space. This thinking relates to "politics of place" in which place is seen as a site of tension, contestation, and resistance. This sort of critical thinking fruitfully intersects with work on food justice by questioning how the spatial organization of our food system generates economic inequality, health disparities, social oppression, and uneven environmental burdens. It also points to the role of places like school, homes, community gardens, and farmers' markets as sites of resistance within the global food system.

Praxis and reflexivity are both important aspects of a critical approach to the study of food and place. Indeed, many researchers are involved in projects that seek to change the food system and engaged in reflection over these practical experiences to identify promising ways to promote food security, food justice, or food sovereignty. Given the importance of these three ideas in critical food studies and in the chapters included in this volume, it may be worthwhile to briefly define and contrast these goals.

Food security typically refers to having access to nutritious, safe, affordable, and culturally appropriate food (World Food Summit 1996). **Food justice** has become a very common term that is often used loosely and inconsistently. Generally, it implies that material resources and power are shared equitably so that people and communities can meet their food needs and lead secure, food-based livelihoods with dignity now and into the future (Allen 2010, 297). Therefore, in addition to having basic food needs met, food justice also requires access to equal opportunity, freedom from oppression and exploitation, and environmental sustainability.

Lastly, **food sovereignty** is often defined by relying on the Declaration of Nyéléni (Nyéléni Food Sovereignty Forum 2007), which was signed in Mali by more than five hundred representatives of landless peasants, indigenous people, urban farmers, and fishing communities, mostly from the Global South. For them, "food sovereignty is the right of peoples to healthy and culturally appropriate food produced through ecologically sound and sustainable methods, and their right to define their own food and agriculture systems." As such, it privileges local economies and the needs of those involved in growing food. It decidedly takes on the current corporate and trade food regime as the major force undermining food sovereignty. It fights against "imperialism, neoliberalism, neocolonialism and patriarchy, [. . . and their] agents [. . . ,] including international financial institutions, the World Trade Organization, free trade agreements, transnational corporations, and governments that are antagonistic to their people" (Nyéléni Food Sovereignty Forum 2007). These goals inform very different politics, with food sovereignty motivating much more radical interventions than the usually more-benign forms of assistance driven by food security objectives.

Over the past decade, a number of individuals, communities, and organizations have mobilized around food, leading some observers to announce a food revolution, heralding the emergence of an **alternative food system** and the pending demise of the corporate industrial food regime. Yet, upon closer observation, it is clear that the alternative food movement is far from being unified, and that there are indeed many different ways that people can challenge and resist the contemporary food system. To some, this may include purchasing ethical products—food labeled as fairly traded, organic, or sustainable. To others, it might entail participating in a localized food economy—shopping at the farmers' market and participating in community-supported agriculture. It may also involve doing things differently at home—growing food, reducing waste, and being mindful of the gender inequalities associated with the preparation of food.

To many, including several authors in this volume, these types of activism are not enough to promote food justice. In some cases, these individualized or localized choices even reproduce or exacerbate inequalities, as when a new community garden brings about gentrification, or when efforts to improve the local food environment lead to the stigmatization of people and places. What is required for food justice is a structural transformation of the capitalist food system that would enable people to control how food enters their lives, whether as producers or consumers. Without attending to the political and economic structures and the cultural hierarchies that divide people by class, race, gender, and other differences, people's agency within the food system will remain constrained. For these reasons, as noted above, organizations working toward food sovereignty tend to adopt anticapitalist, anti-imperialist, and anti-patriarchal agendas. These radical approaches to food activism, however, have the danger of discouraging smaller acts of dissent and resistance. Although it is important to understand how persistent social inequalities may curtail the effects of collective action, we must also acknowledge the transformative potential of spontaneous, small-scale, and grassroots initiatives.

Research on social movements and activism has emphasized the importance of place in influencing the aspirations, mobilizations, practices, and successes of social action (Bosco 2001). For example, occupying a place and making a cultural, legal, or economic claim to it is often a key aspect of social movements. Similarly, as noted above, changing spatial arrangements to improve access to resources is also a key aspect of spatial justice (Soja 2010). At the same time, the ability to connect horizontally to other actors engaged in similar struggles or vertically to different levels of power is decisive. Place and networks are particularly relevant in the realm of food justice, where food and place are so intimately linked yet connected to broader geographies. The chapters in this volume all address in different ways the roles of place and networks in changing our relationships to food and promoting food justice.

Key Terms

alternative food system
body
body politics
capitalism
culture
difference
embodiment
food justice
food landscape/foodscape
food regime
food security
food sovereignty
food system
foodways

geographical imaginaries
globalization
landscape
neoliberalism
othering
place
race
representation
resistance
scale
space
spatial justice
visceral

Summary

- Studying food from a place perspective draws attention to the embeddedness of food and its dynamic relationship to the physical environment, social relations, economic structures, cultural practices, and political institutions.
- Place has multiple and debated meanings as a location, a locale, and a sense of place. It is constituted by numerous intersecting relations unfolding at a variety of scales, from the global to the body.
- The study of food has become a respected, relevant, and interdisciplinary field, partly motivated by discontentment with the contemporary food system. It rests on a number of key concepts, such as food system, foodways, food regime, food landscape, and the body, which all have connections to theoretical understandings of place.
- A critical perspective on food and place requires that we question the spatial organization of our food production and consumption and its relationships to economic inequality, health disparities, social oppression, and environmental burdens. It also involves praxis and reflexivity toward the creation of food justice and sovereignty.

References

Agnew, John A. 1987. *Place and Politics: The Geographical Mediation of State and Society.* Boston: Allen and Unwin.

———. 2011. "Space and Place." In *The Sage Handbook of Geographical Knowledge*, edited by John A. Agnew and David N. Livingstone, 316–30. Los Angeles: Sage.

Allen, Patricia. 2010. "Realizing Justice in Local Food Systems." *Cambridge Journal of Regions, Economy and Society* 3(2): 295–308.

Appadurai, Arjun. 1981. "Gastro-Politics in Hindu South Asia." *American Ethnologist* 8(3): 494–511.

———. 1990. "Disjuncture and Difference in the Global Cultural Economy." *Theory, Culture and Society* 7: 295–310.

Barthes, Roland. 1961. "Pour une Psycho-Sociologie de l'Alimentation Contemporaine." In *Annales. Économies, Sociétés, Civilisations* 16(5): 977–86.

Belasco, Warren. 2008. *Food: The Key Concepts.* New York: Berg.

Bell, David, and Gill Valentine, eds. 1997. *Consuming Geographies: We Are Where We Eat.* New York: Routledge.

Bosco, Fernando J. 2001. "Place, Space, Networks and the Sustainability of Collective Action: The Madres de Plaza de Mayo." *Global Networks* 1(4): 307–29.

Coles, Ben. 2016. "The Shocking Materialities and Temporalities of Agri-Capitalism." *Gastronomica: The Journal of Food and Culture* 16(3): 5–14.

Cook, Ian, Peter Jackson, Allison Hayes-Conroy, Sebastian Abrahamsson, Rebecca Sandover, Mimi Sheller, Heike Henderson, Lucius Hallett, Shoko Imai, Damian Maye, and Ann Hill. 2013. "Food's Cultural Geographies: Texture, Creativity and Publics." In *The Wiley-Blackwell Companion to Cultural Geography*, edited by Nuala C. Johnson, Richard H. Schein, and Jamie Winders, 343–54. Oxford: Wiley-Blackwell.

Cosgrove, Dennis E. 1998. *Social Formation and Symbolic Landscape.* Madison: University of Wisconsin Press.

Cresswell, Tim. 2015. *Place: An Introduction.* 2nd ed. Malden: Wiley.

Cummins, Steve, and Sally Macintyre. 2002. "A Systematic Study of an Urban Foodscape: The Price and Availability of Food in Greater Glasgow." *Urban Studies* 39(11): 2115–30.

Douglas, Mary. 1972. "Deciphering a Meal." *Daedalus* 101: 61–81.

Echánove, Flavia. 2005. "Globalisation and Restructuring in Rural Mexico: The Case of Fruit Growers." *Tijdschrift voor Economische en Sociale Geografie* 96(1): 15–30.

Friedman, Thomas L. 2005. *The World Is Flat: A Brief History of the Twenty-First Century.* New York: Farrar, Straus and Giroux.

Friedmann, Harriet. 1982. "The Political Economy of Food: The Rise and Fall of the Postwar International Food Order." *American Journal of Sociology* 88: S248-S286.

———. 1993. "The Political Economy of Food: A Global Crisis." *New Left Review* 197: 29–57.

Friedmann, Harriet, and Philip McMichael. 1989. "Agriculture and the State System: The Rise and Decline of National Agricultures, 1870 to the Present." *Sociologia Ruralis* 29(2): 93–117.

Gaytán, Marie S. 2004. "Globalizing Resistance: Slow Food and New Local Imaginaries." *Food, Culture & Society* 7(2): 97–116.

Goodman, David, and Michael Watts (Eds.). 1997. *Globalising Food: Agrarian Questions and Global Restructuring.* London: Routledge.

Guthman, Julie. 2011. *Weighing In: Obesity, Food Justice, and the Limits of Capitalism.* Berkeley: University of California Press.

———. 2012. "Opening up the Black Box of the Body in Geographical Obesity Research: Toward a Critical Political Ecology of Fat." *Annals of the Association of American Geographers* 102(5): 951–57.

———. 2014. "Doing Justice to Bodies? Reflections on Food Justice, Race, and Biology." *Antipode* 46(5): 1153–71.

Harris, Marvin. 1987. "Foodways: Historical Overview and Theoretical Prolegomenon." In *Food and Evolution: Toward a Theory of Human Food Habits*, edited by Marvin Harris and Eric B. Ross, 57–90. Philadelphia: Temple University Press.

Harvey, David. 1973. *Social Justice and the City*. London: Edward Arnold.

Hayes-Conroy, Allison, and Deborah G. Martin. 2010. "Mobilising Bodies: Visceral Identification in the Slow Food Movement." *Transactions of the Institute of British Geographers* 35(2): 269–81.

Hayes-Conroy, Jessica, and Allison Hayes-Conroy. 2013. "Veggies and Visceralities: A Political Ecology of Food and Feeling." *Emotion, Space and Society* 6: 81–90.

Hinrichs, Clare. 2015. "Fixing Food with Ideas of 'Local' and 'Place.'" *Journal of Environmental Studies and Sciences* 6(4): 759–64.

Inglis, David, and Debra Gimlin. 2009. *The Globalization of Food*. New York: Berg.

Johnston, Josée, and Shyon Baumann. 2009. *Foodies: Democracy and Distinction in the Gourmet Foodscape*. New York: Routledge.

Johnston, Josée, Andrew Biro, and Norah MacKendrick. 2009. "Lost in the Supermarket: The Corporate Organic Foodscape and the Struggle for Food Democracy." *Antipode* 41(3): 509–32.

Johnston, Josée, Alexandra Rodney, and Michelle Szabo. 2012. "Place, Ethics, and Everyday Eating: A Tale of Two Neighbourhoods." *Sociology* 46(6): 1091–1108.

LaBianca, Øystein S. 1991. "Food Systems Research: An Overview and a Case Study from Madaba Plains, Jordan." *Food and Foodways* 4(3–4): 221–35.

Lai, Paul. 2008. "Stinky Bodies: Mythological Futures and the Olfactory Sense in Larissa Lai's 'Salt Fish Girl.'" *Melus* 33(4): 167–87.

Lake, Amelia A., Thomas Burgoine, Fiona Greenhalgh, Elaine Stamp, and Rachel Tyrrell. 2010. "The Foodscape: Classification and Field Validation of Secondary Data Sources." *Health & Place* 16(4): 666–73.

Lefebvre, Henri. 1972. *Le Droit à la Ville*. Paris: Anthropos.

Lévi-Strauss, Claude. 1966. *The Raw and the Cooked*. Penguin.

Long, Lucy M. 2010. "Culinary Tourism in and the Emergence of Appalachian Cuisine: Exploring the 'Foodscape' of Asheville, NC." *North Carolina Folklore Journal* 57(1): 4–19.

Longhurst, Robyn. 2005. "Fat Bodies: Developing Geographical Research Agendas." *Progress in Human Geography* 29(3): 247–59.

Longhurst, Robyn, and Lynda Johnston. 2012. "Embodied Geographies of Food, Belonging and Hope in Multicultural Hamilton, Aotearoa New Zealand." *Geoforum* 43: 325–31.

Longhurst, Robyn, Lynda Johnston, and Elsie Ho. 2009. "A Visceral Approach: Cooking 'at Home' with Migrant Women in Hamilton, New Zealand." *Transactions of the Institute of British Geographers* 34(3): 333–45.

MacKendrick, Nora. 2014. "Foodscape." *Contexts* 13(3): 16–18.

Marston, Sallie A., John Paul Jones III, and Keith Woodward. 2005. "Human Geography Without Scale." *Transactions of the Institute of British Geographers* 30: 416–32.

Massey, Doreen. 2005. *For Space*. Los Angeles: Sage Publications.

McMichael, Philip, ed. 1994. *The Global Restructuring of Agro-Food Systems*. Ithaca: Cornell University Press.

———. 2009. "A Food Regime Analysis of the 'World Food Crisis.'" *Agriculture and Human Values* 26(4): 281–95.

Mead, Margaret. 1943. "The Factor of Food Habits." *The Annals of the American Academy of Political and Social Science* 225: 136–41.

Mintz, Sidney. 1986. *Sweetness and Power: The Place of Sugar in Modern History*. New York: Vintage.

Morgan, Kevin, Terry Marsden, and Jonathan Murdoch, eds. 2006. *Worlds of Food: Place, Power and Provenance in the Food Chain*. Oxford: Oxford University Press.

Nyéléni Food Sovereignty Forum. 2007. *Declaration of Nyéléni*. https://nyeleni.org/spip.php?article290.

Pechlaner, Gabriela, and Gerardo Otero. 2010. "The Neoliberal Food Regime: Neoregulation and the New Division of Labor in North America." *Rural Sociology* 75(2): 179–208.

Poe, Melissa R., Joyce LeCompte, Rebecca McLain, and Patrick Hurley. 2014. "Urban Foraging and the Relational Ecologies of Belonging." *Social and Cultural Geography* 15(8): 901–19.

Probyn, Esther. 2000. *Carnal Appetites: FoodSexIdentities*. London: Routledge.

Slocum, Rachel. 2013. "Race in the Study of Food." In *Geographies of Race and Food: Fields, Bodies, Markets*, edited by Rachel Slocum and Arun Saldanha, 25–60. Farnham: Ashgate.

Soja, Ed. 2009. "The City and Spatial Justice." *Spatial Justice* (1): 1–5.

———. 2010. *Seeking Spatial Justice*. Minneapolis: University of Minnesota Press.

Thrift, Nigel. 2008. *Non-Representational Theory: Space, Politics, Affect*. London: Routledge.

Tuan, Yi-Fu. 1974. "Space and Place: Humanistic Perspective." *Progress in Human Geography* 6: 211–52.

Wilk, Richard, ed. 2006. *Fast Food / Slow Food: The Cultural Economy of the Global Food System*. Walnut Creek, CA: Altamira Press.

World Food Summit. 1996. *Rome Declaration on World Food Security*.

Zukin, Sharon. 2010. *Naked City: The Death and Life of Authentic Urban Places*. Oxford: Oxford University Press.

Where Does Your Breakfast Come From?

What did you eat for breakfast this morning? How did you decide what to eat? Was your choice motivated by convenience, affordability, health, or other factors? Make a list of all the key ingredients in your breakfast and identify their geographic origin. Consider the multiple actors that have been involved in making this meal available to you.

For example, you might have eaten granola today. It has long been considered a healthy breakfast and snack. Made popular by "hippies" and "health freaks" in the 1960s, it has now become a common staple on supermarket aisles throughout the Western world. Even fast-food restaurants serve granola in an effort to revamp their image. As a dish made of several different ingredients, it illustrates the many relationships embodied in food. It raises questions about where our food comes from, how it is produced, and by whom. It also prompts us to think about what healthy food means, and how we construct those notions by emphasizing certain qualities, like nutritional content or organic farming, while ignoring other less-obvious aspects, such as environmental impacts, labor issues, and geopolitics.

The recipe below outlines a simple method to make granola. You can make many different versions, however, by adding a number of optional ingredients in various combinations (e.g., almonds, orange zest, cardamom, and apricots; pecan, cherries, flax, and cocoa nibs; walnuts, raisins, and cinnamon).

Granola

Ingredients

3 cups old-fashioned rolled oats
⅓ cup raw nuts, such as almonds, pecans, pistachios, hazelnuts, or walnuts
½ cup sweetener, such as maple syrup, honey, or agave syrup
¼ cup oil, such as canola or coconut
1 teaspoon salt

Optional ingredients

2 tablespoons quinoa or wheat germ
1 cup seeds, such as pumpkin, sunflower, flax, or sesame
1 cup unsweetened coconut flakes
1 cup dried fruits, such as cranberries, raisins, cherries, blueberries or chopped apricots,
    figs, pineapple or mango
2 tablespoons orange zest
1 teaspoon cinnamon, cardamom, or ginger
¼ cup cocoa nibs

Preparation

Preheat oven to 300 degrees Fahrenheit. Mix grains, nuts, seeds, salt, zest, and spices in a large bowl. Add sweetener and oil. Mix well and spread the mixture on a large baking sheet. Bake for 30 to 45 minutes, stirring after 20 minutes, and then every 10 minutes. Be vigilant at the end, as the granola could easily burn, and keep in mind that it will not become crunchy until it cools off. Add the dried fruits and cocoa nibs as soon as you take it out of the oven, and let the granola cool off completely. Store in an airtight container. Eat with milk, yogurt, fresh fruit, or by itself.

PART I

FOOD REGIMES

CHAPTER 3

Networks of Global Production and Resistance

MEAT, DAIRY, AND PLACE

Alida Cantor, Jody Emel, and Harvey Neo

Textbox 3.1. Learning Objectives

- Explore territorialized networks and social, environmental, and political impacts of meat production and consumption.
- Trace flows of materials and nodes of activity that comprise complex global meat production networks.
- Critically consider cultural, ethical, and animal welfare dimensions of meat production and consumption.

"Meat Is Horrible!" announced the headline of a recent *Washington Post* editorial. Meat production and consumption is spreading globally, more than tripling over the past fifty years (see figure 3.1). Today, over sixty billion animals per year are slaughtered globally, and domesticated animals for food have become 97 percent of the nonhuman, non-plant biomass on the planet (Emel and Neo 2015). This "meatification" of diets is a relatively recent phenomenon (Weis 2013) which carries significant environmental impacts, including production of greenhouse gases and other pollutants, as well as negative impacts on land and water resources (see textbox 3.2). No wonder the United Nations International Resource Panel, comprising thirty-four scientists and thirty governments, recently recommended a "meat tax" to reduce production and demand for meat (Vaughan 2016).

Meat production can be either extensive or intensive. An **extensive production system**—for example, chickens pecking in the yard, cattle or goats foraging, or pigs rooting for food in the forest—requires few inputs other than pasture, grazing land, or other food sources, such as waste from human food systems. **Intensive production systems** involve high concentrations of animals in small spaces, with feed transported in and waste transported out. These concentrations purportedly allow for efficient production and economies of scale, but they also create significant problems for the animals and the environment. Intensive systems are spreading rapidly throughout the world, and the production of animal products—dairy, eggs, and meat—is considered ripe for foreign direct investment (Schneider 2014). The global

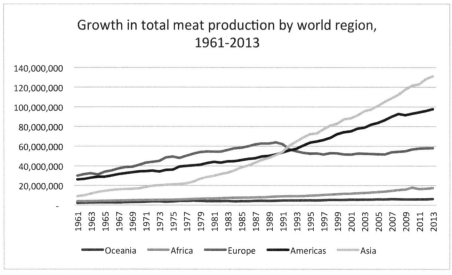

Figure 3.1. Growth in total meat production by world region, 1961–2013
Source: Authors, based on data from FAOSTAT (2016).

"land grab" (the acquisition of large pieces of land by transnational corporations and governments, mostly in the Global South) is largely centered on obtaining land to produce grains, forage, and other feeds for animal production.

Studying food from a **place** perspective allows us to not only see how certain **commodity chains** or networks impact specific places; it also allows us to examine the infrastructures supporting commodities produced in a place. As Evans and Joassart-Marcelli show in chapter 6, commodity networks are built on economic, political, social, and cultural relations that unfold at various scales, both globally and locally, within particular nodes. This approach is useful to consider social, environmental, and animal-welfare impacts of those systems in specific places, as well as the politics and networks of resistance against impacts that are viewed negatively. The concept of **networks of resistance** highlights how activism against particular modes of production and consumption of meat has increasingly relied on ideas that circulate globally (e.g., "Meatless Monday" has been replicated in dozens of cities around the world), as well as enrolling transnational political actors and allies to specific local causes (e.g., the consumption of dog meat in China, discussed later in this chapter). Finally, we can

---

Textbox 3.2. Environmental Impacts of Livestock Production

- Livestock production uses one-third of the world's freshwater and one-third of available cropland (Herrero et al. 2013).
- Livestock produce 18 percent of global greenhouse gas emissions—more than transportation (Steinfeld et al. 2006).
- Industrial livestock production is responsible for localized environmental justice issues, including air and water pollution from nitrogen compounds, heavy metals, E. coli, and more.
- Livestock expansion causes biodiversity reduction and extinction (Steinfeld et al. 2006).

examine differences between places in terms of impacts and politics. In this chapter we focus on several dimensions of the myriad contradictions of the growing global production and consumption of animal products, including the territorialized impacts of livestock commodity networks and the cultural and moral foment around dog eating, along with the complex political movements and resistance accompanying each of these practices. We consider how these networks produce, and are produced by, place.

Place, Scale, and Networks of Meat Consumption and Resistance

Globally, the production of meat has increased dramatically over recent decades. However, meat and dairy consumption are geographically uneven, and the variance in demand for meat globally is significant. For instance, among the top three most popular meats in the world (beef, poultry, and pork), only poultry is embraced consistently by meat eaters, with substantive portions of the globe eschewing beef and pork for religious and cultural reasons. Similarly, other types of meat, like goat, are popular among meat eaters in specific regions and places such as Africa and South Asia. Consumption of even less conventional meats such as rat meat and dog meat are confined to pockets of places across the world. Dairy products have traditionally been consumed and produced at relatively high levels in South Asia (India and Pakistan), Europe, and North America. Demand for dairy is increasing rapidly in all areas, however, as populations increase and diets are homogenized through retailers and advertising. For example, drinking milk imports into China increased from 15,000 tons in 2010 to 195,000 tons in 2013 (Euromonitor International 2016). Figure 3.2 shows the growth of total

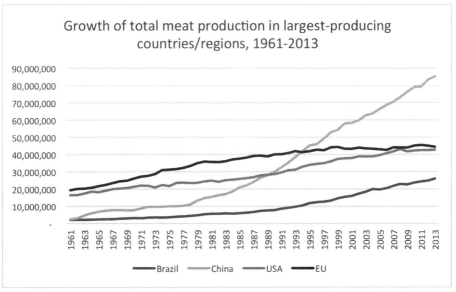

Figure 3.2. Growth of total meat production in largest-producing countries/ regions, 1961–2013
Source: Authors, based on data from FAOSTAT (2016).

meat production over the past fifty years for the world's largest-producing countries/regions: Brazil, China, the United States, and the European Union. While meat production has leveled off in the EU, the rapid growth of meat production particularly in China is apparent.

Just as meat and dairy producers rely upon complex networks to promote the consumption of meat globally, **resistance** to meat and dairy consumption benefits from global networks. Resistance to modern processes of meat consumption and production has grown over time. Some individuals and organizations advocate for meat production systems that are more environmentally friendly and/or that make provisions for animal welfare, such as raising animals on pasture (grass-fed), raising animals according to organic standards, and/or giving animals more space to roam freely (free-range). Certification systems have been developed in an attempt to provide third-party verification of these claims. These systems include legally defined certification standards, such as the organic standards established by the US Department of Agriculture in 2002, as well as independent programs developed by nonprofit organizations, such as the Humane Farm Animal Care's "Certified Humane Raised and Handled" program, developed in 1998.

Others eschew the consumption of meat altogether, advocating vegetarianism or veganism (see textbox 3.3). The first group to agitate for the nonconsumption of meat—"The British and Foreign Society for the Promotion of Humanity and Abstinence from Animal Food" (the precursor for the United Kingdom's "Vegetarian Society")—was formed in 1843. An Englishman coined the word *vegan* in 1944 when he cofounded the first vegan society. The American Vegan Society was founded in the 1960s and linked to the concept of *ahimsa*, a Buddhist, Jainist, and Hindu concept of "noninjury" and compassion. The rise of industrial dairies and accompanying education by animal welfare and animal rights groups has pushed veganism into the mainstream in Europe and North America. With meat consumption becoming more prevalent across the world, this movement has become increasingly global. Additional international organizations, such as the International Vegetarian Union (IVU), formed in 1908, have been created to strategize and share knowledge about how to moderate the demand for meat. The IVU holds an annual world congress—most recently held in Dresden (Germany), Jakarta (Indonesia), and Brasilia (Brazil)—to promote vegetarianism and veganism.

Textbox 3.3. Vegetarianism and Veganism

For some people, vegetarianism (not eating meat) or veganism (not eating or using any animal products, such as dairy, eggs, or honey, in addition to meat) is a choice motivated by an individual's desire to maintain a healthy lifestyle. Others pursue meat-free or animal-free diets as a form of social movement, motivated by concern for animal rights and/or environmental sustainability. Vegetarianism is not always an all-or-nothing proposition; for example, the recent "Meatless Monday" initiative attempts to reduce meat consumption (for both health and environmental reasons) by encouraging those who do eat meat to go vegetarian for one day every week.

Spread of CAFOs and Globalized Livestock Production Networks

Concentrated animal feeding operations, or **CAFOs**, bring together large numbers of animals in small areas. From their origination in the United States, CAFOs have spread to every continent but Antarctica. Populations of cattle, pigs, goats, and sheep increased 23 percent between 1980 and 2010, and 80 percent of this growth in the livestock sector has come in the form of CAFOs (World Watch Institute 2016). China has the largest dairy farm in the world, with 40,000 cows. The cows are entirely housed indoors, their only exposure to the outside world via sometimes-open walls (as in most poultry and pig confinement systems). Al Safi in Saudi Arabia hosts 37,000 cows, while the largest dairy in the United States houses 30,000 cows. China and Russia are planning a dairy CAFO to top them all—one that will house 100,000 cows. This CAFO dairy will primarily serve Russia, which has cut trade with European Union and US agricultural partners. Russia will use 284,000 acres to grow feed for the multibillion-dollar operation (Blackmore 2015).

Industrial meat and dairy production are growing rapidly, and their supply chains are highly globalized. Countries and companies are buying land for feed, pasture, and water rights, as well as slaughtering and processing facilities and distribution systems. For example, a Chinese billionaire bought Australia's biggest dairy company in 2015. Smithfield Foods, a US company that is the world's largest pork producer, was acquired by a Chinese government–backed company for nearly $5 billion in 2013. A Brazilian company, JBS, bought out Swift and Co. and Smithfield beef businesses and is now the biggest beef meatpacker (and slaughterer) in the United States, and the world. JBS also owns feedlots in the United States and Canada. American-held Tyson Foods is still the biggest meat and poultry producer in the United States, just slightly ahead of JBS in sales as of 2015.

Some countries outsource food supplies while others are exporting. In particular, portions of industrial meat and dairy production networks are outsourced by China, Japan, and some countries of the Middle East, which have elected to import much of their livestock and feed from other countries (Schneider 2014). Not only are supply and consumption networks governed by environmental, welfare, and economic institutions and norms, but they are also subject to food security and geopolitical concerns; for example, China's purchasing of Smithfield Foods was deemed something of a security issue by the US Congress, and hearings were held to determine whether or not to let the purchase go forward. Outsourcing the production of meat, dairy, and animal feed means that social and environmental costs of production, such as poor treatment of workers or intensive use of water resources, are borne disproportionately by the producing regions rather than the consumers.

In the section that follows, we detail two contrasting case studies of meat consumption and production in two diverse locations: the United States and China. While the meat in question (beef and dog) for the two case studies could not be more different, the centrality of place and networks and how they intersect with politics, culture, and history is apparent in both cases.

Case 1: The Water-Alfalfa-Dairy Cow-Feedlot-Meat Production Network in Imperial Valley, California

California's Imperial Valley, located just north of the US–Mexico border (see figure 3.3), is one of the most productive agricultural areas in the United States. The Imperial Valley is one of the primary sites of Cesar Chavez's farmworker movement, and one of the most policed border crossings. It is also home to one of the largest irrigation canals in the world, and the source of over half of the United States' winter vegetables. It is a desert, once inhabited sparsely by the Cahuilla and other Native American groups, and still home to a number of small reservations. The area was colonized first by the Spanish and then by the United States.

Despite the long, eleven-month frost-free growing season, rainfall in the Imperial Valley is only two to three inches per year, not nearly enough to grow crops. Early in the twentieth century, the Imperial Valley's developers imported water from the Colo-

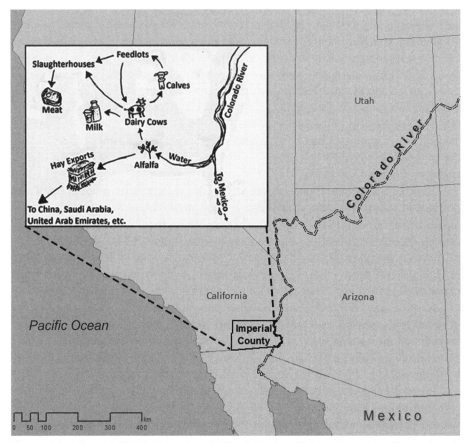

Figure 3.3. Imperial Valley's water-alfalfa-dairy-feedlot-meat production network
Source: Authors.

rado River, which travels through seven states before entering Mexico, where it once fed into the Gulf of California. They developed the region with distant capital and advertised it as prime farmland. The Imperial Irrigation District, which holds one of the oldest and largest water rights on the Colorado River, receives nearly three-quarters of California's allocation, almost 20 percent of all Colorado River allocations, and twice as much water as Mexico.

The Imperial Valley has put these water rights to work in order to become the largest alfalfa-growing region in the world (UCCE 2010). Alfalfa is a legume that is high in protein, more so than many other forage sources. It is used as a feed crop for livestock, especially lactating dairy cows. High-producing milk cows, bred and engineered to produce five to six times as much milk as their forebears, have problems eating enough to keep up with the energy output it takes to produce so much milk. These cows live only two to four years compared with the twelve to thirteen years they could live if they were not pushed to reproduce so often and to yield so much milk. Alfalfa uses large quantities of water, and is grown in great quantities in some of the driest places on the planet (like the Imperial Valley), where it must be irrigated. Alfalfa is California's single largest agricultural water user, with seasonal applications ranging from 4 to 5.5 million acre-feet per year. (In comparison, total annual urban and industrial use of water in California is about 9 million acre-feet.)

Recent drought has brought the Imperial Valley's water-use practices under scrutiny. In particular, the region has been criticized for using a large portion of the Colorado River's water flow to irrigate alfalfa and hay for shipment around the globe. While about two-thirds of the alfalfa and other hay crops grown in the Imperial Valley support the dairies of southern and central California, the remaining third is shipped from California's Long Beach port to Mexico, China, Japan, Taiwan, the United Arab Emirates, and South Korea (see Jervey 2014). These countries (except for Mexico) either forbid or do not concede land to grow forage for livestock production, choosing instead to buy it from farms in California, Arizona, and other Western US states. For example, a Saudi Arabian company, Fondomonte, purchased 1,800 acres of land in California near Blythe, and Fondomonte's parent company, Almarai, purchased 10,000 acres fifty miles away in Arizona. These land purchases are for growing forage that Saudi Arabia forbids growing at home in order to feed its expanding dairy industry. Al Dahra ACX, the number-one exporter of forage from the United States in 2015, is a United Arab Emirates company that operates alfalfa farms in Imperial Valley and buys hay from eleven Western US states.

China is now the biggest buyer of US alfalfa, second only to the UAE as the world's top importer. Dairy consumption has increased in recent decades in China as the Western diet became more popular due to rising incomes and marketing. Because of shipping networks, logistics, and trade patterns, it is cheaper to ship alfalfa from the Imperial Valley to China than it is to ship the same load to California dairies just a few hundred miles to the north (Pierson 2014). For every two shipping containers that come into Long Beach, one goes back empty. This trade imbalance has lowered the cost of shipping to China and made possible the "disarticulation of production into component parts that can be stretched out and rearranged in more complex configurations" (Cowen 2014, 103).

The Imperial Valley's system of alfalfa production for export raises questions for some observers. The Colorado River is a stressed and over-allocated river system; in most years the river does not even reach its terminus at the Gulf of Mexico because so many users are drawing from the river. Should this extremely valuable water, part of one of the most disrupted ecological systems, be used to irrigate water-intensive alfalfa for other countries that do not want to use their own land and water for it? Is it ethical to use valuable water to irrigate alfalfa for industrial dairies anywhere? Is it racist to give special scrutiny to Chinese and Middle Eastern ownership of land, water, and animals within US borders? And should people far removed from nodes of production be deciding what goes on in those places?

DYNAMIC COMMODITY NETWORKS: ETHICS AND ECONOMICS IN THE DAIRY PRODUCTION NETWORK

Commodity production networks represent the relations between producers in the construction of a final product and its distribution to the consumer (see also chapter 6 for a discussion of global commodity chains). Networks of production are located in specific places, and also connect far-flung places together (Rocheleau and Roth 2007). These geographically located networks can be represented by nodes of activity and flows of product (Coe and Yeung 2015). A dairy commodity network may be local or transnational. Traditionally, dairies were located close to urban areas in order to keep the milk and other dairy products fresh (Friedberg 2009; DuPuis 2002), but today's dairy production networks stretch much further—particularly when we look beyond the milk itself and consider the flow of milk products (like cheese and yogurt) and animals throughout the production network.

Not all contemporary dairies are scenic, small-scale, family farms. The dairy sector is California's most lucrative agricultural industry. Most of California's dairies are drylot: The cows are kept in relatively small enclosures and fed with feed from the Imperial Valley, the Corn Belt, or more local farms. Replacement calves (about half the female cows) from these drylots are separated from their mothers almost immediately and are shipped out to operations of up to nine thousand head in Idaho and Utah. These female calves will, if they survive, end up back in Southern California dairies. The remaining female calves and all of the males are raised by calf ranches and purchased by feedlots where they are "finished" (grown to a marketable weight) for slaughter.

In 1980, Imperial Valley was home to more than half the livestock feedlot activity in the state of California. Beef cattle herds moved into the region as early as the 1880s, with concentrated feeding operations beginning in the 1940s. By the 1980s, the farmers and ranchers of the area developed a niche feeding dairy calves, called "junk steers," which were considered lesser beef. The warm weather allowed for longer feeding of lighter calves. With ample sources of forage and water, this was a successful venture, especially with the presence of a local slaughterhouse. Cattle ranked as the number-one product by value in Imperial County in 2014, with alfalfa the second-largest earner.

Commodity production networks can be disrupted by the disappearance of an important node, however. The Imperial Valley network was disrupted when the local Brawley, California, slaughterhouse, owned and operated by National Beef, was closed in 2015. The causes for the closure were both multinational and local. When the Brazilian company JBS bought the 130,000 head–capacity McElhaney Feedyard in Wellton, Arizona, the Arizona cattle that had been coming to Brawley for slaughter were instead routed to JBS's slaughterhouse in Tolleson, Arizona. The Brawley slaughterhouse closure resulted in the transport of Imperial Valley cattle 225 miles east to the Tolleson plant and elsewhere for slaughter, raising costs and lowering animal welfare. The closure of the slaughterhouse, a central node in the Imperial Valley production network, impacted the local economy as well as the production network. It meant not only the loss of 1,300 jobs, augmenting already-high levels of unemployment among mostly Latino/a workers, but also the moving of cattle feeding to other parts of California, or out of state, to Texas or Kansas (Artsy 2014).

Commodity production networks encompass ethical issues as well as economic issues. Because dairy cows are so used up after a few short years of constant reproduction and high levels of milk giving, they are often lame or sick when they get shipped to slaughter. At least two of the dairy-cow slaughterhouses linked to the Imperial Valley agricultural network and other Southern California dairy sites have been investigated, undercover, by various animal welfare groups. These groups have filmed the abuse of sick and "downed" cows, illustrating the use of high-pressure hoses forced into their mouths, electric prods, and even forklifts to get them up and walking. Since the mad cow disease scare of 2003 (caused by feeding cows to cows), US federal law required animals to be able to walk at least until Food and Drug Administration inspection—though they could collapse afterward and still be slaughtered. Employees of the plants were filmed kicking cows, letting cows trample each other, dragging cows with chains, allowing cows still alive to move through the de-hiding stations, and having as many as five bolt gunshots to the head before finally achieving unconsciousness.

At the most notorious plant, Hallmark/Westland in Chino, California, two employees were arrested and sentenced. One of the two was an undocumented immigrant who ended up being deported. Both claimed the owner knew of the ongoing situation, but the owner was not charged. The owners of the Hallmark/Westland slaughterhouse were later sued for fraud by the US Department of Justice because much of their meat went to the federal school lunch program and the company was not compliant with the federal slaughter laws. It was the first-ever federal government fraud case for abuse of animals. The plant is now owned by another company and is still slaughtering cows. Some legal changes did result: Following the Chino plant abuse and meat recall, the Obama administration stipulated that no "downed" cows could be slaughtered, even if they were able to stand at inspection.

This case of networked and territorially embedded alfalfa-dairy-meat production illustrates the shifting dynamics of networks and products, both geographically and in terms of **governance** (including law, ownership, norms, and protest groups). It also raises complex ethical questions. The closure of an inhumane slaughterhouse (assuming any are humane) means that workers are disadvantaged and cows must be transported farther, resulting in more stress and injury. Consumer-led approaches (e.g., consumer boycotts of genetically modified foodstuffs, or consumers choosing to buy fair trade–labeled coffee) and corporate social responsibility (companies demonstrating their social and environmental awareness by, for example, purchasing only cage-free eggs) are the most traditional ways of addressing social and environmental issues in global production networks (Hughes et al. 2008). These methods are difficult to implement in the case of global meat and dairy production systems, which involve long and complicated supply chains. Any sort of governance of production networks is generally the result of long and difficult campaigns by nonprofit and other political groups. And it is actually a reduction in overall meat and dairy consumption that is necessary, not just changes in production practices. Does the responsibility lie with the consumer, or elsewhere? How should questions of food security, animal welfare, labor rights, and immigration be addressed?

Case 2: Dog Meat Consumption in Yulin

Compared with beef and dairy, the consumption and production of dog meat is minuscule. Nonetheless, dog meat is still consumed by segments of populations in countries such as China (Kerr and Yu 2015), Vietnam (Avieli 2011), Korea (Czajkowski 2014), Indonesia (Parker 1991), and even Switzerland (Hall 2013). In China, dog consumption has a long history dating back to the Zhou Dynasty, more than three thousand years ago. Then, it was a form of meat enjoyed by all segments of society. Today, it is a fringe consumption practice found only in selected places in northeastern and southwestern China.

The town of Yulin is located in the southwestern province of Guangxi in China. The province has a significant number of ethnic minorities, with the Zhuang minority comprising more than 30 percent of its overall population of 47.5 million. While dog consumption is not unheard of in Guangxi, since the late 2000s it has coalesced into a summer festival of sorts, which culminates in a ten-day "canine culinary culture" event, where an estimated 10,000 to 15,000 dogs are slaughtered. By any standards, such an event would attract global media attention (not unlike the annual slaughter of dolphins in Taiji, Japan) because of the way an unconventional meat is made the object of conspicuous consumption. The debate over the Yulin Dog Meat Festival engages with the concepts of place, culture, and ethics in several ways.

First, local organizers and participants of the festival argue that dog consumption has always been a practice in their culture. Hence, to disrupt and deny this practice smacks of **cultural imperialism**. Such cultural imperialism in effect denigrates other cultures for no defensible reason. However, opponents argue that cultural imperative does not excuse cruel practices, and charge that the slaughter of dogs constitutes undue cruelty and suffering to the animals. They further argue that many of the dogs destined for slaughter are actually captured from other places, many of them lost or stolen pets. In terms of the actual slaughtering of the animals, opponents of the festival have charged that many dogs are beaten before being killed, as it is thought this helps to tenderize the meat.

In response, others have argued that the consumption of dog and the ways the animals are slaughtered and processed is no less cruel than the methods used to produce more-conventional meat in CAFOs (as detailed earlier in this chapter). In that sense, a political commentator writes that it is hypocritical to condemn dog meat consumption while excusing the consumption of other meat forms:

> Others might have been motivated by the pictures of dogs crammed to-
> gether in cages. This is indeed cruel, but this is how animals are abused in
> many parts of the world. If you don't like how the Chinese treat their dogs,
> then protest against their pork and chicken farming, too. Remember also
> that in westernized industrial farming, animals are often kept in similar
> conditions all their lives, not just on market day. (Baggini 2016)

The objection to dog consumption is arguably strongest if it focuses on the cruel aspects of its production, as well as any hint of illegality in which dogs are sourced. Conversely, it becomes weaker when the objection is centered on how "dogs are humans' best friends," as such an argument is ineffective in places like South Korea, where dog farms specifically breed a particular kind of dog (called *nureongi*, or "yellow dog"), destined for the dinner plate and seldom kept as pets (Podberscek 2009). Indeed, the idea of strong bonds between humans and their pet dogs is hardly a universal one, and is a product of a specific cultural and historical context. In that sense, many Koreans believe that consuming dogs is no different from consuming other forms of meat.

Indeed, for places such as Korea and Yulin, place identity is critical in understanding the politics of dog consumption. While opponents of the practice tend to stereotype entire populations as dog eaters, the fact is that even in Yulin, not all residents consume dogs. This leads to two interesting reactions. First, locals who do not partake in the festival feel aggrieved that their town has been maligned as a town of dog eaters. Second, the deep politicization of the festival actually results in unintended consequences. As an employee of a dog meat restaurant explains, "In the past, at best 50 percent of Yulin residents consume dog. But now with increasing media attention, more people actually start to consume it" (Phoenix Web 2016).

Elsewhere, there have been similar cases where intense opposition toward livestock farming has actually valorized place and ethnic identity. Such recourse can happen largely because food consumption practices are often culturally inflected. Hence, objections toward ways in which a particular food (such as meat) is produced and consumed are often taken to be a cultural affront by consumers. For instance, activism against factory farms in the United States is sometimes taken as an assault on the American way of life, resulting in consumers actually consuming even more meat as an act of cultural symbolism (Willard 2002). In Malaysia, a country where consumption of pork is forbidden by the majority of the population, who are Muslim, Chinese pig farmers have banded together in the face of increased discrimination over their farming practices (Neo 2012). While the opposition toward pig farming in Malaysia stems from local Muslim elites, in the case of Yulin, opposition comes from both near and far-flung places.

DYNAMIC POLITICAL NETWORKS OF RESISTANCE

A simple keyword search of "Yulin" on YouTube will throw up numerous videos aimed at rousing opposition toward the festival. Countless animal rights organizations and individuals have documented and led the fight against the Yulin festival. For some, such as the Animal Hope and Wellness Foundation, enlisting Hollywood stars like Matt Damon and Pamela Anderson to their cause is common practice.

The politics against the Yulin festival stretch across space, both physical and virtual. The festival has attracted online attention as well as physical protests at Chinese embassies around the world (Snowdon 2015). The hashtag #StopYulinForever has, since August 2015, generated thousands of tweets and retweets on Twitter. The range of opposition to the festival is such that activists from different places come together (often virtually), sometimes in unity, other times acting on their own to save the Yulin dogs. Individuals have been known to visit the festival to buy live dogs to avert their imminent fate. The persistent circulation of cruel images, slogans, and acts of saving the dogs is what keeps the outrage current.

However, not all activist groups subscribe to these tactics of shaming and rescuing, attesting to the dynamism of politics in opposing the festival. For example, several local Chinese groups, including Animals Asia Foundation and China Small Animal Protection Association, refused to stage protests or purchase dogs for rescue because they believed that any form of publicity would only attract more consumers from the town, as well as from surrounding areas. They also believed that purchasing dogs would only encourage more dogs to be led to the festival, where sellers hope they will be bought off, leading to the formation of a dog trade (Lin 2016).

Despite the regular protests, the festival has continued, albeit with the central government explicitly distancing itself from it. In 2016, the Chinese foreign spokesperson stated that city officials in Yulin have never supported nor organized the Yulin Dog Meat Festival (Dongwang News 2016). Clearly, the fight against the festival requires a nuanced understanding of place, along with a politicized network that draws in local Chinese activists as well as government officials. Enrolling the support of locals is essential if supporters of the festival continue to see opposition as stemming from faraway places and people who do not "understand" the local culture.

Conclusion

Why do people who know that farm animals are oppressed and violated not change their behavior? Mitchell (2011) argues that they are morally disengaged. In both of our examples, such disengagement has resulted in a business-as-usual state of affairs that does not disrupt conventional practices. Moreover, both of the cases described in this chapter involve networks of consumption and resistance that stretch across considerable distances. Distance makes for a disjointed politics of governance, but media can go some length toward more evenly distributing knowledge of faraway places and practices.

In the case of the cattle industry, consumers are morally disengaged because significant and fundamental changes seem challenging in the face of complex global commodity networks. This is especially true when demand for beef and dairy are likely to remain high in the foreseeable future. The long supply chain involved in beef and dairy production means that a change in governance would require a networking of activism across distant places.

In the second case, activist networks across places exist, but a different approach to politicizing and opposing the Yulin festival might yield better and more-sustained results. For example, the strengthening and enforcement of local animal welfare laws could disrupt the organizing of the festival in material ways. Opposition to the Yulin festival highlights the two kinds of politics: "symbolic" and "information" politics. In the case of the Yulin Dog Meat Festival, resistance has always leaned slightly toward symbolic politics, where visceral images and stories of dogs destined to be slaughtered are propagated through social media. Yet, information politics is crucial when explaining how the Yulin Festival has come to be seen as a cultural-historical event, when in reality, that is not the case. Drawing on both kinds of politics would provide the necessary justification to enact appropriate laws.

This chapter emphasizes the important issues of environmental and animal welfare that are tied to meat consumption. In recognition of these concerns, some argue that meat can be ethically consumed by using lower-input extensive production systems rather than intensive production systems. However, while intensive animal production systems magnify animal welfare problems, extensively raising animals—which might improve their welfare—requires more land. Others argue that meat and dairy consumption should be avoided altogether. Both those who advocate for extensive animal production systems and those who advocate to reduce or eliminate meat and dairy consumption typically agree that the problem is one of too much reliance on animal products, especially in wealthier countries where per capita consumption of animal products is higher. If meat and dairy consumption continue to increase, then greenhouse gas emissions, water use, and land use for feed provision will increase as well. The only real solution is to decrease dependency upon animal products.

This chapter also shows that the ethics of eating, including cultural differences around animal consumption practices, are a knobby terrain: A careful and reflective analysis is required to avoid the pitfalls of stereotyping and racism. A sensitivity to place, place identities, and networks of production and consumption will go a long way toward developing sustained and effective solutions for the betterment of meat animals—be they common, like cows, or unconventional, like dogs.

Key Terms

CAFO
commodity chain / commodity
    production network
cultural imperialism
extensive production system

governance
intensive production system
networks of resistance
place
resistance

Summary

- The production and consumption of meat varies widely around the world. Rising global demand for meat and animal products has significant environmental, economic, and social impacts.
- Meat commodity production networks are geographically located in particular places and territories that are connected by flows of materials. These commodity production networks are dynamic and can be disrupted when a node or flow changes.

- Meat production and consumption raises complicated questions around ethics, culture, and animal welfare that have sparked local and global networks of resistance.

Additional Resources

Several nonfiction books address environmental, health, and other ethical issues related to eating animals, including Foer (2009), Schlosser (2001), and Joy (2010). The novel *My Year of Meats* by Ruth Ozeki (1998) is also useful in raising similar questions regarding meat eating.

Food Inc. (2008) and the SAMSARA food sequence (2011), available at https://vimeo.com/73234721, are thought-provoking documentaries.

The Meatless Monday website (www.meatlessmonday.com) provides practical information on reducing meat consumption.

References

Artsy, Avishay. 2014. "Imperial Valley Slaughterhouse Closure Worries Locals." KCRW (National Public Radio member broadcasting from Santa Monica College), April 1. http://curious.kcrw.com/2014/04/imperial-valley-slaughterhouse-closure-worries-locals.

Avieli, Nir. 2011. "Dog Meat Politics in a Vietnamese Town." *Ethnology* 50(1): 59–78.

Baggini, Julian. 2016. "China Dog Meat Festival: Is it Really So Bad to Eat Dog?" CNN, June 20. Accessed July 25, 2016. http://edition.cnn.com/2016/06/19/opinions/china-dog-meat-festival-hypocrisy.

Blackmore, Wiley. 2015. "The World's Largest Dairy Farm Will Be Home to 100,000 Cows." *Takepart*, July 9. www.takepart.com/article/2015/07/09/world-largest-dairy-farm.

Coe, Neil M., and Henry Wai-Chung Yeung. 2015. *Global Production Networks: Theorizing Economic Development in an Interconnected World.* Oxford: Oxford University Press.

Cowen, Deborah. 2014. *The Deadly Life of Logistics: Mapping Violence in Global Trade.* Minneapolis: University of Minnesota Press.

Czajkowski, Claire. 2014. "Dog Meat Trade in South Korea: A Report on the Current State of the Trade and Efforts to Eliminate It." *Animal Law* 29: 30–64.

Dongwang News. 2016. "Foreign Ministry: The Government Does Not Support Yulin Festival." http://hk.on.cc/cn/bkn/cnt/news/20160621/bkncn-20160621231757605-0621_05011_001.html.

DuPuis, E. Melanie. 2002. *Nature's Perfect Food: How Milk Became America's Drink.* New York: New York University Press.

Emel, Jody, and Harvey Neo. 2015. *Political Ecologies of Meat.* London and New York: Routledge.

Euromonitor International. 2016. "Dairy in China." www.euromonitor.com/dairy-in-china/report.

FAOSTAT. 2016. Food and Agricultural Organization of the United Nations Statistics Division. http://faostat3.fao.org/home/E.

Foer, Jonathan Safran. 2010. *Eating Animals.* London: Penguin UK.

Friedberg, Susanne. 2009. *Fresh: A Perishable History.* Cambridge, MA: Belknap Press of Harvard University Press.

Hall, Allan. 2013. "Farmers in Switzerland Routinely Eating Cats and Dogs with Their Meals." *UK Daily Mail*, March 18. www.dailymail.co.uk/news/article-2255684/Farmers-Switzerland-routinely-EATING-cats-dogs-meals.html.

Herrero, Mario, Petr Havlík, Hugo Valin, An Notenbaert, Mariana C. Rufino, Philip K. Thornton, Michael Blümmel, Franz Weiss, Delia Grace, and Michael Obersteiner. 2013. "Biomass

Use, Production, Feed Efficiencies, and Greenhouse Gas Emissions from Global Livestock Systems." *Proceedings of the National Academy of Sciences* 110(52): 20888–93.

Hughes, Alex, Neil Wrigley, and Martin Buttle. 2008. "Global Production Networks, Ethical Campaigning, and the Embeddedness of Responsible Governance." *Journal of Economic Geography* 8: 345–67.

Jervey, Ben. 2014. "Exporting the Colorado River to Asia, Through Hay." *National Geographic.* http://news.nationalgeographic.com/news/2014/01/140123-colorado-river-water-alfalfa-hay-farming-export-asia/.

Joy, Melanie. 2010. *Why We Love Dogs, Eat Pigs, and Wear Cows: An Introduction to Carnism.* San Francisco: Conary Press.

Kerr, Andrew, and Dan Yu. 2015. "Tradition as Precedent: Articulating Animal Law Reform in China." *Journal of Animal and Natural Resources Law* 11: 71–86.

Lin, Gene. 2016. "Animal Activists and Locals Quarrel at Yulin Dog Meat Festival." *Hong Kong Free Press.* www.hongkongfp.com/2016/06/23/animal-activists-and-locals-quarrel-at-yulin-dog-meat-festival/.

Mitchell, Les. 2011. "Moral Disengagement and Support for Nonhuman Animal Farming." *Society & Animals* 19(1): 38–58.

Neo, Harvey. 2012. " 'They Hate Pigs, Chinese Farmers . . . Everything!': Beastly Racialization in Multiethnic Malaysia." *Antipode* 44(3): 950–70.

Parker, Lynette. 1991. "The Dog Eaters of Bali." *Canberra Anthropology* 14(1): 1–23.

Phoenix Web. 2016. "The Controversial Yulin Dog Meat Festival." http://news.ifeng.com/a/20160622/49216248_0.shtml#p=1.

Pierson, David. 2014. "US Farmers Making Hay with Alfalfa Exports to China." *Los Angeles Times,* June 8. www.latimes.com/business/la-fi-feeding-china-hay-20140609-story.html.

Podberscek, Anthony. 2009. "Good to Pet and Eat: The Keeping and Consuming of Dogs and Cats in South Korea." *Journal of Social Issues* 65(3): 615–32.

Rocheleau, Dianne, and Robin Roth. 2007. "Rooted Networks, Relational Webs and Powers of Connection: Rethinking Human and Political Ecologies." *Geoforum* 38(3): 433–37.

Schlosser, Eric. 2001. *Fast Food Nation: The Dark Side of the All-American Meal.* Boston: Houghton Mifflin Harcourt.

Schneider, Mindi. 2014. "Developing the Meat Grab." *Journal of Peasant Studies* 41(4): 613–33.

Snowdon, Kathryn. 2015. " 'Horrible' Yulin Dog Meat Festival Protest Outside Chinese Embassy in London Attracts Hundreds." *Huffington Post UK.* June 26. www.huffingtonpost.co.uk/2015/06/26/yulin-dog-meat-festival-embassy-protest_n_7672656.html.

Steinfeld, Henning, Pierre Gerber, Tom Wassenaar, Vincent Castel, Mauricio Rosales, and Cees de Haan. 2006. *Livestock's Long Shadow: Environmental Issues and Options.* Rome: Food and Agriculture Organization.

University of California Cooperative Extension (UCCE). 2010. "Imperial County Agriculture." http://ceimperial.ucanr.edu/files/96429.pdf.

Vaughan, Adam. 2016. "UN Export Calls for Tax on Meat Production." *The Guardian.* May 25. www.theguardian.com/environment/2016/may/25/un-expert-calls-for-tax-on-meat-production.

Weis, Tony. 2013. *The Ecological Footprint: Global Burden of Industrial Livestock.* London and New York: Zed Books.

Willard, Barbara. 2002. "The American Story of Meat: Discursive Influences on Cultural Eating Practices." *Journal of Popular Culture* 36(1): 105–18.

World Watch Institute. 2016. "Rising Number of Farm Animals Poses Environmental and Public Health Risks." www.worldwatch.org/rising-number-farm-animals-poses-environmental-and-public-health-risks-0.

Animals as Food

Do you eat meat? Why or why not? What animals do you typically eat? Are there certain types of animal that you would refuse to eat? Why? What distinguishes pets from meat?

In Western foodways, cows, pigs, sheep, chicken, and fish are among the most common animals eaten by humans. What meat is culturally acceptable, however, varies over time and space. For instance, hunters in the United States eat deer, bear, and squirrels; insects are eaten in many different cultures in Africa, Asia, and Latin America; camels and goats are consumed in the Middle East; and the French seemingly enjoy frogs and snails. What makes eating beef more ethical than dog? Some argue that judging dog-eating by Western standards is a form of cultural imperialism.

The recipe below is from China, where, as we learn in chapter 3, dogs are consumed by some as meat. We certainly do not encourage you to make this dish with dog meat; it is meant to provoke critical thinking about the ethics of eating animals.

Clay-Pot Dog Meat Stew

Ingredients

1 pound dog hind leg meat
1 bunch mint leaves, finely chopped
1 tablespoon sugar
1 tablespoon dried chili
¼ cup Chinese white wine
1 shallot, finely chopped
1 tablespoon grated fresh ginger
1 star anise
½ teaspoon amomum (a cardamom-like spice)
¼ teaspoon peppercorns
1 teaspoon salt
1 cup vegetable oil
3 tablespoons soy sauce
1½ cups beef or chicken stock

Preparation

Dice dog meat into small cubes and rinse/wash in water twice, then pat dry. Heat oil in a wok and stir-fry all the spices, ginger, sugar, and shallot on medium heat, for 2 minutes. Add dog meat and soy sauce and fry for 20 minutes. Add stock and wine and transfer ingredients to a clay pot. Cover and simmer for 1 hour. Garnish with chopped mint leaves before serving.

Source: http://baike.baidu.com/view/6274.htm#4, recipe translated from Chinese.

CHAPTER 4

Genetically Modified Crops and the Remaking of Latin America's Food Landscape

Elizabeth Fitting

Textbox 4.1. Learning Objectives

- Learn about the role of GM crops in the global "food regime."
- Critically evaluate the use of GM crops in Latin America.
- Understand the concept of food regime and food sovereignty.
- Articulate a few of the ways that context and place shape the adoption of, and resistance to, GM crops.

GMOs are a central part of the new global food system. As a concept concerned with scale and political economy, the **food regime** provides a window onto **capitalism** and helps us understand both how biotech crops contribute to the uneven remaking of place, and how place also shapes the adoption and understanding of agricultural biotechnology. Genetically engineered or biotech crops were first commercialized in 1996 and grown on 1.7 million hectares.

By 2016, cultivation had reached 185.1 million hectares (James 2016). The United States remains the country that grows the most biotech crops today, followed by Brazil, Argentina, Canada, and India. In the Global South, Latin America is the region with the largest area devoted to biotech crops (James 2016). The cultivation of biotech crops has transformed agricultural practices and agrarian relations in those countries where it has been widely adopted. However, associated regulations and trade of GMOs have also influenced regions where they are not commercially grown on a large scale.

As is the case with all technology, in order to understand its impact, we need to understand context—the cultural, political, and economic contexts—in which GM crops are introduced, accommodated, adopted, or rejected. This chapter briefly discusses three cases from Latin America—Argentina, Mexico, and Colombia—in order to illustrate a few of the ways such crops have transformed these regions and to show how **place** influences if, and how, GM crops are adopted.

> ### Textbox 4.2. GMOs: Genetically Modified Organisms
>
> *Agricultural biotechnology* refers to recombinant DNA techniques that use organisms, their parts, or their processes to modify or create living organisms with particular traits. This technology includes genetic engineering and tissue culture techniques. Genetically modified organisms (GMOs) or transgenic plants are the products of such techniques, and include plants whose genomes contain inserted DNA material from other plants or species. Conventional plant breeding and farming practices also produce new gene characteristics in plants, but what makes plant breeding and farming different from genetic engineering is that they work at the level of the whole plant. In contrast, genetic engineering has the capacity, at least in theory, to overcome the sexual incompatibility of different species and to identify, isolate, and relocate any gene from one organism to a recipient plant's genome.

Food Regimes and GMOs

The concept of food regime focuses our attention on policies and practices related to food production, provisioning, and consumption, including alternative or counter practices (see chapter 2; Friedmann and McMichael 1987). The first global food regime emerged with industrial capitalism and colonialism. Food was instrumental in establishing world hegemony for Britain in the nineteenth century. The emergence of industrial capitalism was connected to the development of regions around the world as exporters of inexpensive food. Following World War II, a second food regime developed as the United States used food aid to generate political alliances and a market for its agro-industrial goods. The current food regime, or set of food policies and practices, and its role in neoliberal capitalism, has pushed small-scale farmers and agricultural laborers into a casual global workforce for capital (see chapter 5 on farmworkers). Scholars debate whether the term *corporate* or *neoliberal* best captures the contemporary regime, and the extent to which corporations or neoliberal state policies play a role in the expansion and concentration of the agro-food sector, including seeds and agricultural biotechnology (Otero 2012). From a political economy perspective, both are intimately related, since the **neoliberal** state and corporate power work in tandem to reproduce the economy in general and global food regimes in particular.

The contemporary food regime is characterized by an increase in liberalized trade, nontraditional food exports from the Global South (fruits, vegetables, meat), the continued export of subsidized grain from the Global North, the consolidation of agribusiness, and an increase in the precariousness of rural livelihoods (McMichael 2006). Farming remains important to rural households in many parts of the world, but often in conjunction with other income-generating activities, such as labor migration within and across national borders (see chapter 5).

The food regime is also characterized by the rise of genetic engineering as a key technology for capitalist agriculture, and by changes in regulation at national and international levels, which accommodate this technology (Pechlaner and Otero 2008). Neoliberal agricultural and trade policies have facilitated the rise of GM agriculture, and this has involved market concentration in the food system, notably among seed corporations. Three corporations, Monsanto, DuPont Pioneer, and Syngenta, control more than half of the world's commercial seed market, and the top ten corporations control over three-quarters (ETC Group 2013, 4). Yet despite this market concentration, many of the world's small-scale farmers do not rely on the corporate seed industry but rather save, use, and improve local or "traditional" varieties of seed (ETC Group 2013).

Agricultural biotechnology has the potential to aid small-scale, subsistence agriculture in diverse environments, and numerous plant breeders and institutions work on projects targeting smallholder farmers in the Global South. However, critics worry that corporate interests have too much influence over the research agenda of crop science. While scientific plant breeding in North America and Europe was first developed in public institutions, agricultural biotechnology has been led by industry from its early development (Kenney 1986).

Debates over GMOs are often presented in the media as starkly polarized, but it is important to remember that supporters and critics may have more complicated and nuanced positions on the topic—for instance, in opposition to (or support of) a *particular* type of GM crop, like transgenic corn or herbicide-resistant soy. Similarly, the benefits and problems of GMOs are unevenly experienced and distributed. Finally, it is worth remembering that the category of GMO captures different types of varieties from herbicide-tolerant (Ht) varieties, pest-resistant (Bt) varieties, stacked varieties (which are both herbicide-tolerant and pest-resistant), or those with other characteristics such as added nutritional content (e.g., "golden rice" with vitamin A).

Supporters and advocates of biotechnology argue that GMOs provide an important tool for increasing food production and the nutritional content of crops, particularly as our climate changes and the world population increases. Bt seed varieties were developed in the 1990s and seen to increase crop yields; however, there is debate about whether yield increases in Bt corn and soy are the result of GM technology or conventional plant breeding (Gurian-Sherman 2009). Herbicide-resistant crops are promoted as environmentally friendly because they require, at least initially, less agrochemicals than conventional crops. They are also promoted as a more-efficient use of labor and inputs, because they can lower the labor required, as in the case of soy, discussed below.

Resistance to GMOs: Places and Networks

The neoliberal food regime has not only involved the growth of transnational agribusiness and food conglomerates, but also transnational **networks of resistance** and social movements as well (see also chapter 3 for examples related to global meat networks). In Western Europe, early campaigns against GMOs were quite effective in mobilizing consumers around issues of food safety, ideas about preserving rural society, and ethical concerns about genetic engineering as "playing God" or defiling the natural boundaries between species (Schurman 2003, 9–10).

In the Global South, **resistance** to this technology focuses on the effects of GMOs on the environment and small-scale farmers' livelihoods, as well as the interconnected issues of property rights and biopiracy—or the appropriation of traditional knowledge and biological resources (Schurman 2003, 10–11). These issues have increasingly been adopted among activist networks spanning the Global South and North. An important actor in this movement is the peasant rights group La Via Campesina, which was founded in 1993 and works to promote **food sovereignty**, or "the right of peoples to healthy and culturally appropriate food produced through ecologically sound and sustainable methods, and their right to define their own food and agriculture systems" (2007).

Textbox 4.3. Food Sovereignty

Since its founding in 1993, Via Campesina has grown to 164 member organizations in 73 countries in the Global North and South. In its 2007 Declaration of Nyéléni, the organization defined food sovereignty as:

> the right of peoples to healthy and culturally appropriate food produced through ecologically sound and sustainable methods, and their right to define their own food and agriculture systems. It puts those who produce, distribute and consume food at the heart of food systems and policies rather than the demands of markets and corporations. [. . .] It offers a strategy to resist and dismantle the current corporate trade and food regime, and directions for food, farming, pastoral and fisheries systems determined by local producers. Food sovereignty prioritises local and national economies and markets and empowers peasant and family farmer–driven agriculture, artisanal-fishing, pastoralist-led grazing, and food production, distribution and consumption based on environmental, social and economic sustainability. Food sovereignty promotes transparent trade that guarantees just income to all peoples and the rights of consumers to control their food and nutrition. It ensures that the rights to use and manage our lands, territories, waters, seeds, livestock and biodiversity are in the hands of those of us who produce food. Food sovereignty implies new social relations free of oppression and inequality between men and women, peoples, racial groups, social classes and generations.

The idea of food sovereignty and the global networks of resistance in which it is embedded have been influential in Latin America, where anti-GM activists express concerns heard in other parts of the world, yet also highlight ones specific to their region. Activists portray GMOs—or particular GM crops, such as transgenic corn or soy—as a symbol of contemporary imperialism or neoliberal capitalism. In contrast, "traditional" and creolized varieties (which together are often referred to as *criollos* in Spanish) represent the food sovereignty of the community, country, and region. In Mesoamerican countries—the center of biodiversity, and where maize originated—biotech corn has been the focus of anti-GM activism. The notable case is Mexico, where an anti-GM network and movement formed around the controversial finding of GM corn growing in traditional cornfields, despite the fact that the testing and commercial cultivation of GM corn was prohibited at the time. The commercial cultivation of GM corn in Mexico remains prohibited today except in authorized test plots. Maize is also the focus of anti-GM campaigns in Colombia, where indigenous groups are resisting GMOs by establishing "territories free of transgenics."

In the next sections, we turn to three Latin American case studies to illustrate why the history of place and the symbolic meaning of traditional varieties and particular food crops connected to place are central to understanding the acceptance or rejection of GMOs.

Case 1: The Soy Boom in Argentina

Why and how did GM soy take off in Argentina? The cultivation of (non-GM) soybeans was introduced in the agricultural Pampa region of Argentina in the 1970s. The area devoted to monocrop soy fields grew steadily in the following two decades, supplanting the production of corn, sorghum, and livestock (Teubal 2008, 192–94). Soy is often used as animal feed, and the expansion of soy in the Americas is a consequence of the increased global consumption of meat (see chapter 3) for which Argentina, Brazil, and Paraguay have become important suppliers. In the 1990s, government policies supported agribusiness and encouraged the expansion of export-oriented soy production and the use of GM crops, both as export cash crops and as feed for the growing Argentinean meat industry (Newell 2009).

In 1996, Monsanto's herbicide-resistant Roundup Ready (RR) soybean was introduced. RR is resistant to the company's brand of the herbicide glyphosate. By 2012, GM soy was grown on 18.9 million hectares, and annual use of glyphosate reached 200 million liters (Leguizamón 2014, 152; Lapegna 2016, 518). This boom transformed the agricultural landscape in Argentina, and has had an impact across the border: GM seed was smuggled into neighboring countries, including Paraguay and Brazil, where it was illegal to grow until 2004 and 2005, respectively. A decade later, Brazil and Paraguay had become the second- and sixth-largest producers of soy in the world (Ezquerro-Cañete 2016; Motta 2016).

In the 1990s, President Carlos Menem implemented economic liberalization policies which affected the agricultural sector, and pegged the Argentine peso to the US dollar. The cheap US dollar, weak regulations on GM seed, and no import taxes on agricultural products acted as incentives for growing GM soybeans (Leguizamón 2014, 150). The seed sector was also reorganized in a way that favored private-sector seed research and facilitated the concentration of the seed market (Newell 2009).

Farmers took up GM soy because it was the least expensive and most profitable crop to plant; the price of glyphosate was lower than other herbicides, RR seed was inexpensive, and the no-tillage method reduced labor and fuel costs. The main benefit of RR soy is that it simplifies agricultural production, as it can be sown without plowing the land. The glyphosate eliminates the weeds but not the RR plants (Lapegna 2016, 518).

The social and economic benefits of the soy boom have been unequally distributed and experienced. While large farmers and agribusiness saw their profit margins expand, along with their political and economic influence, other Argentines benefited from the boom both directly and indirectly, such as medium-size farmers who rented out their land, or the recipients of social programs paid for with the tax revenue on exports. Indeed, the economic growth and profit generated by soy exports is heralded as a successful development model for the Global South. Researchers have rightly asked, however, at what cost is this economic success to the environment, smaller-scale farmers, and public health? (Leguizamón 2014; also Lapegna 2016 and Teubal 2008). Those sectors of society that did not benefit from the boom yet bore the brunt of social, economic, and environmental problems include small-scale farmers and peasants, rural workers, and indigenous communities.

The shift to agriculture for export rather than the production of basic foodstuffs for domestic consumption undermined Argentina's position as one of the twentieth century's "breadbaskets"—that is, a country that was self-sufficient in food, and a supplier of food to the world economy (Teubal 2008, 191). Specifically, the soy boom helped to consolidate agribusiness and contributed to the disappearance of small- and medium-size farms. Soy farming is largely undertaken by agribusiness via "sowing pools," which involve capital from investors and a team of managers who are in charge of renting land, labor, and machinery (Leguizamón 2014, 153). As the scale of farms expands and the number of farms declines, there are fewer agricultural employment and livelihood opportunities available—what some have referred to as "farming without farmers" (see Teubal 2008, 207).

The shift to soy also generated interest in land and rising land values, exacerbating social tensions and violence against indigenous farmers and *campesinos* (peasants). For a decade, violent confrontations over natural resources have erupted as transnational and national corporations (interested in agribusiness, and mining and drilling for oil) clash with the local residents, *campesinos*, and indigenous peoples (Lapegna 2013, 2016).

The boom has also had environmental repercussions. The clearing of rain forests in several northern provinces, which had begun prior to the soy boom, accelerated with the cultivation of large-scale monocrop GM soy. In the Chaco region, deforestation also entailed a loss of access to the forest as a means of subsistence for residents. Another deleterious effect of the soy boom has been the rise in agrochemical use and public health concerns about herbicides drifting onto people's farms, residences, and water supplies. Although initially adopted by farmers in part because of the reduction in agrochemicals required for planting, over time the growing tolerance of weeds to the herbicide and the continuous cultivation of soybeans (without crop rotation) necessitated an increase in the amount and type of chemicals applied. One of the successes of anti-GM activism in the country is the attention now given to the issue of agrochemicals and their impact on human health and the environment (Leguizamón 2016).

Environmental, *campesino*, and women's groups, as well as concerned citizens, have organized around the expansion of GM soy agriculture as part of a critique of neoliberalism and the health effects of agrochemical drifts (Ibid.). However, despite gaining momentum in recent years, anti-GM activism in Argentina has not had the same widespread support or resonance it has had in places like Mexico—at least, not yet. Why would this be the case? Some have suggested that the funding of much-needed social programs through taxation of soy production has contributed to the acceptance of the negative impacts of the boom (Lapegna 2016). Following an economic crisis, the government redirected policies toward "export-oriented populism" in the 2000s (Richardson 2009, in Lapegna 2016). Taxes were established on agricultural exports, and the government used the revenue on GM soy exports to garner support for their social programs in urban areas. Such taxes were met with protests by the medium to large landowners and agribusinesses that grow soy. These growers, along with the media, promoted the idea that "what is good for agribusiness is good for the country." Medium and large growers portrayed themselves as representative of the countryside, minimizing the role of *campesinos* and indigenous smallholders in national agriculture, along with their concerns about GM soy's environmental and social impact (Lapegna 2016, 522). In other words, the concerns of small indigenous and *campesino* groups, and anti-GM activists, did not make it into the public debates about the soy boom at that time.

In contrast to Argentina, Mexico has been the site of sustained anti-GM activism which has resonated beyond indigenous, *campesino,* and environmental groups. This is so for many reasons, including the cultural significance of maize, and the fact that GMOs do not undergird export-oriented populism, as is the case in Argentina.

Case 2: Anti-GM Activism in Mexico: In Defense of Maize

> Without corn there is no country (Sin maíz, no hay país).
>
> —Slogan from Mexican anti-GM network, In Defense of Maize

When evidence of GM corn growing among traditional cornfields was found in the highlands of Oaxaca in 2001, a controversy erupted about the import of GM corn and its environmental, and then later, its social and economic, consequences. Although there was a de facto moratorium on the scientific field-testing of GM corn at the time, and growing it was prohibited, the country imported GM corn from the United States for use as animal feed, grain for tortillas, and in industrial processing. Small-scale Mexican cultivators likely encountered these imports in regional markets. Under NAFTA, Mexican imports of US corn dramatically increased, and imports now surpass ten million metric tons per year. It is a bitter irony of the neoliberal food regime that countries of the Global South, like Mexico, import basic foods that they themselves have historically produced, and in this case, such a culturally significant one.

In response to the controversy, an anti-GM campaign and network, In Defense of Maize, emerged and expanded, drawing together over three hundred environmental, food activist, independent peasant, and indigenous rights organizations, most of which are Mexican. Numerous academics, researchers, and scientists are also involved in the network. Two transnational organizations with offices in Mexico City—Greenpeace Mexico, and the Action Group on the Environment, Technology, and Concentration (ETC Group), important participants and founding members of the network—had been voicing concerns about GM corn imports in the years just prior to the controversy.

In 2002, in response to the controversy, some government officials and advocates of GM corn suggested that the flow between GM corn and *criollos* would help improve the performance of the latter. Yet, as one maize scientist explained: "Promoters of biotech say how wonderful it is that Bt corn was found in Oaxaca because it's going to help peasants. But this is incorrect because in Mexico we don't have the pests that Bt was designed to attack" (Interview, Dr. José Antonio Serratos, January 28, 2002). Interviews conducted with scientists involved in the In Defense of Maize network indicate that they were not against agricultural biotechnology per se, but rather against the testing and cultivation of transgenic corn *in Mexico*. According to these scientists, GM corn, including the Bt variety, is not suited to this particular *place*.

Activists emphasize the cultural importance of traditional maize, and in doing so, highlight the specificity of place. Biotech crops like cotton have been grown in Mexico without the same degree of public attention or concern that has been given to maize. Since 2012, however, GM soy has generated concern for Mayan honey producers in the Yucatán because GM pollen was found in honey samples destined for export. A district judge overturned Monsanto's permit to grow GM soy in 2014.

Maize is the main crop grown throughout the country, the cornerstone of rural livelihoods, a key ingredient of culinary traditions and the national diet, and a powerful and longtime symbol of the Mexican nation (see figure 4.1). At times, maize invokes elements of shared culture across different scales of place, ranging from the small rural community or region to the nation-state, but also beyond the borders of Mexico to indigenous and rural Latin America. For example, while indigenous *campesinos* of the Tehuacán Valley in Mexico may refer to themselves as the "people of maize," so too might urban-based maize consumers, and some farmers, seed activists, and indigenous groups elsewhere, such as the Zenú, in Colombia. While there is place-based cultural attachment to maize in various places in Latin America, such as Mexico, Guatemala, and Colombia, this is not the case with soy in Argentina.

Figure 4.1. Corn is life
Corn is a powerful symbol of rural livelihoods and indigenous culture. Although many varieties have historically been grown, they are now being threatened by commercial agriculture.
Source: Author.

Although yellow corn, which tends to be imported or grown in the north, is used as animal feed or to make industrial tortillas in Mexico, traditional varieties of white, blue, and red maize are preferred for taste and texture in rural communities, smaller towns, and among urban foodies; these varieties are grown by *campesinos* and indigenous producers for food. Cultivated on some eight million hectares, most maize agriculture is rain-fed and involves nonindustrial farming (Turrent Fernández, Wise, and Garvey 2012, 7). Maize is considered hardier than other cash crops in the valley, no doubt because *criollos* tend to be well adapted to local conditions and environments. In some regions, it is less expensive for farmers to buy imported corn than it is to grow *criollos*. With multiple, flexible uses, maize provides a social safety net because it can be eaten by the farmer's family in the form of tortillas or other foods, or sold, albeit possibly at a loss.

An elderly *campesino* who had traveled quite a distance to attend the first In Defense of Maize forum in 2002, organized in the aftermath of the GM corn scandal, explained the importance of maize for him and his community: "I am too old to do any other work [other than maize farming] and what will I leave my children and their children? Maize is life for us" (Campesino interview, January 24, 2002). Similarly, when I asked residents of Tehuacán Valley why they grew corn even when it is not profitable, they explained that "There is no work here [for us older folk] except in the fields." Younger residents in their teens and twenties migrate to the north or across the border to the United States for work (Fitting 2011). Additionally, residents noted their preference for the taste of *criollo* white maize for tortillas.

At that first 2002 forum, an activist from the National Support Center for Indigenous Missions (CENAMI)[1] also spoke, explaining how the government views small-scale corn producers: "[T]he government perspective is: We don't need peasants, nor do we need indigenous communities. We need people that can work in the *maquiladoras* [factories]."

Maize represents numerous struggles that Mexico—particularly rural Mexico—faces under a neoliberal food regime. By linking GM corn imports, regulation, and cultivation to neoliberal policies that undermine the livelihood of small-scale farmers, such as trade liberalization, cuts to rural subsidies, the commercialization of the seed, and a lack of political transparency, In Defense of Maize creates and extends connections between environmentalists, anti-neoliberal activists, peasant and indigenous groups, and concerned scientists and academics both within and across national borders (Fitting 2014). These connections are centered around place and the symbolic role of maize in rural livelihoods and indigenous cultures.

Starting in 2009, the government has permitted experimental plots of GM corn to be planted. Since then, Monsanto, Dow Chemical, and DuPont's Pioneer have applied to enlarge their small experimental plots of transgenic corn with the goal of planting the first commercial plots in northern Mexico (Reuters, September 19, 2011). Following these applications to plant 1.4 million hectares in Sinaloa and over 1 million hectares in Tamaulipas, Mexican activists and their international supporters intensified their efforts to garner support for a government rejection of these corporate applications to grow transgenic corn (GRAIN 2012, 3). The National Union of Autonomous Peasant Organizations (UNORCA) held a sit-in and hunger strike at Mexico City's Angel of Independence monument in January 2013, and thousands joined the anti-GM protests in January and May. Farmers' organizations from Oaxaca named 2013 "the year of resistance to transgenic maize." That same year in Colombia, transgenic crops and the protection of traditional seed varieties began to receive considerable media and public attention.

---

1. CENAMI is a nonprofit based in Mexico City that works to support indigenous pastors and churches in various regions of the country. Beyond this, their mission includes supporting indigenous projects to defend and promote indigenous culture, territory, and rights (see www.cenami.org).

Case 3: Seed Regulations and Activism in Colombia

> Colombia, especially in the Caribbean, is an important center of biological diversity for maize and other plants, where an enormous diversity of maize races and *criollos* exist, the fruit of the collective labour of thousands of generations of agriculturalists, who have developed these varieties adapted to different regions and cultural, socio-economic and agricultural conditions. [. . .] For the indigenous communities of the Zenú, maize is a fundamental element, a support of our culture, our productive systems and the food sovereignty of our people.
>
> —Excerpt from the *Zenú Declaration of their Territory as Transgenic Free,* Resguardo indígena Zenú Córdoba y Sucre, Colombia (October 7, 2005; my translation)

Colombia is one of eighteen countries in the world growing more than 50,000 hectares of transgenic crops, primarily maize and cotton (James 2016, 4). Beyond activist circles and some indigenous communities, there was little public debate weighing the benefits and risks of genetically engineered crops up until 2013, when a national agrarian strike and a documentary about a recent law regulating seeds used in Colombian agriculture brought the issue to the fore.

In 2005, San Andrés de Sotavento, in the northern departments of Córdoba and Sucre in Colombia, was the first indigenous community, or **resguardo**, to declare itself a transgenic-free territory (TFT). This Zenú territory is also home to the Caribbean Agroecology Network (Red Agroecológica del Caribe, or RECAR), which has been the driving force behind the national "Seeds of Identity" campaign to promote the conservation and exchange of *criollo* seed in Colombia. Initiated in 2002, the campaign is the work of RECAR, the Bogotá office of SwissAid, and the Colombian NGO Grupo Semillas (the Seed Group). These nonprofits are part of the Red de Semillas Libres (RSL), a network of grassroots and activist organizations in Colombia that promote the use of *criollos* and "seed sovereignty," or farmers' ability to share, save, breed, replant, and make autonomous decisions about seed. The network challenges the cultivation of GMOs, including the privatization and commercialization of seed, and promotes saving and exchanging *criollos*.

In their 2005 declaration, Zenú leaders point to Colombia as a center of biological diversity of maize, and emphasize the cultural, alimentary, and socioeconomic importance of the crop for the Zenú. They refer to themselves as "the children of maize," and contend that the import of transgenic maize and other products generates "negative impacts on our seeds, our agriculture and our food sovereignty."

Key participants in the Colombian anti-GM campaign looked to Mexico's anti-GM organizing in 2002 for information and strategy (Fitting 2014). In both Mexico and Colombia, where maize is representative of the "nation"—be it the nation-state or an indigenous people and territory—the import and cultivation of transgenic corn is seen to undermine political, economic, cultural, and food sovereignty. Indeed,

Colombia's imports of corn, largely from the United States, and up to 90 percent of which is used for animal feed, increased in the 1990s, and reached 4.5 million metric tons in 2016 (USDA 2016).

Since the Zenú Declaration, five other indigenous *resguardos* have established their communities as transgenic-free territories. However, the real turning point for media and public attention to questions related to seed in Colombia was in 2013, when Resolution 970 gained notoriety through a documentary that went viral online, and then was taken up as an issue during the national agrarian strike. The Colombian Agricultural Institute (ICA), a branch of the Ministry of Agriculture and Rural Development responsible for the regulation of seed and genetically modified organisms, implemented Resolution 970 in 2010. It required that all seeds in the country used by small-scale farmers and in indigenous territories be registered and certified for reasons of quality, productivity, and plant disease management and prevention.

Across Latin America and elsewhere, new seed laws and regulations help the expansion of the corporate seed industry, and create seed registration and certification requirements which may prohibit the traditional practice of local farmer seed exchange and sale (Santilli 2012, 49). Such laws and regulations challenge what is referred to as "farmers' rights" or "farmers' privilege"—the common practice of farmers to save and replant their seeds.

Colombia made legal and regulatory changes on intellectual property and phytosanitary controls in part to meet the requirements of the free trade agreement with the United States, which took effect in 2012. Resolution 970 prohibited the production, saving, selling, sharing free of charge, and using of seeds not registered or certified by ICA, and without breeder's authorization. Registration and certification represent a costly and time-consuming process that many small-scale farmers cannot afford. Yet, if the seed is not registered and certified, the resolution prohibited farmers from saving and replanting their seed.

The Red de Semillas Libres submitted a challenge to Resolution 970 to the Constitutional Court, arguing that it had not previously consulted indigenous and Afro-Colombian communities. The RSL's position was supported in late 2013 by agrarian strike leaders, who included the repeal of the resolution in their own list of demands forwarded during negotiations with the government. During the agrarian strike, which involved marches and roadblocks, *campesino* leaders, truckers, miners, and coffee growers called for a reduction in fuel and fertilizer prices and the cancellation of free trade agreements, among other issues. In response to the negative publicity and the agrarian strike, the government suspended the Resolution in order to rewrite it.

In September 2015, ICA released Resolution 3168 as a replacement to 970. It contains small changes that address some of the concerns articulated by activists and farmers. ICA eliminated the requirement to register seed in its information system, and it states that it does not apply to creole or native seed; however, it does not define these kinds of seeds, leaving the door open for ambiguity. The RSL argues that Resolution 3168 is similar to its predecessor in that it mandates that all seed used in the country must be certified seed, indirectly prohibiting *criollos*, and that it maintains the restrictions on saving and commercializing certified seed, which helps to ensure market control for seed companies (Gutiérrez and Fitting 2016).

Similar to seed activists elsewhere, the RSL sees the struggle to maintain farmers' rights to replant and exchange seed as part of a longer and larger struggle against imperialism, neocolonialism, and an agrarian structure in which the big capitalist landowners continue to thrive at the expense of small-scale farmers. Thus, the RSL pursues seed sovereignty because it sees defending *criollo* seeds as resistance to corporate agriculture and the commodification of seeds, but also as political autonomy, cultural survival, and food sovereignty.

Conclusion

GMOs provide a lens through which to see changes taking place in agriculture and food at various scales of analysis; the role of international trade agreements comes into focus, along with regulatory frameworks (on seed and intellectual property rights), the expansion of transnational agribusiness, and the creation and expansion of activist networks. At regional (and local) levels of analysis, we see how particular crops and foods represent a sense of place and way of life. While activists argue that GMOs undermine that sense of place and its culture, and erode the livelihood of small-scale farmers—or public health, as with the use of glyphosate—others argue that such technology provides important benefits, like economic opportunity. Clearly, in order to understand why GMOs engender support, acquiescence, or resistance, we need to understand something about the context and history of place.

This chapter suggests a few possible reasons why GM soy does not (yet) resonate more broadly in Argentina when compared to Mexico and Colombia: because soy does not carry the same cultural significance that maize does in Mexico or Colombia; because regulatory changes on seed have not yet captured mainstream media attention in the same way they did in Colombia, with Resolution 970; and because medium- and large-scale growers and agribusiness not only have political influence on government—as arguably they have in Mexico and Colombia, albeit perhaps not to the same extent—but they also successfully mobilize narratives about representing the countryside.

The anti-GM activist groups and networks discussed here share several characteristics with other contemporary social movements in Latin America: First, these anti-GM networks involve people who are often excluded from the formal institutions of their societies, particularly peasants, indigenous peoples, and women's groups (Bosco 2016), in addition to the participation of NGOs and professional activists and environmentalists.

Second, like other movements, GM activists strategically use place and a sense of place to mobilize beyond their immediate group (Ibid.). Not only do activists use physical places like a city plaza or highway to make their demonstrations and marches visible to the public, but they also focus on foods, seeds, and crops as symbols of a culture or way of life associated with place—including both those with clearly demarcated territories, such as a *resguardo* or country, and those without, such as the "countryside," or Mesoamerica.

A third similarity with other social movements in the region is that these anti-GM groups involve networks *across* scales, from the local community level, to national, and transnational networks. The Internet is a key technology employed by these networks to communicate and get their message out, and the success of these anti-GM campaigns depends on whether their concerns resonate beyond the particular and the local with non-activists at home and abroad.

Finally, and connected to this, anti-GM groups and networks, similar to—and even as a part of—other social movements in Latin America, engage alternative or conflicting definitions and approaches to nature, justice, and other concepts (Bosco 2016). Although some campaigns are more successful in mobilizing support beyond activist circles, and in influencing government regulations and policy, in general, anti-GM networks in Latin America engage and contribute to ideas about food and seed sovereignty as a counternarrative and critique of neoliberalism.

Key Terms

capitalism
food regime
food sovereignty
GMO
neoliberalism

networks of resistance
place
resguardo
resistance

Summary

- The cultivation of GMOs has increased dramatically over the past decade, leading to profound changes in agricultural practices.
- The rise in GMOs can be linked to the contemporary global food regime and its associated neoliberal food policies.
- Resistance to GMOs takes on different forms in different contexts, as illustrated by the examples of Argentina, Colombia, and Mexico. Deep connections between a particular crop and a sense of place help activists to mobilize support from the ground up, creating transformative networks of resistance across places where food sovereignty is similarly threatened.

Acknowledgments

Many thanks to my interviewees from the Red de Semillas Libres, and the activists and maize farmers in Mexico City and Tehuacán areas, respectively. Thank you to anthropologist Laura Gutiérrez Escobar for our writing collaborations about the Red, and to Pablo Lapegna for his feedback. Thanks also go to the editors of this collection for their thoughtful suggestions.

References

ABColombia (Christian Aid, CAFOD, Oxfam GB, SCIAF, Trócaire). 2010. "Caught in the Crossfire: Colombia's Indigenous Peoples." Report, October. London: ABColombia. www .abcolombia.org.uk/downloads/Caught_in_the_Crossfire.pdf.

Bosco, Fernando. 2016. "Latin American Social Movements: Places, Scales and Networks of Action." In *Placing Latin America: Contemporary Themes in Geography*, edited by Ed Jackiewicz and Fernando J. Bosco, 159–74. Lanham, MD: Rowman and Littlefield Publishers.

Campesino. Interview with author. January 24, 2002. In Defense of Maize Forum, Mexico City.

Dowd-Uribe, Brian, Dominic Glover, and Matthew Schnurr. 2014. "Seeds and Places: The Geographies of Transgenic Crops in the Global South." *Geoforum* 53: 145–48.

ETC Group. 2013 *Putting the Cartel before the Horse . . . and Farm, Seeds, Soil, Peasants, etc. Who Will Control Agricultural Inputs, 2013*. Communiqué No. 111, September. www.etcgroup .org/putting_the_cartel_before_the_horse_2013.

Ezquerro-Cañete, Arturo. 2016. "Poisoned, Dispossessed and Excluded: A Critique of the Neoliberal Soy Regime in Paraguay." *Journal of Agrarian Change* 16(4): 702–10.

Fitting, Elizabeth. 2011. *The Struggle for Maize: Campesinos, Workers, and Transgenic Corn in the Mexican Countryside*. Durham: Duke University Press.

———. 2014. "Cultures of Corn and Anti-GM Activism in Mexico and Colombia." In *Food Activism: Agency, Democracy and Economy*, edited by Carole Counihan and Valeria Siniscalchi, 175–92. London and New York: Bloomsbury.

Friedmann, Harriet, and Philip McMichael. 1987. "Agriculture and the State System: The Rise and Fall of National Agricultures, 1870 to the Present." *Sociologia Ruralis* 29 (2): 93–117.

GRAIN, 2013. *Hands Off Our Maize! Resistance to GMOs in Mexico*. Report, May 16. www .grain.org/article/entries/4725-hands-off-our-maize-resistance-to-gmos-in-mexico.

Gurian-Sherman, Doug. 2009. *Failure to Yield: Evaluating the Performance of Genetically Engineered Crops*. Union of Concerned Scientists. www.ucsusa.org/sites/default/files/legacy/assets/ documents/food_and_agriculture/failure-to-yield.pdf.

Gutiérrez Escobar, Laura, and Elizabeth Fitting. 2016. "The *Red de Semillas Libres*: Contesting Biohegemony in Colombia." *Journal of Agrarian Change* 16(4): 711–19.

James, Clive. 2016. "Global Status of Commercialized Biotech/GM Crops: 2016." ISAAA Brief, No. 52-2016. Ithaca, NY: ISAAA. www.isaaa.org/resources/publications/briefs/52/ download/isaaa-brief-52-2016.pdf.

Kenney, Martin. 1986. *Biotechnology: The University-Industrial Complex*. New Haven: Yale University Press.

Lapegna, Pablo. 2013. "Notes from the Field: The Expansion of Transgenic Soybeans and the Killing of Indigenous Peasants in Argentina." *Societies Without Borders* 8(2): 291–308.

———. 2016. "Genetically Modified Soybeans, Agrochemical Exposure, and Everyday Forms of Peasant Collaboration in Argentina." *The Journal of Peasant Studies* 43(2): 517–36.

Leguizamón, Amalia. 2014. "Modifying Argentina: GM Soy and Socio-Environmental Change." *Geoforum* 53: 149–60.

———. 2016. "Environmental Injustice in Argentina: Struggles Against Genetically Modified Soy." *Journal of Agrarian Change* 16(4): 684–92.

McMichael, Philip. 2006. "Peasant Prospects in the Neoliberal Age." *New Political Economy* 11 (3): 204–418.

———. 2009. "A Food Regime Genealogy." *Journal of Peasant Studies* 36(1): 139–69.

Motta, Renata. 2016. "Global Capitalism and the Nation State in the Struggles over GM Crops in Brazil." *Journal of Agrarian Change* 16 (4): 720–27.

Newell, Peter. 2009. "Bio-Hegemony: The Political Economy of Agricultural Biotechnology in Argentina." *Journal of Latin American Studies* 41: 27–57.

Otero, Gerardo. 2008. *Food for the Few: Neoliberal Globalism and Biotechnology in Latin America*. Austin: University of Texas Press.

———. 2012. "The Neoliberal Food Regime in Latin America: State, Agribusiness Transnational Corporations and Biotechnology." *Canadian Journal of Development Studies / Revue Canadienne d'Études du Développement* 33(3): 282–94.

Otero, Gerardo, and Pablo Lapegna. 2016. "Transgenic Crops in Latin America: Expropriation, Negative Value and the State." *Journal of Agrarian Change* 16(4): 665–74.

Pearson, Thomas. 2012. "Transgenic-Free Territories in Costa Rica: Networks, Place, and the Politics of Life." *American Ethnologist* 39(1): 90–105.

Pechlaner, Gabriela, and Gerardo Otero. 2008. "The Third Food Regime: Neoliberal Globalism and Agricultural Biotechnology in North America." *Sociologia Ruralis* 48 (4): 1–21.

Reuters. September 19, 2011. "Mexico Set to Expand GMO Corn Planting-Group. Mexico City." www.reuters.com/article/be-mexico-corn-idUSS1E78I1MJ20110920.

Santilli, Juliana. 2012. *Agrobiodiversity and the Law: Regulating Genetic Resources, Food Security and Cultural Diversity*. New York: Earthscan.

Schurman, Rachel. 2003. "Introduction. Biotechnology in the New Milennium: Technological Change, Institutional Change, and Political Struggle." In *Engineering Trouble: Biotechnology and Its Discontents*, edited by Rachel Schurman and Dennis T. Kelso, 1–23. Berkeley: University of California Press.

Serratos, Dr. José Antonio. Interview with author. January 28, 2002. Chapingo, Mexico.

Teubal, Miguel. 2008. "Genetically Engineered Soybeans and the Crisis of Argentina's Agriculture Model." In *Food for the Few: Neoliberal Globalism and Biotechnology in Latin America*, edited by Gerardo Otero, 189–216. Austin: University of Texas Press.

Turrent Fernández, Antonio, Timothy A. Wise, and Elise Garvey. 2012. Achieving Mexico's Maize Potential, Global Development and Environment Institute Working Paper No. 12-03. October 2012. Medford, MA: Tufts University. www.ase.tufts.edu/gdae/Pubs/wp/12-03TurrentMexMaize.pdf.

USDA Foreign Agricultural Service. 2016. "GAIN Grain and Feed Annual Report." March 15. http://gain.fas.usda.gov/Recent%20GAIN%20Publications/Grain%20and%20Feed%20Annual_Bogota_Colombia_3-15-2016.pdf.

Via Campesina. 1996. "The Right to Produce and Access Land." Rome, Italy, November 11–17. www.acordinternational.org/silo/files/decfoodsov1996.pdf.

———. 2007. "The Declaration of Nyéléni." Selingue, Mali. February 27. https://viacampesina.org/en/index.php/main-issues-mainmenu-27/food-sovereignty-and-trade-mainmenu-38/262-declaration-of-nyi.

———. 2011. "The International Peasant's Voice." February 9. https://viacampesina.org/en/index.php/organisation-mainmenu-44.

I Don't Want GMOs!

Is your food genetically engineered? Pick a food item you recently purchased and determine whether or not it contains genetically modified ingredients. How do you know? Is it labeled in a way that makes this information clear and readily available? Why is it so difficult to obtain this information? What would it take to avoid genetically engineered food entirely? Consider different strategies, including education campaigns, regulations, labels, and grassroots initiatives.

For example, in their book *Decolonize Your Diet*, Luz Calvo and Catrióna Esquibel (2016) make a case for ancestral diets as a way to avoid GMOs and resist other ills of the contemporary food regime. They argue that Latin American foodways have been eroded by colonizing forces, including the introduction of wheat bread by Spanish missionaries, the devaluation of corn and beans as indigenous and morally inferior food, the contamination of corn by GMOs, the free-trade agreements that encourage production for exports, and the flooding of local markets with Coca-Cola and other mass-produced imported food. They argue that people of Latin America, including Latino immigrants in the United States, must "decolonize" their diets in order to reclaim their health and culture.

The following recipe is inspired by one provided on Calvo and Esquibel's website: http://decolonizeyourdiet.org/2013/11/chiles-poblanos-rellenos.html. It is based on ingredients and techniques that are native to Mexico and symbolize a form of resistance.

Chiles Poblanos Rellenos

Ingredients

4 poblano chiles
1 ear of sweet corn
1 onion, finely chopped
1 tablespoon olive oil
½ cup cilantro
1 cup quinoa, cooked
¼ cup pumpkin seeds
salt and pepper to taste
½ cup yogurt
1 pomegranate

Preparation

Grill corn and poblano chiles on the barbecue or in the oven until lightly charred. Place the chiles in a paper bag and let them rest for a few minutes until they cool off. This will help you peel them more easily. Peel the thin skin off with your fingers, make one long incision on the side, and remove the seeds.

Heat the oil in a pan, fry the onion, and transfer to a large bowl. Use the same pan to toast the pumpkin seeds and add to the bowl. With a large knife, cut corn kernels off the cob and add to the onions, along with quinoa and cilantro. Season with salt and pepper. Fill the chiles with this mixture and bake in an ovenproof dish at 375 degrees Fahrenheit, for 15 minutes. Serve each pepper topped with 1 tablespoon of yogurt and 2 tablespoons of pomegranate seeds.

CHAPTER 5

Farm Labor, Immigration, and Race

Lise Nelson

Textbox 5.1. Learning Objectives

- Identify and explain the unique labor demands of modern, industrial food systems.
- Describe the conditions of work and social reproduction for farm labor within such systems.
- Articulate the reasons why farmworkers are often immigrants, and explain how immigration policy shapes labor conditions and practices.
- Identify and analyze the central role of race and racial hierarchies within these labor systems.
- Reflect on the multiple ways farmworkers resist these conditions.

The rise of the modern farm and global industrial food systems explored in previous chapters is closely connected to the reconfiguration of farm labor, as well as to new patterns of global migration. On one hand, over the past century, the growth of industrial agriculture in different times and places has usually signaled a process of labor and livelihood *displacement*. Machinery replaces human hands and, as explored in more detail in chapters 4 and 7, industrial agriculture tends to squeeze out small-scale farmers. Peasants and small-scale family farmers often end up as "surplus" population as industrial agriculture expands.

On the other hand, the growth of industrial and globally integrated agriculture creates a new set of labor *needs* often characterized by high but short-term demand for human labor—during harvest, for pruning, or for the processing of highly perishable goods. These two dynamics work together: Processes of displacement create a pool of "available" workers, while new kinds of labor demand mobilize these workers, often across regional and national borders, into agro-food industrial complexes.

From Zimbabwean farmworkers laboring in South Africa, Cambodians working in the fields of Thailand, indigenous women supporting Chile's export agriculture sector, to Albanians employed on German farms, industrial agriculture across the globe relies on regular—but often seasonal—access to a low-paid and highly marginalized workforce. *How* this marginalization is produced—in relation to immigration law, racial or gender hierarchies, and/or poverty—varies across space and through time, yet the effect on workers can be numbingly similar. Farmwork remains, in our "modern"

Figure 5.1. Farmworkers harvesting in California
Maria Perez in a crew of indigenous Oaxacan farmworkers, picking strawberries in a field near Santa Maria, California.

Source: David Bacon (copyrights paid). Available at http://fresnoalliance
.com/wordpress/thousands-of-farmworkers-cant-make-a-living/. Reprinted
with permission.

industrial agricultural system, one of the most backbreaking, dangerous, and low-paid
jobs on the planet (see figure 5.1). Given its seasonality, these labor systems often
produce an itinerant population whose lives and families have tenuous connections to
place, dignity, and basic human rights.

This chapter examines the relationship between labor and industrial agriculture
systems. It touches briefly on the ways industrial agriculture displaces people from livelihoods in some regions. The focus, however, is on how these systems recruit economically displaced people—often across national boundaries—into **industrial farmwork**.
The term *industrial farmwork* is used to differentiate it from family and local farm
labor systems characteristic of peasant agriculture and other nonindustrial food and
agriculture systems. Industrial farmwork is a system in which labor on farms becomes
proletarian as well as spatially and temporally flexible—characteristics maintained
through hierarchies of class, race, gender, and immigrant legal status.

This chapter also explores the conditions of work within industrial agriculture
systems, as well as the conditions of **social reproduction** for industrial farmworkers.
The term *social reproduction* refers to the daily activities and spaces outside of work
that are nevertheless essential to the functioning of the economy, as well as to life and
well-being. Key spaces of social reproduction include homes, schools, parks, clinics,
and churches. The chapter considers closely how hierarchies of race and ethnicity, as
well as workers' legal status as immigrants, function to produce a highly vulnerable and
flexible workforce attuned to the needs of production, but profoundly constrained in
terms of workers' social reproduction and well-being.

Finally, the chapter looks at how farmworkers and farmworker advocates organize
to resist these dynamics, claiming rights and a space of **belonging**.

The chapter takes a place-based approach to understanding this topic, using the case of farm labor flows between Mexico and the United States and the situation of farmworkers in the Northern Willamette Valley of Oregon, many of whom live in or near the town of Woodburn. A place-based approach allows us to connect the specific history of farm labor and farmworker social reproduction in the Northern Willamette Valley to broader, structural processes visible at regional, national, and global scales. Specifically, the chapter traces the connections between large-scale events such as the debt crisis and structural adjustment in Mexico, or US federal immigration policy, to the economic activities, social relations, and struggles over the meaning of community in the Northern Willamette Valley.

Out of the Shadows: Latino/a Immigrant Farmworkers in Woodburn, Oregon

Lying about twenty miles south of Portland, the town of Woodburn is the largest majority-Latino city in the state of Oregon (see figure 5.2). According to the 2014 American Community Survey, 56 percent of the community identifies as Latino—a census category that includes US-born citizens of Latin American descent, foreign-born naturalized citizens, legal immigrants, and undocumented immigrants (undocumented residents are likely undercounted in the census, but not absent). Among those that identify as Latino/a on their census forms, 55 percent in Woodburn are foreign-born (US Census Bureau 2014). If we narrow our focus on Latino residents employed primarily in farmwork in the Northern Willamette Valley, these numbers change dramatically: Nearly all are foreign-born, and upward of 80 to 90 percent are undocumented. This part of the chapter will explore the history of farmwork in the region, and help you understand why the majority of farmworkers today are immigrants, most likely undocumented, and how that shift to a migratory labor regime happened, as it did in most agricultural regions across the United States.

The history of farm labor recruitment in the Northern Willamette Valley produced these contemporary demographic patterns. A rich agricultural region, the area has depended on the seasonal availability of Latino farm labor since the 1940s. Woodburn became a "settling out" point for some Latino farmworkers (who at the time were mostly Mexican-American citizens arriving from Texas—not immigrants) in the 1950s and 1960s, even as most farmworkers at that time remained *migratory*—moving across regions depending on the seasonality of harvests or other labor demands.

Woodburn witnessed a more-dramatic demographic shift in the 1980s and 1990s when the demand for industrial farmworkers became increasingly year-round, and many began to settle permanently in the community (the nature and cause of this shift will be explored further below). If in 1980 the Latino population of Woodburn was estimated at 17 percent, it grew to 33 percent by 1990, and to over 50 percent by 2000. Today Latino residents are not exclusively employed in farmwork, and are as likely to work in larger proximate cities such as Salem or Portland, within the burgeoning service sector. Yet farm labor remains a central presence and key cultural and political

Figure 5.2. Map of Northern Willamette Valley (top) and image of downtown Woodburn (bottom)

Source: Map created by Maylian Pak and Jacob Bartruff; photo by author.

focus of identity for Latino residents in the area. (A large number of Latino residents have parents or other relatives who were or are farmworkers.) The **cultural landscapes** of downtown Woodburn reflect this economic and demographic history, as Spanish is the lingua franca, and most of the stores have signage in Spanish (see figure 5.2).

Like many agricultural regions across the United States, the Northern Willamette Valley first became exposed to Latino immigrants as a labor source in the context of the **Bracero Program**, a guestworker program negotiated between the governments of the United States and Mexico during World War II to fill wartime labor shortages.

Between 1942 and 1947 the Bracero Program imported 47,000 workers from Mexico to the Pacific Northwest, and local newspapers at the time hailed Mexican workers as saving the region's agriculture sector (Gamboa 2000). The program in much of the country continued long after the war, until 1964, resulting in the importation of five million Mexican workers into the United States over its twenty-two-year life.

Why is it important to start our story with the Bracero Program? In the case of Woodburn, and in much of the United States—beyond those states such as Texas that physically border Mexico—the Bracero Program marked the beginning of a process that transformed regional farm labor markets, ones that had previously relied on proximate labor sources (primarily family labor, or the seasonal work of poor white, African-American, and/or Mexican-American citizens), depending on the region.

Initiated by the US government, the Bracero Program stimulated a turn toward a primarily *transnational* labor force, mostly of Latin-American origin, across the entire country. The program created strong relationships between specific growers and workers, as many workers returned to the same farm year after year. In 1964 when the Bracero Program formally ended, these labor and employment relations in practice usually changed little: Growers had begun to rely on a set of workers, and those workers had already oriented their lives around seasonal and geographically dispersed employment. Transnational labor flows and employment relations that were for decades legal became "illegal."

From the perspective of evolving industrial agriculture systems, the arrival of *braceros* (Spanish term for "manual laborers") and the establishment of transnational farm labor regimes came at a critical moment. Industrial agriculture in the United States was expanding after World War II, with farmers gaining new access to machinery and chemical inputs, as well as hybrid seeds and plants. It was also during this period that farmers gained access to a disciplined workforce that fit the needs of large-scale, industrial agriculture. Machines and other technologies favored the decline of family farms and the growth of large-scale operations run on an industrial model.

While technology could often replace certain labor needs, it also often created new ones, requiring labor at peak moments—and usually at a higher level, compared to historical needs, simply because the size of farms had grown. Thus for many crops and products, the industrial agricultural model requires the ability to mobilize a lot of workers at times of high need. A side "benefit" of relying on a mobile and transnational workforce for short periods is that neither farmers nor local communities were responsible for the year-round upkeep and social reproduction of workers so critical to the functioning of the overall system.

In the case of the Northern Willamette Valley, key crops throughout the mid-twentieth century included berries that needed to be picked and canned at a particular moment of ripeness, as well as filberts/hazelnuts, cucumbers, and grapes—among others. Growers learned to expect crews of workers to arrive on short notice and be willing to perform arduous labor in the summer heat for twelve to sixteen hours a day during these key periods in the production process. Under this system, for which farm labor was exempt from most labor laws, growers were often not compelled to invest in bathrooms, water, or protective gear. Most strove to keep their costs down as much as possible, contributing to very difficult working and living conditions for workers.

In sum, the industrial farm labor force in the Northern Willamette Valley following World War II through the 1970s was highly **disciplined** (meaning compliant with grower demands and needs despite arduous conditions), and mobile.

How was a disciplined and mobile labor force, suited to the needs of a modernizing industrial food system, produced? Scholarly research on the topic suggests that the intersection of immigration and guestworker policies, racism, and poverty worked together to create discipline and mobility. The Bracero Program, while nominally providing Mexican workers some rights during their tenure in the United States, in practice delivered workers to growers and limited their ability to change employers or demand fair wages and better conditions. (For a history of the Bracero Program in the Pacific Northwest, see Gamboa 2000.) After the Bracero Program ended, many farmworkers became "illegal," which increased their vulnerability in relation to employers and to the broader society. Most people accepting employment in farmwork do so because they have few options, and poverty usually motivates their willingness to accept the difficult working conditions associated with farm labor. As low-wage immigrants, most do not speak much English— a situation that exacerbates their ability to speak out and contest conditions.

The labor camp is the iconic space associated with the labor regime of modern, industrial agriculture. Since the early twentieth century, farm labor camps have been used to house farmworkers during their seasonal stays. Isolated and usually under the ownership of the grower, the labor camp in the United States has operated as essential infrastructure for a labor regime based on mobility and seasonality (see Mitchell 1996). Camps are critical infrastructure because they increase farmers' access to, and control over, workers. The camps allow employers round-the-clock access to workers—with the potential to call people up with little notice. In this context, if farmworkers quit a job, they also lose a space to sleep. Moreover, the camps keep the presence of thousands of farmworkers much less visible to wider communities. Figure 5.3 is an image of a farm labor camp in the Northern Willamette Valley taken in the 1950s, at a time when various state investigations found that over half of the labor camps in Oregon did not meet building codes, and one-quarter of them were unfit for human habitation (Nelson 2008). The image helps make concrete the key spaces of social reproduction available to farmworkers throughout the twentieth century and beyond—the reality of precarious living conditions and little or no access to services.

Yet in the Northern Willamette Valley, like other agricultural regions across the United States, a profound shift in the nature of farmwork and social reproduction for farmworkers began taking place in the 1980s. This shift was characterized by the expansion of demand for agricultural labor, numerically and temporally (e.g., length of season), a process driven by the emergence and consolidation of new crops and agricultural systems. In Oregon, the production of greenhouse nursery crops (i.e., plants and trees for landscaping) rose dramatically in the 1970s and 1980s, requiring year-round workers for pruning, transplanting seedlings, and performing a variety of other timely tasks under the cover of a greenhouse. The 1970s and 1980s also witnessed the expansion of Christmas tree farming, which requires regular pruning. National and state forests began to use Latino immigrant labor (hired through subcontractors) for the large-scale reforestation in the wake of clear-cutting (Sarathy 2012). Additional canning and food-processing facilities opened in the Northern Willamette

Figure 5.3. Farmworker housing in Oregon, circa 1960
Source: Oregon Historical Society (reprinted with permission).

Valley during the 1980s, many of which hired Latino immigrants—documented and undocumented—at high rates. Even farmworkers who did not garner year-round employment with one employer (e.g., with a greenhouse nursery farm or food-processing plant) were able to cobble together year-round employment in the same region in ways less feasible prior to the 1980s. Farmworkers could settle in Woodburn or other small towns and move between jobs harvesting crops, processing food, pruning Christmas trees, or planting trees in the National Forest.

Under this restructuring of agriculture and forestry in Oregon, the labor camp became a less-viable option, since living in any camp was usually tied to working with a particular grower for a short season. Equally important, labor camps were being closed down due to liability concerns—decreasing available housing spaces at a time when demand for farm labor was increasing. A perfect storm was created, producing a "farmworker housing crisis" by the mid-1980s—circumstances to which we will return in the final section when we examine the transformation of social reproduction for farmworkers as they transitioned from migratory workers to year-round and in-town residents throughout the Northern Willamette Valley.

To summarize, the 1980s was characterized by the expanding recruitment of low-wage and often undocumented immigrants, largely from Mexico, to work and settle permanently in the Northern Willamette Valley. This pattern emerged in stark contrast to the preceding era, when immigrant farmworkers were less-visible sojourners in the region—recruited as temporary workers and housed in isolated labor camps. For towns such as Woodburn, the "settling out" of farmworkers in the 1980s entailed the growing and highly visible presence of low-wage Latino immigrants living in apartments and neighborhoods in town (often in overcrowded conditions), and a rapid rise in immigrant children enrolled in public schools. For many white residents, these changes generated anxiety and resentment.

Before turning to an account of these local changes, it is important to consider, from a relational perspective on place, broader political and economic processes that helped shape these dynamics visible in the Northern Willamette Valley. These "nonlocal" factors include federal immigration policy on one hand and economic changes in Mexico on the other—changes that pushed more people onto the labor migration trail between Mexico and the United States.

Political Economy of Farm Labor Regimes: 1980s and Beyond

Federal immigration policy shaped the settlement patterns and labor regimes in Woodburn primarily in the form of the Immigration Reform and Control Act (IRCA), legislation promoted and passed by President Ronald Reagan in 1986. IRCA provided an opportunity for millions of undocumented immigrants in the United States to legalize their status by showing multiple years of continuous residence and employment, as well as a lack of criminal record. Policymakers assumed that IRCA, which also included increased border control and enforcement, would slow the unauthorized movement of workers across the US–Mexico border. Although millions of Latino immigrants did become legalized through IRCA, the legislation did very little to slow the flow of undocumented immigrants across the US–Mexico border, largely because globalization processes driving the displacement of workers (in Mexico) and recruitment of workers (in the United States) continued unabated (see Cornelius 1989).

The expansion of border enforcement following IRCA had an unintended consequence directly relevant to understanding the demographic history of Woodburn: It encouraged low-wage immigrant workers to settle permanently in the United States by making **circular migration** more difficult. Before then, the movement of labor across the US–Mexico border flowed fairly easily, making it relatively inexpensive and safe for a Mexican worker to spend periods of time working in the United States (whether as a farmworker or in other sectors) while maintaining a home base in Mexico—what scholars of migration call circular migration. Efforts to fortify the border continued to expand with Operation Gatekeeper (1994) and the Secure Fence Act (2006), militarizing the border with patrols, physical barriers, and surveillance technology. (For a detailed history of the US–Mexico border, see Nevins 2010.) As a result, since the early 1990s, crossing the border became expensive, requiring many low-wage migrants to pay smugglers exorbitant fees, and dangerous, as border crossers were pushed from fortified urban spaces into remote areas. The ethical considerations of this border militarization are profound, as the number of deaths while crossing skyrocketed in the 1990s and beyond. Despite the human and fiscal cost, the overall number of undocumented immigrants arriving in the United States showed no sign of decline while the US economy was growing and there was demand for their labor. In the Northern Willamette Valley, farmworkers were recruited into expanding and diversifying rural employment, and as circular migration became costly and extremely dangerous, these workers began to call Woodburn and nearby communities home.

A final piece of the puzzle for understanding the growing presence of farmworkers in the Northern Willamette Valley during that historic period in the 1980s—one characterized by a shift from largely migratory/seasonal farm labor to a largely year-round farmworker resident population—was the economic changes happening in labor-sending regions of Mexico and other countries in Latin America. In migration theory the term *push factor* refers to the economic, political, or even cultural factors that encourage and sometimes compel people to leave their homes in search of work. Such push factors were deepening during the 1980s throughout Latin America, as the region underwent the ravages of the debt crisis and ensuing economic restructuring designed to open national economies to the global market. Economies throughout the region contracted, and inequality deepened (see Green 2003). For many residents of Mexico and other places, undertaking the arduous journey to the United States for work became a key strategy for families confronting this economic crisis.

Most relevant to this story, however, is the fact that many rural residents in Mexico and throughout Latin America were displaced as a result of industrial agricultural expansion linked to **globalization** and debt-related **structural adjustment programs**. Starting in 1982, at the behest of the International Monetary Fund, Mexico restructured its economy, opening it up to globalization, and drastically cut government spending. While Mexican peasant farmers did not live a plush existence before 1982, prior to debt crisis restructuring there had been agriculture price supports, subsidized credit, and protected markets (e.g., the protection from international competition in key commodities like corn and coffee) that in combination allowed peasant agriculture to survive. Economic restructuring based on neoliberal and free trade ideals removed these protections and supports, displacing rural **livelihoods** that were estimated at the time to support three million peasant families. Also at the behest of global creditors, Mexico expanded further its large-scale agro-export sector during the 1980s, stimulating more production of winter fruits and vegetables as cash crops destined for the US market. Such large-scale agricultural enterprises did lower the cost and improve the year-round availability of fruits and vegetables for US consumers, but they also displaced small-scale farmers and sent many of them in search of work to the North. (For an excellent discussion of Mexico's agro-export sector and labor, see Marosi 2014.)

In sum, three factors converged in the 1980s and beyond to expand the resident Latino immigrant population in the Northern Willamette Valley: 1) a shift in the kinds of crops and the organization of agriculture and forestry in Oregon that began to offer year-round demand for farm labor; 2) federal immigration policy that encouraged the settlement of previously circular cross-border low-wage migrants; and 3) an economic crisis in Mexico and other labor-sending regions, directly linked to globalization and economic restructuring, which displaced millions of people and deepened flows of labor migrants across the US–Mexico border.

The Politics of Place, Race, and Resistance

The previous section helps to explain the structural economic and political conditions that led to an increasingly sedentary farm labor force in the Northern Willamette Valley, a process that helped produce a "farmworker housing crisis" by the late 1980s. Here we turn to cultural politics and the renegotiation of place and belonging precipitated by the expansion of the Latino population in Woodburn. It is here, in this new rural landscape, that **race** becomes increasingly visible, as does the active role farmworkers and farmworker advocates have in resisting the marginalization and invisibility of farmworkers within the agro-food industrial system. In short, the farmworker housing crisis, and the struggle to build safe, decent, and affordable housing for farmworkers within the municipal boundaries of Woodburn in the 1990s, represent an important entry point into struggles over place, race, and belonging during the midst of these agricultural and demographic changes.

As noted previously, for many decades white residents of Woodburn, and the Valley more generally, did not see or interact with farmworkers on a regular basis—except perhaps for seeing them bent over in the strawberry fields and other landscapes of production while driving down the highway. Yet as the hiring of farmworkers grew numerically in the 1980s, and as farmworkers began to garner year-round employment and to rent housing in towns such as Woodburn, their relative invisibility within social landscapes shifted. Some landlords saw an opportunity: Many began renting single rooms to entire families for upward of $400 per month, crowding four families or more into single-family homes. Farmworkers reported that one way to lower their rent was to live in the garage of a house—despite the cold in the winter that left their children with repeated respiratory issues. Those unable to afford the rent often turned to sleeping in even less permanent shelter. For both farmworkers and many white local residents, the situation was reaching a crisis level by the late 1980s (see textbox 5.2 for farmworker testimonies).

By that time the local newspaper, the *Woodburn Independent*, began to cover the "farmworker housing crisis" regularly, reflecting the shock that longtime, mostly white residents often felt in observing the effects of this process in their daily lives and sense of place. If the previous spatial organization of farmworker social reproduction—the labor camp—kept the presence and experiences of farmworkers largely outside of the eyes and minds of local citizens, the 1980s was the reverse. The newspaper regularly published stories of farmworkers sleeping in public parks, under bridges, or in their cars, with additional stories bemoaning the conditions of overcrowded rental properties in town. While some readers responded to the situation of farmworkers with charity and concern, the dominant public narrative was one of acrimony and fear that mobilized to keep farmworkers out of town. Public narratives frequently blamed the situation on the farmworkers themselves, rather than on the landlords or the lack of low-income housing in a region profoundly dependent on low-wage labor.

In response to the farmworker housing crisis, a number of farmworker advocacy organizations, including health, labor, housing, and legal aid associations, joined forces to found a new nonprofit group, the Farmworker Housing Development Corporation (FHDC). Their goal in founding the FHDC was to build subsidized farmworker housing in the City of Woodburn, within reach of needed services for farmworker families. After a long struggle, they built Nuevo Amanecer (New Dawn) in 1994 and Esperanza (Hope) Court in 1997. One of the FHDC's first board members, Nargess Shadbeh, describes the motivation of these activists and organizations:

Textbox 5.2.   Farmworker Testimonies

Testimony from a farmworker who spoke at a Northern Willamette Valley hearing on labor camp conditions, organized by the Oregon Bureau of Labor and Industries in June 1985 (cited in Nelson 2007):

> I live in a labor camp in this area. . . . There are four wooden out-houses in the labor camp. There are approximately thirty-five to forty men living there at the camp. Nothing but men. The houses are really old. They are falling down. The grower gives us a hammer and the nails and we look for lumber. We repair the leaks in the roof or we repair the floor to get them to be in living condition. . . . The boiler or hot water heater, there is one in the shower room [the only hot water in camp,] and they [the workers] told the man if he didn't fix it, they were going to cooperate and pitch in the money and pay for the hot water heater . . . So they [the workers] pitched in the money and then the grower fixed the hot water heater.
>
> They do not like to complain, like they have in the past; he has told them that they had better leave the camp if they do complain. They don't have any place to go, that is why they don't do anything or complain.

Excerpt of an interview from August 2002, conducted by Lise Nelson with "Elvira" (age thirty-eight), in which she described her living conditions upon arriving in the early 1990s to the Northern Willamette Valley. Her main source of work when she arrived was picking cucumbers and berries, as well as working in a berry-processing plant:

> I came to Oregon because I had a cousin who moved to Gervais, Oregon [about ten miles from Woodburn]. I moved into her garage with my daughters, for seven years. I paid two hundred dollars in rent. They fixed it up, putting in a little kitchen, but we had to go inside the house to use the bathroom. I remember that it was so cold, the concrete floor. We had a little heater, but it was so cold in the winter. I still preferred it to living with other families in an apartment, because in the apartment there were many strangers and I was afraid for my children.

I will tell you a bit about what motivated us to form *Nuevo Amanecer*. . . . Day after day in my work I see farmworkers who have spent all day in the field, hands stained with the juices of fruit they pick and their backs in pain from the hard work but no place to go to sleep in safety or to call their home. . . . Farmworkers live in overcrowded conditions whether it is within the city or in the labor camps, and yes, they do pay outrageous rents compared to what they get in return. The cabins are often controlled by the farmer or the labor contractor. The labor contractor puts as many farmworkers in a cabin as he wants, tells the workers who to work for, where and when to work, and even who they can invite to the cabin for a chat after a long day.

The farmworkers of our community should not live in constant fear of retaliation and eviction from dilapidated shelter. This is not the treatment that a labor force, which supplies most of the riches of this community, deserves. What if you the farmworker did not have to look to the labor contractor or the farmer/employer for the housing? What if the housing was available and within the city? And what if you had a voice in the operation and administration of housing for farmworkers in this community? (FHDC 1992, quoted in Nelson 2007)

The eventual construction of farmworker housing in town by the FHDC—housing developments that have received national recognition for their design and participatory management strategies—represent a material enactment of farmworkers' right to belong, to claim a place of dignity in the Northern Willamette Valley.[1]

Despite the eventual success and national recognition of these two housing projects, the process of getting approval to build these units was very difficult, and reflects the struggle over place-making. In 1991 and 1992 FHDC founders lined up funding for Nuevo Amanecer fairly quickly, using low-income-housing tax credits and support from the Oregon Housing Authority. They found a piece of developable land within walking distance of downtown, land owned by the City of Woodburn due to a foreclosure of a public-private partnership a few years prior. For several years the city had eagerly looked for buyers, few and far between given the economic recession. Nevertheless, when the FHDC offered to buy the property, the city council vigorously resisted. They delayed the decision for several months, and when the issue finally came to a head in June 1992, city council members claimed that they could not sell the land to the FHDC, in order to protect the city's "taxpayers" (although no local taxpayer money was used to fund the project; for more details, see Nelson 2008). They only agreed to approve the sale after receiving a letter from Governor Barbara Roberts stating that the city would no longer be eligible for community development block grants (which had funded the failed public-private partnership) if they refused to sell. The resistance to the FHDC may seem surprising, given that the city desperately needed to solve its housing crisis and to sell the land, the latter absolving them of a large debt. However, the intersection of race, class, and legal status help to explain it, marking farmworkers as subjects without rights to belong. Their presence in labor camps far from town was acceptable, but a living space in town, within reach of schools and other services, proved threatening to many in the white-majority community. Within public spaces and dialogues, questions of race and xenophobia were not *explicit*, but instead cloaked in a language of "taxpayers' rights" and suggestions that farmworkers need to have more housing outside of city limits, but not within them.

Privately, more-explicit invocations of racism and xenophobia emerged in Woodburn. In March 1993, as construction of Nuevo Amanecer was under way, an anonymous letter was sent to the manager of a nearby apartment building, signed "Americans for the Last Crusade":

> The Mexicans are going to have a housing project in Woodburn, right across the street from the high school where their gangs can freely mingle with our kids. If you don't think this housing project will create gangs, just check with police agencies in Southern California. The Mexicans will work the summer season and then spend the winters in living quarters built for them with our money. They will create a bigger dope problem and crime will increase. [. . .] What our politicians (Governor Roberts and her gang) are creating will become a cesspool of humanity. (Rede 1993, cited in Nelson 2008, 49)

---

1. Residents must certify twice per year that a certain percentage of household income is earned from farmwork to remain in these housing units.

This letter was not the first overtly racist message directed at farmworker housing advocates. The day before the groundbreaking ceremony for Nuevo Amanecer in December 1992, FHDC representatives found a spray-painted plywood sign set up at the Nuevo Amanecer site reading: "Future home of Salud's slum." The letter and the graffiti both mark Nuevo Amanecer as a threatening site of criminality and impurity due to the presence of racialized (and poor) others. (See textbox 5.3 for a more-detailed discussion of how scholars theorize about race, and how it applies to this discussion.)

Textbox 5.3. Race as a Social Construct

Scholars in the humanities and social sciences usually start from the presumption that race is "socially constructed." This means that while ideas, words, and images associated with racial categories usually frame differences between so-called racial groups as *biological* (marked on the body by skin color and other physical characteristics), they are, in fact, arbitrary categories invented by human beings in particular historical periods and places in order to justify the exertion of power. Biology is invoked to "naturalize" social, political, economic, and cultural hierarchies, and thus (seemingly) casts these hierarchies as beyond human intention and intervention. However, anticolonial struggles, antislavery politics, and civil rights movements have demonstrated that racial categories are not natural but invented in order to control and manipulate certain groups of people.

The relationship between racial categories and labor exploitation is a long one. Slavery relied on the assumption that "black" was inferior to "white," and people seen as black could be legally treated as the property of white people. Today race operates in more subtle but still insidious ways. In a post–civil rights era in the United States, explicit racism is usually confined to anonymous hate mail, such as the letter sent to Nuevo Amanecer expressing fear and loathing for "the Mexicans." Yet the city council's protracted resistance to authorizing the construction of living spaces for farmworkers in town, within reach of city services—*even when it would have saved them money*—suggests something more than rational economic calculus driving those housing debates. It suggests a racialized fear and loathing, emotions made more complex by the additional challenges of poverty and legal status faced by many farmworkers.

The city council's behavior and language in challenging the Farmworker Housing Development Corporation (FHDC) communicated their shock at the idea that they should facilitate or condone efforts to build housing in town for poor, brown, and "illegal" bodies. That the regional economy relied on, and, in fact, thrived on the backs of poor, brown, and "illegal" bodies did not garner their attention. In this example, one can see how space and place become **racialized**, as many white residents thought it was acceptable to house farmworkers in isolated labor camps, but unacceptable to house them in town, where they would be seen daily and become part of the fabric of the community—of the place.

Today the existence of millions of undocumented immigrants living and working in the United States—some in farmwork, but millions more in a range of urban sectors—raises questions on how "illegality" works *with* racial categories to justify placing a group of workers and longtime residents beyond the bounds of law and human dignity. Public narratives and images discussing "illegals" are heavily laden with images of brown bodies. At every step, "illegality" is racialized in ways that not only affect the everyday lives of the undocumented residents, but also the lives of all Latinos, from fifth-generation Americans to naturalized citizens. These are the hierarchies and narratives that undergird our modern agricultural system, and make its labor system possible.

When neither gangs nor overcrowding materialized at Nuevo Amanecer, and after the housing project won national recognition, one might have expected a more-straightforward approval process for the second project, Esperanza Court. It was more difficult for the overwhelmingly white leaders on the city council and planning commission to stop it, but they still put up a fight. The FHDC purchased a privately owned, empty lot already zoned for multifamily housing before announcing the project publicly. At that point the only means to resist it was in the building approval process, which did force the designers to revise their plan on multiple occasions. Even when every single planning code had been fulfilled, the public remained highly polarized about approving the project. One elected leader testified to the planning commission that "we already have enough farmworker housing," and at the same meeting one commissioner stated to the local newspaper: "I looked hard to find a way to vote against this [. . .] but there is no legal way I can do it [given fair housing laws]." The local paper reported the appearance of protesters at a planning commission meeting, one shouting at farmworker advocates to "go home!" to which they replied, "We are home!" (see Nelson 2008).

The polarized debate came to a head in October 1996 when the city council held a final hearing to discuss and vote on the planning commission's approval for the project. The city council chambers were overflowing, including farmworkers, farmworker advocates, and other citizens both for and against the project. Those against it often asserted that "we need farmworker housing," but argued that *it did not belong in the city*, downtown and across the street from city hall. Farmworkers testified at the meeting about their work and their need for a decent place to live. When the city's lawyer pointed out that any effort to stop the development would be overturned in court, the council voted to approve the project even as one councilor declared he only voted for it because of the "dictatorial powers of the state." In building both Nuevo Amanecer and Esperanza Court, the Farmworker Housing Development Corporation and the cluster of activists working with it were asserting a politics of belonging and place for farmworkers who had long been confined to the margins of the region's social landscapes. Doing so, they resisted and challenged a racialized and nostalgic vision of farming towns as white places.

Conclusion

The rise of industrial agriculture across the globe has relied on the creation of an industrial farm labor force. An agricultural system characterized by larger-scale operations and the use of mechanical, chemical, and genetic technologies *requires* seasonal and sometimes year-round access to a highly disciplined workforce that can arrive on short notice and (seemingly) disappear as needed.[2] For growers, key to the production of a

---

2. I italicize the word "requires" here to problematize it. There is nothing necessary or inevitable about these systems; both the overall system and the labor conditions for farmworkers are choices we make as human beings about the world we live in.

disciplined and flexible workforce is the recruitment of vulnerable transnational workers whose vulnerability is created at the intersection of poverty, racism, and legal status. Without any systematic reform that would bring fair wages and labor conditions to the fields for workers, both documented and undocumented, the life of industrial farmworkers is characterized by long days and low pay, as well as dangerous and unhealthy work conditions brought on by excessive heat, dehydration, lack of sleep, and exposure to dangerous chemicals on a regular basis (see Holmes 2013).

Equally problematic are the conditions faced by farmworkers before and after work—the spaces of social reproduction. For many decades of the twentieth century in the United States and other places, the labor camp was the primary site of farmworker social reproduction—spaces often overcrowded, unsafe, isolated, and marked by unhealthy living conditions. In many parts of the United States today, the persistence of migratory farm labor is complemented by a shift toward the permanent settlement of farmworker families—particularly in regions that through rural diversification or intensification offer year-round employment opportunities. The permanent settlement of many farmworker families challenges the status quo geography of production and social reproduction in industrial agriculture, even as working conditions remain very difficult, and farmworkers still face challenges finding decent housing and access to services.

The struggle over the construction of farmworker housing within Woodburn's city limits reflects the contradictions between an industrial agricultural system that demands and profits from a particular kind of labor system, and a society that seeks to keep industrial farmworkers spatially contained and socially invisible. The efforts by farmworkers and farmworker advocates to construct subsidized farmworker housing in Woodburn could have been seen as a win-win situation for the local political elite in Woodburn, as it addressed a significant and publicly recognized crisis in farmworker housing. Yet because it disrupted the spatial and social status quo that regulated brown laboring bodies as not "belonging" in town, these efforts were resisted vigorously by many city and planning officials. Only through the persistence of advocates, the success of early efforts, and the emergence of city leaders who became allies to the movement did the FHDC thrive and grow. Today the FHDC provides housing to 1,300 individuals in five cities of the Northern Willamette Valley (see www.fhdc.org/about-us). Their example offers hope that through action we can change the exploitative conditions associated with our modern agricultural system.

Key Terms

belonging
Bracero Program
circular migration
cultural landscape
discipline
globalization

industrial farmwork
livelihood
race
racialization
social reproduction
structural adjustment programs

Summary

- The global corporate food regime rests on a flexible and often invisible industrial farm workforce.
- The reliance on immigrants for farmwork is partly explained by structural political and economic factors, such as globalization and structural adjustment programs, which have stimulated migration and increased immigrants' vulnerability.
- The permanent settlement of migrant farm labor is transforming the cultural landscape of rural towns, creating tensions based primarily on race, legal status, and ideas about belonging.
- The exploitation and social exclusion of migrant farmworkers can be observed in the sphere of social reproduction, including the difficulty of securing decent housing and accessing services. However, it is also in the spaces of social reproduction that these forms of oppression can be resisted, as illustrated by the example of migrant community housing initiatives in Woodburn, Oregon.

Additional Resources

This chapter is based on original research described in greater detail elsewhere (Nelson 2007 and 2008).

For an analysis of migrant farm labor in the United States, see the work of Holmes (2013) and Mitchell (1996). The latter offers a geographic perspective that draws attention to the social production of agricultural landscape and the invisibility of labor.

Nevins (2010) provides an analysis of the militarization of the US–Mexico border, which has reduced circulatory migration and led to changes in migrant settlement patterns, with important impacts in agriculture and food production.

Cornelius (1989), Gamboa (2000), and Massey et al. (1990) help to make sense of the impact of immigration policy on migrant flows, while Green (2003) shows the effect of economic restructuring in Mexico.

Several films focus on farm labor in the United States, including *La Cosecha (The Harvest)* (2010) about child labor and migrant families, *Food Chains* (2014) about Florida farmworkers battling a global supermarket industry for fair wages, and *Cesar Chavez* (2014) and *Delano Manongs* (2014), about the farmworker movement in California.

The websites of organizations representing farmworkers provide useful information:

Farmworker Justice: www.farmworkerjustice.org/content/international-labor-rights
United Farmworkers: www.ufw.org/_page.php?menu=research&inc=history/03.html
Global farmworker and farm labor issues: https://migration.ucdavis.edu/rmn/more
    .php?id=785

References

Cornelius, Wayne A. 1989. "Impacts of the 1986 US Immigration Law on Emigration from Rural Mexican Sending Communities." *Population and Development Review*: 689–705.

Gamboa, Erasmo. 2000. *Mexican Labor & World War II: Braceros in the Pacific Northwest, 1942–1947*. Seattle: University of Washington Press.

Green, Duncan. 2003. *Silent Revolution: The Rise and Crisis of Market Economics in Latin America*. New York: New York University Press.

Holmes, Seth. 2013. *Fresh Fruit, Broken Bodies: Migrant Farmworkers in the United States*. Berkeley: University of California Press.

Marosi, Richard. 2014. "Hardship on Mexico's Farms, Bounty for US Tables." *Los Angeles Times*, December 7. http://graphics.latimes.com/product-of-mexico-camps/.

Massey, Douglas S., Katharine M. Donato, and Zai Liang. 1990. "Effects of the Immigration Reform and Control Act of 1986: Preliminary Data from Mexico." In *Undocumented Migration to the United States: IRCA and the Experience of the 1980s*, edited by Frank D. Bean, Barry Edmonston, and Jeffrey S. Passel, 182–210. Santa Monica: Rand Corporation and Washington: The Urban Institute.

Mitchell, Don. 1996. *The Lie of the Land: Migrant Workers and the California Landscape*. Minnesota: University of Minnesota Press.

Nelson, Lise. 2007. "Farmworker Housing and Spaces of Belonging in Woodburn, Oregon." *Geographical Review* 97(4): 520–41.

———. 2008. "Racialized Landscapes: Whiteness and the Struggle over Farmworker Housing in Woodburn, Oregon." *Cultural Geographies* 15(1): 41–62.

Nevins, Joseph. 2010. *Operation Gatekeeper and Beyond: The War on "Illegals" and the Remaking of the US–Mexico Boundary*. New York: Routledge.

Sarathy, Brinda. 2012. *Pineros: Latino Labour and the Changing Face of Forestry in the Pacific Northwest*. Vancouver: UBC Press.

US Census Bureau. 2014. "S0501: Selected Characteristics of the Native and Foreign-Born Populations." *2010–2014 American Community Survey*. US Census Bureau's American Community Survey Office. http://factfinder.census.gov.

Can Farmworkers Afford to Eat the Food They Grow?

When was the last time you ate fresh fruits or vegetables? Where and by whom were they grown? How much did their production depend on immigrant farm labor? What would this produce cost if farmworkers were paid a living wage? Do you find it ironic that many farmworkers cannot afford to eat the fruits and vegetables they pick for a living?

The recipe below is inspired by one provided by Mark Bittman to the Union of Concerned Scientists to celebrate Labor Day and draw attention to the plight of farmworkers (see http://blog.ucsusa.org/karen-perry-stillerman/a-labor-day-recipe-for-a-fairer-food-system). It is a simple dish that makes great use of tomatoes, which are usually perfectly ripe around Labor Day. Tomatoes have been at the center of a farmworker movement in Florida, where the Coalition of Immokalee Workers has led a grassroots campaign and successfully negotiated better wages and working conditions for the thirty thousand workers who pick tomatoes for major retailers and restaurant chains. This recipe celebrates these victories toward building a just food system.

Pasta with Fresh Tomatoes

Ingredients

1 box spaghetti (1 pound)
2 cups diced fresh and ripe tomatoes
2 tablespoons olive oil
2 cloves garlic, minced
salt and pepper to taste
¼ teaspoon red chili flakes (optional)
¼ cup pine nuts (optional)
½ cup fresh basil leaves
1 ball of fresh mozzarella, cut in small pieces

Preparation

Combine the tomatoes, olive oil, and garlic in a large bowl. Season with salt, pepper, and red chili flakes. If using, toast pine nuts in a dry frying pan for a minute or so (be careful not to let them burn) and add to tomato mixture. Chop basil and add to salsa. Mix well and set aside. Meanwhile, bring a large pot of salted water to boil and add pasta. Cook according to package instructions, drain, and toss in tomato salsa. Top with cut mozzarella.

CHAPTER 6

Ethical Food and Global Commodity Chains

Hannah Evans and Pascale Joassart-Marcelli

```
┌─────────────────────────────────────────────────────────────────┐
│               Textbox 6.1.  Learning Objectives                   │
│                                                                   │
│  • Contextualize the rise of ethical consumption in market-based economies. │
│  • Link consumer ethics to global commodity chains, emphasizing unequal positions of │
│    power at various nodes along the chain.                        │
│  • Explore how ethical food is socially produced, both materially and discursively. │
│  • Question the extent to which labeling schemes unsettle global connections between con- │
│    sumers in the Global North and producers in the Global South.  │
└─────────────────────────────────────────────────────────────────┘
```

Recent years have witnessed a rapid growth of ethical consumerism, with food being at the center of many initiatives meant to encourage consumers to shop "responsibly." Relying on labels and certificates, nonprofit organizations have become key actors in promoting the consumption of products that they identify as being produced in fair and sustainable ways. These efforts aim primarily at connecting Global North eaters to growers in the Global South, where much of our food originates and the negative effects of modern production on labor and environmental resources are most acutely felt. In this chapter, we explore those power-laden geographic connections, emphasizing both the material and discursive aspects involved in the production of ethical commodities.

After an introduction to ethical consumerism and its recent expansion, we turn to the concept of global supply chains and explore the power relations at various nodes. We emphasize both the material and semiotic process in which ethical food is commoditized, borrowing the concept of geographical imaginaries. We pay particular attention to the actors involved in the production of fair trade and sustainable food narratives and the voices that are silenced by this process. We provide several examples from the literature and include findings from our own ethnographic research on sustainable rum in Chichigalpa, Nicaragua, to illustrate how ethical labeling hides these power relations and therefore may reproduce inequality. We analyze ethical food narratives from the perspective of different actors who, despite being located in close proximity to each other, occupy very different positions along the commodity chain.

Ethical Consumerism

In the face of an increasingly integrated world economy, serious concerns over global economic inequality, labor exploitation, human rights, and environmental degradation have arisen. This is particularly true regarding food—a most intimate object, yet an increasingly distant and alienated commodity. Anxious about what goes into their bodies, a growing number of consumers seem eager to (re)connect with producers and acquire knowledge about where their food comes from. In that context, **ethical consumerism** and consumer-centered innovations have become increasingly popular as a tool for mitigating human and environmental exploitation and drawing attention to the social, political, and economic connections between consumers and producers. This strategy encourages consumers to take advantage of the opportunity to purchase goods that are certified and marketed as ethical. Consumers typically pay a premium for these commodities with the understanding that producers, in particular those operating at small scales, receive the treatment and benefits that allow them to generate a living wage and adopt sustainable production methods.

This has generated a new form of activism that is largely reflective of **neoliberalism**—the political ideology that views markets and free trade as a superior organization of society. Initiatives in ethical consumerism function as market-based solutions, whereby capitalist forces of production and consumption are utilized as primary mechanisms for social change. In other words, they do not challenge economic relations or international trade regimes, but instead help to reproduce them by creating markets for new products and expanding capital accumulation. In fact, as Bryant and Goodman (2004) argue, "resistance itself is commodified," since resisting environmental degradation or social injustice is expressed through new commodities exchanged on the global market for a premium.

One of the central features of ethical consumerism is that the responsibility for a better food system falls almost entirely on the consumer. Instead of addressing social inequities and environmental problems through direct state interventions such as regulation, tax, and subsidy, individuals are invested with that mission through an emphasis on "making the right choices." This devolution of responsibility produces a new form of subjectivity in which people are "[made to feel] responsible for themselves, their families, and sometimes socioeconomic or ethical issues at other spatial scales" (Bell, Hollows, and Jones 2016, 2). Moral citizenship, therefore, hinges on ethical consumerism.

This form of self-regulation is known as **governmentality**—a concept developed by Michel Foucault to draw attention to the government's ability to coerce and manipulate people without actually imposing rules, but by creating moral categories that divide people between "good" and "bad" citizens (see also chapter 14). Governmentality, including its expression through ethical food citizenship, has an important class dimension to the extent that the ability to self-regulate via consumption choices is influenced by income. As several chapters in this volume illustrate (see chapters 8, 9, 13, and 14), low-income people, whose limited budgets constrain their food choices, are seen at best as "ignorant," and at worst, as "irresponsible" and "morally inferior."

In contrast, for elite consumers who can afford to pay the premium associated with alternative products, food choices become a way to reinforce their class position and moral superiority. As sociologist Pierre Bourdieu (1984) argued in his classic work on **taste**, "knowing" good food is an important aspect of class distinction. This emphasis on knowledge underscores the disproportionate focus on education and awareness among consumers in contemporary ethical food initiatives. Yet, as Hayes-Conroy and Hayes-Conroy show in chapter 13, understandings of good foods are socially constructed and vary according to class, as well as other categories, like race and gender. Ethical food commodities tend to normalize the eating habits of white and affluent consumers as superior.

According to Cook (2004), "knowing good food" requires "lifting the veil of the market" to defetishize food and social connections between consumers and producers. In practice, it assumes bridging the distance between these two groups of actors. Shrinking the food system and focusing on the local scale is one way to attempt to create a more transparent and accountable system (see chapter 11). Yet, in a global food economy, localization of production and consumption in the Global North could have devastating effects on farmers and producers in the Global South who depend on exports for revenue. Another strategy consists of unpacking global supply chains to bring to light and unsettle the uneven relations between consumers and producers (Cook 2004). We turn to these concepts in the next section.

Global Commodity Chains and Power Relations

The concept of the **global commodity chain** is useful to understand and visualize the global connections between consumers (primarily located in the Global North) and producers (mostly in the Global South). Commodity chains metaphorically represent multifaceted links between the various stages of design, production, distribution, marketing, and consumption of global commodities, including food staples like coffee, chocolate, bananas, sugar, papayas, etc. They are used broadly as a tool to help explain the political-economic structure and the division of labor underpinning international trade and global capitalism (Gereffi 1999). The commodity chain literature brings to the fore the uneven power relationships between consumers, producers, and institutional actors at multiple scales (Castree 2001; Dolan 2005). These relationships are built on economic relations, political and institutional arrangements, and cultural flows of knowledge.

ECONOMIC RELATIONS

The commodity chain idea is primarily inspired by the assumption that **capitalism** (and its insatiable quest for profit) drives **globalization** and the spatial integration of economic activities. In that framework, commodities typically flow from the Global South to the Global North, while capital investments, including technology, go in the opposite direction. For example, most raw agricultural products, like cocoa, coffee, sugar, and palm oil, come from developing economies, while patented seeds, fertilizers, pesticides, irrigation systems, and farming equipment come from the United States and Western Europe. Value is added to commodities as they move along the chain and are being transformed by processing, packaging, branding, marketing, advertising, and retailing. Because the Global North is rich in capital and the Global South has an abundance of labor, these valorizing tasks, which are more capital-intensive than farming or manufacturing, are typically performed in facilities located in or financed by the Global North. Transnational corporations—firms that have headquarters in one or more countries and operate wholly or partially owned subsidiaries in other countries—have become major actors in controlling the flows of goods and capital. As a result, most of the economic returns accrue to corporate capital owners typically located in the Global North, while producers in the Global South receive a very small share of the profits. Coffee provides a very good illustration of the uneven distribution of return along global commodity chains (see textbox 6.2).

Commodity chains may be structured in many different ways, with firms or corporations playing a key role in shaping their organizational forms. For instance, distinctions are made between buyer-driven and producer-driven supply chains (Gereffi 1999). Major retailers like Walmart typically control the former by purchasing products like toys and clothing for their large domestic markets from competing subcontractors, mostly in the Global South. The latter are coordinated around production activities like car and computer manufacturing that requires the assembly of multiple components. Researchers argue that this distinction has become increasingly blurred, with chains taking on many different forms. Global chains are also differentiated by the number of subcontractors and intermediaries involved. Although information technology and direct purchasing agreements seem to have reduced the number of actors, it is unclear how these changes affect power relationships and benefit producers and farmers.

POLITICAL AND INSTITUTIONAL ARRANGEMENTS

These uneven relations are not purely economic; they are facilitated by international institutions (e.g., the World Bank, the International Monetary Fund, the World Trade Organization) and a policy framework that encourages free trade, foreign investment, and global integration. For instance, the mango industry in western Mexico was encouraged by international and domestic policies that promoted the expansion of cash crops for exports and dismantled local economies (Echánove 2005). These policies include **structural adjustment programs** imposed by the International Monetary Fund and the World Bank as a result of the 1980s debt crisis, which forced governments to eliminate agricultural subsidies, limit public sector investments, remove assistance programs to small farmers, and privatize public assets.

The sugar industry in Nicaragua (see case study below) has been transformed by a similar political structure that favors privatization, export-oriented growth, and trade liberalization. Nicaragua's structural evolution, in large part, has been conditioned by political reforms reflective of privatized, large-scale, and export-based agricultural

Textbox 6.2. Coffee

As a tropical crop, coffee is exclusively produced in the Global South, with the largest producers being Brazil, Vietnam, Colombia, Indonesia, and Ethiopia. Although it is a major source of foreign revenue in these and other poor countries, historically low world prices means that farmers' livelihoods are threatened by the pressure to sell at or below cost. In 2002, the international nonprofit Oxfam produced a report documenting how increased global competition in the coffee market led to widespread poverty among coffee farmers. The vulnerability of coffee farmers in Africa, Asia, and Latin America is linked to their almost powerless position within the global supply chain, since they rarely own land, equipment, or technology. This is a legacy of the colonial system of the plantation, which is still active in many countries and reproduces the dependence of landless peasants on a powerful landowner. Given the deterioration of coffee-farming livelihoods, many men have begun looking for work elsewhere, leaving women and children behind to continue providing low-wage labor for coffee picking.

In the Global North, demand for coffee has not kept pace with production, leading to low world prices. To maximize profit, the market has become bifurcated between mainstream and specialty coffees. The rapid success of Starbucks in the 1990s and the proliferation of various types of high-end coffee shops illustrate the latter segment of the market and our seemingly insatiable thirst and willingness to pay for lattes and cappuccinos. The majority of coffee is distributed by a handful of transnational corporations, including Kraft, Nestlé, and Sara Lee, which are involved at various stages of the production of both low-end and high-end products.

A comparison of the price of coffee as it travels from the farm to the cup highlights disparities along the global commodity chain. Regardless of the type of coffee, the bulk of the value accrues to roasters, who process, package, and market the product to consumers via coffee shops or retailers. Figure 6.1 (adapted from Rueda and Lambin 2013) represents a typical coffee commodity chain and illustrates the uneven distribution of value-added using 2010 data about Colombian coffee. Roasters of single-serve coffee (e.g., Starbucks) earn over forty dollars per pound of coffee and capture more than 90 percent of the total value-added. Coffee certified by the Rainforest Alliance as ethical sells at a lower price and allocates a larger share of its value to farmers, although this represents a smaller amount.

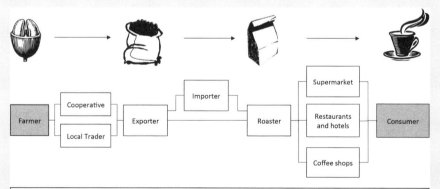

Type of Coffee	Farmer Price/lb.	Farmer Percent Value Added	Exporter Price/lb.	Exporter Percent Value Added	Roaster Price/lb.	Roaster Percent Value Added
Mainstream	$2.34	23%	$0.32	3%	$7.70	74%
Rainforest Alliance Certified	$2.43	25%	$0.52	5%	$6.69	69%
Single Serve	$2.67	6%	$0.96	2%	$43.10	92%

Figure 6.1. The coffee commodity chain
Source: Authors, adapted from Rueda and Lambin (2013).

developments and market-led economic platforms that have undoubtedly served to augment marginalization and exploitation for the majority of the country's working class. For example, sugar production in Nicaragua has received substantial support from the International Finance Corporation, or IFC, which functions as a private lending institution and subsidiary of the World Bank Group. Continued investment in Nicaragua's sugar industry is reflective of one of the IFC's primary objectives: to "harness the power of the private sector to create jobs and drive economic growth in challenging areas" (IFC 2015). In addition to promoting export-led growth, these investments claim to encourage **sustainability** via environmentally sound industrialization and projects like ethanol plants. However, as is discussed later, the legacy of exploitive working practices in the sugar industry contradicts the opportunities presented through free trade and further entrenches uneven power relations in both domestic and international contexts.

CULTURAL FLOWS OF KNOWLEDGE

More recently, scholars have drawn attention to cultural flows of knowledge, including narratives and representations of products and places that help actors along global commodity chains valorize their products, justify their position, and reproduce these inequalities. For instance, Cook (2004) shows how actors along the papaya commodity chain embrace a variety of narratives that hide or justify exploitation. These include abstract and decontextualized depictions of exotic plantations with seemingly happy, self-made farmers, working in pristine landscapes, overlaid with representations of intense and "cutthroat" competition that require business owners and distributors to be extremely knowledgeable and vigilant (see textbox 6.3).

These researchers often draw attention to the spatiality of production and consumption, without prioritizing production. Shifting their analytical gaze away from linear global connections, they have turned their attention to nodes connecting global chains and the particular places where these nodes are situated. "Placing" actors in farms, communities, ports, container ships, corporations, grocery stores, or restaurants, for instance, allows researchers to focus on the local impacts of political-economic processes originating at broader scales. It also emphasizes the contexts in which products acquire exchange value and become **commoditized**. This approach is consistent with the relational place perspective that inspires this volume. Again, Cook's ethnographic research of the papaya commodity chain illustrates this approach by focusing on multiple locales, including a packing plant in Jamaica, a supermarket chain in the United Kingdom, and a flat in North London (see textbox 6.3). He shows how consumer "knowledge" of the papaya as an exotic, unusual, and sophisticated food are constructed in different places, often through **geographical imaginaries**—unconscious or unreflective mental images we have of the world and specific places.

In short, while earlier framings of global commodity chains focused mostly on the political and economic organization of production, more-recent theoretical understanding put greater emphasis on the consumption side, and the cultural process in which commodities become meaningful to consumers. These different conceptualiza-

Textbox 6.3. Multi-Locale Ethnography

Much of the literature on global commodity chains adopts a "value chain" perspective and documents inequalities in income distribution by focusing on economic factors and price differentials (see textbox 6.1). While highlighting a central aspect of the uneven power relations between producers and consumers, this approach may ignore other linkages that an ethnographic approach would likely reveal. Ethnography is a field-based qualitative research method that requires the researcher to spend time in the setting where people live to observe and interact with participants in their daily lives.

Marcus (1995) argued that, in the context of increased global integration, ethnographic methods needed to adapt and focus on multiple sites in order to "spatialize globalization" and better understand how globalization manifests itself differently across space and connects distant places. For Falzon (2016, 1–2), "the essence of multi-sited research is to follow people, connections, associations, and relationships across space (because they are substantially continuous but spatially non-contiguous). Research design proceeds by a series of juxtapositions in which the global is collapsed into and made an integral part of parallel, related local situations, rather than something monolithic or external to them. In terms of method, multi-sited ethnography involves a spatially dispersed field through which the ethnographer moves—actually, via sojourns in two or more places, or conceptually, by means of techniques of juxtaposition of data."

In his classic study of the papaya, Ian Cook (2004) adopts this multi-locale research method to offer a new perspective on global commodity chains. He provides a "series of overlapping vignettes about people who were (un)knowingly connected to each other through the international trade in fresh papaya, and an entangled range of economic, political, social, cultural, agricultural and other processes also shaping these connections in the early 1990s." Cook travels from Jamaica to London and explores how a papaya grown on a Jamaican farm becomes a fetishized commodity for London consumers through "circuits of culture." His research allows the juxtaposition of knowledges about papayas, and provokes ethical questions about consumption. For Mina, a supermarket purchaser, it is an exotic food to be purchased at a decent price and marketed to consumers via free recipes and promotions (just like pineapple or kiwi). For Tony, a fresh produce importer, it is a business opportunity that allows him to support his family. For Philipps, the farm foreman, the fruit embodies tense and ambiguous relations with the white farm owner he responds to and the black workers he supervises. For Pru, a single mother and papaya packer, it is a toxic survival strategy and a symbol of exploitation. For Jim, the farm owner, it is a risky and rewarding business he has carefully built through education, investment, and wise management. Finally, for Emma, the young, educated, and well-traveled consumer in North London, it is a symbol of her eclectic taste and social status. What is striking about these narratives is how they both overlap and contradict each other to create incomplete stories that allow "exotic" papayas to be "picked off the supermarket shelf" without facing inconvenient truths about exploitation and oppression.

tions of commodity chains have in common a desire to "lift the veil of the market" and reveal power inequalities associated with producing and valorizing consumer goods. As an activist strategy, it assumes that, if inequities were revealed to them, consumers would change their consumption behavior in ways that would improve the livelihood of producers in the Global South. This posits the consumer as naive, yet potentially powerful if made socially conscious. Educating consumers and providing them with avenues to make informed choices have been the pillars of fair trade and other ethical

Figure 6.2.   Ethical consumerism
Marketing campaigns encourage consumers to "buy more" in order to support small farmers, solve environmental problems, and end global poverty.
Source: SineadReilyInsomnia and allispossible.org.uk via Flickr.

consumption initiatives (see figure 6.2). This "moral economy" rests on the identification and marketing of ethical commodities through labels and certificates, a political process we discuss in the next section.

Product Labeling, Political-Ecological Narratives, and Geographical Imaginaries

Researchers have suggested that ethical consumption can help to address the inequities inherent to global commodity chains by drawing attention to the exploitation and environmental degradation at the production end (Varul 2009). Certification schemes, such as **fair trade** and sustainable labels, have grown in popularity as mechanisms to reduce inequities while educating consumers. Fair trade programs require that producers be paid a decent or living wage (or receive a "fair" share of income). Sustainable labels demand that goods be produced in ways that preserve environmental resources. Practically, this means that certain standards must be established, enforced, and certified by a third party. For the Fair Trade Foundation (2016), "fair trade is about better prices, decent working conditions, and fair terms of trade for farmers and workers. It's about supporting the development of thriving farming and worker communities that have more control over their futures and protecting the environment in which they live and work." Yet, it is unclear how it supports and empowers communities, aside from the guarantee of a minimum price at or above market price; the payment of a premium managed by a committee that includes NGO, industry, and workers' representatives;

the protection of hired workers' freedom of association and collective bargaining; and the prohibition of certain toxic materials. Establishing tractable standards for sustainability is even more difficult given the ambiguity of this concept, which in its least-demanding version focuses on banning certain chemicals, while in its more-radical form includes goals of economic, social, and environmental justice.

There are incentives for business owners to keep the list as short and equivocal as possible to keep requirements and costs down. The certification process, which is critical in giving consumption goods their ethical value, is therefore a political one. International programs such as Fair Trade, Rainforest Alliance, and others have been established in the past decades to enforce certification and labeling schemes. These organizations function as independent endorsers of particular products and brands that meet certain "ethical" criteria, such as supporting animal and human rights and reducing pollution (Barnett, Cloke, Clarke, and Malpass 2005). These endorsements provide the ethically conscious consumer with the credibility required to legitimate the production process by increasing transparency and producing a feeling of trust (Wright 2009; Bryant and Goodman 2004). Yet, corporate actors have been eager to brand themselves as good social citizens by obtaining certification or seeking alternative (and less-constraining) ways to advertise the virtues of their products. Increasingly, marketing and advertising focus on creating ethical and green products—a process which has been described as "greenwashing." In that context, sustainable and fair trade labels can easily be manipulated due to weak standards and lack of oversight (Wright 2009).

In addition, meeting the list of agreed-upon criteria does not necessarily alter the relations of production or improve the social position of farmworkers. Scholars have become critical of the capacity of fair trade to counter or offset neoliberal and capitalist processes (Raynolds 2000). For instance, according to Harrison (2008), sustainable practices in agro-food activism appear to "adopt neoliberal governmentalities and accommodate—rather than confront—the neoliberalization of environmental governance." Under this interpretation, dissent on behalf of advocacy groups is limited through conformative practices that correspond to "checking boxes" on a list of criteria defining organic farming and fair trade. For example, Trauger (2007) has provided important insights into the ways marginalization and exploitation of immigrant workers remain prevalent in certified organic cooperatives in central Pennsylvania. Similarly, Guthman (2002) shows that the expansion of organic farming in California has created large agricultural corporations, which do not address many of the social and economic justice issues that originally motivated the organic food movement, but profitably meet consumers' growing demand for products that are labeled as organic. Raynolds (2009) has shown how fair trade certification labels, while representative of important steps forward in globalized trade regimes, do little to alter the pervasive social and geographical abstractions that result from the process of **commoditization**.

Fair trade typically claims to "strengthen the influence, income, and security of producer partners" in the South and connect them to the Northern consumer by shortening or even eliminating the social distance between the two actors (Raynolds 2002). By exposing the realities of production, it reduces opportunities for **commodity fetishism** (see textbox 6.3). This can be facilitated in a number of ways, including

Figure 6.3. Political-ecological imaginaries of fair trade production
Representations of people and places associated with fair trade and sustainable labels as pristine and happy.
Source: Rainforest Alliance Guatemala via en.wikipedia.

"fair trade vignettes" used in marketing and packaging, which give a short summary of producers' lives and a description of how they benefit from fair trade (Castree 2001).

In the case of sustainable rum made in Nicaragua, the Sierra Club offers online descriptions of Ingenio San Antonio, the corporation involved in producing rum from sugarcane, its production site, as well as employee benefits (see case study below). However, Wright (2009) argues that this process leads to a sort of refetishization, as the lives of producers become commoditized, "rendered items of consumption in themselves as images and text on the product packaging." This, she argues, perpetuates a slanted view of producers' lives and landscapes—a geographical or political-ecological imaginary (Goodman 2004). For example, fair trade narratives allow consumers to "meet" coffee growers and "visit" the places where coffee is grown (see figure 6.3). This, however, is often a one-way relationship to the extent that farmers do not have the same privilege, and have little control over the production of knowledge.

Case Study: Sustainable Rum from Nicaragua

The corporate-driven quest for socio-ecological equilibrium, especially within the context of international trade and consumption, must always be understood as a political act. With the intention of analyzing the various ways in which understandings of sustainability are produced and interpreted relative to one's "place" along commodity chains, we conducted a case study (Evans 2014) in Nicaragua that focused on sugarcane, and, more specifically, Flor de Caña rum, one of the country's staple commodities. Drawing on ethnographic fieldwork and discourse analysis, we investigated how narratives, especially those related to sustainability, are interpreted differently according to one's place along the rum commodity chain. We show how unique representations of sustainability, in the case of sugar production in Nicaragua, serve to further abstract the consumer from the realities of production at the expense of the rural field worker. In particular, we argue that various forms of violence against workers, such as their blatant exclusion from corporate and media representations of the production practices, are actually produced through sustainability narratives relative to the Nicaraguan sugar industry. This invisibility of labor is especially alarming given the recent onset and proliferation of a particular form of kidney disease linked explicitly with sugarcane production (Wei 2015), known as chronic kidney disease of nontraditional cause (CKDnt).

Our case study centered on interviews conducted with rural cane cutters, living in the sugar-producing city of Chichigalpa, as well as tourists (and rum consumers) traveling from the Global North and residing temporarily in the nearby city of Leon. In addition, we utilized discourse analysis to focus on the narratives and representations produced by the Sierra Club—one of the nonprofit organizations that have independently advertised Flor de Caña rum as a sustainable product of sugarcane—and two corporations in the town of Chichigalpa that have historic roots in sugar and rum production. We focused on the ways in which labor (i.e., local sugarcane cutters) experience the product and the corporation, while also investigating their personal understandings of sustainability and sustainable practices and lifestyles. We compared the workers' interpretations of sustainability with those of ecotourists in the neighboring city of Leon, consumers in the United States, and the Sierra Club, that are interacting with and shaping the sustainability narratives produced by Ingenio San Antonio (ISA), the sugar mill where Flor de Caña is produced, and Grupo Pellas, the corporation that owns it.

Flor de Caña rum represents both a staple commodity and a notorious cultural symbol for Nicaragua. The rum is ubiquitous throughout Central America and is very famously associated with Nicaraguan culture and society. As a product, Flor de Caña has recently been lauded domestically and internationally, specifically by **nonprofits** such as the Sierra Club, for its commitment to sustainable production, including processes such as efficient water recycling and generation and use of renewable energy (SER San Antonio 2015). In fact, as noted above, the International Finance Corporation's direct investment in the sugar industry is reflective of the company's ability to meet the social and environmental standards set forth by the investment firm. However, while the sugarcane industry has reaped the benefits of international investment and endorsement, agricultural workers continue to face marginalization and exploitation in various ways.

For instance, sustainability advertisement, explanation, and endorsement occur only in exclusive places, such as online, at the Flor de Caña headquarters, and at the international airport, which are mostly inaccessible to local workers. In interviews conducted with cane cutters in Chichigalpa, participants were unanimously unaware of the meaning of ethical consumption. Cane cutters in Chichigalpa, largely, were familiar with sustainability and sustainable practice, but not with the fact that Flor de Caña rum is an independently endorsed sustainable product. In contrast, sustainability was referenced largely within the context of community and survival, and more broadly in relation to economic solvency. Indeed, the focus throughout the rural community was on the pervasive and increasingly dangerous CKDnt epidemic, which has ravaged the countryside and contributed to over twenty thousand deaths throughout Central America (Wei 2015). In the past decade, in Chichigalpa, more than three thousand deaths (and 75 percent of deaths among thirty-five- to fifty-five-year-old men) have been attributed to CKDnt, which is itself linked to heavy labor in hot temperatures, as well as exposure to environmental toxins such as pesticides (La Isla Foundation 2016). Given this reality, it is important to note that ISA has continuously denied any links between working conditions and the onset of the disease, despite explicit etiological associations that have been identified and published in both academic and international spheres.

In contrast, knowledge surrounding ethical consumption and sustainable production related to Flor de Caña was most prevalent among Western tourists. The major narrative that is constructed on behalf of ISA and publicized at their headquarters and online relates explicitly to corporate sustainable practice. ISA is instrumental in portraying an image of itself as a company that advances social and ecological responsibility. However, this narrative is exemplified only in particular places and for specific audiences—namely, those who possess the means and knowledge to travel to the distillery and pay to take a tour of the facility. Sustainability advertising here often references ecological innovations in the production process, such as advanced recycling techniques and other waste-management strategies.

However, the headquarters—which also functions as a museum showcasing the company's history—does not include any mention of the employees (and residents of Chichigalpa) that would be identified as field workers. In fact, workers are not referenced even once throughout the entire tour, despite the fact that their relevance to the production process is clearly paramount. That is, while capital-intensive production innovations that highlight various aspects of environmental responsibility are covered widely throughout the tour, labor is not featured as a relevant factor. Yet, it must be socially reproduced or "sustained." This reflects a narrow and static understanding of sustainability that ignores its social aspects and dynamics. It also clearly illustrates the purposeful invisibility of farmworkers that characterizes much of our food system (as discussed in chapter 4).

Despite the contention regarding the invisibility of workers in sustainability narratives in the face of evidence of their marginalization and exploitation, most consumers accept the sustainability narrative presented by ISA. This disconnect can be seen online, through independent blogs that are published by Western tourists, as well as through corporately sponsored endorsements of the product by Western companies. In fact, over the past ten years, Flor de Caña has expanded sales to more than forty countries on five continents, including the United States, Chile, Australia, France, and Canada. As such, in addition to sustainability advertising throughout the Flor de Caña headquarters, independent actors have become instrumental in perpetuating Flor de Caña's brand as a sustainable option for consumers.

One of the most interesting of such endorsements is that of the Sierra Club, which is a well-known environmental nonprofit headquartered in the United States and involved in the promotion and endorsement of sustainable activity and practice. Among the organization's many initiatives is a program specifically targeting ethical consumption. As a subsidiary to the nonprofit, the web-based *Sierra* magazine focuses on providing a guide for "people who care deeply about nature." It encourages a "green" lifestyle, and includes "Act" and "Innovate" links that highlight particular clean technologies, along with "Enjoy" sections focused on promoting the consumption of certain brands deemed "sustainable."

Of interest here is one such publication dedicated to the promotion of "sustainable spirits." This site suggests a variety of brands of alcohol that support a "green lifestyle," including Flor de Caña rum, which is publicly endorsed as an ethical option for consumers, emphasizing production innovations that range from extensive recycling to the repurposing of yeast to create ethanol.

To make their case, *Sierra* magazine (2011) quotes Hamilton, who is presented as an expert on rum:

> Nicaragua's Flor de Caña is the most environmentally friendly distillery I've ever visited. They recycle and reuse 100 percent of their by-products. Spent yeast from the distillation process is converted into ethanol that powers the distillery, and into fertilizer and animal feed. The sugar mill that makes the molasses generates up to 30 percent of Nicaragua's electricity, reducing the country's dependence on foreign oil. The Grand Reserve 7 Year has notes of raw cocoa, cinnamon, and nutmeg and some vanilla and pecan flavors in the finish. About $25 for 750 milliliters.

The website, colored with interesting facts about the alcohol's country of origin and witty references to "mitigated hangovers" and intoxication, paints a misleading picture for the viewer given the environmental and human concerns raised above. It encourages trust and obedience from the presumably conscious consumer through the organization's independent, nonpartisan affiliation and overall mission to make the world a "greener" place. However, no formal certification for Flor de Caña actually exists; the association with sustainability, therefore, is entirely arbitrary, subjective, and independent of domestic or international approval.

It is important to note that this type of certification is not exclusive to the Sierra Club. In fact, many different certification programs are set up and implemented by NGOs with minimal government intervention, including the USDA's Organic label, and the Marine Stewardship Council (MSC) certification program for sustainable seafood. However, given recent developments in worker exploitation within this industry, the Sierra Club's endorsement is particularly troublesome. For example, the concept of ethical consumption here focuses entirely on the Western consumer. As such, products like this one that are used to advance global sustainability are explicitly biased toward those in the advantageous position of choosing the way in which they live, regardless of the production realities.

Consumers' acceptance of the ecosocial narrative put forth by ISA, with the help of international nonprofits, is especially surprising in the case of foreign tourists who are physically closer to the production site. Presumably, this proximity would reduce the distance within the commodity chain and generate sufficient knowledge to "lift the veil of the market." Yet, the dominant narrative is so prevalent and the social distance so wide that it is only rarely challenged by physical proximity.

This case study illustrates that, in the case of Flor de Caña rum, workers are not involved in the production of narratives related to ethical consumption, despite the fact that they are most directly concerned with those issues. Instead, the ethical consumption narrative relative to Nicaragua's sugar industry targets a specific, albeit disconnected group of consumers, and is dependent upon several different actors, such as private corporations and nonprofits, which are primarily located in the Global North. The social implications for arbitrary and independent certification of this product go against the goals of highlighting the poor working conditions and marginalization of workers by conflating these realities with a fabricated notion of sustainability. In fact, independent sustainability labeling of products can be seen, in some cases, as potentially harmful for workers, as consumers are encouraged to purchase a product wrought with historical and contemporary contestations regarding worker rights and protections. In addition, they hinder resistance efforts by silencing local workers or suggesting that any surfacing concerns are being addressed by corporate responsibility and ethical purchases.

The premise behind ethical consumption is to create connections and increase transparency between producers' and consumers' lives as a way of humanizing the production process, while also providing a basis for conscious consumption in globalized economies (Wright 2009; Guthman 2002). However, most of the transparency efforts in Nicaragua's sugar industry are focused on ecological aspects of production, with the goal of showing consumers how to purchase products "responsibly" in order to "help" poor people in Nicaragua. The relationship between cane cutters and consumers is not reciprocal, as workers are left largely unaware of consumer incentives for purchasing, and are not in control of the way they are being represented (Wright 2009).

Conclusion

Ethical consumption—when viewed globally through applications in development initiatives, as well as consumer-based alternatives in trade—is reflective of uneven power relations and carries different meanings depending on who is involved. This chapter has approached the concept of ethical consumption critically, with the intention of highlighting the potential for certification programs to truly offset the normative capitalist processes it advertises against. In contrast, we have shown how ethical consumption narratives can actually reproduce the same structural inequalities it originally set out to oppose. This is most notably visible through narratives that produce geographical imaginaries that are oftentimes exclusive and largely disconnected from the realities of production.

While innovations in ethical consumption represent an alternative to normative capitalist processes that have historically been exploitive, attention should be paid to the uneven opportunities pervasive within these systems. We have argued that current applications in ethical consumption must work within the confines of the market, which can create a precarious future for goals related to social change. As Bryant and Goodman (2004, 360) note, "the political and economic transformative power of these [alternative product] markets will only be taken as far as the market will 'bear.' "

In other words, only those who can afford it will be able to participate in "alternative" consumption. Without redistribution efforts, this means that high-income consumers in the Global North will dictate the direction of these markets.

Key Terms

capitalism

commodification

commoditization

commodity fetishism

ethical consumerism

fair trade

geographical imaginaries

global commodity chains

globalization

governmentality

neoliberalism

nonprofit

structural adjustment programs

sustainability

taste

Summary

- Ethical consumerism has emerged as a form of activism that encourages consumers to purchase products in support of particular goals such as social justice and environmental sustainability. It reflects neoliberalism to the extent that it relies on markets, and shifts social responsibility from governments and corporations to individual consumers.
- In practice, ethical consumerism rests on the identification of ethical products via certification and labeling. This is a political process in which international nonprofits have significant power in the determination of fairness and sustainability, while farmers have a limited voice.
- Although ethical consumerism seeks to increase accountability and transparency by revealing the connections between consumers and producers along global commodity chains, it does so in a partial and biased way. This is partly due to the fact that ethical commodities are materially, but also discursively, produced in ways that fetishize people and places through various geographical imaginaries.
- The case of Flor de Caña rum from Nicaragua illustrates how commodities labeled as sustainable often embody a narrow corporate understanding of sustainability that ignores the perspective of farmworkers. This is illustrated by the invisibility of labor in the sustainable rum narrative, which serves to hide labor exploitation as manifested in the prevalence of chronic kidney disease.

Additional Resources

For photographic documentation of the CKDnt epidemic in Chichigalpa by various artists, see www.facinganepidemic.com/.

A video and additional materials are available on National Geographic: http://video.nationalgeographic.com/video/news/150129-news-under-cane-chronic-kidney-disease-vin.

The Isla Foundation, which is dedicated to fighting CKDnt in Nicaragua and other countries, provides resources on their website, https://laislafoundation.org.

For an overview of supply and commodity chains, see Gereffi (1999) and Mansvelt (2005).

For critical perspectives on ethical consumerism, see Bryant and Goodman (2004) and Wright (2004, 2009).

References

Barnett, Clive, Paul Cloke, Nick Clarke, and Alice Malpass. 2005. "Consuming Ethics: Articulating the Subjects and Spaces of Ethical Consumption." *Antipode* 37(1): 23–45.

Bell, David, Joanne Hollows, and Steven Jones. 2016. "Campaigning Culinary Documentaries and the Responsibilization of Food Crises." *Geoforum*. In press.

Bourdieu, Pierre. 1984. *Distinction: A Social Critique of the Judgement of Taste*. Cambridge: Harvard University Press.

Bryant, Raymond, L., and Michael K. Goodman. 2004. "Consuming Narratives: The Political Ecology of 'Alternative' Consumption." *Transactions of the Institute of British Geographers* 29(3): 344–66.

Castree, Noel. 2001. "Commodity Fetishism, Geographical Imaginations and Imaginative Geographies." *Environment and Planning A* 33(9): 1519–25.

Cook, Ian. 2004. "Follow the Thing: Papaya." *Antipode* 36(4): 642–64.

Dolan, Catherine S. 2005. "Fields of Obligation: Rooting Ethical Sourcing in Kenyan Horticulture." *Journal of Consumer Culture* 5(3): 365–89.

Echánove, Flavia. 2005. "Globalization and Restructuring in Rural Mexico: The Case of Fruit Growers." *Tijdschrift voor Economische en Sociale Geografie* 96(1): 15–30.

Evans, Hannah. 2014. *Sustainable Sugar? Commodity Chains, Ethical Consumption, and the Violent Geographies of Sugar Production in Nicaragua*. Master's Thesis. San Diego: San Diego State University.

Fair Trade Foundation. 2016. *About Fairtrade*. http://amsfairtrade.weebly.com/about-fairtrade.html.

Falzon, Mark-Anthony, ed. 2016. *Multi-Sited Ethnography: Theory, Praxis and Locality in Contemporary Research*. New York: Routledge.

Gereffi, Gary. 1999. "International Trade and Industrial Upgrading in the Apparel Commodity Chain." *Journal of International Economics* 48(1): 37–70.

Goodman, Michael K. 2004. "Reading Fair Trade: Political Ecological Imaginary and the Moral Economy of Fair Trade Foods." *Political Geography* 23(7): 891–915.

Guthman, Julie. 2002. "Commodified Meanings, Meaningful Commodities: Re-thinking Production-Consumption Links through the Organic System of Provision. *Sociologica Ruralis* 42(4): 295–311.

Harrison, Jill. 2008. "Abandoned Bodies and Spaces of Sacrifice: Pesticide Drift Activism and the Contestation of Neoliberal Environmental Politics in California." *Geoforum* 39(3): 1197–1214.

International Finance Corporation (IFC). 2015. Annual Report. http://www.ifc.org/wps/wcm/connect/37e8210049cfbc32b940bbe54d141794/IFC_AR15_Section_2_Private_Sector_Impact.pdf?MOD=AJPERES

La Isla Foundation. 2016. *The Epidemic.* https://laislafoundation.org/epidemic/

Lorimer, Jamie. 2010. "International Conservation 'Volunteering' and the Geographies of Global Environmental Citizenship." *Political Geography* 29(6): 311–22.

Mansvelt, Jane. 2005. "Connections." In *Geographies of Consumption*, 101–26.

Marcus, George E. 1995. "Ethnography In/Of the World System: The Emergence of Multi-Sited Ethnography." *Annual Review of Anthropology* 24: 95–117.

Raynolds, Laura T. 2000. "Re-embedding Global Agriculture: The International Organic and Fair Trade Movements." *Agriculture and Human Values* 17: 297–309.

———. 2002. "Consumer/Producer Links in Fair Trade Coffee Networks." *Sociologia Ruralis* 42(4): 404–24.

———. 2009. "Mainstreaming Fair Trade Coffee: From Partnership to Traceability." *World Development* 37(6): 1083–93.

Rueda, Ximena, and Eric F. Lambin. 2013. "Linking Globalization to Local Land Uses: How Eco-Consumers and Gourmands Are Changing the Colombian Coffee Landscapes." *World Development* 41: 286–301.

SER San Antonio. 2015. Company Website. Grupo Pellas. www.nicaraguasugar.com.

Sierra Club. 2011. "Enjoy: Worth a Shot." *Sierra Magazine.* http://vault.sierraclub.org/sierra/201101/enjoy.aspx

Trauger, Amy. 2007. "Un/Re-Constructing the Agrarian Dream: Going Back-to-the-Land with an Organic Marketing Co-operative in South-Central Pennsylvania, USA." *Tijdschrift voor Economische en Sociale Geografie* 98(1): 9–20.

Varul, Matthias Z. 2009. "Ethical Selving in Cultural Contexts: Fairtrade Consumption as an Everyday Ethical Practice in the UK and Germany." *International Journal of Consumer Studies* 33(2): 183–89.

Wei, Clarissa. 2015. *The Silent Epidemic Behind Nicaragua's Rum.* https://munchies.vice.com/en/articles/the-silent-epidemic-behind-nicaraguas-rum.

Wright, Caroline. 2004. "Consuming Lives, Consuming Landscapes: Interpreting Advertisements for Cafédirect Coffees." *Journal of International Development* 16(5): 665–80.

———. 2009. "Fairtrade Food: Connecting Producers and Consumers. In *The Globalization of Food*, edited by David Inglis and Debra Gimlin, 139–60. Oxford: Berg.

What Sorts of Connection Does Fair Trade Create?

Pick a fair trade product (you can select one in a store or online) and explore the way it is marketed to consumers. Does it include pictures or stories about producers? Is place featured in these descriptions? How are the producers represented? Who controls the narrative? What sorts of feelings does it elicit? How would you characterize the relationship it seeks to establish between consumers and producers? Is the relationship emotional, social, economic, and/or political?

The fair trade movement attempts to shed light on the supply chains connecting consumers in the Global North to producers in the Global South. Through labeling and marketing, it hopes to "educate" consumers and create a market demand for ethical products, which in turn will generate support for farmers and producers. As we show in chapter 6, this demand rests on geographical imaginaries that distort the relationship between consumers and producers.

The recipe below relies on two of the most commonly fairly traded commodities—coffee and cocoa. Indeed, various fair trade schemes promise to reduce child labor, pay living wages, and encourage sustainable farming practices. This recipe is meant to encourage us to consider the benefits and limitations of fair trade and reflect on the sorts of connection we, as consumers, create with producers.

Chocolate and Coffee Brownies

Ingredients

10 ounces dark fair trade chocolate, roughly broken up
1½ sticks unsalted butter
4 large eggs
2 cups unrefined golden fair trade sugar
1 cup all-purpose flour
1 teaspoon baking powder
pinch of salt
1 teaspoon fair trade vanilla extract
1 very strong fair trade espresso-style coffee (2 ounces)

Preparation

Preheat oven to 375 degrees Fahrenheit. Grease a 15-by-10-by-1-inch baking pan with 1 tablespoon butter. Melt remaining butter with half of the chocolate in a large metal bowl placed over a pan of simmering water. Stir constantly until melted and smooth. Remove from heat and mix in sugar, vanilla extract, espresso, and salt (mixture will be grainy); then add eggs one at a time. Add flour and remaining chocolate pieces to the batter and mix gently. Spread batter evenly in the greased baking pan and bake in the oven on the middle rack until the top is firm, about 18 to 20 minutes. Do not overbake; the brownies will taste better if they remain moist. Cool in the pan for 10 minutes, then cut into squares. Lift brownies off the pan with a spatula and serve warm or at room temperature. Brownies will keep for a few days in an airtight container.

CHAPTER 7

Global Hunger

POVERTY, INEQUALITY, AND VULNERABILITY

Daniel Ervin, Cascade Tuholske, and David López-Carr

Textbox 7.1. Learning Objectives

- Define the terminology used to study hunger, including hunger, undernourishment, undernutrition, malnutrition, hidden malnutrition, food insecurity, and overnutrition.
- Describe the current situation and recent trends of under- and overnutrition at the global and regional scale, including where and whom these affect the most.
- Consider various explanations of hunger and malnutrition, including theories based on population, entitlements and vulnerability, and political economy.
- Understand the role of various types of inequalities in shaping hunger.

We have all seen pictures of hungry people: refugees crammed in makeshift camps with little to eat, homeless people waiting in line for a bowl of soup, and skinny infants and young children with distended bellies—all seemingly victims of unpredictable and random natural disasters that have disrupted the production and/or distribution of food. Media attention to hunger is sporadic, and surfaces when earthquakes, droughts, floods, political conflict, or other disasters hit. More often than not, images are linked to fund-raising campaigns by nongovernmental organizations (NGOs).

While appealing to our empathy, these **representations** tend to create symbolic boundaries and distance between the "self" and "others" in thinking about poverty and hunger (Lamers 2005). As Farmer (2004, 271) argues, "the suffering of individuals whose lives and struggles recall our own tends to move us; the suffering of those who are distanced, whether by geography, gender, race, or culture, is sometimes less affecting." As such, these popular representations may lead to a process of **othering** and limit our ability to care and our willingness to ask inconvenient questions. Images of hunger also reproduce Western ideas about the Global South as a place of endless turmoil, conflicts, and disasters that is incapable of generating economic growth and political stability without international intervention from NGOs and multinational agencies. Similarly, the people displayed in these images, mostly children, exhibit such vulnerability that it reinforces the idea of hungry people as ignorant, helpless, and passive. Furthermore, these images typically capture desolate and barren landscapes

Figure 7.1. Representations of hunger
Images of hunger tend to portray individuals as victims of their environments; many show children and young people in desert landscapes. This picture was used by Oxfam to draw attention to the plight of children in Dadaab (Kenya), where many people walked to find food and refuge during a severe drought in 2011. On the edge of the camp, a young girl stands amid the freshly made graves of seventy children, many of whom died of malnutrition.

Source: Andy Hall/Oxfam. Available via Wikimedia Commons at: https://com mons.wikimedia.org/wiki/File:Oxfam_East_Africa_-_A_mass_grave_for_chil dren_in_Dadaab.jpg.

(see figure 7.1), suggesting that hungry people are victims of geography—not human actions—reflecting the same sort of "geographic determinism" that Guthman describes in chapter 9. As Escobar (2011) shows, perceptions and knowledge about development matter, because they shape policy responses, including those aimed at reducing hunger.

In short, the reality is not as simple as these images may convey. There is no doubt that people are hungry because they don't have enough food, but that statement requires follow-up questions. One might ask why some people don't have enough food while others have plenty; why some places are so vulnerable to natural disasters or external shocks while others rebound quickly; why market stalls are empty while storage facilities are full; why international food distribution fails to alleviate long-term hunger; or why impoverished peasants grow food for exports but cannot grow food to feed themselves and their communities.

These questions point to the importance of embedding hunger in broader economic, social, cultural, and political geographies. In that framework, economic inequality and poverty become obvious contributors to food insecurity, since poorer people generally spend a greater proportion of their income on food and have fewer means to cope with any external shocks. But other types of inequalities, such as those based on gender, age, ethnicity, race, religion, and other social distinctions, are important too in explaining hunger. Many of these inequalities unfold spatially, with certain places much more likely to experience hunger than others because of their historical and current position in local and global hierarchies of political and economic power. In this chapter we consider the role of structural forces and their interaction with place-specific conditions in causing a collapse of regular mechanisms of food provision and livelihoods, which produces widespread hunger and malnutrition.

We begin by providing detailed definitions of key terms related to hunger, including undernutrition, malnutrition, and food insecurity. We then turn to the current global hunger crisis and describe its impacts and extent, emphasizing the uneven distribution of hunger both geographically and across population groups. Next, we consider different explanations of hunger, paying attention to how poverty and inequality make certain people and places more vulnerable and less resilient, and therefore more likely to suffer from hunger. Rather than privileging a single cause of hunger, we conceptualize it as a place-based cumulative systemic failure.

Defining Hunger, Malnutrition, and Food Security

Most of us have experienced temporary hunger pangs, but chronic or persistent hunger is a complex phenomenon that is challenging to measure (Jones et al. 2013). Indeed, there is much disagreement about the definition of hunger and the related ideas of undernourishment, undernutrition, and famine. These terms reflect different understandings of what hunger means and what causes it. Therefore, they are often used politically to support different policy agendas. The FAO defines **hunger** "as an uncomfortable or painful sensation caused by insufficient food energy consumption" (FAO 2008), a sustained level of which leads to **undernutrition**: "a state, lasting for at least one year, of inability to acquire enough food, defined as a level of food intake insufficient to meet dietary energy requirements" (FAO 2015). Because hunger is a more commonly used term, associated with strong emotional and physical sensations, it is often preferred by activists and scholars, who attempt to highlight its debilitating and oppressive effects—what Watts (2013) describes as a "silent violence."

Undernutrition can be the result of undernourishment, and includes being "underweight for one's age, too short for one's age (stunted), dangerously thin for one's height (wasted), and deficient in vitamins and minerals (micronutrient malnutrition)" (FAO 2015). We should note that undernutrition can be caused by other factors outside of food consumption, such as genetics, disease, or parasites (Harcourt 2012; Stephenson, Latham, and Ottesen 2000). Finally, **famine** is undernourishment at a population scale. It implies systemic and chronic undernutrition. Webb and von Braun (1994) define famine as "a catastrophic disruption of society as manifested in a cumulative failure of production, distribution, and consumption systems."

In addition to the problem of not having enough to eat, the world is facing a new and related issue called **overnutrition**: too much to eat, or, more accurately, too many calories but not enough nutrients, as in added sweeteners, highly refined grains, and high levels of salt and trans fats that are usually delivered in the vehicle of packaged and pre-prepared foods and beverages (Malik, Schulze, and Hu 2006; Vartanian et al. 2007; Sinha et al. 2009; Walker et al. 2005). Overnutrition has recently surfaced as an important and highly politicized issue (see chapters 9, 13, and 14). It is estimated that two billion people are overweight or obese worldwide, with one in twelve of those suffering from diabetes. What some have described as a nutritional "pandemic" does not occur only in wealthy places. Overnutrition and its attendant health issues are present around the globe, even in some of the poorest places.

Overnutrition is troubling because it seems to be on the rise just as the global community is making progress on addressing undernutrition. In fact, there is evidence that both phenomena occur simultaneously, with many hungry people being paradoxically overweight. As Patel (2007) puts it, the world is both "stuffed and starved." This presents an entirely new set of challenges and foes that our current nutrition response systems, which consist primarily of international emergency food aid, are not set up to handle (Campbell 2012). Yet, the recognition that both undernutrition and overnutrition—the two main aspects of **malnutrition**—are related to the same sort of systemic failures and shaped by similar political, social, and economic inequalities shall help to develop less-superficial solutions than those typically advocated.

Food insecurity, often used synonymously with hunger, emphasizes the lack of access to adequate nutrition. As Patel (2012) argues, "the concept of 'food security' attempts to capture the notion of hunger as a deficit not of calories [as in undernutrition], but as a violation of a broader set of social, economic, and physical conditions." From the United Nations' (UN) Food and Agricultural Organization's (FAO) 1996 World Food Summit, "Food security exists when all people, at all times, have physical and economic *access* to sufficient safe and nutritious food that meets their dietary needs and food preferences of an active and healthy life" [emphasis added] (FAO 2008).

This definition includes four interlinked dimensions that form the foundation of food security: physical *availability* of food, economic and physical *access* to food, food *utilization*, and the *stability* of the prior three dimensions over time. An individual, household, region, or nation is food secure when all four dimensions are realized. Given the range of factors that contribute to these four dimensions, food security remains a complex and difficult phenomenon to measure, much less compare across and between different scales. Jarosz (2011) argues that the shift in the policy literature from the concept of hunger to food security signals a scalar shift "away from national and regional levels of self-sufficiency to individual purchasing power and investment strategies which serve to further the neoliberal agenda dedicated to free market strategies of poverty alleviation" (121). Considering the scale of analysis and place-based contexts that influence the four dimensions of food security is pivotal to understand *who* is food (in)secure, as well as *where* and *why* people are food (in)secure.

A recent review of the food security literature shows that at least eighteen different metrics and indices exist to measure food security, each focusing on slightly different components and operating at various scales of analysis (Jones et al. 2013). National-scale measurements tend to focus on total food availability or supply; a common metric is national food balance sheets, which are (usually yearly) sums of the total amount of food produced and imported. Household-scale measurements often focus on access and utilization of food, such as total food expenditures in a set period of time. These can also include aggregations of individual scale-measurements, like the recall of recent or usual diet, and dietary diversity assessments. Researchers also use measures of the body (anthropometrics), such as height, weight, and body mass index (BMI), which reflect medium- or long-term effects of nutrition status. Finally, more-narrow measures of individual nutrient intake, such as vitamin A deficiency tests, can be used to examine particular deficiencies (Ibid.).

Each metric has strengths and weakness and should be chosen to match the particular research question. We argue that scale is particularly important in this choice. If we are to study hunger from a place perspective, we need to have data that allow us to measure differences across places and assess the role of local factors such as culture, gender relations, political participation, and social relations that are likely to influence people's ability to access and use food. For example, national-level estimates assume homogeneity for the entire country's population and do not accurately reflect differing food availability and consumption habits at smaller scales. These national statistics hide disparities between places (e.g., urban vs. rural), especially as they relate to socioeconomic status, ethnicity, age, or gender (Ibid.).

Programs that monitor food security take many forms. The World Bank Living Standards Measurement Study and USAID Demographic Health Surveys are long-running, multi-country, household-level projects that include questions on food access and utilization, and anthropometrics. These datasets distinguish between urban and rural households and allow for subnational analysis. However, they do not provide fine-scale geographic information that would allow, for example, assessing disparities between households within a city. The Famine Early Warning System, an important tool in predicting food insecurity, illustrates the challenges and benefits of creating reliable and comparable measurements (see textbox 7.2).

There has been a notable push in the international community to reduce the number of people in the world who are hungry and food insecure. This was partly prompted by the 2000 United Nations' Millennium Summit where member states and international organizations agreed upon eight Millennium Goals to be reached by 2015, with the "eradication of extreme poverty and hunger" at the top of the list. As we describe in greater detail below, the global prevalence of undernourishment has dropped significantly during the past fifteen years, from 18.2 percent in 2000 to 12.9 percent in 2014–15 (FAO 2015). Yet, **hidden hunger**, or micronutrient deficiency, affects nearly two billion people worldwide, and is often overlooked by policymakers and development practitioners (IFPRI 2014).

People who experience micronutrient deficiency are not necessarily hungry; they may in fact consume sufficient calories to survive, but lack adequate essential vitamins and minerals. Hidden hunger may actually coincide with overnutrition or the excessive consumption of low-nutrient foods, which can result in chronic diseases, like obesity (Ibid.). Micronutrient deficiency can have long-term negative health and socioeconomic outcomes, restricting people from reaching their full physical and mental potential. Physical and intellectual disabilities, deteriorated immune systems, and child and maternal mortality are among a host of negative effects caused by hidden hunger (IFPRI 2014; Girard et al. 2012). Communities affected by hidden hunger are often caught in a cycle of poverty, and many theorize that poor nutrition leads to lower educational achievement, and, in turn, reduced economic output. The cycle perpetuates itself in a loop of poor nutrition, bad health, low productivity, enduring poverty, and stunted economic growth (IFPRI 2014; Stein and Qaim 2007; Tanumihardjo et al. 2007).

Textbox 7.2. Food Security Monitoring

The Famine Early Warning Systems Network (FEWS NET), led by USAID, in partnership with private-sector and other government agencies, provides rapid forecasting of food security in more than thirty-five at-risk countries in order to allow rapid and appropriate mobilization of resources. Combining agro-climatology, market, socioeconomic, and nutrition data, FEWS NET creates an in-depth "knowledge base" for each county and region. They evaluate the food security situation in countries of concern, combining local, national, and international data about short-term factors, such as current food prices and recent and predicted rainfall, to assess "conditions and outcomes, make assumptions about the future, and forecast likely outcomes." They release "food security outlooks" each quarter based on these scenarios (see figure 7.2). Concurrently, they actively monitor for potential acute food insecurity situations, based on a standardized and internationally recognized scale, in order to provide governments and humanitarian organizations with accurate and clear information to quickly gauge current and potential food security crises and take action. Finally, FEWS NET offers these decision makers resources to develop response plans to food security challenges.

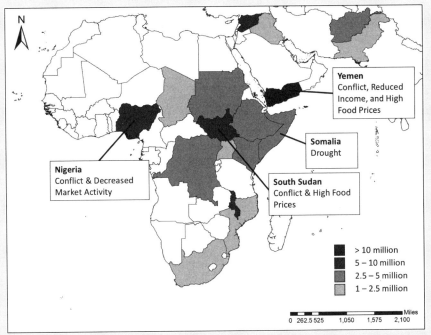

Figure 7.2. Famine Early Warning Systems Network estimates of acutely food-insecure populations for fall 2017

This map identifies several areas with high levels of food insecurity, including Nigeria, Somalia, South Sudan, and Yemen, which are considered at risk for famine.

Source: Map created by authors using data from the Integrated Phase Classification 2.0 (www .fews.net/IPC).

Patterns and Trends of Hunger and Overnutrition

Globally, undernutrition (persistent hunger) affects almost 800 million people—more than one out of ten people on the planet (IFPRI 2016). Even worse, out of the roughly 675 million children on the planet, approximately 160 million, or almost 25 percent of them, exhibit physical signs of undernutrition, which have troubling long-term negative effects (IFPRI 2016). The global distribution of hunger, however, is highly uneven, and reflects deep inequalities in the global **food regime** that are tied to geographic differences in political, economic, financial, and social power (see chapter 2).

Similar patterns can be observed at the regional or national scale, with poorer and less powerful places being home to more hungry people (Smith et al. 2000; Weber and Kwan 2003). For example, Sub-Saharan Africa as a region has a much higher prevalence of undernourishment than other world regions like Latin America and South Asia, where economic development and specific policies have helped to reduce hunger dramatically in recent years. Within this region, in 2014–15, countries like Zambia and the Central African Republic had extremely high rates of undernourishment (i.e., 48 percent of the population). If we continue to zoom in, we can observe significant differences within each country, where certain rural areas, urban neighborhoods, or particular population groups are much more severely affected by a lack of availability and access to food. For example, in Zambia, hunger is especially prevalent in the more-remote northern and southern provinces (IFAD 2016). In the Central African Republic, political and religious conflict has created a dire situation, especially in the northern and western parts of the country (World Food Program 2013).

In middle- and high-income countries, a lack of power can also result in hunger (see chapter 10), which is often manifested alongside overnutrition, leading to obesity, diabetes, and other attendant and deadly consequences of unhealthy diets. Malnutrition is more likely to be prevalent in socially and economically marginalized places, such as poor urban neighborhoods, communities of color, and neglected or transitioning rural areas (see chapter 9). It is worth pointing out that, in high-income countries, malnutrition is paradoxically high in rural areas, where agriculture is concentrated and many people are employed in farming, processed meat, and related occupations (Weis 2011).

Hunger affects those at the bottom of social hierarchies: the poor, the landless, women, children, disenfranchised ethnic or indigenous groups, and those with less education. Various forms of oppression linked to gender, race, class, religion, age, ethnicity, race, etc., intersect each other in producing food-insecure places. To go back to our example about Sub-Saharan Africa, regional and national trends hide the fact that in Zambia, for instance, as in many other countries, female-headed rural households, including those decimated by HIV/AIDS, migration, and economic restructuring, are much more vulnerable to hunger (IFAD 2016).

There has been some progress in fighting hunger during the last twenty years; the number of hungry people has been reduced by about 200 million. This progress has occurred despite the addition of two billion people to the world population during this time, mostly in middle- or low-income areas and among the disadvantaged. This has resulted in the percentage of undernourished people dropping globally, from about 23 percent in 1990–92, to 13 percent in 2014–15 (FAO 2015). The world's two largest countries, India and China, have contributed significantly to the decline in absolute numbers of undernourished people, as they both have undergone tremendous economic growth over this period.

Almost all regions have made significant progress in reducing the number of undernourished people in the last twenty years (see figure 7.3). Latin America has cut its percentage of undernourished people by almost two-thirds, from 14 percent to 5 percent. East Asia (China, Korea, Japan, and neighbors) and Southeast Asia (Indonesia, the Philippines, and neighbors) have made tremendous progress as well, cutting levels of hunger from approximately 30 percent or 25 percent, to under 10 percent. Southern Asia (India, Pakistan, and neighbors) has reduced hunger from 24 percent to 16 percent. In Africa, progress has been slower, and the record is less positive. Northern Africa has maintained its very low levels of undernourishment, and Sub-Saharan Africa has reduced it from 33 percent to 23 percent. However, the Central African subregion has experienced increases in hunger. Another region where hunger has increased, albeit from a lower baseline of 6 percent to 8 percent, is Western Asia (or the Middle East). These increases in undernourishment are likely related to ongoing political conflicts in these regions.

The relatively "good" news illustrated in figure 7.3 hides dramatic disparities in *who* the remaining 800 million people affected by hunger are, and *where* this phenomenon is most acute. It also masks the explosive rise in overnutrition, which now far exceeds undernutrition globally, and accompanies hunger in almost every place, at every scale. Fewer than twenty countries in the world do not experience simultaneously some significant level of undernutrition in women and children *and* a substantial

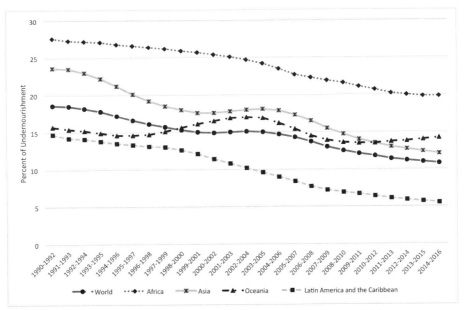

Figure 7.3. Percent undernourished by world region, 1990 to 2016
Source: Figure created by authors using data from the FAO (2016).

number of adults who are overweight or obese (IFPRI 2014). This "double" or "dual" burden of hunger and overnutrition is a new, but widespread, phenomenon (Doak et al. 2005; Kennedy et al. 2006).

These patterns and trends, including the unequal distribution of hunger around the world, suggest that a number of factors are at play, including global patterns of uneven development and climate change, as well as more-localized processes linked to state capabilities, environmental resources, cultural practices, gender equality, and ethnic and religious relations. We turn to these factors in the next section as we consider various theoretical explanations of hunger.

Explaining Hunger: Environment, Population, Poverty, and Vulnerability

ENVIRONMENT, POPULATION, AND FOOD INSECURITY

Poor nutritional status perpetuates poverty and poverty perpetuates hunger and food insecurity, creating a deleterious feedback loop. Surprisingly, connecting the relationship between poverty, hunger, and food insecurity is a relatively new concept. As late as the 1980s, most research identified demographic factors (e.g., rapid population growth) or environmental events (e.g., drought, floods, pests) as the major causes of hunger (Baro and Deubel 2006). Because drought, floods, pests, crop failure, and a host of other supply-side issues are perceived as temporary, hunger was primarily addressed on a short-term emergency basis via international food aid. Indeed, most policies aimed at reducing hunger and food insecurity focused solely on distributing emergency food aid during acute famines. In addition, policymakers concluded that people were hungry because not enough food was being produced. Therefore, long-term interventions consisted primarily of increasing national-level food supply, yields, and productivity via capital investments, which often originated from international agencies, such as the World Bank and the International Monetary Fund, or foreign corporations.

The problem of hunger has also long been framed as a problem of "too many people"—too many mouths to feed. The most widely known theories concerning the relationship between population and agriculture have not changed notably over the last two centuries. Thomas Malthus famously wrote at the end of the eighteenth century that increasing population would inevitably lead to famine and death. **Malthusian theory** predicts that unchecked population growth increases "geometrically" (exponentially), while food production can only increase "arithmetically" by cultivating more land to produce additional food (Bilsborrow and Carr 2001; Malthus 1803). This theory and its modern "Neo-Malthusian" versions call for population growth to be halted, or at least controlled, to prevent mass hunger.

Yet, the fact that global population has doubled nearly three times since the publication of Malthus's work without a global collapse of population suggest that there may be flaws in his predictions. Of course, there have been numerous and devastating famines in various places, but none at the scale predicted by Malthus and others. The ability to increase the amount and quality of food while population rose at a never-before-seen rate is usually attributed to industrialization and mechanization, which allowed for energy to substitute for other forms of labor. The invention of chemical fertilizer and pesticides and other advances in agriculture have led to what is often called the "green revolution," which fostered exponential increases in agricultural productivity. It is important to note that these unprecedented productivity increases, which primarily rely on technology developed and financed in the Global North, reflect increased control of transnational corporations and multilateral organizations in the global food regime, which limit food sovereignty in Global South nations (see chapters 2 and 4).

There is also evidence that the green revolution and related technologies, such as genetically modified crops, have imposed significant costs to the environment. Indeed, today, many Neo-Malthusians point to the loss of natural lands and biodiversity due to agriculture, the potential exhaustion of fossil fuels, and resultant climate change, expounding that we are at another critical period when we must dramatically reduce population. Others argue that lowering our consumption, especially by moving away from animal-derived foods, may be sufficient, while still others are optimistic that the resulting pressures upon society will force new technologies and innovations.

In that context, it is also important to recognize that food consumption and production varies significantly across places, requiring different amounts of resources to grow, process, and transport. The environmental impacts of food production and global supply chains are discussed elsewhere in this book, but in general, meat, milk, and cheese, as well as highly processed food, require far more land and other resources than whole plant-based foods (see chapters 3, 4, and 6, in particular). Residents in higher-income places consume more food per person and far more red meat, animal products, and processed food. In one study, per capita consumption of calories was found to be more than 250 percent higher and protein consumption 430 percent higher when contrasting the richest and the poorest nations (Tilman et al. 2011). Urban residents in middle- and low-income countries, who are increasingly alienated from the places where food is produced, also consume many more total calories and resource-intensive foods than do their rural counterparts. More-informed decisions about what food to produce, including a switch away from animal protein and crops with a high ecological footprint, may help to prevent or delay Malthusians' dire predictions.

ENTITLEMENTS, VULNERABILITY, AND RESILIENCE

In his 1981 seminal work, *Poverty and Famines: An Essay on Entitlement and Deprivation*, Nobel laureate Amartya Sen uprooted the supply-side argument. Sen contended that starvation is not a result of a lack of food at the national or even regional level. To understand hunger, he posited that we need to better understand *why* some groups do not have enough food. Lack of income may be one simple explanation as to why people do not have enough food. Sen, however, was not satisfied with this answer, and asked: "Why don't people have the income?" and "Why is their current income insufficient to purchase food?" These questions draw attention to the role of markets and to factors that may prevent them from functioning as expected. Sen proposed that a person's ability to command food depends on a suite of **entitlements** that each person or group has in a given society. What a person owns, what exchange possibilities are available, what is free and what is taken from a person determine his or her entitlements.

Such entitlements can be direct or indirect. For example, a cassava farmer in Ghana can directly produce food to feed herself and her family. Alternatively, she can also sell some of her crop at the local market and purchase food, or she can do a combination of both. An urban slum street vendor's entitlement may solely be his ability to make an income by selling items at his stall. Because he does not have access to land and cannot grow food, his entitlements are more limited and require him to purchase food. Any factor that reduces these entitlements, and people's capacities to participate in the market, reduces a person's ability to secure enough food for a healthy life (Sen 1981).

What Sen's work and subsequent research have continued to show is that entitlements are influenced by one's position in society and the functioning of global, national, and local institutions. Institutional factors, including well-established property rights and operating markets, exercise a significant impact on entitlements. Sen's work was also instrumental in drawing attention to the role of **gender** in limiting entitlements in India and elsewhere. Girls' and women's access to adequate food, including their ability to grow food, is hampered by the laws restricting their rights to own or inherit land, borrow money, or engage in contracts; by the social norms underlying gendered domestic and child-rearing responsibilities; by persistent gender discrimination in paid employment; and by political exclusion from decision-making processes (Watson 2015). More recently, others have emphasized the constraints imposed by religion, class, race, ethnicity, and sexuality, which create difference and are used to limit entitlements.

As the discussion of food security and hunger has shifted toward the relationship between entitlement failure and poverty, there has been an increased emphasis on understanding who is vulnerable to hunger and food insecurity, as well as why and where **vulnerability** is common. The concept of vulnerability has gained traction in theory and policy because of its usefulness in combining the idea of entitlements with external stressors and risk factors like climate change, conflict, or global economic crises. In that framework, groups or individuals vulnerable to food insecurity face exposure to stresses, environmental or social, without the capacity to *adapt* in order to mitigate or manage these stresses (Adger 2006). **Resilience**, which includes the capacity to adapt, refers to the amount of stress a system—which could be a country, region, city, social group, household, or individual—can withstand before a reduction in food security occurs (Adger 2006). Some have raised concerns, however, about applying a concept initially used in the context of natural disasters to situations caused by systematic inequalities and political-economic decisions. In the latter cases, resilience might "be deployed as an inducement to putting up with precarity and inequality and accepting the deferral of demands for change, and as a means of relocating responsibility" (Diprose 2015, 45).

A household may be vulnerable to food insecurity if one or more entitlements are exposed to a hazard or risk. For example, a teenage subsistence fisherman in Samoa is vulnerable to food insecurity if he becomes sick and cannot fish in a similar way a factory worker's family in São Paulo is vulnerable to food insecurity if she loses her job and cannot buy food. However, the factory worker may have the ability to secure other employment to cope with the loss of income, whereas the fisherman may not have other avenues. The fisherman, however, may be connected to a tighter fishing community, where social networks of reciprocity provide a safety net, in contrast to the factory worker living in the large and fragmented metropolis of São Paulo. The role of the state in providing a safety net, either through direct food assistance, or indirectly, through social and economic policy, may also differ. Thus, while both individuals may be equally impoverished, they are differently vulnerable to food insecurity. While risks can be economic, cultural, political, or environmental, food insecurity arises as a consequence of human activity, and can be prevented by behavior change or political action (Adger 2006). This perspective is a significant advance over earlier approaches that envisioned hunger as a result of external forces and ignored the social factors that shape the way people are able to respond and adapt to these shocks.

Poverty and vulnerability, especially in the context of food security, are not synonymous. Poverty suggests a spatiotemporally static concept, whereas vulnerability describes a dynamic process of change in a person's condition (Moser 1998). A person can be poor but not vulnerable (e.g., Amazonian subsubsistence farmers), or vulnerable but not absolutely or comparatively poor (e.g., Syrian refugees to Turkey). Vulnerability is more than a lack of tradable currency or goods; it includes potential exposure to risks, hazards, shocks, and stresses, as well as the ability to adapt to these. Defining vulnerability requires an understanding of the sensitivity to risks, the ability to avoid these risks, as well as the potential resilience to recover from or cope with negative events. Using Sen's concept of entitlement, short-term solutions may help people cope with a loss of entitlements, but decreasing vulnerability and promoting resilience requires long-term solutions that reduce social inequalities and empower people (Moser 1998).

POLITICAL ECONOMY

More-radical understandings of entitlements and hunger critique Sen's approach for emphasizing institutional factors underpinning the functioning of food markets and neglecting the role of political and economic structural factors in creating conditions of vulnerability (Baro and Deubel 2006). Scholars have highlighted the significance of uneven economic development, neoliberal policies, and the social disruption they create in increasing vulnerability, poverty, and inequality (Escobar 2011; Lawson 2014; Watts 2013). Many point specifically to the negative consequences of trade agreements, foreign direct investment, and **structural adjustment programs** undertaken since the mid-1970s underlying the contemporary global food regime (see chapter 2). The removal of agricultural subsidies and trade barriers, along with a shift toward export-oriented cash crops, has significantly weakened local livelihoods and subsistence agriculture in the Global South. Global price instability, including fluctuations to both extremes of low and high global prices for commodities, has had severe consequences on Third World countries that depend on food export for revenue and food imports for food. Neoliberal policies, once advocated as an effective way to reduce hunger by increasing productivity, seem to have failed and instead exacerbated the vulnerability of people and places.

Studies of hunger within the political-economic perspective tend to adopt a place-based approach in which they connect localized histories of hunger to structural processes unfolding at various scales. Watts (2013) in his research on famine, through a detailed case study of a village in northern Nigeria, sheds light on the relationship between famine, climate, and political economy. He shows how the incorporation of African peasants into the global circuits of capitalism, starting in the colonial era and continuing today, has threatened rural **livelihoods**. Watts critiques the concepts of vulnerability or entitlements developed by Sen (1981) for being too narrow and static. First, they are primarily focused on factors affecting command over food in a market system, and fail to consider the structural political, economic, and social factors "that allocate or deprive households and individuals of assets and endowments" and "mark the onset of the famine process" (2013, lxx). Second, they ignore historical processes and "explain neither what transpires in the wake of mass starvation nor the lineaments linking a single famine to earlier or later crises" (2013, lxx). Instead of vulnerability based on individual entitlements, Watts and Bohle (1993) write about "spaces of vulnerability," which are shaped by the political-economic structures of capitalism and relations of power.

Echoing the concept of **structural violence** (Farmer 1996, 2004), Watts describes hunger as a sort of "silent violence" imposed on the powerless—"the permanency and normalization of hunger, [. . .] the reduction of human existence to bare life, [. . .] a slow death by attrition" (2013). In the case of Nigeria, he links this silent violence to agricultural decline and increased dependence on global food markets prompted by the postcolonial state's pursuit of oil wealth, which reshaped the economic, social, and political lifeblood of Nigeria. Much of the country's oil wealth has been exported, stolen, and wasted; it has encouraged corruption, political instability, and ethnic strife; and it has contributed to hunger and malnutrition among peasants who have lost their livelihoods. Hunger needs to be understood as the result of these historical and economically driven processes of social inequality. For Farmer, who studied health and poverty in Haiti's Central Plateau, "structural violence is violence that is exerted systematically—that is, indirectly—by everyone who belongs to a certain social order" (2004, 308). Systematic oppression is linked to large-scale social forces—"racism of one form or another, gender inequality, and above all brute poverty in the face of affluence" (2004, 317)—and becomes *embodied* as individual experiences of hunger, disease, and suffering (see chapter 2 for a discussion of embodiment).

Another example comes from Mexico, where the North American Free Trade Agreement (NAFTA) has led to the dismantling of the *ejidal* communal land system; the consolidation of landholdings in the hands of foreign corporations; and the expanded industrial cultivation of crops, including genetically engineered varieties of corn (see chapter 4) and fruits for exports (Echánove 2005). This has resulted in a loss of rural livelihoods, leading to rapid urbanization and migration—two processes with important ties to vulnerability (FAO 2016).

Indeed, globally, we are experiencing an unprecedented growth in urbanization, with more than half of the world population now living in cities—many in slums and disadvantaged areas (Reba, Reitsma, and Seto 2016). This is partially accounted for by our current "age of migration," wherein billions have migrated from rural to urban areas within their own countries, and hundreds of millions have migrated internationally in search of opportunities (Castles and Miller 1993). These two interlocking processes mean that a growing number of people live in places where they can no longer grow food and must rely on imported and mass-produced staples. This shift signals a decline in **food sovereignty**, defined as the tandem rights of people "to healthy and culturally appropriate food produced through ecologically sound and sustainable methods" and "to define their own food and agriculture systems" (Nyéléni Forum for Food Sovereignty 2007). In that political-economic framework, hunger cannot be dissociated from the structural forces that disempower people in the global food system. As such, it calls for resistance to the current global and corporate food regime as the basis for the fight against hunger, and seeks to "empower peasant and family farmer–driven agriculture, artisanal fishing, pastoralist-led grazing, and food production, distribution, and consumption based on environmental, social, and economic sustainability" (Nyéléni Forum for Food Sovereignty 2007).

Conclusion

With rapid urbanization, changing migration flows, mounting environmental pressures associated with climate change, feeble institutions, growing economic inequality, and persistent social injustices linked to gender, race, ethnicity, and religion, we face a daunting challenge. How will we feed more people in a way that sustains their health, culture, and livelihoods while preserving the environment for future generations? How will we cope with the millions of people suffering from hunger and malnutrition?

In this chapter, we have shown that the underlying drivers of various types of malnutrition are linked to a lack of access, which results from inequality and limited power. Many of these inequalities unfold spatially, with certain places much more likely to experience hunger than others because of their historical and current position in local and global political and economic relations of power.

While undernutrition has declined globally and regionally, both as a total number and as a percentage of the population since World War II, this has not occurred evenly across places and population groups. Moreover, hidden hunger, a chronic lack of micronutrients, has not experienced the same decline in this time period, and overnutrition has actually increased globally, with marginalized people more likely to suffer from malnutrition.

A place perspective allows us to conceptualize hunger and malnutrition as a localized phenomenon shaped by larger-scale processes. While population growth and environmental disasters reduce food production and may lead to famine, contemporary explanations agree that hunger is less about a lack of food than a person, group, or region's ability to access food and control resources needed to do so.

To make progress in solving persistent hunger and malnutrition, we need to move beyond emergency assistance and address the deep inequalities that underlie poverty and vulnerability. It is also becoming increasingly important to recognize the similarities in the causation of undernutrition and malnutrition and treat them simultaneously.

In recent years, food movements have emerged around the world, encouraging people to eat locally; to eat less animal products and processed and packaged foods; to eat fairly traded food that provides growers with their fair share of revenue; to protect farmers and farmland; and to encourage sustainable systems of all types and at all scales. These new or reinvented relationships to food are likely to reduce the environmental impacts of food production, generate a more equitable distribution of food and resources, and support food-based livelihoods. As such, they will address some of the causes of hunger and malnutrition. We encourage you to search for your own answers and to keep a critical perspective.

Key Terms

entitlements
famine
food regime
food insecurity
food sovereignty
gender
hidden hunger
hunger
livelihood
malnutrition

Malthusian theory
othering
overnutrition
representation
resilience
structural adjustment programs
structural violence
undernutrition
vulnerability

Summary

- Despite recent progress in reducing worldwide hunger, it remains a very important problem with severe health and social consequences.
- Hunger is associated with food insecurity and several aspects of malnutrition, including undernutrition and overnutrition, which in the contemporary food regime seem to be increasingly connected.
- Defining hunger is a political act that shapes how we respond to its various manifestations, from hidden hunger to famine.
- There are three main theoretical explanations of hunger: Malthusian theory focuses on population growth and limited natural resources; entitlement theory emphasizes individual capacities to access food, as well as vulnerability and resilience to hazards; political economy suggests that hunger is a form of structural violence created by the inequalities inherent to global capitalism and neoliberalism.

Additional Resources

Most of the statistics presented in this chapter came from the International Food Policy Research Institute (IFPRI 2016) and the Food and Agriculture Organization (FAO 2015). These recent reports from reliable international agencies provide useful data on the state of malnutrition globally, by region, and by country. Much valuable information can be gathered on the FAO website associated with its annual report on food insecurity, at: www.fao.org/hunger/en.

Sen (1981) and Watts (2013) are seminal works that have advanced our theoretical understanding of hunger from the different perspectives of institutional economics and political economy.

Weeks (2014) has written a comprehensive textbook on population, which includes a discussion of hunger and the environment, and offers a geographic perspective.

We Feed the World (Grasser and Wagenhofer 2009) is a visually striking documentary about commercial food production and its worldwide effects.

References

Adger, W. Neil. 2006. "Vulnerability." *Global Environmental Change* 16 (3):268–81.

Baro, Mamadou, and Tara F. Deubel. 2006. "Persistent Hunger: Perspectives on Vulnerability, Famine, and Food Security in Sub-Saharan Africa." *Annual Review of Anthropology* 35: 521–38.

Bilsborrow, Richard E., and David L. Carr. 2001. "Population, Agricultural Land Use and the Environment in Developing Countries." In *Tradeoffs or Synergies? Agricultural Intensification, Economic Development and the Environment*, edited by David R. Lee and Christopher B. Barrett, 35–56. Wallingford: CABI.

Campbell, Hugh. 2012. "Let Us Eat Cake? Historically Reframing the Problem of World Hunger and Its Purported Solutions." In *Food Systems Failure: The Global Food Crisis and the Future of Agriculture*, edited by Christopher J. Rosin, Hugh Campbell, and Paul V. Stock. Abingdon: Earthscan.

Castles, Stephen, and Mark J. Miller. 1993. *The Age of Migration: International Population Movements in the Modern World.* New York: Guilford Press.

Diprose, Kristina. 2015. "Resilience is Futile." *Soundings* 58(58):44–56.

Doak, Colleen M., Linda S. Adair, Margaret Bentley, Carlos Monteiro, and Barry M. Popkin. 2005. "The Dual Burden Household and the Nutrition Transition Paradox." *International Journal of Obesity* 29(1): 129–36.

Echánove, Flavia. 2005. "Globalization and Restructuring in Rural Mexico: The Case of Fruit Growers." *Tijdschrift voor Economische en Sociale Geografie* 96(1): 15–30.

Escobar, Arturo. 2011. *Encountering Development: The Making and Unmaking of the Third World.* Princeton: Princeton University Press.

Famine Early Warning Systems Network. *About Our Work.* www.fews.net/our-work.

FAO. 2008. *An Introduction to the Basic Concepts of Food Security.* Food and Agricultural Organization of the United Nations. www.fao.org/docrep/013/al936e/al936e00.pdf.

———. 2015. *The State of Food Insecurity in the World 2015: Taking Stock of Uneven Progress.* Rome: Food and Agriculture Organization of the United Nations. www.fao.org/3/a-i4646e.pdf.

———. 2016. *Immigration and Protracted Crises*. Food and Agricultural Organization of the United Nations. www.fao.org/3/a-i6101e.pdf.

Farmer, Paul. 1996. "On Suffering and Structural Violence: A View from Below." *Daedalus* 125(1): 251–83.

———. 2004. "An Anthropology of Structural Violence." Sidney Mintz Lecture. *Current Anthropology* 45(3): 305–25.

Girard, Amy W., Julie L. Self, Corey McAuliffe, and Olafunke Olude. 2012. "The Effects of Household Food Production Strategies on the Health and Nutrition Outcomes of Women and Young Children: A Systematic Review." *Paediatric and Perinatal Epidemiology* 26(s1): 205–22.

Grasser, Helmut, and Erwin Wagenhofer. 2009. *We Feed the World*. Documentary Film. New York: Kino International.

Harcourt, Alexander H. 2012. *Human Biogeography*. Berkeley: University of California Press.

IFAD. 2016. *Rural Poverty in Zambia*. International Fund for Agricultural Development. www.ruralpovertyportal.org/country/home/tags/zambia.

IFPRI. 2014. *Global Nutrition Report 2014: Actions and Accountability to Accelerate the World's Progress on Nutrition*. Washington, DC: International Food Policy Research Institute.

———. 2016. *Global Nutrition Report 2016: From Promise to Impact: Ending Malnutrition by 2030*. Washington, DC: International Food Policy Research Institute.

Jarosz, Lucy. 2011. "Defining World Hunger: Scale and Neoliberal Ideology in International Food Security Policy Discourse." *Food, Culture and Society* 14(1): 117–39.

Jones, Andrew D., Francis M. Ngure, Gretel Pelto, and Sera L. Young. 2013. "What Are We Assessing When We Measure Food Security? A Compendium and Review of Current Metrics." *Advances in Nutrition* 4(5): 481–505.

Kennedy, G., G. Nantel, and P. Shetty. 2006. "Assessment of the Double Burden of Malnutrition in Six Case Study Countries." In *The Double Burden of Malnutrition: Case Studies from Six Developing Countries*, FAO Food and Nutrition Paper 84:1–20.

Lamers, Machiel. 2005. "Representing Poverty, Impoverishing Representation? A Discursive Analysis of an NGO's Fundraising Posters." *Graduate Journal of Social Science* 2(1): 37–74.

Lawson, Victoria. 2014. *Making Development Geography*. New York: Routledge.

Malik, Vasanti S., Matthias B. Schulze, and Frank B. Hu. 2006. "Intake of Sugar-Sweetened Beverages and Weight Gain: A Systematic Review." *American Journal of Clinical Nutrition* 84(2): 274–88.

Malthus, Thomas Robert. 1803. *An Essay on Population*. London: JM Dent and Sons.

Moser, Caroline O. N. 1998. "The Asset Vulnerability Framework: Reassessing Urban Poverty Reduction Strategies." *World Development* 26(1): 1–19.

Nyéléni Forum for Food Sovereignty. 2007. *Declaration of Nyéléni*. https://nyeleni.org/spip.php?article290.

Patel, Rajeev C. 2007. *Stuffed and Starved*. London: Portobello.

———. 2012. "Food Sovereignty: Power, Gender, and the Right to Food." *PLoS Medicine* 9(6): e1001223.

Reba, Meredith, Femke Reitsma, and Karen C. Seto. 2016. "Spatializing 6,000 Years of Global Urbanization from 3700 BC to AD 2000." *Scientific Data* 3: 160034.

Sen, Amartya. 1981. *Poverty and Famines: An Essay on Entitlement and Deprivation*. Oxford: Oxford University Press.

Sinha, Rashmi, Amanda J. Cross, Barry I. Graubard, Michael F. Leitzmann, and Arthur Schatzkin. 2009. "Meat Intake and Mortality: A Prospective Study of over Half a Million People." *Archives of Internal Medicine* 169(6): 562–71.

Smith, Lisa C., Amani E. El Obeid, and Helen H. Jensen. 2000. "The Geography and Causes of Food Insecurity in Developing Countries." *Agricultural Economics* 22(2): 199–215.

Stein, Alexander J., and Matin Qaim. 2007. "The Human and Economic Cost of Hidden Hunger." *Food and Nutrition Bulletin* 282: 125–34.

Stephenson, L. S., M. C. Latham, and E. A. Ottesen. 2000. "Malnutrition and Parasitic Helminth Infections." *Parasitology* 121(S1): S23–S38.

Tanumihardjo, Sherry A., Cheryl Anderson, Martha Kaufer-Horwitz, Lars Bode, Nancy J. Emenaker, Andrea M. Haqq, Jessie A. Satia, Heidi J. Silver, and Diane D. Stadler. 2007. "Poverty, Obesity, and Malnutrition: An International Perspective Recognizing the Paradox." *Journal of the American Dietetic Association* 107(11): 1966–1972.

Tilman, David, Christian Balzer, Jason Hill, and Belinda L. Befort. 2011. "Global Food Demand and the Sustainable Intensification of Agriculture." *Proceedings of the National Academy of Sciences* 108(50): 20260–64.

Troy, Lisa M., Emily Ann Miller, and Steve Olson. 2011. *Hunger and Obesity: Understanding a Food Insecurity Paradigm: Workshop Summary.* Institute of Medicine of the National Academies. Washington, DC: National Academies Press.

Vartanian, Lenny R., Marlene B. Schwartz, and Kelly D. Brownell. 2007. "Effects of Soft Drink Consumption on Nutrition and Health: A Systematic Review and Meta-Analysis." *American Journal of Public Health* 97(4): 667–75.

Walker, Polly, Pamela Rhubart-Berg, Shawn McKenzie, Kristin Kelling, and Robert S. Lawrence. 2005. "Public Health Implications of Meat Production and Consumption." *Public Health Nutrition* 8(4): 348–56.

Watson, Lori. 2015. "Food Is a Feminist Issue." In *Just Food: Philosophy, Justice, and Food*, edited by J. M. Dieterle. Lanham, MD: Rowman and Littlefield.

Watts, Michael J. 2013. *Silent Violence: Food, Famine, and Peasantry in Northern Nigeria.* 2nd ed. Athens: University of Georgia Press.

Watts, Michael J., and Hans G. Bohle. 1993. "Hunger, Famine and the Space of Vulnerability." *GeoJournal* 30(2): 117–25.

Webb, Patrick, and J. von Braun. 1994. *Famine and food security in Ethiopia: lessons for Africa.* Chichester, UK: John Wiley & Sons Ltd.

Weber, Joe, and Mei-Po Kwan. 2003. "Evaluating the Effects of Geographic Contexts on Individual Accessibility: A Multilevel Approach." *Urban Geography* 24(8): 647–71.

Weeks, John R. 2014. *Population: An Introduction to Concepts and Issues.* 12th ed. Boston: Cengage Learning.

Weis, Tony. 2011. "Breadbasket Contradictions: The Unstable Bounty of Industrial Agriculture in the United States and Canada." In *Food Security, Nutrition and Sustainability*, edited by Geoffrey Lawrence, Kristen Lyons, and Tabatha Wallington. London: Earthscan.

World Food Program. 2013. "Conflict in Central African Republic Puts More than a Million at Risk of Hunger." *News.* www.wfp.org/news/news-release/conflict-central-african-republic-puts-more-million-risk-hunger.

World Food Summit. 1996. *Rome Declaration on World Food Security and World Food Summit Plan of Action.* World Food Summit, November 13–17. Rome, Italy: Food and Agriculture Organization of the United Nations.

Can We Solve the Global Food Crisis with Indigenous Crops?

What is the ecological footprint of your food? Does our diet impose a disproportionate burden on the planet and its resources? Identify the main components of your diet and assess roughly its carbon and water footprints using online resources such as the Food Carbon Emissions Calculator (www.foodemissions.com/foodemissions/Calculator.aspx), the Nature Conservancy (www.nature.org/greenliving/carboncalculator/index.htm), or Shrink that Footprint (http://shrinkthatfootprint.com/food-carbon-footprint-diet) for the carbon impact, and the Water Footprint Network (http://waterfootprint.org/en/resources/interactive-tools/personal-water-footprint-calculator/) or the Water Footprint Calculator (www.watercalculator.org) for water.

What would happen if nine billion people were to eat the same diet? How can we reduce our ecological footprint and use natural resources more sustainably to feed the world's population?

As the Worldwatch Institute (2011) points out, we do not need to rely on imported technology such as engineered crops to alleviate hunger in the Global South. Indigenous plants can play a significant role in enhancing nutrition, reducing environmental degradation, limiting the use of agro-chemicals, restoring biodiversity, sustaining local livelihoods, and preserving local cultures. The recipe below (adapted from Schmidt 2016) includes millet and purslane, two promising crops. Millet has been cultivated for thousands of years and is a staple grain in East Africa and South Asia. It is one of the most nutritious and versatile cereal crops, naturally gluten-free, and high in fiber, vitamin B, folic acid, calcium, iron, potassium, and magnesium. Purslane is a plant native to India and Persia that produces tasty and small dark green leaves containing an unusual amount of vitamin E and essential omega-3 fatty acids. Although purslane is considered a weed in many parts of the world, it is relatively drought-resistant, and may offer a reliable and affordable alternative to meat or imported foods.

Spiced Millet and Chickpea Burgers with Lemon Yogurt and Purslane

Ingredients

½ cup millet (or quinoa)
1 pinch salt
1 cup water
3 tablespoons olive oil
1 onion, finely diced
2 cloves garlic, minced
⅓ cup parsley, finely chopped
¼ cup mint leaves, finely chopped
1 teaspoon each of ground cumin, turmeric, and coriander
½ teaspoon all spice
salt and pepper to taste
zest and juice from 1 lemon
⅓ cup breadcrumbs
½ cup chickpeas (cooked or canned), roughly chopped
2 eggs
½ cup yogurt
1 large tomato, diced
1 cup purslane (or other dark leafy greens like arugula, baby spinach, watercress, or lamb's lettuce)
3 pitas, cut in half

Preparation

Toast the millet in a saucepan over medium heat until golden, for 3 to 4 minutes. Add water and 1 pinch of salt, reduce heat to low, and cover and cook for 15 minutes. Remove from heat and let stand covered for another 10 minutes. Meanwhile, fry onion on medium heat in a large frying pan with 1 tablespoon of olive oil until it begins to soften—about 3 minutes. Add garlic and spices and stir for 1 minute. In a mixing bowl, combine the cooked millet, onion and spice mixture, half of the lemon juice and zest, breadcrumbs, and chickpeas. Season with salt and pepper. Mix in the eggs with a wooden spoon. Using your hands, make six burger patties. Make the yogurt sauce by combining yogurt, remaining half of lemon juice and zest, and 1 tablespoon of olive oil. Season with salt and pepper. Using the same frying pan, heat the remaining 2 tablespoons of oil on medium heat. Fry the burgers until golden brown, about 4 minutes per side. Serve the millet burgers inside the pita halves, topped with yogurt sauce, chopped tomato, and purslane.

References

Echánove, Flavia. 2005. "Globalization and Restructuring in Rural Mexico: The Case of Fruit Growers." *Tijdschrift voor Economische en Sociale Geografie* 96(1): 15–30.

Schmidt, Jennifer. 2016. "Spiced Millet and Chickpea Burgers." *Delicious Everyday: Vegetarian Recipes*. www.deliciouseveryday.com/spiced-millet-chickpea-burgers/.

Worldwatch Institute. 2011. "Africa's Indigenous Crops." *Supplement to State of the World 2011*. Innovations that Nourish the Planet. www.worldwatch.org/system/files/NtP-Africa%27s -Indigenous-Crops.pdf.

PART II

FOODSCAPES

CHAPTER 8

Food and Gentrification

HOW FOODIES ARE TRANSFORMING URBAN NEIGHBORHOODS

Pascale Joassart-Marcelli and Fernando J. Bosco

Textbox 8.1. Learning Objectives

- Understand the role of food in "making" places, including urban neighborhoods.
- Use the concept of foodscape to analyze how food landscapes are materially and culturally produced.
- Identify ways in which food places and practices reproduce difference.
- Explore how food contributes to gentrification.

What we eat, where we obtain our food, and how we cook reflect identities and reveal differences. Similarly, food distinguishes places; food stores, public markets, restaurants, street vendors, and other food spaces give neighborhoods character and value. In a context where culture has become a key determinant of the economic success of cities, food projects have emerged as powerful tools of urban renewal and neighborhood transformation. Public officials and business leaders are joining forces to create food districts and host food festivals that will attract both residents and tourists. Along with music and art, food is a central tenet of so-called creative cities—a newly embraced model of urban development in cities around the world.

In this chapter, we consider a variety of urban food projects and assess their impact on urban life. To do this, we first introduce the concept of foodscape as a framework in which to think about the urban food environment spatially and temporally. We specifically focus on the material and cultural production of urban food landscapes and the way they divide city dwellers along lines of class and race. Second, we turn our attention to various food trends (e.g., food trucks, farm-to-table dining, comfort food, cosmopolitanism) and explore how they contribute to an evolving foodscape. Specifically, we focus on the commoditization of dining and other related food experiences. Third, we investigate how these trends relate to physical displacement as well as cultural marginalization of specific groups of residents in urban places around the world. Our examples point to the effects that the cultural food economy has, transforming and gentrifying urban communities, working primarily through cultural appropriation and displacement.

The Urban Foodscape

The **foodscape** includes the built environment, such as supermarkets, corner stores, restaurants, farmers' markets, food trucks, and school cafeterias, but also encompasses the cultural and political space where food takes on meaning. As MacKendrick (2014, 16) puts it, it is "the places and spaces where you acquire food, prepare food, talk about food, or generally gather some sort of meaning from food." Because it includes institutional arrangements and cultural discourse, this concept is broader than the idea of food environment, which typically refers to the built environment alone (see chapter 12). In their studies of foodies, Johnston and Bauman (2014) use the concept of foodscape to capture the cultural spaces and material places that underpin food cultures, such as television sets and social media.

The concept of foodscape rests on the idea of **landscape**, which cultural geographers have long understood as socially produced. Those scholars suggest that urban landscapes hold clues about local cultures and social relations, which can be "read" through careful examination of the spatial arrangement of buildings, signs, and symbols. Mitchell (2000) argues that the imprint of humans on the land is shaped by economic imperatives and unequal relations of power, suggesting that landscapes are purposely created to maintain capital accumulation. As a result, landscapes are uneven, segmented, and exclusionary. For instance, the decline of public space in contemporary cities reflects capital flows that dictate land use, with important consequences for the way we interact with each other and experience urban life. The idea of landscape brings together the material and the cultural, which are deeply intertwined.

Returning to the concept of foodscape, it is important to draw attention to the two-way relationships between **food culture** (the food and eating practices we desire and value) and food materiality (what, how, and for whom food is produced). For example, a particular restaurant may be valued for its fashionable cuisine, celebrity chef, and casual but trendy atmosphere, which provide its consumers with a sense of distinction. The location of this restaurant in an up-and-coming area of the city may also contribute to its attractiveness by creating a sense of adventure. At the same time, the neighborhood could be energized by the restaurant's presence, which could in turn help to attract other businesses, visitors, and new residents. This example suggests that the cultural production of place (i.e., the restaurant, the neighborhood) is intimately connected to the process of capital accumulation. However, it also hints at the exclusionary characteristics of foodscapes: the fact that access to this restaurant and the social and sensory experiences it offers is restricted by physical, economic, and cultural barriers. As Cook and Crang (1996, 140) put it:

> Foods do not simply come from places, organically growing out of them, but also make places as symbolic constructs, being deployed in the discursive construction of various imaginative geographies. The differentiation of foods through their geographies is an active intervention in their cultural geographies rather than the passive recording of absolute cultural geographic differences.

In other words, the relationship between food and place is not static. Burgers don't simply come from America. Although they often symbolize America, they have been fashioned by a history of immigration and "creolized" by globalization, as witnessed in the rapid expansion of restaurants serving gourmet burgers (with ingredients as diverse as grass-fed Kobe beef, foie gras, or roasted poblano chilies) and the spread of this trend to Paris, London, and other world cities (see chapter 12). New elevated burger joints do not resemble their fast-food counterparts, which are typically relegated to suburbia and lower-income urban neighborhoods. Instead, their unique decor, location, service, and menu provide customers with a distinctive experience.

In this chapter, we use the idea of foodscape and focus specifically on the relationship between food and place in generating economic value, differentiating food cultures, and generating social exclusion. We use a number of examples to illustrate this argument.

The Cultural Economy of Food: Commoditization of Eating

Food sells. Basic foodstuffs, like bread and oil, are not the only commodities traded. In the Global North, a seemingly endless supply of new products is reaching markets, including premium and exotic ingredients, highly processed novelty food items, cookbooks, appliances, and various kitchenware items. In addition, shopping for food and eating out have become **commoditized**—turned into an experience that can be traded for an exchange value. The very places where these activities are performed are instrumental in this valorization process and contribute to the creation of marketable and recognizable experiences.

The marketability of food (and other cultural activities like music and art) has been associated with the rise of a **cultural economy** linked to postfordism, neoliberalism, and postmodernism. These "isms" respectively relate to economic, political, and cultural trends and conditions that have unfolded in the past two decades. **Postfordism** signifies a shift away from mass production and consumption toward flexible manufacturing and services. **Neoliberalism** describes a political system in which the post–World War II welfare state has been replaced by an entrepreneurial state whose primary role is to promote markets. Finally, **postmodernism** refers, among other things, to the decentering of the subject away from rigid categories of race, class, gender, and sexuality in favor of individual experiences and lifestyles. Together, these set the stage for the idea of the "creative city," where "talent, technology, and tolerance" intersect to generate economic growth (Florida 2002). According to its numerous advocates, building the **creative city** requires attracting young, educated, diverse, and creative people (associated with the growing service and technology sectors) via a cultural economy based on entertainment, art, and other lifestyle amenities in which food figures prominently. Expanding this cultural economy has justified a new approach to **urban governance** and planning in which state and local governments focus their energy and resources on branding the city and attracting private investors that would contribute to that brand.

Urban branding includes place-based efforts to market cosmopolitan foodways and eateries as signs of a desirable urban lifestyle. Being able to "walk to cafés and restaurants" seems to be a major selling point for urban real estate, as witnessed in advertising from Berlin to Brooklyn. Indeed, cities are increasingly described in terms of their food scene. For example, a 2014 article entitled "The Best American Cities for Foodies" published in Condé Nast's *Traveller* makes the following sweeping claims: "Just as the city of Portland has transformed itself from scruffy to sophisticated, so too has its cuisine"; "Austin has never been short on good food [. . .] But these days, chefs are adding all sorts of culinary twists to the Texas capital [. . .] The East Austin food truck scene deserves a Zagat guide unto itself"; "[Chicago]'s food scene has never been hotter, thanks to a healthy ratio of stalwart restaurateurs [. . .] and a smattering of ethnic eateries reflecting the city's diversity"; and "It's no surprise that New York landed in the No. 1 spot on the list [. . .] This is, after all, a city of culinary experts and of culinary upstarts. It's the foodie mecca where other chefs come to learn to be chefs, and where regular citizens learn to be food critics [. . .] But it's not all about famous chefs in this town—it's about authentic international cuisine and small mom-and-pop kitchens too."

This form of food boosterism is primarily directed at **foodies** who exemplify the urban creative class by embracing cultural identities built on a lifestyle centered on "good food." It should therefore not be surprising that food ratings have now been added to the list of indices used by Livability (2015) to rank the quality of life of US cities. Although the idea of livability has made its way into research on urban health, it has mostly served the political and economic purpose of promoting small and midsize cities by marketing them as creative cities. Alongside bike lanes, historic buildings, green parks, and good schools, food and drinks have become essential in marketing cities.

Among these various politically motivated accounts of urban foodscapes, several common elements stand out. First, *aesthetic* is a key aspect, with small, independent, chic, and hip places winning over franchised or corporate establishments. As Zukin et al. (2009) argue, with the example of the Williamsburg neighborhood in Brooklyn, New York, the bohemian urban aesthetic found in restaurants, art galleries, and boutiques provides "cultural means of social distinction" to new consumers who are able to distance themselves from older and poorer residents who patronize different types businesses. For instance, the livability ranking mentioned above is based on data measuring the number of critically acclaimed restaurants (including James Beard, Michelin, and Yelp award winners), the percentage of residents who prefer independent restaurants, and the level of access to healthy food and farmers' markets. As discussed in chapter 12, these indicators tend to reflect the food environment of white and affluent neighborhoods.

Second, *diversity* appears to be highly valued. Popular food destinations are often described as cosmopolitan, consisting of an assemblage of restaurants serving a variety of ethnic food and a combination of low- and high-brow culinary styles. This is particularly true in global cities like London and New York, where immigrants have historically been involved in the food and restaurant industry as a way to make a living. However, **cosmopolitanism** is also becoming a trademark of smaller cities seeking the aura of tolerance and multiculturalism associated with contemporary urbanism. In his ethnographic study of Vietnamese restaurants in Cabramatta, a suburb of Sidney, Hage (1997) observes that **multiculturalism** is increasingly marketed as a tourist attraction. Yet, in that context, **difference** is consumed by white diners as a means to acquire cultural capital, distinguish themselves, and validate their own identity, rather than a way to understand and engage with other cultures. This narcissistic project can lead to "multiculturalism without migrants," in which ethnic food is marketed for and by white people, and migrants' struggles with poverty and prejudice become invisible (see chapter 12).

Third, media accounts of popular urban food places often emphasize their *sociality*. This can be observed in the popularity of communal tables where strangers eat side by side, open kitchens where diners can interact with bartenders, servers, and chefs, and pop-up supper clubs where meals are prepared for larger groups of people brought together by a shared interest. The expectation of social interaction is also an important aspect of food festivals and farmers' markets. These sorts of eating places and practices are imbued with nostalgic visions of cities as "objects of bourgeois desire, in which is realized the dream of social solidarity among a community of strangers in an authentic public realm" (Goss 1996, 223). Bell (2007) argues that spaces in which to eat, drink, and "engage in hospitable encounters at the table or across the bar" (p. 8) are at the core of postindustrial cities' attempts to redefine urban living and sell themselves as spaces of leisure and pleasure. Sociality is also central to farmers' markets and community gardens associated with an alternative food movement that often defines itself by its emphasis on local communities (see chapter 11).

Fourth, simple eateries appear to be on the same footing as fancier and more-exclusive restaurants in pleasing food critics and consumers. In fact, so-called casual restaurants are the fastest-growing segment of the industry. Toques, bowties, white tablecloths, silver cloches, and dessert carts seem to have been pushed aside for a more-casual eating experience. This may suggest a *democratization* of **taste**. But as Johnston and Baumann (2014) argue, it reflects a false egalitarianism, which hides a desire, especially among foodies, to assert their distinction through their food choices "in a cultural context that endorses democratic ideals and rejects overt snobbery" (p. 2). Although foodies may be willing to try all kinds of food, not every food is equally appealing. Local, organic, authentic, homemade, and artisanal foods all convey a sense of distinction. The tension between democracy and distinction is also apparent in the eateries that symbolize the creative city, including "holes in the wall" and food trucks (see textbox 8.2).

Taken together, these four trends suggest a constant search for differentiation through repositioning of food and restaurants. Paradoxically, they have also contributed to a homogenization of food across place. While the seeming democratization of food has led to a revival of regional cuisines, it has done so in the "same generically cosmopolitan direction," pointing to a "dire situation [in which] the cuisines of the world are merging into one giant, amorphous mass" (*Food and Wine* 2015). Food critics argue that the very same meal could be served in Mumbai, Mexico City, Cape

Textbox 8.2. The Food Truck Revolution

In the past decade gastro trucks have taken over the streets of many cities, signaling their locations on social media to dedicated followers who line up for sustainably harvested fish tacos, grass-fed beef cheeks, and locally sourced beet salad. These are not traditional lunch trucks; they are often owned by chefs who have been trained in the best culinary schools and have worked in highly ranked restaurants. The reinvented food truck is often credited to Los Angeles's Roy Choi and his Kogi BBQ truck empire.

Mobile kitchens signal a changing foodscape that reflects larger social issues, including increased mobility and temporariness, the rise of the "foodie," growing concerns about health and sustainability, changing eating patterns, and the spread of communication technologies into everyday spaces. The gathering of food trucks on any given night indicates neighborhood stardom. For example, the numerous "food trucks parked outside of bars and music venues every night" are cited in a *Forbes* article as one of the reasons that "East Austin unseated [other neighborhoods] as Austin's newest hipster home base" (Brennan 2012). Urban planners, public officials, business leaders, and food critics have encouraged this trend as a way to revitalize or market neighborhoods.

Hanser and Hyde (2014) in their study of food trucks in various North American cities argue that the "food truck revolution" has had an ambivalent effect on urban neighborhoods. To some, this is a form of "street activation," where the food truck reinvigorates street life by bringing people together and strengthening communities. Others, however, point to the growing tension among food truckers competing for space, with hot-dog carts and traditional taco trucks being devalued as "roach coaches" selling "cheap food" compared to high-end trucks serving "good food." Other businesses that are less mobile and have higher fixed costs, like rent and utilities, also find it difficult to compete with the influx of trendy mobile kitchens. As a result, neighborhood demographics change, leading to social exclusion.

Cities of the Global South are also part of this trend, and Buenos Aires, the capital of Argentina, is a good example. Gastro trucks selling cosmopolitan versions of gourmet food have become popular in the city. With names like "Delicious Machine," "Hollywood Dogs," "Bon Bouquet Creperie," "Nomade," and "Retro Food Truck," gastro trucks sell everything from organic lamb burgers and cheese fondue in sourdough bread bowls to gourmet donuts and cupcakes (see figure 8.1). None of these foods are common to Argentine cuisine, and the food trucks and food scene around them could just as well be taking place in Brooklyn or San Francisco. Social media is the main conduit to generate customers, who are mostly made up of a cohort of young and mobile urbanites who fit the foodie profile and who grew up watching international and local versions of cable TV programs such as *The Great Food Truck Race* and *Food Truck Wars*.

Gastro trucks have elevated street food in Buenos Aires, which until recently had been mostly limited to hot dogs, popcorn, candy, and ice cream. Unfortunately, rather than democratizing street food by providing more variety and tastier street food options to the entire urban area, the impact of gastro trucks in the city's foodscape has been uneven. Existing municipal legislation restricts food truck sales to already prepackaged or not-cooked food, such as candy or cold sandwiches, and the city government has shown little interest in changing the law. Thus, rather than being in regular city streets or public parks, gastro trucks gather at food truck festivals in private lots and at private events, usually charging an entrance fee. The festivals often take place in upscale or rapidly gentrifying neighborhoods, reaching only a limited public, and leaving other people in other neighborhoods out of the equation. Children in public parks or workers in middle-class or blue-collar neighborhoods are left with fewer options and lower-quality street food. As in the case of North American cities, the restricted location of food trucks in Buenos Aires further emphasizes social, class-based differences of food access in the city.

Figure 8.1.   The "Delicious Machine" food truck in Buenos Aires, Argentina
This type of gourmet food truck, which serves cosmopolitan food, has become popular in Buenos Aires's affluent neighborhoods.
Source: Photo by Fernando Bosco.

Town, Sidney, Shanghai, London, Los Angeles, or Paris. "In most cities with a vibrant food scene, you could take some of this year's hottest new restaurants—the ones with the most ambitious chefs, the best real estate, the most stunning design—and plop them down in another city, another country, another continent, and no one would notice" (see textbox 8.3).

Foodies and Gentrification

One of the most insidious consequences of the contemporary cosmopolitan foodscape relates to its association with the process of **gentrification**. Since the 1980s, scholars have shown how urban renewal policies, including private and public investment to refurbish the housing stock of "blighted" areas, have led to the displacement of low-income and minority residents who can no longer afford to live in those revitalized neighborhoods. The resulting class remake of the urban landscape—the influx of white and affluent residents and the exodus of poor people of color—is a central tenet of the concept of gentrification (Smith 1996). Yet, with a few exceptions, it is only recently that researchers began looking beyond housing production into the realm of consumption for a broader understanding of the causes and processes of gentrification.

Textbox 8.3. The American *Bistrot* in Paris / The French *Bistro* in New York

The Parisian bistro (or bistrot) has come to symbolize casual French dining with its combination of traditional dishes, zinc countertops, and gruff waiters in long white aprons. "The entire English-speaking world comes to Paris on an enthralled mission to eat the great bistro dishes so lovingly described by writers like Elizabeth David and Julia Child" (Lobrano 2011). Since the 1990s, as people grew disenchanted with the perceived arrogance and fussiness of nouvelle cuisine, bistros have received renewed interest from consumers and food critics. Chefs have been encouraged to dig out old recipes and add new ones, leading to what is known as "bistronomie" (i.e., bistro and gastronomie). While kidneys, livers, tongues, brains, and "légumes oubliés" (forgotten vegetables, such as Brussels sprouts, rutabaga, turnips, beets, and chard) figure prominently on most menus, chefs are also taking liberties by adding worldly ingredients such as chili oil, coconut, and lemongrass.

A surprising recent appearance on menus in Parisian bistros and other restaurants is the hamburger, or "le burger," which, according to news media, seems to have "conquered Paris" by having "transcended its fast-food origins to seduce more refined French palates" (Zaleski 2016). This is not unrelated to a similar trend in the United States, where gourmet burgers have become very popular (Caldwell 2014).

Today, many renowned bistro-style restaurants in Paris, such as Verjus, Buvette, Spring, and Frenchie are run by American or American-trained chefs. The irony of American chefs redefining "traditional" French cuisine and "reviving [its] artisanal spirit" has not gone unnoticed by food critics (Steinberger 2014).

On the other side of the Atlantic, French cuisine has long been synonymous with "haute cuisine," as most expatriate French chefs specialize in fine dining. Yet, the modest French bistro (along with the Italian trattoria) has been a feature of urban neighborhoods like New York's Greenwich Village since the early twentieth century. Today, it continues to shape casual dining in the city through an increasingly global circulation of ideas via magazines, guidebooks, websites, and highly mobile diners that ratify what French bistro fare ought to be. Some of the most successful and "typical" Parisian bistros in New York City, including Balthazar, Buvette, and Dirty French, are products of American and English restaurateurs. Paradoxically, dishes showcasing the humble and regional origins of foods have gained global notoriety and can be enjoyed in Paris's Left Bank and Bastille neighborhoods, as much as they are in New York's Tribeca, SoHo, and Lower East Side (see figure 8.2). Although all claim to be authentic, this convergence of style across place suggests that the French bistro has become a pastiche or a simulacrum—a stylistic imitation of the original bistro.

Figure 8.2.   French bistros in Paris and New York

The top picture shows a typical Parisian bistro. In recent years, as eating out has become more casual, such bistros have experienced a revival in Paris. For tourists, they represent the typical Parisian dining experience. "Super-authentic" and "Disneyfied" versions of French bistros have become increasingly common in other cosmopolitan places, as illustrated by the success of Balthazar in New York City, shown in the bottom photo.

Source: Top photo by Pascale Joassart-Marcelli; bottom photo from Google Creative Commons (2016).

Zukin's work (2009) has drawn attention to the role of commercial gentrification in ushering in urban growth. Focusing on various areas of New York City, she showed how the replacement of traditional stores by art galleries, restaurants, and boutiques changed both the physical and the **cultural landscape** of neighborhoods. New spaces of consumption normalize the elitist lifestyle of fashionably clad, latte-sipping, gallery-hopping, and tech-savvy urbanites, which clashes with the everyday life of older and poorer residents who feel unwelcome and excluded.

A recent online article about the gentrifying area of North Brooklyn in New York City illustrates the view that an influx of new and trendy restaurants is to be celebrated as the sign of an urban renaissance when it states:

> Lifelong New Yorkers and startlingly attractive European ex-pats brave the G, L and JMZ trains to taste the future in neighborhoods like Williamsburg, Greenpoint and Bushwick. Filled with warehouses, factories and Polish- and Italian-American community centers, these formerly industrial districts now launch global food trends, thanks to a constant influx of game-changing cooks, craftsmen and purveyors. Whether you're craving innovative pizza, whimsical soul food or serious single-origin coffee, North Brooklyn never disappoints. (Saladino 2014)

As is common in narratives of urban renewal, those leading the transformation are portrayed as pioneers with adjectives like "brave" and "game-changing." In contrast, little consideration is given to former residents who are often described in static and negative ways. What is unique about this new wave of consumption-led gentrification, however, is not just the cultural emphasis on lifestyle—a key to creative cities—but the concealing of displacement that is facilitated by a pretense of simplicity and multiculturalism. "Innovative pizza or whimsical soul food" exemplifies the cosmopolitan ethos and lifestyle of the post-race / post-class city, where **race** and **class** are no longer seen as relevant or meaningful social categories. Yet, as Zukin et al. (2015) argue, these categories are re-inscribed in the "omnivore's neighborhood" (see textbox 8.4).

Food critics and city officials around the world, but especially in large postindustrial cities, have fostered the type of urban food revolution described in this chapter, contributing to an "ethos of urban entrepreneurialism" characteristic of neoliberal urbanism (MacLeod 2002). As a result, the homogenization of food described above has been accompanied by a similar standardization of urban spaces of food consumption. Industrial and neglected neighborhoods are being reinvented as cultural districts, themed leisure zones, and shopping destinations where eating and drinking are important profit-generating activities. Famous examples include Canary Wharf in London, Times Square in New York City, Faneuil Hall in Boston, and Barcelona's Las Ramblas. Lesser-known neighborhoods in cities across the world are adopting this strategy of "festivalization" as a way to attract capital from consumers and investors. In that "place-making" process, social spaces are being transformed and everyday activities, like shopping for food or eating out, are turned into a spectacle that is performed for consumption and marketed for an exchange value. The commoditization of culture produces a sense of dispossession and displacement for residents who either cannot afford to participate in these new forms of consumption or do not feel comfortable doing so.

Textbox 8.4. Race in the Omnivore's Neighborhood

Online reviews of restaurants have become an important source of cultural capital production. Yelp, for example, provides an online platform where millions of diners share comments about the food, service, and atmosphere of restaurants in over twenty countries, influencing the commercial success of these eateries. Through an in-depth analysis of Yelp content, Zukin, Lindeman, and Hurson (2015) showed that the reviews' impact extends to the neighborhood scale. In revealing their tastes for certain places, reviewers may initiate or accelerate processes of gentrification by attracting like-minded consumers to these neighborhoods and triggering capital investment. Because the majority of people who post comments on Yelp are young, white, and self-identified foodies, they bring certain biases to their online entries, including racialized perceptions of "good" and "bad" neighborhoods.

To explore the role of race in shaping place-based food discourse, Zukin and her colleagues compared Yelp reviews for the top ten "most reviewed" and "traditional" restaurants in two Brooklyn neighborhoods with similar trends in gentrification but different racial histories. While Greenpoint is viewed as a primarily white neighborhood—in part because of its large Polish immigrant community—Bedford-Stuyvesant has had a majority-black identity for decades. In Yelp reviews, both neighborhoods are seen as "up-and-coming," in part because of new restaurants and unique food scenes. In Bedford-Stuyvesant, however, reviewers expressed an ideology of "neo-imperialism," in which the new trendy restaurants were perceived as improving a "contested neighborhood" by imposing good tastes in spite of the dark, dangerous, and ghetto conditions. In contrast, descriptions of cozy, authentic, and European restaurants in Greenpoint helped to build a narrative of "cultural preservation," where "authentic" working-class restaurants contribute to an "imagined homeland" that helped valorize the neighborhood and its residents. Zukin et al. (2015) equate this "discursive investment" process to a form of "cultural redlining," in which black neighborhoods are marked as less valuable than "more interesting" white neighborhoods.

Spatial exclusion is a significant concern about this simultaneous commoditization of space and culture. For instance, in many cities across the Western world, farmers' markets have become very popular and highly marketed events (see chapter 11). Purchasing food is only a small element of a larger consumer experience that rests on a classed and raced identity of educated, responsible, and/or sophisticated consumer. Although these spaces recall the simplicity of street markets, distinction is created by the focus on specialty products (e.g., organic produce, local seafood, craft beer), the importance of entertainment (e.g., live music, decorations, and costumes), and the increasing use of privatized public space. As such, farmers' markets are heavily regulated both by local ordinances, enforced via increased policing and surveillance, and by symbolic everyday practices and norms that delineate acceptable behavior and define who belongs. Indeed, researchers have argued that farmers' markets tend to be much more exclusionary than organizers and participants typically claim (see chapter 11).

Those "festivals," however, create an allure of diversity and a sense of place and community that hides the marginalization and exclusion of certain residents (see textbox 8.5). Guy Debord in *The Society of the Spectacle* (1973) deplored the transformation of social relations into a mere spectacle dominated by leisure, consumption, and entertainment that seduce people and distract them from the social inequalities

Textbox 8.5. Berlin's Food Scene

The fall of the Berlin Wall in 1989 and the reunification of Germany transformed Berlin and launched a search for collective symbolic and cultural capital. According to Jakob (2010), public leaders have embraced the idea of Berlin as a creative city with a lively nightlife and an innovative art scene, emphasizing low rents and the availability of space and vacant buildings. Neighborhoods like Mitte and Prenzlauer Berg led the way to gentrification via arts and culture two decades ago. Today, others are trying to replicate their success by publicizing creativity and livability, with food playing an increasingly important role. Kreuzeberg, for example, is known as "Euro Hipster Central," and is "famous for its boutique shops, diverse mix of international cuisine, gourmet coffee houses and trendy bars" (Cable 2014) that serve a "sophisticated but totally unstuffy [. . .] crowd" (Edelstein 2013).

"In Berlin, food is the new party," announces Sachs (2014) in an online article about Berlin's booming food scene. Citing the Neue Heimat Berlin Village Market, where former popular techno club owners now run a weekly food market, as an example, she argues that food is a sort of social glue that brings young people to Berlin. This includes "expats and techies" involved in the "startup scene," and those trying to "catch the real bohemian vibe." Other food-centered events or places, such as Markthalle Neun's Street Food Thursday (see figure 8.3), Bite Club, and Berlin Food Week capitalize on people's desire "to have a feeling that [they] are in a place with like-minded people."

Despite the optimism about Berlin's growing food (and art) scene and the associated revitalization of its neighborhoods, some argue that creativity strategies have counterproductive effects. Instead of promoting alternative social and economic arrangements that would benefit all residents, Jakob (2010, 195) argues that festivals and other consumption-led approaches tend to "homogenize the urban landscape [. . .] and undermine the very nature of the creative city they aim to build." He interprets these strategies as "developments that value public perception and illusionary images of creativity over inclusion and equality." The local government's choice to promote creativity by subsidizing festivals and encouraging the temporary use of vacant space for pop-up dinners and weekly markets does not address the need for investments in jobs, education, and housing that would benefit lower-income Berliners.

Figure 8.3. Markthalle IX in Berlin, Germany
The temporary use of old factories and other abandoned buildings to create spaces of conviviality has become a current trend in many cities experiencing a transition from a Fordist to a postfordist economy.
Source: Øystein Vidnes on Flickr: www.flickr.com/photos/oysteinv/8056654064.

inherent to capitalism. Many urban scholars have echoed his concern with the transformation of cities into theme parks and "urban villages where [. . .] everyone can relate in a civil and urbane fashion to everyone else" (Harvey 2000, 170). These images of multiculturalism—the hallmarks of the creative city—make the new wave of consumer-oriented gentrification difficult to oppose or resist, let alone identify.

Conclusion

Eating is a common and banal activity; everybody must eat. Perhaps it is this banality that has allowed food to become a symbol of distinction while conveying values of democracy and social inclusion. Casual restaurants, food trucks, ethnic eateries, and farmers' markets distinguish themselves by offering food that reflects the ethos of authenticity, simplicity, and community embraced by foodies. In addition to transforming the eating experience, this trend is altering urban foodscapes both physically and culturally. In particular, the influx of new food shops, restaurants, and informal retail arrangements in previously ignored neighborhoods has attracted visitors and would-be residents to those areas, prompting further investments in retail and housing. A number of actors, including public officials, new business owners, and residents, investors, and professional and amateur food critics, are involved in the production of this new urban foodscape, which normalizes the eating practices of white and affluent residents and exemplifies the ideals of the creative city. The resulting landscape, however, generates cumulative processes of displacement of older and poorer residents who cannot afford to live there anymore, and whose everyday lives, including food provision activities, conflict with the lifestyles of new residents. While the effects of this mode of gentrification are very localized, its dynamics are linked to global processes, including the relentless commoditization of consumption culture, as well as the neoliberalization of urbanism. Together, these have encouraged models of urban development that focus on attracting a creative class of young professionals without attending to the needs of low-income residents.

Key Terms

class
commoditization
cosmopolitanism
creative city
cultural economy
cultural landscape
difference
food culture
foodie
foodscape

landscape
gentrification
multiculturalism
neoliberalism
postfordism
postmodernism
race
taste
urban governance

Summary

- Food has become an important symbol and maker of identity and place.
- The significance of food in the production of urban places is linked to the rise of a cultural economy and new forms of urban governance under postfordism, neoliberalism, and postmodernism. In that context, urban food practices and experiences are commoditized in order to be sold and consumed.
- City foodscapes are both materially and discursively produced in ways that reflect and reproduce difference and social relations of power. While embracing seemingly inclusive ideals of multiculturalism, community, and authenticity, foodies often use taste as a way to distinguish themselves and exclude others.
- Food is playing an active role in the gentrification of urban neighborhoods by transforming the character of places and changing their demographic composition.

Additional Resources

Johnston and Baumann (2014) provide an in-depth analysis of foodies and the contemporary cultural foodscape they help to create.

Zukin's work, including her 2009 book *Naked City*, centers on consumption-driven gentrification and its cultural aspects. Some of her articles address specifically the role of food and restaurants in that process. For a classic treatment of gentrification that emphasizes its political and economic nature, see Smith (1996).

Acknowledgments

This chapter is based on research supported by the National Science Foundation under Award No. 1155844.

References

Bell, David. 2007. "The Hospitable City: Social Relations in Commercial Spaces." *Progress in Human Geography* 31(1): 7–22.

Brennan, Morgan. 2012. "America's Hippest Hipster Neighborhoods." *Forbes*. September 20. www.forbes.com/sites/morganbrennan/2012/09/20/americas-hippest-hipster-neighborhoods/.

Cable, Simon. 2014. "The Hipster Guide to the World! The Poor Inner-City Districts that Have Become Achingly Cool." *Daily Mail* Online. November 26. www.dailymail.co.uk/travel/travel_news/article-2837916/The-hipster-guide-world-poor-inner-city-districts-achingly-cool-beards-optional.html.

Caldwell, Melissa. 2014. "The Rise of the Gourmet Hamburger." *Contexts* 13(3): 72–74.

Condé Nast *Traveler*. 2014. "Best American Cities for Foodies." CNTraveler.com. August 15. www.cntraveler.com/galleries/2014-04-28/best-food-cities.

Cook, Ian, and Peter Crang. 1996. "The World on a Plate: Culinary Culture, Displacement and Geographical Knowledges." *Journal of Material Culture* 1(2): 131–53.

Debord, Guy. 1973. *The Society of the Spectacle*. London: Bread and Circuses Publishing.

Edelstein, J. H. 2013. "A Day in . . . Kreuzberg, Berlin. Berlin Holidays. Experts' and Readers' Tips." *The Guardian*. November 20. www.theguardian.com/travel/2013/nov/29/a-day-in -kreuzberg-berlin.

Florida, Richard. 2002. *The Rise of the Creative Class: And How It's Transforming Work, Leisure, Community and Everyday Life*. New York: Basic Books.

Food and Wine. 2015. "The Insidious Rise of Cosmo Cuisine." www.foodandwine.com/articles/ the-insidious-rise-of-cosmo-cuisine.

Goss, Jon. 1996. "Disquiet on the Waterfront: Reflections on Nostalgia and Utopia in the Urban Archetypes of Festival Marketplaces." *Urban Geography* 17(3): 221–47.

Gutowski, Jörn. 2015. "TRY Berlin's Food Scene." *Go-PopUp*. www.gopopup.com/magazine/ try-berlins-food-scene

Hage, Ghassan. 1997. "At Home in the Entrails of the West: Multiculturalism, Ethnic Food and Migrant Home-Building." In *Home/World: Space, Community and Marginality in Sydney's West*, edited by Helen Grace, Ghassan Hage, Lesley Johnson, Julie Langsworth, and Michael Symonds, 99–153. Annandale: Pluto.

Hanser, Amy, and Zachary Hyde. 2014. "Foodies Remaking Cities." *Contexts* 13(3): 44–49.

Harvey, David. 2000. *Spaces of Hope*. Berkeley: University of California Press.

Jakob, Doreen. 2010. "Constructing the Creative Neighborhood: Hopes and Limitations of Creative City Policies in Berlin." *City, Culture and Society* 1(4): 193–98.

Johnston, Josée, and Shyon Baumann. 2014. *Foodies: Democracy and Distinction in the Gourmet Foodscape*. New York: Routledge.

Livability. 2015. 10 Best Foodie Cities. https://livability.com/top-10/food-and-drink/10-best- foodie-cities/2015.

Lobrano, Alexander. 2011. "Ten of the Best Bistros in Paris." *Guardian*. May 5. www.theguard ian.com/travel/2011/may/06/top-10-bistros-in-paris

MacKendrick, Norah. 2014. "Foodscape." *Contexts* 13(3): 16–18.

MacLeod, Gordon. 2002. "From Urban Entrepreneurialism to a 'Revanchist City'?: On the Spatial Injustices of Glasgow's Renaissance." *Antipode* 34(3): 602–24.

Mitchell, Don. 2000. *Cultural Geography: A Critical Introduction*. Malden: Blackwell.

Sachs, Katherine. 2014. "Berlin's Blooming Food Scene." *Deutsche Welle*. October 8. www.dw .com/en/berlins-booming-food-scene/a-17983026.

Saladino, Emily. 2014. "You Travel, You Eat: North Brooklyn." *Food Republic*. New York City. July 7. www.foodrepublic.com/2014/07/07/you-travel-you-eat-north-brooklyn/.

Smith, Neil. 1996. *The New Urban Frontier: Gentrification and the Revanchist City*. New York: Routledge.

Smith-Love, Jade. 2015. "Eats in Austin." *The College Tourist*. www.thecollegetourist.com/eats -in-austin/.

Steinberger, Michael. 2014. "Can Anyone Save French Food?" *The New York Times Magazine*. March 28. www.nytimes.com/2014/03/30/magazine/can-anyone-save-french-food.html.

Zaleski, Erin. 2016. "How Paris Became Obsessed with the Hamburger." *The Daily Beast*. May 8. www.thedailybeast.com/articles/2016/05/08/how-paris-became-obsessed-with-the -hamburger.html.

Zukin, Sharon. 2009. *Naked City: The Death and Life of Authentic Urban Places*. Oxford: Oxford University Press.

Zukin, Sharon, Scarlett Lindeman, and Laurie Hurson. 2015. "The Omnivore's Neighborhood? Online Restaurant Reviews, Race, and Gentrification." *Journal of Consumer Culture* 0(0): 1–21.

Zukin, Sharon, Valerie Trujillo, Peter Frase, Daniel Jackson, Tim Recuber, and Abraham Walker. 2009. "New Retail Capital and Neighborhood Change: Boutiques and Gentrification in New York City." *City & Community* 8(1): 47–64.

Are You a Foodie?

Do you consider yourself a "foodie"? How would you define one? Are there foodie places in your city? What are they, and where are they located? If possible, gather pictures and draw a map. What kind of people do these places attract? Do they appeal to cosmopolitan, democratic, or alternative values? How have they influenced the surrounding neighborhood and the community? Are they generally inclusive or exclusive? Who may be excluded from those spaces?

One of the common characteristics of the contemporary urban food culture is its reinvention of older countercultural ideas, including community, justice, and sustainability. Many foodies embrace these ideas in new ways, mostly through their consumption practices and lifestyle choices. For instance, in the 1960s, veganism was considered a radical rejection of capitalism and the modern food regime. Today, this sort of resistance has become commoditized, as vegan lifestyles can be "purchased" in a growing number of restaurants, fancy food trucks, and high-end stores. Vegan diets are particularly popular among hipsters and other young, highly educated, and primarily white urbanites whose practice of veganism is motivated by personal health reasons rather than environmental, social, and animal justice issues. Those who eat differently may feel excluded both spatially and socially.

This recipe below is inspired by Thug Kitchen (2014), *The Official Cookbook: Eat Like you Give a Fu*k*. The irreverent style of the book reinforces this image of rebellion, yet it is merely superficial, since "giving a fu*k" is reduced to eating creative, tasty, and healthy food, but does not entail addressing any of the structural issues underlying injustices in our food system.

Vegan Roasted Cauliflower Tacos with Lime-Cilantro Slaw

Ingredients (for four people, three tacos each)

For the roasted cauliflower:

1 head cauliflower, cut into small florets
1 teaspoon ground coriander
1 teaspoon mild chili pepper
1 teaspoon smoked paprika
1 teaspoon ground cumin
½ teaspoon salt
½ red onion, thinly sliced
2 garlic cloves, minced
3 tablespoons olive oil

For the lime-cilantro slaw:

½ head of green cabbage, very thinly sliced and cut into small strips (about 3 cups)
1 small carrot, shredded, or cut in thin matchsticks (about 2 inches long)
2 tablespoons lime juice
2 tablespoons rice vinegar
2 tablespoons olive oil
2 green onions, thinly sliced (white and green parts)
1 serrano chili, minced
⅓ cup chopped cilantro

For the salsa:

1 can (14.5 oz.) fire-roasted diced tomatoes
½ white onion, finely chopped
⅓ cup green onions
½ cup cilantro
2 to 3 serrano or jalapeno peppers, seeds removed and minced
3 cloves garlic, minced
Juice of ½ lime
½ teaspoon salt

To assemble:

12 fresh corn tortillas
1 large avocado cut in half, pitted, peeled, and thinly sliced
Limes

Preparation

Begin by making the salsa. Put all the salsa ingredients in a food processor or blender and blend until desired consistency. We prefer it smooth and not too chunky. Keep refrigerated in a jar for up to five days.

Preheat oven to 450 degrees Fahrenheit. Place cauliflower florets on a large baking sheet and toss with spices, salt, garlic, onions, and olive oil. Bake for 15 minutes, stirring once after 10 minutes, until browned.

Meanwhile, make the slaw by mixing the lime juice, vinegar, and oil together in a medium bowl and adding all the other ingredients. Mix well.

Warm up the tortillas in a microwave or one by one in a very hot, dry skillet for about 15 seconds per side. Top each tortilla with some roasted cauliflower, slaw, salsa, and slices of avocado. Serve with lime wedges on the side.

Reference

Thug Kitchen. 2014. *The Official Cookbook: Eat Like you Give a Fu*k*. New York: Rosdale.

CHAPTER 9

Can Place Cause Obesity?

A CRITICAL PERSPECTIVE ON THE FOOD ENVIRONMENT

Julie Guthman

Textbox 9.1. Learning Objectives

- Understand the main tenets of the obesogenic environment thesis, including the idea of the food desert.
- Critique the methodology and major assumptions of this type of research.
- Explore alternative conceptualizations of the relationship between place and obesity that take into account the connections between race, class, place, and health.
- Consider the policy ramifications of the obesogenic environment thesis and alternative perspectives on the relationship between environment and obesity.

Over the past two decades, **obesity** has surfaced as a major societal concern, regularly described as an "epidemic," in light of its alleged consequences on medical conditions such as heart disease, type 2 diabetes, and particular cancers. Evidence of rising obesity, measured through a simple weight-to-height ratio known as the body mass index (BMI), has launched a frenzy of responses, including a financially successful diet and fitness industry, a series of television programs and self-help publications, and weigh-ins at schools and workplaces. These efforts largely blame and objectify individuals for being overweight (see figure 9.1).

In response, researchers, particularly in the relatively well-respected field of public health, have turned their attention to environmental factors as an explanation for the rise in BMI. Hundreds of studies have been completed based on the theory that people are obese because they are surrounded by cheap, fast, and nutritionally inferior food. This theory was first formalized in the academic literature as the "**obesogenic environment**" thesis. As stated by Hill and Peters (1998, 1371), "our current environment is characterized by an essentially unlimited supply of convenient, relatively inexpensive, highly palatable, energy-dense foods, coupled with a lifestyle requiring only low levels of physical activity for subsistence. Such an environment promotes high energy intake and low energy expenditure."

Along with generating research, the thesis has animated various planning, advocacy, and educational interventions to address the obesogenic qualities of the built environment. These have included creating outlets for fresh fruits and vegetables in "inner-city" food deserts, redesigning (or remarketing) public spaces to encourage walking and bicycle riding, and city-sponsored educational campaigns to achieve obesity reduction.

The focus on the built environment in explaining and attempting to prevent obesity is in certain respects salutary. Deemphasizing individual behaviors would seem to diminish the moral scrutiny and invocations of personal responsibility that typically accompany discussions of obesity's causes (Guthman 2011). Moreover, a built-environment perspective brings some focus to food industry and regional planning practices, which potentially assigns culpability to powerful and malignant actors.

Despite their appeal, studies in this vein have as a whole generated inconclusive or marginal results. Furthermore, there is little evidence that the policy interventions to which the thesis leads work effectively in reducing obesity. The

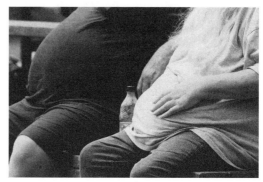

Figure 9.1. The objectification of obese bodies
Representations of obesity typically show portions of large bodies. As in this picture, these headless bodies are depicted sitting and consuming high-calorie and low-nutrient food or drinks, suggesting that their condition is a direct result of a lack of exercise and poor diets. Such representations turn obese bodies into objects that become devalued, blamed, and disciplined.
Source: Tony Alter (2009), Flickr.

problem is in part methodological: Studies are limited by the availability and commensurability of useful data to test the thesis, and tend to rely on questionable proxies. But it is also conceptual: These studies embed several untested assumptions about the character of the problem. In this chapter, I focus on two such assumptions: 1) that the built environment determines people's eating behaviors; and 2) that people's eating behaviors determine obesity.

Narrow conceptualizations of the relationship between the food environment, race/class, and obesity reduce the range of potential explanations and solutions, and tend to reproduce existing disparities. Indeed, much of the current research related to the obesogenic environment thesis suffers from what science studies scholars call "**problem closure**." This occurs when a specific definition of a problem is used to frame subsequent study of the problem's causes and consequences in ways that preclude alternative conceptualizations of the problem (Hajer 1995, 22). It may entail embedding assumptions about a scientific object's character into the research of that object. For example, the obesogenic environment thesis thoroughly embeds the energy-balance model in assuming that the environment is responsible for causing obesity by promoting high energy intake and low energy expenditure. This assumption prevents researchers from investigating alternative ways in which the environment might cause weight gain—for instance, through class-related stress or toxic exposures.

Problem closure can also entail defining the cause of the problem in relation to socially acceptable solutions. Studies of the obesogenic environment do this as well. By focusing on the built environment as a cause of obesity, they suggest that certain supply-side solutions, such as farmers' markets, community gardens, and financial incentives to attract large retailers, will reduce obesity. Such solutions are often more politically palatable and doable than those that might be raised by alternative conceptualizations of the problem, which might require addressing significant income inequality, or insufficient environmental regulation.

To make my case, I begin by defining the obesogenic environment, focusing specifically on the foodscape. In the following section, I turn to representative research on the **food environment**, primarily in North American cities, and problematize key assumptions. I then introduce alternative conceptualizations of the relationship between food, place, and obesity, including recent work on race, class, and place, and research on noncaloric etiologies that question the energy-balance concept. Throughout this chapter, I argue that, in the case of the food environment, problem closure stems from a myopic view of place that ignores its social production, dynamic characteristics, and various capacities to shape bodies.

Defining and Operationalizing the Obesogenic Food Environment

The obesogenic environment thesis, as it relates to the built environment, contains two core claims: one about the ubiquity of affordable, fast, junk food, relative to fresh, "healthy" food (energy intake); and the other about the dearth of opportunities for physical activity (energy expenditure). Here, I focus on the former, which in the United States and the UK is intimately tied to fast food and the idea of "food deserts." While physical activity spaces are an important component of the obesogenic environment thesis—especially considering it embeds the energy-balance model—that aspect is less relevant to this volume, which focuses on the relationship between food and place.

The term **food desert** is generally used to describe urban neighborhoods with a paucity of supermarkets and other venues where it's possible to purchase healthful fruits, vegetables, meats, and grain products (see textbox 9.2). This is often coupled with an abundance of liquor and convenience stores where only snack food and highly processed, ready-to-eat meals can be purchased. In the United States, food deserts are primarily inhabited by African Americans and recent immigrants (Short et al., 2007). The other problematic food environment is the endless strips of "big-box stores" (large, warehouse-style discount stores) and fast-food and chain restaurants in which supersizing / value-meal practices figure prominently. Unlike food deserts, these "food swamps" are defined by excess, not scarcity (see figure 9.3). Such strips tend to be located in newer suburbs, inhabited primarily by working-class and middle-class whites.

With the concepts of food desert and food swamp in mind, it is worth considering how researchers might go about trying to demonstrate a relationship between obesity and features of the built food environment. Most turn to two established scientific

Textbox 9.2.   Food Deserts

Food desert is a term used to describe neighborhoods where residents do not have access to affordable and healthy foods. This powerful metaphor has become popular among policy-makers, researchers, and advocacy groups. For instance, the US Department of Agriculture (2015) publishes an online Food Access Research Atlas, which displays census tracts (small geographic areas of approximately four thousand people, as defined by the US Census) with limited access to supermarkets, for policy, planning, and research purposes. Similarly, the Centers for Disease Control and Prevention (CDC 2011), in an effort to understand fac-tors contributing to childhood obesity, computed a modified retail food environment index (mRFEI), which is a ratio of healthy to less-healthy food retailers by census tract, categorizing supermarkets, large grocery stores, supercenters, and produce stores as healthy retailers, and fast-food restaurants, small grocery stores, and convenience stores as less-healthy. Numerous other studies document the existence of food deserts in low-income urban neighborhoods as well as in rural communities.

There are growing concerns, however, that these measures fail to capture the complexity of food environments by focusing almost entirely on supermarkets, relying on classed and racialized distinctions between healthy and unhealthy stores, and ignoring the important role that ethnic markets and small retailers play in the everyday food-provision activities of low-income people. As such, the food desert concept may stigmatize places as unhealthy, further contributing to devaluation, disinvestment, poverty, and, potentially, obesity.

The maps in figure 9.2, reproduced from a study of community food security in the City Heights neighborhood of San Diego (Joassart-Marcelli, Rossiter, and Bosco 2016), contrast a typical representation of food deserts that relies on supermarket data (panel a), with a finer-grained depiction that includes other types of stores (panel b). Despite being labeled as a food desert, this neighborhood has a vibrant commercial center with numerous small markets, including many ethnic stores, within walking distance of most residences.

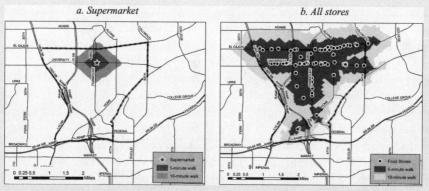

Figure 9.2. Walking distance to food stores in City Heights, San Diego, California

Source: Maps designed by Jamie Rossiter.

Figure 9.3. The obesogenic landscape
The concentration of fast-food restaurants in low-income neighborhoods has been blamed as a cause of obesity. This picture shows a commercial street in Bowling Green, Kentucky, with numerous fast-food restaurants side by side.
Source: Ross Uber (2006) via Wikimedia Commons. Available at https://commons.wikimedia.org/wiki/ File:Fastfood.jpg.

methods for identifying relationships between health outcomes and place: geographic information systems (GIS) and spatial analysis. These involve the use of spatial statistics and mapping to demonstrate correlative relationships between places with higher obesity prevalence and environmental features that might contribute to obesity. Both approaches, however, must rely on available data to make these correlations—data which themselves lead to certain kinds of explanations and not others.

First, researchers would need to ascertain variations in the prevalence of obesity across space in order to establish that some neighborhoods, places, and/or regions have higher obesity prevalence than others. They would tend to use body mass index (BMI) as a measure of obesity, since height and weight (the two size measurements used to compute BMI) are collected in various surveys. Surveys, however, differ in their sample size, geographic scale (e.g., state, region, city, neighborhood), time frame (i.e., longitudinal vs. cross-sectional), and number of additional variables collected (e.g., health behaviors, socioeconomic status). Thus, the choice of survey influences the depth and breadth of the findings. Alternatively, researchers could use self-reported data on weight and height. To show that BMI values vary across space, they would need to sort individual BMI values by geocodes—codes that link the individual to a particular state, county, postal code, and/or census tract. Although fine-grained scales are preferable for measuring neighborhood environmental influences, researchers might find that it is very difficult to obtain statistically reliable measures of BMI below the state, metropolitan area, or county scales. They might then map this variation to identify clusters of high obesity prevalence.

Thus far, however, the analysis would only have identified geographic variation in obesity—or, perhaps, clusters of obesity for further study. The next step would be to identify statistical associations between higher obesity rates and environmental features. The researchers would need to hypothesize what features might actually contribute to obesity and turn them into variables. With regard to the food environment, they would want to ascertain differences in availability of good-quality and bad-quality food. Researchers might thus be interested in the proximity, density, and mix of grocery stores, fast-food restaurants, big-box stores, and so forth.

But it would not be enough to conceptualize features of the built environment that contribute to obesity. The researchers would also need to find data to approximate those features. They would likely turn to business censuses or remote sensing technologies to obtain data by geocode. Researchers might also do their own surveying, perhaps walking and driving to estimate travel times to different sorts of business. Or they could forgo these "objective" data, as they are often referred to in this research, and collect "subjective" data by asking research subjects about their perceptions of these qualities in their neighborhood.

Finding data would not be the only challenge researchers face. They would also have to make their data geographically commensurate, which might entail aggregation to the largest common geographic scale used. Too coarse a scale, though, would provide very little information. To get that more fine-grained analysis, researchers might make compromises in other dimensions of the research. For example, the North American Industry Classification System (NAICS) used in the business census does not differentiate fine dining from family-oriented chain restaurants in the "full-service restaurant" category. Whether that restaurant is a Denny's (a national budget chain in the United States) or the upscale and award-winning Topolobampo in Chicago would seem to matter greatly. Many studies use variables that are not sharply defined in this way.

In actuality, few projects include all of these steps or a comprehensive array of variables. In the understandable interest of feasibility, most bite off a certain chunk, use variables that approximate environmental features, forgo variables for which data are lacking or incommensurate, and otherwise reduce "noise" by focusing on relatively few elements. This perhaps is one of the reasons why overall, the results of these sorts of studies have been marginal (Cummins et al., 2007). Even when they are robust, however, they do not necessarily prove what they are intended to prove.

Limitations of Existing Studies

Thus far, studies relating different foodscapes to obesity have found inconclusive or inconsistent evidence. The few empirical studies claiming to support the thesis that both food deserts and concentrations of fast-food restaurants are associated with higher obesity rates have reported very marginal findings. In most cases, differences in BMI were minimal, and researchers were unable to pinpoint which characteristics of the food environment contributed to these slim variations.

This can be explained by three methodological concerns.

Untested Assumptions about the Relationship between Environmental Characteristics and Obesity

One of the most surprising features of this area of research is that many studies do not actually measure obesity in place or space, although they still assume the tenets of the obesogenic environment thesis. Since 2000, a large number of studies have been published documenting the geographic relationship between food deserts or fast-food restaurants with low-income neighborhoods of color in a variety of contexts (e.g., Block et al. 2004; Morland et al. 2002; Pearce et al. 2007). Many of these studies do not directly measure this in relation to obesity, yet extrapolate about this relationship, concluding that these environmental disparities cause higher obesity rates among racial minorities and low-income groups without actually testing that hypothesis.

Even evidence that greater access to supermarkets increases the consumption of fruits and vegetables is not sufficient to conclude that additional supermarkets in a neighborhood cause reduction in the prevalence of obesity among its residents. In short, the majority of studies tend to overreach their conclusions by pegging one set of correlations (between features of the built environment and neighborhood deprivation) to another (between low socioeconomic status and obesity), without actually examining the correlations that are at the center of their claims.

Coarse Variables to Test Environmental Features

One great limitation of these studies is the absence of appropriate data with which to test possible hypotheses about the food environment. Even when health surveys provide data to measure obesity rates for specific geographic areas, features of the built environment—including the number and characteristics of grocery stores and restaurants—must almost always be approximated. As such, it appears that data availability has driven much of the research, and sometimes the data available are quite coarse. For example, a study might find an association between restaurant density and BMI, but since the data do not allow the researchers to identify the type of restaurant that predicts higher BMI, their ability to draw relevant conclusions about causality is severely limited.

Rather than attempt to quantify the environment "objectively," several studies have relied on people's perceptions of the built environment. Environmental characteristics are ascertained by subjects' responses to questions about satisfaction with supermarket access and fruit and vegetable availability in their neighborhood. Findings from these types of studies are often anomalous, especially at fine-grained scales—a problem if one is trying to make claims about neighborhood influences. In those cases, researchers typically argue that the problem lies with "local influences" not captured in the data, but rarely entertain the possibilities that either perceptions were not adequate to the task, or the relationship between the food environment and obesity simply does not hold.

Sometimes the data are so coarse that the findings veer toward spurious correlation. One oft-cited study found a relationship between numbers of fast-food restaurants per square mile and rates of obesity (Maddock 2004). However, this was based on statewide obesity rates—a measure too global to test the significance of the built environment in daily life.

Likewise, longitudinal studies that find correlations between the rise of obesity in recent decades and changes in the food environment (e.g., increase in fast-food restaurants) ignore so many other factors that may have changed during that period (e.g., suburban sprawl, immigration), that it seems a major supposition to attribute growth in obesity to just one set of changes. In general, data availability limits the claims that can be legitimately derived from these sorts of studies.

Untested Assumptions about Cause from Correlation

Despite the issues discussed thus far, some studies have yielded robust results (e.g., Morland et al. 2006; Babey et al. 2008). Nevertheless, the robustness is in association— not in establishing cause and effect. The fact that fast-food density, for example, is positively associated with obesity prevalence does not necessarily imply that the former causes the latter. Many studies interpret this positive correlation as a sign that proximity or density of fast-food restaurants is decisive in people's eating habits and that, effectively, living in certain neighborhoods made people bigger than they otherwise might have been. However, there may be other factors that explain this relationship, including economic, political, and social forces shaping neighborhoods. Companies that own fast-food restaurants and convenience stores that are considered obesogenic may choose to locate their outlets in particular neighborhoods in order to reach potential customers, including people who may already be overweight and presumably consume the food those businesses supply. Similarly, zoning regulations, which are shaped by political actors with uneven powers, may restrict the location of less-desirable food outlets in high-income neighborhoods while encouraging their siting in low-income communities. In a context where affordable housing is limited, it is also possible that people who are already obese and have low socioeconomic status move to areas with high fast-food density because the real estate may be cheaper.

There is an overarching assumption in these studies that **place** determines behavior or weight status. Yet, place is typically understood in a static way, without attending to the factors that produce differences between places, including capital flows, population movements, social relations of race and class, political decisions, and urban planning, which are deeply interrelated. Several geographers have argued for a relational perspective on place that requires researchers to consider more than just a list of geographically specific indicators when analyzing the impact of place on social outcomes (Cummins et al. 2007). To the extent that place is the ever-changing product of social relations, these very relations must form the basis of analysis. No studies have looked, for example, at unemployment rates, housing prices, proximity to cultural centers and institutions of higher learning—data that are available at the neighborhood level and could reasonably be used to draw statistically significant associations with weight status.

Conventional representations of place and space also inform different arguments, suggesting that it may be the personal characteristics and behaviors of people who happen to cluster in a space that are the basis of the correlations between obesity and space or place. In that perspective, place only matters in influencing obesity because of the people inhabiting it, suggesting a "population (or composition) effect" rather than a "place (or context) effect." Yet, from a relational perspective, the clustering of fat bodies in particular places is not accidental or separate from the broader processes that create places and produce uneven food landscapes. Nevertheless, the obesogenic environment thesis mostly ignores these recent "composition or context debates" that have animated the field of health geography (see Curtis and Riva 2010; Tunstall et al. 2004), by assuming that it is the built environment that produces obesity, not the socioeconomic characteristics of people inhabiting that place or the social relations embodied in it.

Those who emphasize the importance of gaining a better understanding of place often point to the limitations of quantitative research in understanding causality, arguing that local context cannot be deduced from spatial variables. In general, quantitative studies of the obesogenic environment pay scant attention to how these environments actually affect human behavior and influence individuals differently, because they are methodologically incapable of doing so (Lake and Townshend 2006). Still, even those who consider more-localized causes of obesity through qualitative research assume that the built environment plays a determinative role.

In short, the obesogenic environment thesis suffers from what has been described as **geographic determinism**—the idea that geographic conditions, not human agency or social structures, determine human behavior and social outcomes (see textbox 9.3). This perspective has received much criticism from scholars who argue that environments and geographic places are not fixed or given, but shaped by social relations, including class and race relations. Given the close association between weight status and socioeconomic status, the argument that race and class influence food environments and may therefore underlie spatial variations in obesity rates deserves consideration.

Textbox 9.3. Geographic Determinism

In its early version, geographic determination (also known as environmental determinism) is the belief that the physical environment shapes societies. For instance, many have argued that work ethics and productivity are influenced by climate, providing a simple explanation for the relatively low level of economic development in tropical regions—and a moral justification for intervention (or lack thereof). Despite criticism that environmental determinism negates the role of human agency and the possibility of other explanations, such as historical political and economic relations, it became a central feature of behavioral geography—a field that emerged in the mid-twentieth century, built on the notion that human behaviors are determined by environmental stimuli. The obesogenic environment thesis fits within this theoretical and analytical tradition by emphasizing how mere "exposure" to certain environments produces fat bodies, without asking how these environments were themselves discursively and materially produced, or questioning the multiple ways they may shape body sizes (Colls and Evans 2014).

The Raced and Classed Food Environment

Implicit in most of these studies is the argument that different environments can explain the close correlations between socioeconomic status and weight status. Specifically, people of low socioeconomic status become bigger because they live in neighborhoods with fewer recreational amenities and an abundance of cheap, fast food. Yet, there are problems with this line of reasoning. For one, it neglects the possibility that weight status is a cause of class status rather than a consequence of it. Many studies have demonstrated that weight bias affects people across the life course, including student–teacher relations, college admissions, marital prospects, and job advancement (Puhl and Brownell 2001). Although thinness does not guarantee high status, fatness pretty much guarantees low status. If this is the case, people who are obese are more likely to locate in places where real estate is cheaper—not as a rationally chosen trade-off, but as a necessity. More generally, this corollary of the thesis ignores what makes environments "obesogenic" in the first place—and that, too, has to do with class and race.

Contemporary geographers emphasize that spatial patterns in housing, commercial development, and public land access are a reflection of social relations of **race** and **class**, rather than a producer of them (Schein 2006). These spatialized patterns of race and class have been accentuated in an era when many economic development opportunities stem from the buying power and taxability of local residents (Lipsitz 2006). Consider the origins of the two kinds of urban environments associated with obesogeneity discussed herein: food deserts and food swamps. In the United States, the existence of food deserts is rooted in racist insurance and lending practices (redlining), which have historically made it difficult to develop and sustain businesses in certain areas (Eisenhauer 2001). Importantly, the food-desert phenomenon is also attributed to white flight and the net loss of supermarkets to suburbs with larger sites, fewer zoning impediments, and customers with higher purchasing power.

Conversely, food swamps are partly associated with contemporary suburban sprawl, which has also been driven by developers and mortgage bankers encouraging a struggling, debt-ridden, middle class to move far from the urban core to take advantage of cheaper housing. These expansive working/middle-class suburbs also owe much to new waves of regional economic development that encourage localities starved for tax revenue to provide location incentives to box stores, malls, and outlet centers (Schrag 1998). In other words, to the extent that some places have many features that are supposedly obesogenic, this often reflects the financial resources of those who inhabit such places and the waves of investment/disinvestment that have produced such environments. So the prevalence of obesity in sprawling, working-class suburbs may have less to do with the food environment and more to do with who lives in those suburbs in the first place.

The point can also be argued from the obverse. Much of the research pinpoints mixed-use areas as places where thin people live. Yet these gentrified urban cores that contain upscale and thus, presumably, healthier eating venues, as well as ample public space amenable to walking, are themselves products of particular economic development strategies to attract capital (see chapter 8). Indeed, to the extent that towns and cities with artistic, independent, and healthful restaurants, beautiful outdoor amenities, and unique character are *leptogenic* (causing thinness), it is because they are able to attract businesses to meet the food tastes of residents and generate the taxes needed to improve and maintain those enjoyable public spaces. Yet the more wealth they attract, the more they become inaccessible to many, as home prices follow. So, if thinness is a requisite for higher class status, this means that those who can afford to live in these leptogenic environments are almost necessarily thin.

What I am suggesting is that what may be "predicting" the prevalence of obesity in certain places is, in fact, already existing (but unexamined) bodily differences associated with race and class, indicating that features of the built environment are as much an effect of that spatial patterning as a cause. Rather than arguing that composition trumps context, however, I am concurring with Cummins et al. (2007), who have called the "composition and context debate" a false dualism, in recognition that "there is a mutually reinforcing and reciprocal relationship between people and place" (page 1835). Indeed, it is precisely the inseparability of composition and context that leads to confusion over causal direction and possibly explains the limited statistical significance of spatial models, such as those dominating the obesogenic environment literature reviewed here.

Tipping the Energy Balance

There is another possible reason that the obesogenic environment thesis has yielded results that are modest at best: This has to do with its fundamental reliance on the **energy-balance model** of obesogenesis. Eating too much and exercising too little is widely accepted as the explanation for obesity in Western societies (see chapter 13). Except for admitting some variation in obesity related to genetic predisposition, most hold the energy-balance model as axiomatic. Even when researchers show skepticism about the operationalization of the obesogenic environment thesis, they do not budge on this most primary presumption. Yet, it appears that the energy-balance model has met some challenges, as well.

Empirically, the assumption that since 1980 people have increased the number of calories they take in relative to those they expend has simply not been demonstrated. The literature on food intake is quite contradictory, with some studies suggesting even a reduction in energy intake over the past several decades. More to the point, the degree and direction of such changes are just not known, especially in the absence of good longitudinal data. Epidemiological data are based on recollection and food diaries, which tend to underreport food intake. Supply measures, such as food-availability indices, rely on estimates of farm production, adjusted for exports and imports, nonfood uses, and food waste. These are gross estimates at best. Nor has the putative decline in physical activity been convincingly demonstrated, with most studies of physical activity based on notoriously unreliable self-reporting.

Additionally, cross-sectional studies that compare behaviors across populations debunk assumptions that certain groups eat more calories than others—the corollary of the thesis. For example, data published by the USDA and the USDHHS (2012) on "What We Eat in America" show remarkable similarity among racial and income groups with respect to daily caloric intake. These surprising findings may be written off to self-reporting, but that would assume that certain groups are more prone to under-reporting food intake than others.

Furthermore, a significant array of emerging research on the biological etiology of obesity at least complicates the energy-balance model and potentially topples it as the primary factor determining weight status. The human metabolism, which regulates the digestion of food and its transformation into energy, appears to be influenced by sleep patterns, as well as the timing and distribution of meals. Researchers are also positing that chronic stress has powerful metabolic effects through constant release of the hormone cortisol. Perhaps most significant in understanding the relationship between place and obesity is research that points to the role of environmental toxins in contributing to the rise in obesity (Baillie-Hamilton 2002). The field of **epigenetics** identifies multiple ways in which environmental factors can increase susceptibility to weight gain, and offers promising insights into environmental causes of obesity (see textbox 9.4). Crucially, this research points to biological pathways to obesity that are almost entirely independent of calories. The most paradigm-shifting research is about the role of endocrine-disrupting chemicals, such as Bisphenol-A (BPA). It is worth noting that people with lower socioeconomic status tend to be exposed to more toxins in their

---

Textbox 9.4. Epigenetics

Epigenetics is a relatively new field that considers the interface of gene–environment interactions and focuses on changes in gene expression that occur without modifying the DNA sequence. Within that framework, researchers have begun studying the effects of various environmental factors and adverse conditions, even in early stages of life, on gene expression or regulation, including individual susceptibility to gain or lose weight. Long-term and early exposure to stress and chemicals, as well as past nutritional deprivations, have been shown to alter gene regulation, making certain populations prone to obesity and having transgenerational effects on phenotypes (Kuwaza and Sweet 2009).

Both animal and laboratory experiments have found that maternal exposure to a range of chemicals can alter genetic pathways for fetuses in ways that generate adult obesity. For instance, mice with identical genomes and diets, but different exposure to the synthetic chemical Bisphenol-A (BPA) during gestation and immediately following birth, differ significantly in body weight at adulthood (Adams 2008). This difference is attributed to an epigenetic effect that alters gene expression, acting like an "on/off switch" that turns on a particular gene and results in obesity. BPA is found in many widely used plastics, such as bottles and food containers, raising alarming concerns for human health.

Epidemiological data have provided some empirical support for how these mechanisms might affect humans (for an overview, see Hatch et al. 2010). For example, scientists in North Carolina (Gladen et al. 2000) found that children exposed to higher levels of PCBs (polychlorinated biphenyls) and DDE (a breakdown product of DDT) before birth had higher BMIs than those exposed to lower levels. Together, these studies suggest alternative ways in which environment and obesity relate to each other, challenging the notion that higher obesity prevalence among people of lower socioeconomic status is simply a consequence of their current dietary habits.

workplaces and homes, including some of the agricultural chemicals that have been identified as probable obesogens.

These studies embed their own assumptions, of course, and can be critiqued both ontologically and ethically for their reliance on genetically identical laboratory animals. So it would be folly at this point to suggest that this science presents a higher truth. Nevertheless, such findings do cast doubt on the strength of the energy-balance model that is the very basis of the obesogenic environment thesis. As put by two leading scientists in this research, "the existence of chemical obesogens in and of themselves suggests that the prevailing paradigm, which holds that diet and decreased physical activity alone are the causative triggers for the burgeoning epidemic of obesity, should be reassessed" (Grun and Blumberg 2006, S54). In other words, there are other possible explanations for the rise of obesity and for variations in obesity related to socioeconomic status. Yet, this research is entirely outside of the frame of the obesogenic environment thesis.

At some level, of course, it is to be expected. Researchers on the obesogenic environment are working in entirely different epistemic communities and, to their credit, are attempting to understand social-political dimensions of obesity. It nevertheless appears that researchers are so wedded to the energy-balance model that when results are inconclusive they tend to look for methodological shortcomings rather than question the model itself. The problem is that in neglecting these other possible causes, which also have social-political dimensions (see chapter 13), they re-inscribe a thesis that also has social-political consequences. That is the risk of premature problem closure.

Conclusion: Beyond the Built Environment and Supply-Side Interventions

Where most studies fall short is in assuming that the problematic features of the built environment exist independently of who lives there. I have suggested, instead, that the relationship between the built environment, spatial variation in obesity, and spatial variation in race and class are all of a piece. Gentrified urban cores are thin and wealthy, but it is unclear which begets which. Conversely, features associated with obesogeneity are precisely what make other urban neighborhoods affordable and thus available to those whose class status may exist by virtue of being obese. Yet, the quantitative spatial research that attempts to demonstrate the relationship between the built environment and obesity cannot account for this inseparability, which leads to marginal, or sometimes less than credible, results. Much more damning to the thesis is evidence that points to other possible causes of obesity having little to do with eating and physical activity, much less the built environment.

Despite their less-than-robust results, most studies end with the suggestion that obesity in low-income neighborhoods of color might be ameliorated by increasing the number of produce markets and sidewalks. This is the other aspect of problem closure: not only foreclosing other explanations, but defining problems in relation to socially acceptable solutions. While so-called supply-side data that measure features of the built environment related to the availability of food or opportunities for physical activity are more readily available and therefore form the basis of most studies, they also speak to imaginable interventions. In general, the obesogenic environment thesis, with its focus on access and proximity to grocery stores, restaurants, parks, gyms, and public transportation, leads to the conclusion that, if these conditions are changed, behaviors will follow and body sizes will transform. Other kinds of data might suggest deeper cultural and economic causes of bodily difference that are far less tractable. Arguably, that is the reason that public health professionals and food-system advocates have embraced the thesis.

Supply-side interventions are relatively palatable politically and provide clarity about what to do, such as asking corner liquor stores to sell fruits and vegetables, supporting farmers' markets in underserved neighborhoods, or regulating the sale of soda in proximity to schools. Yet, if obesogenic environments are as inseparable from race and class as I contend they are, picking out particular features of the built environment and making them more leptogenic is unlikely to be efficacious. In effect, these are attempts to make obesogenic environments more like the kind in which thin people live, without questioning whether people were made thin by living there. Such an approach also neglects to consider that the very conditions and amenities that make certain places sites of "the good life" also make them unobtainable to most. Furthermore, championing such environments can only contribute to their economic valorization (i.e., gentrification) and the reciprocal devaluation of obesogenic environments, with the real potential to exacerbate some of the inequalities they are designed to redress (see chapter 8 in this volume).

These two paradigmatic aspects of problem closure exist at our peril. Not only does the obesogenic environment thesis reinforce a supply-side focus, with little thought as to how that might affect real estate values in ways that could replicate class and race inequalities; it also reinforces the idea that people of low socioeconomic status are somehow responsible for obesity, rather than recognizing how weight discrimination affects their class status. Finally, it neglects to consider the possibility that chemicals are remaking bodies in serious ways, regardless of whether they contribute to obesity. Given the evidence for a much more complex etiology of obesity than too much food and too little sidewalk, the "doable" interventions may be doing more harm than good.

Key Terms

class
energy-balance model
epigenetics
food desert
food environment
geographic determinism

obesity
obesogenic environments
place
problem closure
race

Summary

- The food environment has become the dominant explanation for the extent and patterns of overweight and obesity in many settings, especially US cities.
- The obesogenic environment thesis suffers from three important methodological and theoretical concerns. In addition to using coarse data and extrapolating from analyses that actually do not include direct measures of obesity or related health outcomes, existing studies rest on a series of unsubstantiated assumptions that preclude other explanations and restrict the range and effectiveness of policy interventions.
- To address the growing health disparities that negatively affect people of color and low socioeconomic status, we need broader conceptualizations of the food environment and its relation to obesity and illness. In particular, we need to avoid geographic determinism, consider how the built environment is socially produced, and investigate other potential pathways in which environmental factors affect overweight and obesity, including the role of toxins and their epigenetics effects.

Additional Resources

A review of the literature on the obesogenic environment thesis is provided in Lake and Townshend (2006), Black and Macinko (2008), Giskes et al. (2011), and Townshend and Lake (2009).

For research on the relationship between place and health, see Cummins et al. (2007), Curtis and Riva (2010), and Tunstall, Shaw, and Dorling (2004).

For other critical perspectives on the obesogenic environment thesis, see Colls and Evans (2014). Guthman (2011) provides a critical overview of obesity politics.

An overview of the role of epigenetics in influencing obesity is available in Adams (2008) and Hatch et al. (2010).

The USDA provides data on food environments in the United States in its Food Environment Atlas (www.ers.usda.gov/data-products/food-environment-atlas.aspx) and its Food Desert Locator (www.ers.usda.gov/data/fooddesert#).

A number of popular documentaries focus on obesity in the United States, including *Super Size Me* (2004), *Bite Size* (2014), *Fat Head* (2009), *Fed Up* (2014), *Fat, Sick and Nearly Dead* (2010), and the documentary series *The Weight of the Nation* (2012). Although these tend to rely uncritically on the obesogenic environment thesis and energy-balance model, they may provide an opportunity to discuss this issue and consider alternative explanations.

References

Adams, Jill U. 2008. "Obesity, Epigenetics, and Gene Regulations." *Nature Education* 1(1): 128.
Alwitt, Linda F., and Thomas D. Donley. 1997. "Retail Stores in Poor Urban Neighborhoods." *Journal of Consumer Affairs* 31: 139–64.

Babey, Susan H., Allison L. Diamant, Theresa A. Hastert, and Stefan Harvey. 2008. "Designed for Disease: The Link between Local Food Environments and Obesity and Diabetes." *UCLA Center for Health Policy Research*. http://escholarship.org/uc/item/7sf9t5wx.

Baillie-Hamilton, Paula F. 2002. "Chemical Toxins: A Hypothesis to Explain the Global Obesity Epidemic." *Journal of Alternative and Complementary Medicine* 8: 185–92.

Black, Jennifer L., and James Macinko. 2008. "Neighborhoods and Obesity: The Roles of Area Socio-Demographics, Food Availability and the Physical Environment." *Nutrition Reviews* 66(1): 2–20.

Block, Jason P., Richard A. Scribner, and Karen B. DeSalvo. 2004. "Fast Food, Race/Ethnicity, and Income: A Geographic Analysis." *American Journal of Preventive Medicine* 27(3): 211–17.

CDC. 2011. *Census Tract Level State Maps of the Modified Retail Food Environment Index (mRFEI)*. US Centers for Disease Control and Prevention. National Center for Chronic Disease Prevention and Health Promotion. Division of Nutrition, Physical Activity, and Obesity. ftp://ftp.cdc.gov/pub/Publications/dnpao/census-tract-level-state-maps-mrfei_TAG508.pdf.

Colls, Rachel, and Bethan Evans. 2014. "Making Space for Fat Bodies? A Critical Account of 'the Obesogenic Environment.' " *Progress in Human Geography* 38(6): 733–53.

Cummins, Steven, Sarah Curtis, Ana V. Diez-Roux, and Sally Macintyre. 2007. "Understanding and Representing 'Place' in Health Research: A Relational Approach." *Social Science and Medicine* 65(9): 1825–38.

Curtis, Sarah, and Mylène Riva. 2010. "Health Geographies I: Complexity Theory and Human Health." *Progress in Human Geography* 34(2): 215–23.

Eisenhauer, Elizabeth. 2001. "In Poor Health: Supermarket Redlining and Urban Nutrition." *GeoJournal* 53: 125–33.

Giskes, Katrina, F. van Lenthe, M. Avendano-Pabon, and J. Brug, J. 2011. "A Systematic Review of Environmental Factors and Obesogenic Dietary Intakes Among Adults: Are We Getting Closer to Understanding Obesogenic Environments?" *Obesity Reviews* 12: e95–e106.

Gladen, Beth C., N. Beth Bagan, and Walter J. Rogan. 2000. "Pubertal Growth and Development and Prenatal and Lactational Exposure to Polychlorinated Biphenyls and Dichlorodiphenyl Dichloroethene." *The Journal of Pediatrics* 136(4): 490–96.

Grun, Felix, and Blumberg, Bruce. 2006. "Environmental Obesogens: Organotins and Endocrine Disruption via Nuclear Receptor Signaling." *Endocrinology* 147(6): s50–s55.

Guthman, Julie. 2011. *Weighing In: Obesity, Food Justice, and the Limits of Capitalism*. Berkeley: University of California Press.

———. 2013. "Too Much Food and Too Little Sidewalk? Problematizing the Obesogenic Environment Thesis." *Environment and Planning A* 45(1): 142–58.

Hajer, Marteen A. 1995. *The Politics of Environmental Discourse: Ecological Modernization and the Policy Process*. New York: Oxford University Press.

Hatch, Elizabeth E., J. W. Nelson, R. W. Stahlhut, and T. F. Webster. 2010. "Association of Endocrine Disruptors and Obesity: Perspectives from Epidemiological Studies." *International Journal of Andrology* 33(2): 324–32.

Hill, James O., and Peters, John C. 1998. "Environmental Contributions to the Obesity Epidemic." *Science* 280 (5368): 1371–74.

Joassart Marcelli, Pascale, Jamie S. Rossiter, and Fernando J. Bosco. 2017. "Ethnic Markets and Community Food Security in an Urban Food Desert." *Environment and Planning A* 49(7): 1642–63.

Kuzawa, Christopher W., and Elizabeth Sweet. 2009. "Epigenetics and the Embodiment of Race: Developmental Origins of US Racial Disparities in Cardiovascular Health." *American Journal of Human Biology* 21(1): 2–15.

Lake, Amelia, and Tim Townshend. 2006. "Obesogenic Environments: Exploring the Built and Food Environments." *Journal of the Royal Society for the Promotion of Health* 126(6): 262–67.

Lipsitz, George. 2006. *The Possessive Investment in Whiteness: How White People Profit from Identity Politics*. Philadelphia: Temple University Press.

Maddock, Jay. 2004. "The Relationship between Obesity and the Prevalence of Fast-Food Restaurants: State-Level Analysis." *American Journal of Health Promotion* 19(2): 137–43.

Morland, Kimberly, Ana Diez-Roux, and Steve Wing. 2006. "Supermarkets, Other Food Stores, and Obesity: The Atherosclerosis Risk in Communities Study." *American Journal of Preventive Medicine* 30: 333–39.

Morland, Kimberly, Steve Wing, Ana Diez Roux, and Charles Poole. 2002. "Neighborhood Characteristics Associated with the Location of Food Stores and Food Service Places." *American Journal of Preventive Medicine* 22(1): 23–29.

Pearce, Jamie, Tony Blakely, Karen Witten, and Phil Bartie. 2007. "Neighborhood Deprivation and Access to Fast-Food Retailing: A National Study." *American Journal of Preventative Medicine* 32(5): 375–82.

Puhl, Rebecca, and Kelly D. Brownell. 2001. "Bias, Discrimination, and Obesity." *Obesity* 9(12): 788–805.

Schein, Richard H. 2006. "Race and Landscape in the United States." In *Landscape and Race in the United States*, edited by Richard H. Schein, 1–21. New York: Routledge.

Schrag, Peter. 1998. *Paradise Lost: California's Experience, America's Future*. Berkeley: University of California Press.

Short, Anne, Julie Guthman, and Samuel Raskin. 2007. "Food Deserts, Oases, or Mirages? Small Markets and Community Food Security in the San Francisco Bay Area." *Journal of Planning Education and Research* 26(3): 352–64.

Townshend, Tim, and Amelia A. Lake. 2009. "Obesogenic Urban Form: Theory, Policy and Practice." *Health & Place* 15(4): 909–16.

Tunstall, H. V. Z., M. Shaw, and D. Dorling. 2004. "Places and Health: Glossary." *Journal of Epidemiology and Community Health* 58: 6–10.

US Department of Agriculture and US Department of Health and Human Services. 2012. *What We Eat in America, NHANES 2011–12 Data: Nutrient Intakes from Food and Beverages*. www.ars.usda.gov/SP2UserFiles/Place/80400530/pdf/1112/Table_2_NIN_RAC_11.pdf.

US Department of Agriculture. 2015. *The Food Access Research Atlas*. www.ers.usda.gov/data/fooddesert#.

Can We "Read" Class and Race in the Food Landscape?

Pick an issue of a popular food magazine such as Bon Appétit, Food & Wine, Edible, *or* Gourmet, *and find an article focused on food in a particular place (e.g., an urban neighborhood, a travel destination, someone's home, a restaurant). This can be done online. Analyze how the place is described in terms of class and race. Who lives there? Are they affluent or poor? Are the origins of their wealth or poverty described? To what extent does the description of the place give value to the food displayed? Imagine the same food in a very different context; how would that change your perception?*

Burgers may provide a useful example of the role of place in shaping the way food is interpreted and categorized along the lines of class, race, and other differences. As the cultural backlash against fast food (and fast-food eaters) has intensified, ironically, the burger has been reinvented as gourmet food. Throughout Europe and the United States, burgers are being served in casual eateries and acclaimed food establishments, and from trendy food trucks. Despite a similarly elevated number of calories, these gourmet burgers distinguish themselves as sophisticated (and often pass for healthy) because of the unique ingredients they use and the places where they are being served. This recipe points to the hypocrisy in the way we judge food, and eaters. It also emphasizes the time, money, skills, and equipment required to prepare this type of burger. The 99-cent fast-food burger alternative might be a bit more affordable and convenient.

Gourmet Beef Burger with Pickled Red Onions, Tarragon Russian Dressing, Swiss Cheese, and Bacon

Ingredients (to make four burgers)

For the pickled red onions:

1 medium red onion, peeled and very thinly sliced
½ cup apple cider vinegar (or plain vinegar)
1 tablespoon sugar
1 teaspoon salt

For the tarragon Russian dressing:

½ cup mayonnaise
¼ cup ketchup
1 teaspoon mustard
1 teaspoon Worcestershire sauce
2 tablespoons finely chopped tarragon

For the burger:

4 brioche buns (or regular burger buns)
4 slices of Swiss cheese
4 thick slices of bacon
2 pounds ground beef (blend of chuck and sirloin)
1 teaspoon salt
pepper to taste
1 tablespoon chopped parsley

Preparation

To make the pickled onions, whisk vinegar, salt, and sugar together. Pack thinly sliced onions in a jar and pour vinegar mixture on top. Cover and let sit at room temperature for at least 1 hour. Can be kept in the fridge for up to two weeks.

To make the dressing, mix all ingredients together. Cover and refrigerate.

To prepare the burgers, mix the ground meat, salt, pepper, and parsley in a bowl. Divide into four equal portions and form patties. Start the grill and while it heats, cook the bacon in a skillet until crispy and drain on paper towels. Grill burgers for approximately 5 minutes per side for medium (cooking time will vary depending on your grill and desired doneness). Top each burger with a slice of cheese and place the bun halves (facedown) on the grill to toast, for 1 minute or so. Remove buns from grill, spread dressing on bottom halves, top with burgers, bacon, and pickled onions. Cover with top half of bun and serve with fries and/or greens.

CHAPTER 10

Food Banks and the Devolution of Anti-Hunger Policy

Daniel N. Warshawsky

Textbox 10.1. Learning Objectives

- Learn the multiple roles that local food organizations play in urban food systems.
- Comprehend how food banks have grown in influence globally.
- Relate the expansion of food banks to neoliberal forms of urban governance.
- Recognize the strengths and weaknesses of civil society organizations in cities.

In many parts of the world, food assistance to the hungry has been provided by a combination of government agencies and voluntary or nonprofit organizations. In recent decades, as the role of the welfare state has declined, civil society has taken up an increasingly large share of the responsibility to confront food insecurity—the insufficient access to affordable, nutritious, and culturally appropriate food that many low-income people experience (Food and Agriculture Organization 2008). **Local food organizations** (LFOs) have emerged as one of the most important civil society institutions to address these needs in the world's cities. **Civil society** includes social activities that are not part of the state, private sector, or households (Tostensen, Tvedten, and Vaa 2001). As such, LFOs consist of the range of formalized, professionalized, and resource-rich nongovernmental organizations; informal, basic-needs, and resource-poor community-based organizations; and social movements focused on transforming society (Warshawsky 2016a). Very often, LFOs provide key social welfare, contribute to broader social movements, and change urban governance, with profound impacts on community food systems (Moragues-Faus and Morgan 2015; Sonnino 2016).

The growing role of LFOs in addressing urban hunger needs to be contextualized in global food insecurity (see chapter 7). According to the Food and Agriculture Organization of the United Nations (2015), there are approximately 795 million food-insecure people across the world, which is one in nine people. While the food insecurity rates vary dramatically from region to region, most of the globe's food-insecure population lives in lower-income regions, such as Asia or Africa (see chapter 7). In seemingly wealthy countries like the United States, however, a shockingly large share of the population is also considered "food-insecure," the term preferred by policymakers today.

Although **food insecurity**, **hunger**, and **malnutrition** have different connotations, they are all used to measure or characterize the extent of food inaccessibility. As discussed in textbox 10.2, however, the term *food insecurity* has a different connotation than the more-visceral term, *hunger*. According to Berg (2008), the concept of food insecurity allows policymakers to focus on individual food access and ignore the broader political and economic structural inequalities that produce hunger as a social phenomenon. While economic opportunity and government support have helped to reduce extreme food insecurity in the United States, 15 percent of the US population remains food-insecure, with deep concentrations of food insecurity in urban neighborhoods and isolated rural areas (Feeding America 2016b), where poverty rates are well above the national average.

While some suggest that LFOs are instrumental in providing food equity (Gottlieb and Joshi 2010), others argue that LFOs fill service gaps left by the state or private sector (Lambie-Mumford and Jarvis 2012). Although many LFOs have a strong mission, it is unclear whether they can meet their institutional goals, given that, as with most **nonprofits** working for social causes, they often lack adequate financial and human resources, are constrained by donor mandates, and confront increased demand levels (Milligan and Conradson 2006). Although some LFOs have engaged in fundraising campaigns, increased their membership fees, or collaborated with corporate sponsors, it is uncertain whether LFOs can balance institutional stability and mission.

Moreover, some critical scholars have suggested that LFOs, including those involved in the so-called alternative food movement, romanticize the power of local organizations and reinforce inequality along the lines of race and income (see chapter 11). Growing reliance on LFOs appears to fit a **neoliberal** policy framework, which facilitates the **devolution**, privatization, and decentralization of state policy to local actors and exacerbates existing inequalities (Guthman 2008). Recent research suggests that food banks in particular have become integral to the neoliberalization of **urban governance**, which Brenner and Theodore (2002) describe as a movement toward multisector collaborations among public, private, and nongovernmental institutions and away from a so-called welfare state. In that framework, social services are increasingly provided by civil society through coalitions of local, community-driven, nongovernmental, market-friendly, and economically self-sustaining organizations. As a result, service delivery has become more fragmented, narrowly focused on food provision, and increasingly disconnected from the larger political and economic issues of hunger, poverty, and inequality (Warshawsky 2010).

To examine these arguments in more detail, in this chapter, I critically analyze the roles that LFOs play in urban food systems through the case of urban **food banks**. Originally started in the United States in the 1960s, urban food banks now collect, systematize, and deliver unused, surplus, or donated food to poor urban communities in over forty countries on six different continents as a way to reduce food insecurity and food waste (Global FoodBanking Network 2016). In this food banking model, food is donated from government agencies, food industries, and individuals to regional food banks to food bank network beneficiary organizations

Textbox 10.2. Malnutrition, Hunger, Food Insecurity, and the Politics of Counting

Berg in his 2008 book *All You Can Eat: How Hungry Is America?* argues that defining and counting hunger is political. Although most politicians in the United States declare hunger an "embarrassing and intolerable" (Nixon) "national disgrace" (Glickman) that "we have a moral obligation to fight" (Obama), many are reluctant to fund programs needed to truly eradicate it. It was not until the late 1960s that the government first collected national data on hunger, generating media attention and public outrage at the extent of malnutrition (i.e., lack of caloric intake and key nutrients) in America. In the face of disturbing results, however, this survey program was quickly ended, presumably for budgetary reasons. It took much effort by anti-hunger organizations, like the Food Research and Action Center (FRAC), to lobby for official surveys by continuing to document hunger on their own. Eventually, Congress mandated the USDA to collect and publish national data on hunger, producing a first report in 1995. These data are now published annually, but definitions of food insecurity have been revised to political ends.

While many anti-hunger advocates prefer the term *hunger*, which describes the physically and emotionally painful state of people lacking sufficient food, it has been replaced by the term *food insecurity* in the social sciences and within policy contexts. *Hunger* produces a visceral reaction among the general public; most people are almost universally repulsed at its persistence amid affluence. *Food insecurity*, in contrast, is more abstract and less political, implying a lack of food, at times, for an active and healthy lifestyle. Yet, it is a concept that is relatively easy to define and measure via a series of questions designed to assess numbers of meals skipped, involuntary changes in caloric intake, and various concerns about having enough food by household. People are classified as either "food insecure" or "food secure" based on responses to these questions. While in its early version, more extreme food insecurity overlapped with hunger, eventually *hunger* was dropped altogether.

Nevertheless, the public and the media continue to use the term *hunger*, leading to confusion and misuse of data for political aims. For instance, conservative organizations point out that food-insecure households may only lack food for a few days each year, suggesting that the problem is less rampant than otherwise thought. In contrast, progressives tend to exaggerate the extent of food insecurity by labeling all people with any food insecurity, including those who occasionally substitute cheaper food or reduce their caloric intake, as hungry. As a result, the same USDA data allow pundits to claim numbers of hungry people ranging from 17.6 million (Heritage Foundation 2010) to 42.2 million (Feeding America 2016b).

Armed with these numbers, conservatives and liberals push different policy agendas. Conservatives often minimize the extent of hunger by linking it to obesity and arguing that "most adults in food insecure households actually consume too much, not too little, food" (Heritage Foundation 2007), and suggesting that public food assistance programs encourage unhealthy choices and reproduce poverty. This sort of argument, which is not new (see figure 10.1), not only ignores the importance of having access to nutritionally adequate food, but further stigmatizes and punishes the poor (see chapters 9 and 13). In contrast, liberals argue that hunger is a major social problem that cannot be solved only with food assistance, but requires policies to reduce poverty, unemployment, and inequality (see chapter 7). With such different agendas and little bipartisan support, it is not surprising that the provision of anti-hunger services has shifted to the third sector.

Figure 10.1. The politics of food assistance

This political cartoon, entitled "Hard Times," suggests that government assistance is a waste of public money; it does not serve those in need, and instead encourages indulgence, corruption, and laziness. Uncle Sam is depicted working at the "Free Pie Kitchen," symbolically handing out pies to a long line of wealthy and overweight people. While not specific to anti-hunger programs, this cartoon's depiction of food distribution and obese bodies as symbols of government inefficiency and its negative effect on personal responsibility and morality is illustrative of the politics surrounding food assistance.

Source: L. M. Glackens (1908), Library of Congress. Available at: www.loc.gov/pictures/item/2011647297/.

within their respective food bank networks. In the last phase, food is served or distributed to people at beneficiary organizations.

Two research questions are central to this chapter. First, what role do urban food banks play in urban food system governance? Second, what do these findings suggest for the viability of LFOs and their capacity to reduce food insecurity and food waste in cities? To answer these research questions, I present findings from two case studies based on in-depth interviews and participant observation of key food bank stakeholders I conducted in North American and African cities between 2009 and 2014 (see Warshawsky 2010 and 2011 for more detail on these methods and results).

My research suggests that food banking may streamline food donations, increase the amount of food delivered, and reduce food waste in many contexts. However, it is unclear whether food banks can reduce food insecurity or food waste in cities, as they often function in tandem with neoliberal policies, which devolve, decentralize, privatize, and commercialize food policy; reduce the size and scope of welfare programs; and promote market logics over social equality. Moreover, given that many food banks suffer from severe funding shortfalls, excessive corporate and state influence, and problematic implementation in the Global South, the impact of urban food banking may be limited in some contexts.

The structure of this chapter is as follows. To begin, I examine the development of food banking in North America and its growth across the globe. Then, through case studies of urban food banks in Chicago and Johannesburg, I analyze the roles of LFOs in urban food systems. In particular, I utilize a critical political-economic theoretical framework to explore the structure of LFOs and examine how food banks operate within the broader food system. As I argue, food banks operate at a broader scale than beneficiary organizations, which typically work at the community level and are more connected to the places where hungry people live. These different scales of operation create tensions and disconnect between the missions of both types of agencies and limit the overall impact of food banks in the community.

The Political Economy of Food Banking: From a Temporary Institution to a Global Powerhouse

THE EMERGENCE AND STRUCTURE OF FOOD BANKS IN THE UNITED STATES

In the late 1960s, a retired Phoenix businessman named John van Hengel decided to store food donations in a regional warehouse where he could deliver food to the hungry. As illustrated in figure 10.2, this concept of food banking is based on the redistribution of food to people in communities via the aggregation of unused, surplus, or donated food from a variety of food sources. These sources include small-scale and corporate farms and fisheries; supermarkets, restaurants, and other food retailers; food manufacturers, wholesalers, and distributors; and wealthy individuals. Government food programs are also major contributors to food banks. In fact, as discussed in textbox 10.3, some argue that agricultural surpluses resulting from changes in US farm policy starting in the 1970s and managed by the USDA have been a key factor in the expansion of food banks. In particular, the USDA's Emergency Food Assistance Program provides a "dumping ground" for excess food products as a way to stabilize the agricultural commodities market. In this way, the USDA is fundamentally a market-driven program designed to support agro-food corporations. The reduction of food insecurity is an indirect goal of the USDA program, but it is not the driving force that determines the type, amount, and scale of food production and consumption (Henderson 2004; Poppendieck 2014).

The centralization of food donations from these various sources and their subsequent redistribution through regional or community food banks is a relatively new development that represents the most important nonprofit emergency food distribution system in the United States (Feeding America 2016a). As the third-largest charity in the United States, with private support totaling more than $1.8 billion yearly (*Forbes* 2015), Feeding America now serves all fifty states and more than forty-six million people annually through its two hundred regional Feeding America–affiliated food

Textbox 10.3. American Cheese

According to the USDA (2003), American cheese "is a blend of fresh and aged natural cheese (such as cheddar, Colby, etc.) that has been melted, pasteurized, and mixed with an emulsifier according to FDA's Standard of Identity." These two-pound packages of cheese symbolize the political economy of food assistance in the United States.

American cheese was designed by the USDA as a way to repurpose dairy surplus associated with its farm policy. Since the 1930s, the US government had been buying, storing, and distributing agricultural commodities in order to support farmers and stabilize prices. This policy expanded dramatically after the 1973 Farm Bill, which, amid fears of food scarcity and rising food prices, dismantled the previous system of price support through loans and instead encouraged farmers to grow more with direct payments to farmers for any shortfall in the price of commodities like corn, wheat, and dairy (Pollan 2006).

As a result, farmers ramped up production, knowing that they would receive a certain price for their commodities regardless of any drop in price that an oversupply might generate. In the early 1980s, public outrage followed media attention over the fact that "government warehouses bulged with surplus cheese, butter and dried milk" (King 1982) while people were going hungry as a result of deep cuts in public assistance, combined with a severe economic recession. In response, the Reagan administration established a Special Dairy Distribution Program in 1981, and created the Temporary Emergency Food Assistance Program (TEFAP) in 1983 to allocate various commodities to voluntary agencies (Poppendieck 1998).

Huge quantities of cheese (i.e., 190 million pounds in 1981 alone) were distributed to churches and community centers, where people lined up to receive blocks of cheese. This prompted the expansion and consolidation of food organizations, which had to adapt to this massive influx of cheese and deal with storage and find proper uses for this product. Yet, these programs were described as temporary assistance, threatening the sustainability of these expanding agencies, which became increasingly dependent on federal food programs.

This example suggests that food banks did not emerge solely out of voluntarism, but expanded as a result of political decisions that, on the one hand, reduced assistance for the poor through welfare cuts, and, on the other hand, increased support for farmers, leading to both higher demand and larger donations of food channeled through consolidated food pantries.

REFERENCE

Rathe, Caitlin. 2016. "Making Hunger a Temporary Emergency." Paper presented at the Sixth International Conference on Food Studies, University of California, Berkeley, California, October 13.

banks and sixty thousand local food bank network beneficiary organizations, including food pantries, feeding schemes, and soup kitchens; care centers for the young, aged, disabled, sick, or homeless; schools, day-care facilities, and centers for vulnerable children; and, development centers for educational or job training (Feeding America 2016a; Global FoodBanking Network 2016).

Although it is not the only food bank system in the United States, Feeding America is by far the largest in terms of size, influence, and food delivered. As delineated in figure 10.2, Feeding America–affiliated regional food banks receive financial and food donations from multiple and often distant places, including municipal, county, state,

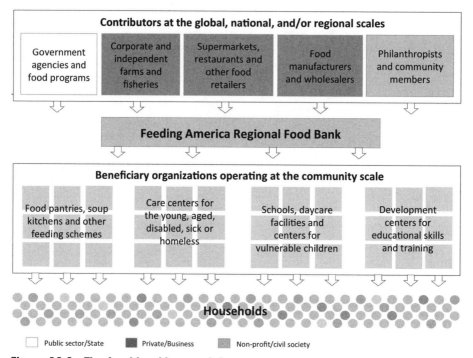

Figure 10.2. The food banking model
Source: Author.

and federal government food programs, surrounding agricultural regions, proximate food retail markets and distribution regions, and local community members.

While the voluntary sector has always played a key role in providing poverty relief in US history (see figure 10.3), the scale and intensity of welfare state restructuring radically transformed the role of emergency food organizations (Wolch 1990). Starting with Reagan-era funding reductions and rollbacks in the 1980s, especially reductions in Food Stamp allotments and other key feeding programs, food banks emerged as temporary relief mechanisms to confront growth in emergency food demand (Poppendieck 1998 and 2014). The need for nonprofit food banks was further intensified as the economy weakened and poverty rose in the 1970s and 1980s. Later, through the Personal Responsibility and Work Opportunity Act of 1996, the Clinton administration's welfare reform policies further reduced the amount and eligibility for key federal programs, such as Food Stamps (Peck 2001). Government retrenchment and devolution reduced resources for social programs and shifted demand onto nonprofits. Increased competition among both nonprofits and for-profits for public funds and philanthropic resources resulted in higher expectations for nonprofits to be financially sound. This led to an increase in corporate partnerships, private-sector fund-raising, and membership fees in order for nonprofits to achieve financial sustainability and community legitimacy as viable organizations (Grønbjerg and Salamon 2012).

With federal funding and food surplus acquired in these early years, America's Second Harvest (now known as Feeding America) developed into a key clearinghouse for food donations. Food banks continued to flourish with the passage of the Tax

Figure 10.3. Community soup kitchen in Chicago (1931)
Until the development of large-scale food banking, food assistance was primarily provided through nonprofits, faith-based organizations, and private donors. These were
particularly active during the Great Depression era. This image shows unemployed
men waiting in line in front of a Chicago soup kitchen presumably established and
funded by notorious gangster Al Capone.
Source: National Archives and Records Administration. Available at: https://catalog.archives.gov/
id/541927.

Reform Act of 1976 and the Good Samaritan Food Donation Act in 1996, as these
laws provided key tax incentives and protected corporations from liability for donating
food (Poppendieck 1998). As food manufacturers and retailers consolidated into fewer
but larger corporations and federal agricultural policies continued to encourage the
production of food surplus, the food banking process became further streamlined. By
the 1990s, Feeding America emerged as the largest US network of food banks, one of
the largest US charities, and a permanent US institution. It is now a key stakeholder
in the US food system, as it helps to manage its surplus and waste while attempting to
address some of its most blatant inequities.

FOOD BANKING IN THE GLOBAL SOUTH

As food banking expanded in size and influence in the United States, demand for international food banking led to a spin-off organization called the Global FoodBanking

Network, also located in Chicago, Illinois. Founded in 2006 in conjunction with leaders from US, Canadian, Argentinean, and Mexican food banks, the Global FoodBanking Network is a nonprofit organization funded by global food corporations and wealthy individuals (Global FoodBanking Network 2006).

Over the past ten years, the Global FoodBanking Network has developed food banking systems in over forty countries on six continents (Global FoodBanking Network 2016). While on-site in each country, the Global FoodBanking Network provides leadership support, technical training, and financial and human resources in consultation with local needs. Importantly, the Global FoodBanking Network promotes Feeding America's system of food banking as the best practice model in local contexts (Global FoodBanking Network 2015). Although food banks in each country are primarily supplied with food and money from local sources within their own country boundaries, the Global FoodBanking Network and its member food banks have often received some start-up funding from food corporations, such as Cargill, General Mills, and Kellogg Company (Global FoodBanking Network 2015).

THE POLITICAL ECONOMY OF FOOD BANKS

With its relatively rapid growth and importance, food banking has been subject to increased scrutiny by scholars. As in other areas of civil society, food banks across the Global North have been embraced for their nongovernmental funding, proximity to communities, and organizational flexibility. Additionally, food banks have been touted for expanding the number of institutions committed to food security, streamlining food donation processes, increasing the amount of food delivered, and reducing waste (Lambie-Mumford 2013; Riches and Silvasti 2014). However, as noted by Poppendieck (1998) in her landmark study on food bank development in the 1980s and 1990s, food banks have been critiqued for reinforcing a false notion that charity and volunteerism can reduce food insecurity and social inequality. The belief that volunteerism can reduce social inequality is arguably related to the physical and social distance that exists between donors and recipients within an increasingly centralized system. The fact that donors, especially large corporate donors and those donating via those corporations, are separated from recipients reduces awareness of hunger, hides its structural causes, and breaks down our ability to care.

Building on this argument, Poppendieck (1998) argues that food banks have depoliticized food insecurity, as food banks prioritize the amount of food delivered, not the causes of structural inequality that underlie hunger. Similarly, Henderson (2004) suggests that the food bank's ability to take political positions on social or economic inequality is limited, since it has to balance the interests of its donors and various stakeholders. Although some food banks have chosen not to join Feeding America's network in order to remain independent (Poppendieck 1998), the majority adopt strategies that allow them to stay in operation. In some cases, food banks have actively promoted neoliberal strategies in order to maintain organizational stability or reinforce their sense of autonomy (Warshawsky 2010). As these food banks commercialize, privatize, and devolve institutional responsibility, their organizational mission risks becoming compromised by funding priorities (Young et al. 2012).

The mission of food banks and Feeding America has changed over time, reflecting both demand factors and resources available, which need to be understood within the larger political and economic system. Food banks initially developed in the United States to confront increased demand due to a stagnant economy in the 1970s and state retrenchment and welfare reform in the 1980s. Since then, Feeding America has consolidated its position as one of the largest charitable organizations in the country, and has adapted its mission. For instance, while food banks were once positioned to reduce food insecurity, they are now central in the battle against food waste and environmental degradation (Global FoodBanking Network 2015). Importantly, each of these mission shifts has privileged institutional self-perpetuation and the long-term institutional viability of the food banking model, possibly at the expense of immediate needs to reduce hunger. It has done so by providing an outlet for federal agricultural surplus and through key partnerships with food manufacturers, wholesalers, retailers, and government agencies. A mutually beneficial relationship has developed between these different sectors to the extent that food banks require food donations, government agencies seek to support farmers and minimize welfare expenditure, and corporations need brand recognition and legitimacy as ethical companies (Ionescu-Somers 2004; Warshawsky 2016b). Yet, although those within Feeding America and the Global FoodBanking Network espouse an increase in food security, reduction of food waste, and empowerment of communities (Feeding America 2016a; Global FoodBanking Network 2015), it is unclear whether food banking can meet these lofty goals. To date, there are no existing studies that point to direct impacts of food banking on food insecurity levels (Riches and Silvasti 2014).

As the US food bank model has begun expanding globally and has received support for expanding the number of institutions committed to food security, streamlining food donation processes, increasing the amount of food delivered, and reducing waste, it is important to examine how food banks develop in other contexts outside North America. Recent studies in South Africa (Warshawsky 2011), Brazil (Rocha 2014), and other countries in the Global North (Riches and Silvasti, 2014) have identified the development and outcomes of food banks in the Global South. However, scholars have only begun to analyze the impact of US-based food banking models in other parts of the world, especially in the Global South.

Urban Food Bank Case Study 1: The Greater Chicago Food Depository

THE STRUCTURE AND DEVELOPMENT OF THE GREATER CHICAGO FOOD DEPOSITORY

As one of the largest and oldest food banks in the United States, the Greater Chicago Food Depository (Depository) distributes sixty-eight million tons of food to the more than 650 food pantries, soup kitchens, shelters, mobile programs, and programs for children and the elderly, for thousands of people across Cook County, Illinois (Greater Chicago Food Depository 2015). The network of emergency food services in Chicago designed to accomplish this enormous distribution task is large and complex, reflecting the organizational structure depicted in figure 10.2 above. The Depository receives food from various growers, processors, retailers, manufacturers, wholesalers, and restaurants. Some of the food received by the Depository is acquired through the federal USDA food programs or local area food drives. State and city governmental offices also provide both financial and food resources to food banks and related metropolitan food organizations. The Depository stores these food products in their warehouse facilities, and donates or sells at a reduced cost these food products to food bank network beneficiary organizations, including pantries, soup kitchens, and shelters, which subsequently give food to people in need in their communities.

In these ways, the Depository is not just a facilitator of emergency food service delivery in Chicago; it also acts as a mechanism to handle food surplus for corporations or government agencies. Since food banking is dependent on the existence of surplus food produced, food banks provide food corporations a critical place to unload their excess food and an opportunity to recast their company as moral and sustainable (Warshawsky 2016b).

Since it started in 1979, the Depository has redesigned its financial structure, commercialized and professionalized its operations, and reduced advocacy as a way to maintain institutional stability. As of 2015, the Depository's operating budget was $111,800,000. Centrally, the Depository has become increasingly dependent on corporate sponsors and membership fees rather than government funding (Greater Chicago Food Depository 2015). This has included the development of an endowment, which was over $40,000,000 as of 2015. Even though user fees account for less than 10 percent of the Depository's funding, this trend suggests that the corporate culture of accountability and performance evaluation is increasingly central to urban food systems (Greater Chicago Food Depository 2015).

In addition to financial reorganization, the Depository has increasingly included shifts in management practice and organizational focus, which are more corporate in nature. For this reason, some have become concerned that its organizational mission may be compromised in the process. Also, given the limits which government imposes on nonprofit activity, many food bank administrators choose not to engage in advocacy, as some worry this could impact government funding contracts (Warshawsky 2010). This has resulted in limited employee engagement in food advocacy and a deliberate depoliticization of food insecurity, hunger, and malnutrition in many cases. While food banks are understandably focused on organizational sustainability, there are concerns that food banks have become permanent nonprofit institutions intended to replace the welfare state and depoliticize the issue of hunger.

FOOD BANK NETWORK BENEFICIARY ORGANIZATIONS IN CHICAGO

The Depository's restructuring into a privately funded powerhouse has resulted in new bureaucratic structures for many of its beneficiary agencies, as it determines many of the ways these organizations work. While the Depository has supported its food bank network beneficiary organizations with reinvestment programs and professional development opportunities, these organizations are arguably not equal partners to the Depository. Many, including the Chicago-based Community Food Pantry (not the actual name) in the West Rogers Park neighborhood have struggled with limited human and financial resources and new bureaucratic limitations. Additionally, as in the case of the Community Food Pantry, the Depository has actually damaged already-existing relationships nonprofits had established with food retailers in their communities (Warshawsky 2010).

Also, many food bank network beneficiary organizations lack the capacity or time to write grants or to attend grant-writing workshops, especially in lower-income communities, which often lack the human capital needed to leverage these fund-raising opportunities. This has been the case with the Neighborhood Food Center (not the actual name) in the Woodlawn neighborhood. These dynamics have reinforced institutional dependencies between the Depository and its beneficiary organizations, such as the Neighborhood Food Center, that are increasingly reliant on any resources available to them. While the Neighborhood Food Center continues to operate, these challenges have led to heightened competition or closure for many food bank network beneficiary organizations.

Although changes in government food policy, persistent structural poverty, and economic inequality have produced many challenges for food bank network beneficiary organizations, the growth of the Depository has exacerbated many problems for these organizations, as seen with the Community Food Pantry in Rogers Park and the Neighborhood Food Center in Woodlawn, creating new bureaucratic structures and producing financial challenges. In this way, the Depository's institutional policies to commercialize its operations have clearly negatively impacted food bank network beneficiary organizations in many contexts.

Urban Food Bank Case Study 2: FoodBank Johannesburg

THE STRUCTURE AND DEVELOPMENT OF THE FOODBANK JOHANNESBURG

As a nascent organization in 2006, administrators in the Chicago-based Global Food-Banking Network were keen to choose food bank locations that were likely to succeed. For that reason, they sought out possible food bank locations in the Global South that had the key components necessary to operate a Feeding America–style food bank. In 2007, the Global FoodBanking Network pinpointed key cities in South Africa as places where food banks could develop given the existing infrastructure, strength of food retailers and manufacturers, and the number of LFOs (Warshawsky 2011). According to recent statistics, 13.8 million people are hungry in South Africa, and approximately one-third of food is wasted there. For these reasons, with the support of the Global FoodBanking Network and key South African governmental departments and LFOs, FoodBank South Africa formed in 2009 and began operating FoodBank Johannesburg. Since then, food banks have opened in numerous other cities across South Africa, including Cape Town, Durban, Port Elizabeth, Rustenburg, Pietermaritzburg, and Polokwane. Through its network of approximately 287 soup kitchens, feeding schemes, schools, old age homes, and HIV clinics (FoodBank South Africa 2016), FoodBank Johannesburg serves about 500,000 meals (1,600 tons) of food per year.

While FoodBank Johannesburg started with significant financial support from the South African government, corporate food retailers, and the Global FoodBanking Network, funding has fluctuated significantly over the past few years. The operating budget has ranged between $1 million and $3.5 million, depending on support from funders and costs of operations in the different urban food banks (FoodBank South Africa 2015). Since its founding, most if not all of its funding has originated from sources within South Africa, as the Global FoodBanking Network only provided a small amount of start-up money. These financial fluctuations have forced FoodBank Johannesburg and its central FoodBank South Africa structure to streamline operations and occasionally reduce the amount or quality of food delivered, or number of beneficiaries assisted. FoodBank Johannesburg has not only reduced its staff and changed management multiple times since 2009, but the LFO has barely enough money to operate in the near future. Although FoodBank South Africa started with aspirations to expand into more than twenty cities across South Africa, this has never materialized due to its perpetual financial crises.

Since 2009, FoodBank Johannesburg has stored damaged, mislabeled, or excess food from South African manufacturers and retailers (FoodBank South Africa 2015). At its warehouse, food is repackaged and then delivered to its network of food bank beneficiary organizations. In addition to its core Food Rescue Programme, FoodBank Johannesburg also runs a Food Procurement Programme to purchase discounted food to balance the quality, quantity, and nutrition of food delivered.

Although it is a nonprofit LFO, the South African state has had a significant impact on the development and continued operation of FoodBank South Africa. To start, the South African state has arguably supported FoodBank South Africa because it fits within its broader political agenda to promote local initiatives in the private or nonprofit sectors—a reflection of neoliberalism. In addition, the South African state has a strong influence over FoodBank Johannesburg's operations through government funding and potential institutional oversight. In particular, state officials have pressured food bank managers to regulate their beneficiary organizations through a memorandum of agreement, which codifies the power relations between the state, FoodBank Johannesburg, and its beneficiary organizations. While some of these changes improve food safety and streamline food donation services, they could lead to a potential micromanagement of beneficiary organizations and delegitimize some food interventions (Warshawsky 2011). As compared to Chicago, the central state in Johannesburg is significantly more involved in FoodBank South Africa's development. This is explained in part by the intense political and social pressure put on the South African state by civil society to reduce food insecurity in a country with a legacy of institutionalized inequality and human rights issues.

Private-sector food manufacturers and food retailers have been essential to Food-Bank Johannesburg through their large-scale food donations to regional food banks. Given that food banking relies on receiving surplus food produced in manufacturing inefficiencies, food banks provide many positive assets to private food businesses, since they not only improve system efficiency, but also improve companies' public image as sustainable and just (Warshawsky 2016b). Even so, some key administrators at prominent South African food businesses remain concerned about brand depreciation from products being sold in secondhand markets and the liability associated with food spoiling.

FOOD BANK NETWORK BENEFICIARY ORGANIZATIONS IN JOHANNESBURG

Of these numerous types of LFOs in the FoodBank South Africa network, beneficiary organizations are the most numerous type (Warshawsky 2011). They are also the last node on the network, as they interact directly with food-insecure households. Primarily, food bank network beneficiary organizations provide hot meals, nonperishable items, or fresh produce, although many others also provide job training or care for vulnerable populations. Beneficiary organizations are funded in numerous ways, with community, church, and individual donations being the most important. Generally, they are funded by community members rather than large grants, for which they are often unable to apply.

Food bank network beneficiary organizations, such as the Katlehong Soup Kitchen (not the actual name) in the mainly lower-income black township of Katlehong in Greater Johannesburg, are deeply embedded in place. It is at the scale of the neighborhood that it is funded, staffed, and managed by community members (Warshawsky 2011). In addition, the relationship between beneficiary organizations like Katlehong and the food bank is very place-specific, as the timing, amount, and type of food delivered at Katlehong and other local beneficiary organizations depends on the micro-scale geographies at its neighborhood or block level. Moreover, the level of need and the cultural and social causes of food insecurity in Katlehong is the result of specific spatial inequalities in that particular township landscape and the place-based processes of social inequality and food insecurity localized in the area proximate to Katlehong's service area.

The tension between FoodBank Johannesburg and its beneficiary organizations has been documented in previous publications, which highlight the top-down approach toward management (Warshawsky 2011). The most common criticism from organizations within the network is that their opinions and experiences were not taken seriously by food bank administrators. According to staff members I interviewed, many key administrators at FoodBank Johannesburg have never visited any food bank network beneficiary organizations in Johannesburg's townships or informal settlements. This not only minimized the credibility of food bank staff, but also limited their understanding of the contexts in which food banks operate. The people who work with the community organizations that distribute food directly to people in need have the best understanding of food insecurity, given that they regularly interact with neighbors and family members who are food-insecure. Moreover, they can assess the types of foods people want to eat, the causes of food insecurity and hunger, and the extent to which certain solutions, such as food banking, actually work in food-insecure environments.

Conclusion

This chapter has examined the role of LFOs in urban food systems through case studies of food banks in Chicago and Johannesburg. While the growth of food banking in these cities may have expanded the number of institutions committed to food security, streamlined food donation processes, increased the amount of food delivered, and reduced waste, it has also produced some concerning outcomes.

In the case of Chicago, the Depository has arguably become an important institution of neoliberal governance as it plays a significant role in food poverty management and further absolves the state from its prior responsibility. In particular, the Depository has commercialized its operations as a way to navigate through uncertain structural forces in emergency food delivery. The Depository plays a major role in defining the problem of food insecurity and the type of interventions that work to overcome the food insecurity crisis. In this way, food banks like the Depository are key players in urban food system management, as they not only provide a significant share of food welfare services in cities, but also play a major role in determining who participates in the process. While the Depository is not explicitly opposed to the alternative food movements (see chapter 11), its operations are clearly more closely aligned with large food corporations and pro-market forces. Financial pressures to commercialize may have weakened the food bank's mission as it becomes increasingly focused on self-perpetuation and system efficiency, not equity. As such, it is has become an integral part of the corporate agro-food system and is instrumental in maintaining the status quo.

As the Depository has grown in size, it has also produced new problems for food bank network beneficiary organizations, including new institutional and financial challenges associated with the increased consolidation and commercialization of food donations. The combination of these challenges and the limits imposed by government lobbying regulations ensure that the Depository and its beneficiary organizations focus mostly on service delivery and less on advocacy or social reforms. Therefore, the broader issue of poverty and the structural inequalities at the origin of food insecurity remain unaddressed (Poppendieck 1998; Warshawsky 2010).

In the case of Johannesburg, FoodBank Johannesburg has experienced mixed results, as its growth has been uneven and has resulted in tensions between the state, private sector, and existing local food initiatives (Warshawsky 2011). The development of FoodBank Johannesburg has allowed the state to reduce its responsibilities toward food insecurity in cities by bringing in non-state actors. It has also depoliticized the issue of hunger through an apolitical approach toward fund-raising and consensus-building. Additionally, the strong participation of food retailers and manufacturers in FoodBank Johannesburg suggests that the food banking process is increasingly under the control of food businesses.

From the perspective of its beneficiary organizations, FoodBank Johannesburg has transformed the landscape of civil society in Johannesburg, as some local food initiatives have been integrated into the food banking structure, while others have been sidelined. Most problematically, FoodBank Johannesburg has implemented a top-down approach in which community-based beneficiary organizations have a limited voice. This has not only minimized the mission of the food bank, but has also limited its ability to fully understand the causes and possible solutions to food insecurity in the communities it serves (Warshawsky 2011).

Although the contexts of Chicago and Johannesburg are quite different, the two case studies presented in this chapter reveal similarities in the operations and impacts of major food banks in their communities. Both fundamentally revolve around a core partnership between large food companies and food banks to redistribute corporate food waste to the food-insecure. Importantly, it is the food corporations, not the food-insecure, that have driven the growth in food banks in each city. As the US food bank model expands to the Global South, where governmental, nonprofit, or corporate resources may not be in place to support their activities, there are growing uncertainties regarding food banks' ability to deal with the global food crisis (see chapter 7) and redistribute food to people and places with the greatest needs.

Key Terms

civil society

devolution

food banks

food security/insecurity

hunger

local food organizations (LFOs)

malnutrition

neoliberalism

nonprofit

urban governance

Summary

- Food banking has become the primary mechanism to address food insecurity in the United States—a trend currently being replicated in other places, including South Africa. It rests on a complex organizational structure in which food donations are channeled to large food banks, such as Feeding America, before being redistributed to local food organizations working directly with people in need.
- Food banking is an important part of the industrial food regime; it provides an outlet for the food surplus generated by large corporations and government agricultural policies.
- The increased reliance on civil society and nonprofit organizations to address food insecurity and hunger reflects a policy shift away from the welfare state toward neoliberalism.

- While food banking feeds millions of people and helps to reduce waste, it fails to address the structural causes of hunger, partly because the dependence of nonprofit organizations on corporations and government limits their willingness to engage in politics.

Additional Resources

For more information on hunger and food assistance in the United States, see Berg (2008), Katz (1986), Poppendieck (1998), and Riches and Silvasti (2014).

For more information on the role of civil society, nonprofits, and nongovernmental organizations in social policy, see Bebbington, Hickey, and Mitlin (2008), Kodras (1997), Salamon (2012), and Wolch (1990).

The relationship between neoliberalism and local food systems is presented in Born and Purcell (2006) and Guthman (2008).

References

Bebbington, Anthony J., Sam Hickey, and Diana C. Mitlin. 2008. "Introduction: Can NGOs Make a Difference? The Challenges of Development Alternatives." In *Can NGOs Make a Difference?*, edited by Anthony J. Bebbington, Sam Hickey, and Diana C. Mitlin, 3–37. New York: Zed Books.

Berg, Joel. 2008. *All You Can Eat: How Hungry Is America?* New York: Seven Stories Press.

Born, Branden, and Mark Purcell. 2006. "Avoiding the Local Trap: Scale and Food Systems in Planning Research." *Journal of Planning Education and Research* 26(2): 195–207.

Brenner, Neil, and Nik Theodore. 2002. "Cities and the Geographies of 'Actually Existing Neoliberalism.'" *Antipode* 34: 349–79.

Feeding America. 2016a. "About Us." www.feedingamerica.org/about-us/.

———. 2016b. "Hunger and Poverty Facts and Statistics." www.feedingamerica.org/hunger-in-america/impact-of-hunger/hunger-and-poverty/hunger-and-poverty-fact-sheet.html.

Food and Agriculture Organization. 2008. *An Introduction to the Basic Concepts of Food Security.* www.fao.org/docrep/013/al936e/al936e00.pdf.

———. 2015. *The State of Food Insecurity in the World.* www.fao.org/3/a-i4646e.pdf.

FoodBank South Africa. 2015. *2015 Annual Report: Changing Lives Together.* www.foodbanksa.org/wp-content/uploads/2015/08/FoodBank-SA-Annual-Report-2015-Final-Online-Version.pdf.

Forbes. 2015. "Top Charities." *Forbes.* www.forbes.com/top-charities/.

Fyfe, Nicholas R. 2005. "Making Space for 'Neo-Communitarianism'? The Third Sector, State, and Civil Society in the UK." *Antipode* 37: 536–57.

Global FoodBanking Network. 2006. "Newsletter: Winter 2006." http://foodbanking.wpengine.com/wp-content/uploads/2014/05/The Global FoodBankingNetwork_Winter06_English-1.pdf.

———. 2015. "2015 Annual Report." www.foodbanking.org/media/publications/annual-reports/annual-report-2015.

———. 2016. "Where We Work." www.foodbanking.org/food-bank-resources/global-food-bank-community.

Gottlieb, Robert, and Anupama Joshi. 2010. *Food Justice.* Cambridge: Massachusetts Institute of Technology.

Greater Chicago Food Depository. 2015. "2015 Annual Report." www.chicagosfoodbank.org/site/DocServer/2015_Annual_Report_Financials.pdf?docID=11963.

Grønbjerg, Karen A., and Lester M. Salamon. 2012. "Devolution, Marketization, and the Changing Shape of Government–Nonprofit Relations." In *The State of Nonprofit America*, 2nd ed., edited by Lester M. Salamon, 549–86. Washington, DC: Brookings Institution Press.

Guthman, Julie. 2008. "Thinking Inside the Neoliberal Box: The Micro-Politics of Agro-Food Philanthropy." *Geoforum* 39: 1241–53.

Henderson, George. 2004. " 'Free' Food, the Local Production of Worth, and the Circuit of Decommodification: A Value Theory of the Surplus." *Environment and Planning D* 22(4): 485–512.

Heritage Foundation. 2007. "Hunger Hysteria: Examining Food Security and Obesity in America." www.heritage.org/Research/Reports/2007/11/Hunger-Hysteria-Examining-Food-Security-and-Obesity-in-America.

———. 2010. "Significant Food Shortages Rare in America." www.heritage.org/Research/Commentary/2010/11/Significant-Food-Shortages-Rare-in-America.

Ionescu-Somers, Aileen. 2004. "The Food and Beverage Industry." In *The Business of Sustainability*, edited by Ulrich Steger, 178–93. New York: Palgrave Macmillan.

Katz, Michael B. 1986. *In the Shadow of the Poorhouse.* New York: Basic Books.

King, Seth S. 1982. "Warehouses Bulge with Surplus Cheese, Butter and Dried Milk." *New York Times.* July 6. www.nytimes.com/1982/07/06/us/warehouses-bulge-with-surplus-cheese-butter-and-dried-milk.html.

Koc, Mustafa, Rod MacRae, Luc J. A. Mougeot, and Jennifer Welsh. 1999. "Introduction: Food Security Is Global Concern." In *For Hunger-Proof Cities: Sustainable Urban Food Systems*, edited by Mustafa Koc, Rod MacRae, Luc J. A. Mougeot, and Jennifer Welsh, 1–7. Ottawa: International Development Research Centre.

Kodras, Janet E. 1997. "Restructuring the State: Devolution, Privatization, and the Geographic Redistribution of Power and Capacity in Governance." In *State Devolution in America*, edited by Lynn A. Staeheli and Janet E. Kodras, 79–96. Thousand Oaks: Sage Publications.

Lambie-Mumford, Hannah. 2013. " 'Every Town Should Have One': Emergency Food Banking in the UK." *Journal of Social Policy* 42: 73–89.

Lambie-Mumford, Hannah, and David Jarvis. 2012. "The Role of Faith-Based Organizations in the Big Society: Opportunities and Challenges." *Policy Studies* 33: 249–62.

Milligan, Christine, and David Conradson. 2006. "Contemporary Landscapes of Welfare: The 'Voluntary Turn'?" In *Landscapes of Voluntarism*, edited by Christine Milligan and David Conradson, 1–14. Bristol: Policy Press.

Moragues-Faus, Ana, and Kevin Morgan. 2015. "Reframing the Foodscape: The Emergent World of Urban Food Policy." *Environment and Planning A* 47: 1558–73.

Peck, Jamie. 2001. *Workfare States.* New York: Guilford Press.

Peck, Jamie, and Nik Theodore. 2010. "Mobilizing Policy: Models, Methods, and Mutations." *Geoforum* 41: 169–74.

Pollan, Michael. 2006. *The Omnivore's Dilemma. A Natural History of Four Meals.* New York: Penguin Press.

Poppendieck, Janet. 1998. *Sweet Charity.* New York: Viking.

———. 2014. "Food Assistance, Hunger, and the End of Welfare in the USA." In *First World Hunger Revisited: Food Charity or the Right to Food?*, 2nd ed., edited by Graham Riches and Tiina Silvasti, 176–90. New York: Palgrave Macmillan.

Rathe, Caitlin. 2016. "Making Hunger a Temporary Emergency." Paper presented at the Sixth International Conference on Food Studies, University of California, Berkeley, California, October 13.

Riches, Graham, and Tiina Silvasti. 2014. "Hunger in the Rich World: Food Aid and Right to Food Perspectives." In *First World Hunger Revisited: Food Charity or the Right to Food?*, 2nd ed., edited by Graham Riches and Tiina Silvasti, 1–14. New York: Palgrave Macmillan.

Rocha, C. (2014). "A Right to Food Approach: Public Food Banks in Brazil." In *First World Hunger Revisited: Food Charity or the Right to Food?*, 2nd ed., edited by Graham Riches and Tiina Silvasti, 29–41. New York: Palgrave Macmillan.

Salamon, Lester M. 2012. "The Resilient Sector: The Future of Nonprofit America." In *The State of Nonprofit America*, 2nd ed., edited by Lester M. Salamon, 3–86. Washington, DC: Brookings Institution Press.

Slocum, Rachel. 2007. "Whiteness, Space and Alternative Food Practice." *Geoforum* 38: 520–33.

Sonnino, Roberta. 2016. "The New Geography of Food Security: Exploring the Potential of Urban Food Strategies." *Geographical Journal* 18(2): 190–200.

Tostensen, Arne, Inge Tvedten, and Mariken Vaa. 2001. "The Urban Crisis, Governance and Associational Life." In *Associational Life in African Cities: Popular Responses to the Urban Crisis*, edited by Arne Tostensen, Inge Tvedten, and Mariken Vaa, 7–26. Uppsala, Sweden: Nordiska Afrikainstitutet.

USDA. 2003. *Pasteurized, Process American Cheese for Use in the USDA Household Commodity Food Distribution Program*. United States Department of Agriculture. https://web.archive.org/web/20060924120852/http://www.fns.usda.gov/fdd/facts/hhpfacts/FS-CheeseProcessed.pdf

Warshawsky, Daniel N. 2010. "New Power Relations Served Here: The Growth of Food Banking in Chicago." *Geoforum* 41: 763–75.

———. 2011. "FoodBank Johannesburg, State, and Civil Society Organizations in Post-Apartheid Johannesburg." *Journal of Southern African Studies* 37: 809–29.

———. 2016a. "Civil Society and the Governance of Urban Food Systems in Sub-Saharan Africa." *Geography Compass* 10: 293–306.

———. 2016b. "Food Waste, Sustainability, and the Corporate Sector: Case Study of a US Food Company." *Geographical Journal* 4: 384–94.

Wolch, Jennifer R. 1990. *The Shadow State: Government and Voluntary Sector in Transition*. New York: Foundation Center.

Young, Dennis R., Lester M. Salamon, and Mary C. Grinsfelder. 2012. "Commercialization, Social Ventures, and For-Profit Competition." In *The State of Nonprofit America*. 2nd ed., edited by L. M. Salamon, 521–48. Washington, DC: Brookings Institution Press.

What Would You Eat on $6 a Day?

Food Stamp benefits in California (known as CalFresh) are $187 per month for a single person with no other income—that is about $6 per day, or $42 per week. With that weekly budget in mind, briefly outline your weekly meal plan (including breakfast, lunch, and dinner each day) and make a shopping list of groceries needed for the week. What is your main strategy to keep the cost down? Do you have to give up anything? Do you think you will have enough to eat? Are you able to include five servings of fruits or vegetables each day? Where and how often do you plan to shop for the week? Will it be easy to find all the ingredients and bring them home? Do you plan to eat out?

For many recipients of food stamps, preparing healthy, tasty, comforting, balanced, diverse, and culturally appropriate meals is a challenge. While food donations from community organizations provide temporary assistance, they tend to lack diversity and nutritious value. The recipe below is inspired by *Fed Up with Lunch* (2012), a website that provides ideas and instructions on how to prepare healthy and budget-friendly meals with the type of ingredients available at many food pantries, including several of the eighteen core items guaranteed to be available at the Chicago Food Depository (e.g., rice, pasta, peanut butter, canned vegetables, canned fruits, hamburger patties, fresh eggs, macaroni and cheese, tuna, and milk).

Fried Rice with Eggs and Veggies

Ingredients (for three)

1 cup uncooked long-grain rice
pinch of salt
2 cups of water
1 can mixed veggies
2 eggs
1 to 2 tablespoons of vegetable oil, plus additional to taste

Preparation

Put the rice in a saucepan with a pinch of salt and cover with two cups of water. Bring to boil over medium heat. Add drained and rinsed veggies to the rice. Turn heat to low, cover with a lid, and simmer for about 20 minutes (until rice is cooked).

Heat two tablespoons of oil in a large frying pan. Add eggs and scramble for a minute. Add cooked rice and veggies to the pan and mix with the eggs. Fry, stirring occasionally, for a few minutes. Serve hot. If desired, season with soy sauce, pepper, or hot sauce.

Reference

Fed Up with Lunch. 2012. "Healthy, Budget-Friendly Recipes Using Food Pantry Staples." http://fedupwithlunch.com/2012/02/healthy-budget-friendly-recipes-using-food-pantry-staples/.

CHAPTER 11

Spaces of Alternative Food

URBAN AGRICULTURE, COMMUNITY GARDENS, AND FARMERS' MARKETS

Fernando J. Bosco and Pascale Joassart-Marcelli

Textbox 11.1. Learning Objectives

- Understand the notion of alternative food practices and the reasons behind them.
- Define and contextualize contemporary forms of urban agriculture.
- Critically analyze community gardens' socio-spatial relations to the urban environment, including its alleged impact on "community."
- Explore food localization efforts, including farmers' markets, and investigate the local scale as a social and political project.

There is a vigorous debate around our contemporary food system, which many see as unsustainable and unfair. In this chapter, we begin by summarizing that debate as a way to frame a discussion of a growing number of alternatives that people pursue to produce and access food differently. We provide an overview of alternative food practices, specifically in the context of growing support for urban agriculture and so-called local food systems in cities in North America and beyond.

Alternative food practices do not occur on the head of a pin; rather, they depend on specific settings and create their own spaces, such as community gardens and urban farms, community kitchens, farmers' markets, and food cooperatives, to name a few. Taking these practices and their spaces into account, we investigate the role they play in the lives of people in the contemporary city and emphasize their **embeddedness** in urban geographies of social, political, economic, and cultural relations. Focusing specifically on *community gardens* and *farmers' markets*, we argue that alternative food spaces are urban projects that resist and respond to inequities in the contemporary global, industrial, and capitalist food system, while simultaneously reproducing the neoliberal logic underlying it. Community gardens and farmers' markets have become popular spaces for growing and distributing food in cities, but they are also spaces for building community and for rethinking the local. However, the types of communities and experiences of the local they engender are typically left unquestioned, except in a small subset of relatively recent research (see Born and Purcell 2006; Dupuis and Goodman 2005; Joassart-Marcelli and Bosco 2014; Mc-

Clintock 2014; Bosco and Joassart-Marcelli 2017). In this chapter, we build on this literature and analyze alternative food practices and spaces geographically, paying attention to both *food politics* and *urban politics*.

Alternative Food Practices

When food scholars, activists, and policymakers discuss the advantages and disadvantages of our contemporary food system, three terms usually take center stage: *industrial, corporate,* and *global.* On the one hand, some argue that our food system, even though dominated by large agribusiness and corporate food manufacturers, is indeed effective, since it can produce and deliver huge varieties and quantities of quality food that can potentially feed the growing world population (Hladik 2012). Investments in agricultural technology, research, and practices developed by agribusiness and the corporate food industry are viewed as beneficial even for smaller producers, for whom these technologies eventually become available.

On the other hand, many others point to abundant and serious problems that arise out of such an approach to food production. One concern, for example, is the large scale at which industrial agriculture and food production takes place—using vast amounts of land, water, and artificial inputs for monoculture, with consequences for health and ecological sustainability (see chapters 3 and 4). Another issue is the scope and reach of global agricultural and food commodity chains that greatly separate the food we eat from the places where it is produced, making farmers as well as their communities, livelihoods, and environments invisible (see chapters 5 and 6). Moreover, under this type of food system many people remain hungry and food-insecure, especially in the Global South (see chapter 7), but not exclusively so (see chapter 10).

Finally, many deplore the deleterious health impacts of our food system, including obesity (see chapter 9) and food-borne illnesses like salmonella and E. coli. In sum, our contemporary food regime may be effective at producing large quantities of food, improving agricultural yields in the short run, and developing new farming and food production technologies that generate huge profits and support further geographic expansion and economic concentration. However, our current food regime is unsustainable over the long term because of the pressures it puts on the environment and the multiple costs it imposes on people and their communities.

Thus, for several decades, consumers, food producers, nonprofits, and policymakers have been searching for a set of alternatives that would allow people to (re)connect with food in transparent ways and reduce some of these alarming concerns. Indeed, many consumers demand to know where their food comes from, how their vegetables are grown, or how the meat they eat is handled, citing health, ecological, or ethical reasons (see chapters 4 and 6). Others want to get closer to the food they eat, or play a more active role in growing their own food to feed family and friends. For many others, finding alternative ways of accessing food is also an issue of *food security*—e.g., supplementing their diets with locally grown produce, saving money, improving access to food. Finally, for some it is about more-radical changes that could democratize the food system and lead to *food justice* and *food sovereignty* (see chapters 16 and 4).

This is a wide spectrum of motives, making it impossible to talk about a single or universal food movement, as it is often portrayed in the popular media. But together, these attempts to change or circumvent our contemporary and conventional food system have come to be known as **alternative food practices**. Alternative food practices may include, for example, the growing of local (and sometimes organic) fruits and vegetables and their distribution in nearby farmers' markets. They also may include the creation of—and participation in—alternative food institutions, such as community-supported agriculture or fair trade networks (see chapter 6). Finally, they may even include the mobilization of larger political movements that either challenge the core of the capitalist food regime, as in the case of many peasant movements in the Global South (see chapter 4), or seek reforms of agricultural, economic, and other governmental policies that underlie inequities.

In general, alternative food practices tend to rely on shorter or localized supply chains that presumably reconnect consumers and producers, thereby increasing the transparency and accountability needed to foster health, justice, sustainability, and other goals. Alternative food practices, therefore, have their own geographies; they create and depend on specific spaces. Following the critical and geographic perspective that informs this collection, in this chapter we focus specifically on these alternative spaces for the production and distribution of food. It would be difficult to cover the characteristics and socio-spatial dimensions of all the settings associated with the wide range of alternative food practices and institutions in a single chapter. Thus, here we pay attention to alternative food practices and their spaces at the urban scale, focusing specifically on community gardens and farmers' markets—two of the most common practices of food **localization**. We consider the context and places where they emerge, and explore how these settings are transformed by key actors and the activities they foster. By considering these changes, we can better understand and assess the benefits, impacts, and consequences that alternative food practices have for people and their communities. This provides a framework for questioning the "alternative" nature of alternative food practices, and pointing out the ways in which they may reproduce socio-spatial inequalities related to class, gender, race, and other social categories of difference that divide cities.

Urban Agriculture

FROM BACKYARD GARDENS TO URBAN FARMS

Urban agriculture has become central to people promoting alternative food practices that reconnect people to their food sources—what is also known as the *food relocalization movement*. Urban agriculture refers to the production, processing, and marketing of food in urban and peri-urban areas, often for consumption in the same area (WinklerPrins 2017). Like *alternative food*, *urban agriculture* is an umbrella term that covers a variety of activities and practices. Common types of urban agriculture include residential growing in yards and rooftops, as well as collective (e.g., a neighborhood group) and institutional (e.g., a hospital, a school) agriculture in gardens and orchards that are often set up in vacant lots, parks, or other available parcels. Urban agriculture may also include commercial and for-profit production in small- to medium-scale plots and farms (McClintock 2014). Finally, it may also include less-common practices, such as "guerrilla" agriculture that takes over unused urban space such as sidewalk fragments, parkways, and vacant lots. Some scholars make distinctions between "gardening" and "agriculture," with gardening thought of more in terms of growing food for leisure, and agriculture in terms of growing food for consumption, or even for commercial distribution; this may also include other practices, such as beekeeping or aquaculture. However, the lines between these two are blurry.

Urban agriculture is embedded in place, with the scale and scope of different practices depending on the social, cultural, economic, and geographic contexts. For example, in cities of the Global South, urban agriculture has typically been associated with a livelihood strategy, as people grow food to feed themselves, often in the context of poverty and marginalization. But mirroring trends in the Global North, many people in cities of the Global South today engage in urban agriculture for the same reasons as people in the Global North: for health, to re-localize food production, to re-appropriate urban spaces, and so on.

Moreover, different types of urban agriculture with different aims and goals may coexist in the same city, whether it is in the Global North or the Global South. For example, many communities in cities across Latin America (e.g., Buenos Aires, Rosario, and Mendoza in Argentina; Sao Paulo and Curitiba in Brazil; and Montevideo in Uruguay, to name a few) have seen a rapid growth of new forms of urban agriculture, such as *granjas urbanas* (urban farms) and *huertas comunitarias* (community gardens—see next section), mostly in middle- and upper-middle-class neighborhoods, as people engage in gardening as a form of leisure and education, and as certain types of consumers became more attuned to the global alternative food movement. Yet, family or neighborhood *huertas* have been prominent in the backyards and empty lots of lower-middle-class and poor urban neighborhoods for a long time, predominantly as a subsistence strategy. A similar situation has developed across cities in the United States, Canada, and Europe, with different types of urban agriculture—reaching different people and with different goals—coexisting in the same urban area.

COMMUNITY GARDENS

Community gardens are one of the forms of urban agriculture that receives the most attention and support from local communities. For example, according to the American Community Garden Association (ACGA), there are an estimated 18,000 community gardens across the United States and Canada (ACGA 2016). The popularity and growth of community gardens has lately been accompanied by changes in local and municipal ordinances for land use that have allowed urban agriculture to flourish. These have often been the result of hard-fought campaigns by urban growers and food activists, but more recently local governments and other actors themselves have been proactive in supporting community gardens in a variety of urban neighborhoods.

Community gardens are often collaborative projects taking place on shared or open spaces (e.g., public parks, vacant lots) where people work together with the aim of obtaining healthful and affordable fresh fruits and vegetables. The United States' Centers for Disease Control and Prevention (CDC) is one of the many agencies and organizations—public or private—that has embraced community gardens as a key strategy for the creation of a healthier food environment and a better food system. According to the CDC, community gardening can offer physical and mental health benefits, since gardening allows people the opportunity to eat healthy fresh fruits and vegetables and to participate in physical activity. Moreover, community gardens create green space, transform brownfield sites, beautify vacant lots or public parks, and may even revitalize communities and support economic development (CCD 2016). There are also potential **sustainability** benefits, including a reduction in pollution if more food is produced locally and does not need to be transported across long distances.

In addition to the benefits mentioned above, perhaps one of the main benefits attributed to gardening is the capacity to foster **community**, either by encouraging stronger connections between neighbors, bringing together marginalized citizens, or expanding social capital and creating opportunities for civic participation (Baker 2004; Kingsley and Townsend 2006). In fact, for the ACGA and all its garden members across North America, "growing community" is more central than growing food. As the ACGA states, its mission "is to build community by increasing and enhancing community gardening and greening across the United States and Canada" (ACGA 2016).

While there are many benefits of community gardens, these seemingly "good" alternative food places can also be appropriated for other means and can further uneven urban geographies in the city (see textbox 11.2). Historically in the United States, community gardens were put in place by activists to address the impacts of racism, social exclusion, and economic inequality in their communities (Eizenberg 2013). Even before then, in the 1890s Depression, cities like Detroit, Chicago, Buffalo, and Boston started programs to convert empty lots to produce food for the unemployed (Broadway 2009). During World War II, most cities experienced food shortages, as both human and other resources were consumed by the war effort. It was then that the Victory Garden Movement encouraged the creation of home and neighborhood gardens, and people of all sorts became involved in food production. But today, despite narratives of **food justice** and alternative food movements, efforts to relocalize our food system are increasingly defined and deployed by urban elites, and are most popular among affluent and white urban residents (Slocum 2007; Guthman 2011). Gardening, shopping, and cooking "local" is being reimagined as an individual creative and therapeutic activity that reflects one's class position (Johnston and Baumann 2009).

As the examples in textbox 11.2 show, community gardens are more likely to emerge in neighborhoods that already have resources (e.g., financing, secure access to land, motivated residents, organized nonprofits), or where real estate developers have interests. While there is nothing intrinsically negative about more community gardens in upscale neighborhoods, the flip side is that these processes may lead to an even more uneven urban landscape of food access and food production—with wealthier or gentrifying neighborhoods benefiting from new alternatives, and poorer neighborhoods—already lacking healthy food access options—being left behind (see chapters 8 and 9).

Moreover, research shows that the neighborhoods with the greatest needs often lack the institutional capacity (e.g., nonprofit organizations or community groups) to

Textbox 11.2. Community Gardens and Gentrification

Is the expansion of community gardens explained primarily by a desire to build community and grow food locally, or are there other motives underlying this trend? At least in the United States, there is growing evidence that the popularity of community gardens is also being appropriated by real estate developers and agents who want to project images of green, progressive, hip, and healthy neighborhoods. The goals are not necessarily about food security or justice, but rather about attracting affluent or middle-class home buyers to a neighborhood or to expand investments into the city.

For example, in northern California, the website for the NOBE (North Oakland/Berkeley/Emeryville) neighborhoods of the San Francisco Bay Area (http://nobeneighborhood.com) tells potential home buyers that the garden movement is in full swing in this area. The catch is that NOBE is a name made up by real estate agents as a way to generate interest in the neighborhood, attempting to attract young, upper-middle-class home buyers who can no longer afford real estate in San Francisco. Moreover, the NOBE "brand" lumps together long-standing neighborhoods inhabited by low- and middle-income African Americans. The aesthetics and activities of the existing community garden, which is run by a local collective, are in fact being appropriated to sell land and homes and to displace people (Markham 2014). Similar situations can be seen in other large cities across the United States—from Washington, DC, to Brooklyn to Detroit—with land previously occupied by community gardens being sold for real estate development, and with urban agriculture shifting from community gardens to urban farms on rooftops, using expensive hydroponic systems (Crouch 2012).

address them (Joassart-Marcelli and Wolch 2003). Starting a community garden is not an easy task. Thus, the assumption that volunteers and resources are readily available (or even that local organizations are best suited to carry on this task) is misleading, and can impose a heavy burden on residents, particularly in low-income areas. All together, this suggests that alternative food practices, despite the best of intentions, can make cities more uneven through processes of social and economic exclusion.

THINKING GEOGRAPHICALLY: GROWING COMMUNITY IN COMMUNITY GARDENS

While "growing community" is central to the mission of the majority of community gardens, this is not a simple task, because communities do not emerge naturally. Thus, it is important to examine the types of communities that gardens may enable and whether and how such communities align with some of the other goals of urban agriculture and alternative food practices. From a geographic perspective, there are a couple of points to keep in mind when thinking about community.

First, we should not confuse community with territory. Although community, neighborhood, and population are often used interchangeably, they are not the same. So, even though community gardens are often associated with specific neighborhoods, we cannot presume a connection with local residents because it may not exist. For example, a community garden may be located in a neighborhood where only a few of the residents participate, or gardeners may come from a different area and have little interaction with those in that community.

Second, we should keep in mind that power relations play a role in community gardens as much as they do in other forms of human organization. Thus, community gardens may be more or less inclusionary depending on the people or organizations involved. Even though neighborhood groups or community-based organizations are often perceived to be more representative than centralized public agencies that function at larger scales, this is not necessarily the case. Nonprofit groups have different missions, goals, and structures. For example, in the case of community gardens, some organizations may be motivated by grassroots ideas about food justice and more connected to the needs of local residents whose participation is central to their success. On the other hand, others may spend more time looking for private donations or government contracts and grants to support their organization, allowing funders to shape the community garden and silencing the voice of residents. In sum, communities do not emerge naturally from community gardens. Rather, gardens and their communities shape each other within a broader political, economic, and geographic context.

Case Study: Community Gardens in San Diego, California

The many community gardens in San Diego today illustrate the points we have made so far about the growing popularity of urban agriculture as an alternative food practice, and about the different communities that emerge out of gardening. Following national trends, community gardens have been growing rapidly in San Diego County, from twenty-seven (and only two permitted) community gardens in 2010 (Ellsworth and Feenstra 2010) to almost ninety active gardens today (SDCGN 2015). The increase in community gardens shows a general interest in urban agriculture, and has been facilitated by institutional and governmental support. For instance, organizations like the San Diego Community Garden Network (SDCGN) have been established to create, support, and grow community gardens. The State of California has recently introduced new legislation favorable to urban agriculture, and the city of San Diego has streamlined its permitting process.

The community gardens operating in San Diego County today represent a variety of practices. Some gardens are geared toward education and training (e.g., those in schools or other institutions), and others fit more squarely within a traditional definition of "community gardens." But this last group includes both private gardens with strict membership requirements as well as those welcoming members of the broader community, masking important distinctions between the communities involved. Textboxes 11.3 and 11.4 describe two community gardens in San Diego and illustrate different ways in which gardens "grow community."

Textbox 11.3.   New Roots Community Farm

In 2009, the International Rescue Committee (IRC)—an international organization involved in refugee resettlement around the world—established the New Roots Community Farm in City Heights, a central and low-income neighborhood in San Diego that is home to many minorities, including recent immigrants and refugees. The garden contains eighty-five plots on 2.3 acres of public land and serves mostly East African refugees and their families, providing them with locally grown and culturally appropriate food, and helping farmers reconnect with land and economic opportunities in the United States.

The garden's farmers are certified to sell their produce at farmers' markets as a way to help them earn income. The farm helped the IRC established itself as a leader in urban agriculture in San Diego, and even drew the attention of former first lady Michelle Obama when she launched her national Healthy Eating campaign with a visit to City Heights. Even though the farm has been a success story, the emphasis on refugee assistance has meant that long-standing residents—including other groups of refugees and immigrants— have not had the same support or benefited from urban agriculture in the same way.

Figure 11.1.   New Roots Community Farm
Source: Fernando Bosco.

Textbox 11.4. Juniper-Front Community Garden

The Juniper-Front Community Garden is located in Bankers' Hill, an old residential neighborhood just a mile north of downtown San Diego that today is home to primarily white and upper-middle-class professionals. The garden was created in 1981 on an empty lot formerly occupied by an apartment building and owned by the San Diego Port Authority. It was originally established as a garden for senior citizens. Today the garden is limited to members only, and there is a long waiting list for those who want to get involved. Only one-third of gardeners are senior citizens, reflecting the changing demographics of a neighborhood that today fits the urban creative-class stereotype often associated with gentrification. In fact, most participants garden as a form of leisure, and tend to see the garden as a cultural amenity that increases the attractiveness of the neighborhood.

Figure 11.2. Juniper-Front Community Garden
Source: Pascale Joassart-Marcelli.

These short descriptions of two gardens illustrate part of the spectrum of contemporary urban agriculture. On the one hand, there is gardening for leisure and for the development of both personal and neighborhood identity. On the other hand, urban farming is a project of **spatial justice**, promoting civic inclusion, food security, and economic opportunity. Despite their different aims and goals, in both cases we can see how creating a community of urban farmers or gardeners leads to both processes of inclusion and exclusion in the same community, and how the missions and goals of the groups involved in running the gardens are embedded in place and shape the direction of urban agriculture.

Farmers' Markets

THE RISE OF FARMERS' MARKETS IN THE UNITED STATES

In the context of alternative food practices, farmers' markets can be seen as the final piece in efforts to relocalize the food system. The benefits of producing food locally, which we highlighted earlier, can be extended and maximized if that same food can be distributed and sold locally as well. Essentially, farmers' markets are places that bring producers and consumers together. They allow farmers to sell what they produce near their farm and provide consumers with a source of farm-fresh and locally grown food. As a result, farmers and consumers, as well as the local economy and environment, all obtain benefits from the relationships that farmers' markets facilitate. Farmers' markets can also be seen as places that contribute toward achieving many of the objectives of the alternative food movement—from eating slow, to eating locally, to eating ethically.

Together with the growth of urban agriculture, growing consumer interest in obtaining fresh food directly from farms has meant that the number of farmers' markets in the United States has more than quadrupled in the last two decades, with over 8,000 farmers' markets listed in the USDA market directory (USDA-AMS 2016). This trend is also part of the attempt to restore the historical connections between human settlements and sites of food production, which urbanization and increased population density in cities, along with the industrialization and globalization of food production, shattered. Today, a few historic sites of connection remain between local farms and cities in US urban landscapes, such as Seattle's Pike Place Market, the Reading Terminal Market in Philadelphia, or even LA's Grand Central Market. However, these places, as well as the many central markets that have recently emerged in other cities, have been dramatically shaped by neoliberal urban policies into sites of consumption that meet consumer demand for fresh and locally produced food, but also attract tourists and help to reinvigorate neighborhoods. As chapter 8 elaborates in more detail, these trends also tie farmers' markets and the local food movement to **gentrification** pressures similar to the ones described in textbox 11.2, in relation to community gardens.

The majority of farmers' markets today are of much more recent origins, smaller in size, and less centralized. In fact, the typical farmers' market today operates at a hyper local scale—mostly at the neighborhood or district scale—rather than as central markets for the entire city. Many urban neighborhoods across the United States now boast weekly farmers' markets, which have become a central feature of the local food movement.

Support for farmers' markets originates from different actors, including neighborhood residents, community organizations, real estate developers, and business associations, as well as federal, state, and local government agencies. At the federal level, the United States Department of Agriculture (USDA) has historically supported US producers of food and specialty crops through various training, marketing, and food-safety programs. The USDA runs its own weekly farmers' market in Washington, DC, which the agency describes as a "living laboratory" that demonstrates and replicates what farmers' markets can accomplish across the entire country: support the local economy, and provide access to local, healthy, and affordable food (USDA-AMS 2016).

At the state and local level, farm bureaus or similar agencies are often involved in supporting the development of farmers' markets, but also in the certification of products for sale at farmers' markets. Farmers' markets nationwide are generally subject to regular inspections for compliance with local regulations regarding the origin of food, processing facilities, storage, etc. However, this type of certification does not guarantee that products sold are grown organically or sustainably, or that farmworkers are fairly paid.

THINKING GEOGRAPHICALLY: FARMERS' MARKETS AND THE LIMITS OF LOCAL FOOD

Despite the stated economic and social benefits of farmers' markets to local communities, there is evidence that such benefits do not reach everyone equally. For example, several scholars have pointed out the racial and class dimensions of the alternative food movement, which in the United States is predominantly white and middle-class (Alkon and Agyeman 2011). Farmers' markets are no exception. The most successful farmers' markets—those offering a wider variety of fresh food and local produce—tend to locate in neighborhoods where they are likely to find customers with enough purchasing power. In addition, produce and fresh food such as meats and cheeses sold at farmers' markets tend to be more expensive than at most grocery stores—mainly as a result of the higher quality and the smaller scale of operations. Together, these factors restrict the ability of people with lower incomes or restricted mobility to shop at farmers' markets.

Studies have shown that racial minorities tend to frequent farmers' markets less often than the majority population. While there are wide variations in these trends depending on the area considered and its demographic characteristics, the issue is not so much about how many nonwhite bodies shop at a particular farmers' market, but rather how farmers' markets tend to be coded as "white" and conceptualized as "white spaces" in ways that exclude others (Guthman 2011). For example, there is a kind of universalism around farm-fresh food (often described as "good food" or "better food"), which assumes that the type of food valued by white people is also widely valued by everyone else (see chapter 13). Because of this, farmers' markets can be spaces that reinforce the material and emotional barriers that people of color face in accessing "better" foods.

Another problem is the tendency to both universalize and homogenize the *local*. The *local* scale is a key component and a critical dimension of alternative food practices. The majority of people involved in alternative food practices believe that encouraging, supporting, and participating in local food systems will lead to greater social and ecological benefits. Farmers' markets are also part of this narrative. However, in accounts of the benefits brought on by the presence of farmers' markets, the local—whether it is defined as the region, the community, or the neighborhood—is often seen as a homogeneous entity whose residents are assumed to benefit equally from local food projects that keep dollars in the community (Cortese 2011; Hewitt 2013; Shuman 2102). In that conflation, the local becomes antonymous of corporate, global, and industrial. However, this is not always the case. While the localization of food production and consumption via urban agriculture and farmers' markets can lead to fresher, healthier, and more sustainable and just food (La Trobe and Acott 2000), it can also lead to the exploitation of labor or to ecologically damaging growing practices.

Finally, another problem with embracing the local as the privileged geographic **scale** for alternative food practices is the unintended embracing of neoliberal ideology—an ideology that the alternative food movement typically rejects. Under **neoliberalism**, political and economic responsibility is removed from central governments and shifted onto cities, communities, and organizations seen as entrepreneurial actors competing for resources (MacLeod and Goodwin 1999; Brenner and Theodore 2002). Thus, by embracing localism, the alternative food movement supports a system of **urban governance** in which neighborhoods compete with each other to gather the resources needed to attract and benefit from a farmers' market, with many struggling or left behind. We described a similar process earlier on in our discussion of community gardens.

We need to understand the local not as something fixed and necessarily good but rather as a *project* that is carried out by actors moved by specific aims (Born and Purcell 2006). In the context of farmers' markets, this means challenging essentialist ideas about these alternative food spaces—whether we think of them as playgrounds for foodies or utopian spaces that can transform our food system. When analyzing farmers' markets, a critical geographic perspective demands that we think of many of the issues highlighted in this section, considering the variety of farmers' markets and actors involved, recognizing their social embeddedness, and acknowledging that there are often tensions and contradictions in their missions and activities.

The next section provides a glimpse of such an approach by examining the growth and aims of farmers' markets in San Diego, California.

Case Study: Farmers' Markets in San Diego, California

Together with community gardens, farmers' markets have become one of the most visible spaces of alternative food practices in San Diego. In 1988, there were five farmers' markets certified by San Diego County's agricultural commissioner. By 2007, there were twenty-five farmers' markets, and today, there are fifty-seven. Their distribution in the metropolitan area, however, is uneven. Farmers' markets are primarily located in densely populated and relatively affluent coastal communities, though in recent years a number of farmers' markets were started in low-income communities, such as City Heights, El Cajon, Southeastern San Diego, Barrio Logan, Imperial Beach, and Santee. These markets came together as a result of the efforts of neighborhood-based organizations. New farmers' markets also emerged in wealthier neighborhoods such as Mission Hills and Little Italy, mostly as a result of real estate development interests. Rural areas, where most farms are located, do not have many regular farmers' markets or direct sale points, underscoring the urban nature of such retail activities (see figure 11.3)

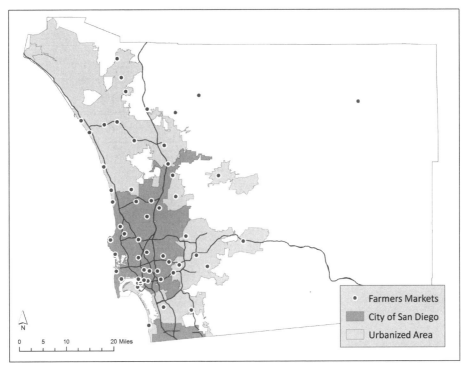

Figure 11.3. Map of farmers' markets in San Diego
Source: Pascale Joassart-Marcelli.

In recent years, the management of farmers' markets has become increasingly centralized and commercialized. Among the fifty-seven certified farmers' markets, approximately half are managed by people and organizations involved in multiple markets. Many of these market managers collaborate with local businesses to gain support for their markets and produce events such as music performances, art walks, food demonstrations, and other community celebrations at the farmers' markets. The emphasis is more on entertainment, business promotion, and place-based consumerism rather than on the essential aim of bringing farm-fresh food to urban residents (see chapter 8). In fact, there is growing presence of noncertified vendors at farmers' markets who sell nonfood items or noncertifiable products such as processed and prepared food.

Despite these trends there are important differences between markets related to the urban geography of the region. Whereas the majority of farmers' markets operate in wealthier coastal neighborhoods and run for four to six hours on Saturdays or Sundays, only a few markets serve lower-income urban areas, and usually only for a couple of hours on a given weekday. Moreover, only a few farmers' markets participate in public programs that promote the consumption of fresh produce for low-income people. For example, the Fresh Fund program was created to match residents' use of the Supplemental Nutrition Assistance Program (SNAP), Women, Infants, and Children (WIC), Supplemental Security Income (SSI), or Social Security Disability

Textbox 11.5. The *Mercato*:
Little Italy's Farmers' Market

The Little Italy farmers' market, known as the *Mercato*, was created in 2008 in a rapidly gentrifying neighborhood close to downtown San Diego. In addition to local residents, it also attracts a large number of tourists and suburbanites. The Mercato builds on the Italian theme of the neighborhood, which is used as a brand by the Little Italy Association, the neighborhood business group that sponsors the market. The market is managed by a private company that hosts four other farmers' markets in San Diego. The market has adopted a business model based on partnerships with local chefs, farmers, artisans, and neighborhood developers under the motto of "Foodies, Meet Farmers." The market's primary goal is to benefit restaurants and other locally based businesses, with the promotion of "a sustainable and healthy environment for San Diego" as an underlying but secondary marketing theme. These business goals are reflected in the atmosphere of the market, the demographics of visitors, and the characteristics of participating vendors and products sold.

In surveys we conducted in 2014, we found that although the market boasts more than 140 vendors, less than 30 are certified farmers. Moreover, several of these producers are not located in San Diego County, do not grow food organically, and are far from affordable to people with limited income. The remaining vendors sell "artisan" foods (e.g., olives, sauces, breads, salt, spices, and chocolate), prepared food and beverages, and specialty products such as clothing, jewelry, and tableware. There are no efforts made to encourage connections with community gardens or other grassroots food initiatives. Yet, all vendors listed on the market website are described as "local," reflecting how the term has been appropriated for economic purposes. City government agencies and the neighborhood business community have capitalized on the currency of local food to attract tourists and residents with significant purchasing dollars to Little Italy.

Figure 11.4. The *Mercato*: Little Italy's farmers' market
Source: Joe Wolf via Flickr. Available at www.flickr.com/photos/joebehr/5647821688.

Insurance (SSDI). Yet, only five markets participate in this program, and less than one-fifth currently accept EBT—the Electronic Benefit Transfer card that allows people to redeem government benefits electronically. Finally, several of the smaller markets that serve lower- or middle-income neighborhoods are struggling to survive because of a lack of ability to attract and retain vendors. All together, this suggests that food security and affordability is not a priority at most farmers' markets in San Diego. The aims are not so much about food access and food justice, but rather represent a more mainstream and homogenized approach of the food movement, which is consistent with some of the criticism we highlighted in the previous section and elsewhere in this volume. Textboxes 11.5 and 11.6 provide vignettes of two farmers' markets in San Diego (the Mercato in Little Italy, and the People's Produce Project in Southeastern San Diego) that illustrate the different contexts and goals of institutional of actors involved in attempts to localize food in the region.

The two San Diego farmers' markets described in textboxes 11.5 and 11.6 illustrate that farmers' markets, like other alternative food institutions, are shaped into different food spaces by the different actors involved and the characteristics of place. All farmers' markets in San Diego, including the two we describe, are characterized by a mixture of vendors, products, consumers, and visitors, who are in turn entangled in multiple social, political, and economic relations. And, as was the case with community gardens, each market includes and benefits certain groups, while also excluding others. Although all farmers' markets describe themselves as "local," the meaning of the term is contingent, contextual, and used to achieve different goals.

Textbox 11.6. People's Produce Farmers' Market in Southeastern San Diego

The People's Produce Farmers' Market opened in November 2010. The market is run by Project New Village, a local nonprofit group with a mission to increase access to fresh and healthy food and to provide economic opportunities to residents in a historically disenfranchised area that has also been described as a "food desert" (Joassart-Marcelli, Bosco, and Delgado 2014). The market participates in the Fresh Fund program, accepts EBT, and gives people an opportunity to purchase relatively affordable fruits and vegetables that tend to be unavailable in neighborhood stores. Central to the mission of the farmers' market is the creation of economic opportunities for residents. By providing a sale point, the hope is to stimulate local farmers and encourage residents to grow food at home or in the organization's community garden.

The market, however, has struggled to attract vendors, since established farms prefer to attend larger markets in affluent neighborhoods where it is assumed that people are willing to pay a premium for local or organic produce. As a result, at the time of our survey in 2014, there were only a few small produce stands and other items sold, including pies, jewelry, soaps, ornamental plants, pastries, and prepared food—perhaps diluting the health impact, but nevertheless creating new economic opportunities for businesses located almost entirely in Southeast San Diego. Making the farmers' market a regular shopping spot for local residents has also been challenging, and has required real grassroots organizing by Project New Village, whose members have engaged in numerous outreach activities, including community events and door-to-door information campaigns.

On the one hand, the Mercato has become instrumental in the gentrification of Little Italy, which continues to displace low-income people both culturally and materially. The local here is a project undertaken by urban real estate developers and civic entrepreneurs in ways that align closely with neoliberal urban governance (Brenner and Theodore 2002; McLeod and Goodwin 1999). On the other hand, the People's Produce Project has strengthened food advocacy in Southeastern San Diego. The local here is a community grassroots movement that has contributed to the creation of an alternative food space where a small but growing group of local residents can meet to shop and mingle. The market also provides an avenue for debating other issues relevant to this marginalized community.

Conclusion

In this chapter, we contextualized alternative food practices in specific urban spaces, focusing specifically on community gardens and farmers' markets, which have gained unprecedented popularity in the past two decades in cities in the United States and elsewhere around the world. We provided examples from San Diego, California, highlighting and problematizing the role and importance of two key geographic concepts—community and the local scale. These two concepts are often used in popular and academic representations of alternative food practices as essential features that contrast with the impersonal, global, and industrial food system. In these representations, local and community become conflated with other "alternative" values, such as food justice, health, and sustainability. This is problematic to the extent that it allows urban managers and policymakers to reclaim urban agriculture and local food systems as parts of a larger neoliberal urban agenda, while maintaining the support of people and organizations that are marginalized by this very process. In that context, far from being progressive, alternative and local food practices tend to prioritize economic growth via gentrification and consumption.

Our goal in this chapter has been to illustrate how community gardens and farmers' markets function to benefit some people and exclude others, thereby contributing to the reproduction of uneven urban geographies, particularly along the lines of race and class. Focusing on the spaces of alternative food practices provides a useful approach to uncover the social, political, economic, and cultural relations underlying them. In our analysis of community gardens, we drew attention to the different type of "communities" that these gardens can produce. Similarly, with our examples of farmers' markets, we showed how "the local" carries a different meaning and represents diverse types of projects based on the actors involved and the location of the market. As support for community gardens and farmers' markets continues to grow, drawing in new actors interested in capitalizing on their popularity, it is important to consider these differences and what they mean for building a truly alternative food system. Alternative food spaces, especially in the United States, have become part of larger processes of urban change that are more about capital accumulation and economic growth and less about food justice and sovereignty.

Key Terms

alternative food practices
community
embeddedness
food justice
gentrification
localization

neoliberalism
scale
spatial justice
sustainability
urban agriculture
urban governance

Summary

- Alternative food practices and spaces seek to reconnect people with food in transparent ways, reducing the ecological, social, economic, and health concerns attributed to the global industrial food system.
- Community gardens and farmers' markets have become popular alternative spaces for growing and distributing food in cities; they are also spaces for building community and for rethinking the local.
- The communities created through these spaces are varied: They can be inclusionary or exclusionary along lines of race and class; they can be progressive and contribute to food security and justice, or they can represent the status quo and encourage consumerism.
- The local scale also carries different meanings and represents different projects based on the actors and locations involved. The local is a project that can support marginalized communities or perpetuate neoliberal urban governance.
- An emerging criticism of alternative food spaces in the United States is their tendency to become appropriated as parts of processes of capital accumulation and urban change instead of fostering food justice and sovereignty.

Additional Resources

The documentary *The Garden* (2008) is about a community garden in South Central Los Angeles. It highlights the politics of establishing and maintaining a garden in a low-income community.

Acknowledgments

This chapter is based on research supported by the National Science Foundation under Award No. 1155844.

References

Alkon, Alison H., and Julian Agyeman. 2011. "Introduction: The Food Movement as Polyculture." In *Cultivating Food Justice: Race, Class, and Sustainability*, edited by Alison H. Alkon and Julian Agyeman, 1–20. Cambridge: MIT Press.

American Community Garden Association (ACGA). 2016. "Growing Community Across the U.S. and Canada." https://communitygarden.org/mission/.

Baker, Lauren E. 2004. "Tending Cultural Landscapes and Food Citizenship in Toronto's Community Gardens." *Geographical Review* 94(3): 305–25.

Born, Branden, and Mark Purcell. 2006. "Avoiding the Local Trap: Scale and Food Systems in Planning Research." *Journal of Planning Education and Research* 26(2): 195–207.

Bosco, Fernando, and Pascale Joassart-Marcelli. 2017. "Gardens in the City: Community, Politics and Place in San Diego, CA." In *Global Urban Agriculture: Convergence of Theory and Practice between North and South*, edited by Antoinette WinklerPrins. Boston: CABI Publishers.

Brenner, Neil, and Nick Theodore. 2002. "Cities and the Geographies of 'Actually Existing' Neoliberalism." *Antipode* 34(3): 349–79.

Broadway, Michael. 2009. "Growing Urban Agriculture in North American Cities: The Example of Milwaukee." *FOCUS on Geography* 52(3-4): 23–30.

CDC. 2016. "Healthy Food Environment." Centers for Disease Control and Prevention. www.cdc.gov/healthyplaces/healthtopics/healthyfood_environment.htm.

Cortese, Amy. 2011. *Locavesting: The Revolution in Local Investing and How to Profit from It*. Hoboken: John Wiley & Sons, Inc.

Crouch, Patrick. 2012. "Evolution or Gentrification: Do Urban Farms Lead to Higher Rents?" *Grist*. http://grist.org/food/evolution-or-gentrification-do-urban-farms-lead-to-higher-rents/.

DuPuis, E. Melanie, and David Goodman. 2005. "Should We Go 'Home' to Eat?: Toward a Reflexive Politics of Localism." *Journal of Rural Studies* 21(3): 359–71.

Eizenberg, Efrat. 2013. *From the Ground Up: Community Gardens in New York City and the Politics of Spatial Transformation*. Burlington: Ashgate.

Ellsworth, Susan, and Gail Feenstra. 2010. *Assessing the San Diego Food System: Indicators for a More Food Secure Future*. UC Davis Agricultural Sustainability Institute. Davis: University of California Research and Education Program.

Guthman, Julie. 2011. *Weighing In: Obesity, Food Justice, and the Limits of Capitalism*. Berkeley: University of California Press.

Hewitt, Carol P. 2013. *Financing Our Foodshed: Growing Local Food with Slow Money*. Gabriola Island: New Society Publishers.

Hladik, Maurice J. 2012. *Demystifying Food from Farm to Fork*. Bloomington, IN: iUniverse, Inc.

Joassart-Marcelli, Pascale, and Fernando Bosco. 2014. "Alternative Food Projects, Localization and Urban Development: Farmers' Markets in Southern California." *Metropoles* 15: 2–22.

Joassart-Marcelli, Pascale, Fernando J. Bosco, and Emanuel Delgado. 2014. *Southeastern San Diego's Food Landscape: Challenges and Opportunities*. A Policy Report. San Diego: Department of Geography, San Diego State University and Project New Village. http://geography.sdsu.edu/Research/Projects/FEP/Docs/Report.pdf.

Joassart-Marcelli, Pascale, and Jennifer Wolch, 2003. "The Intrametropolitan Geography of Poverty and the Nonprofit Sector in Southern California." *Nonprofit and Voluntary Sector Quarterly* 32(1): 70–96.

Johnston, Josée, and Shyon Baumann. 2009. *Foodies: Democracy and Distinction in the Gourmet Foodscape*. New York: Routledge.

Kingsley, Jonathan Y., and Mardie Townsend. 2006. " 'Dig In' to Social Capital: Community Gardens as Mechanisms for Growing Urban Social Connectedness." *Urban Policy and Research* 24(4): 525–37.

La Trobe, Heken L., and Tim G. Acott. 2000. "Localising the Global Food System." *International Journal of Sustainable Development and World Ecology* 7(4): 309–20.

MacLeod, Gordon, and Mark Goodwin. 1999. "Space, Scale and State Strategy: Rethinking Urban and Regional Governance." *Progress in Human Geography* 23(4): 503–27.

Markham, Lauren. 2014. Gentrification and the Urban Garden. *The New Yorker*. May 21. www.newyorker.com/business/currency/gentrification-and-the-urban-garden.

McClintock, Nathan. 2014. "Radical, Reformist, and Garden-Variety Neoliberal: Coming to Terms with Urban Agriculture's Contradictions." Local Environment 19(2): 147–71.

San Diego Community Garden Network (SDCGN). 2016. Community Garden Map. www.sdcgn.org.

Shuman, Michael. 2012. *Local Dollars, Local Sense: How to Shift Your Money from Wall Street to Main Street and Achieve Real Prosperity*. Community Resilience Guides. White River Junction: Chelsea Green Publishing.

Slocum, Rachel. 2007. "Whiteness, Space and Alternative Food Practice." *Geoforum* 38(3): 520–33.

USDA. 2014. "Why Local Food Matters: The Rising Importance of Locally Grown Food in the US Food System." US Department of Agriculture. www.ams.usda.gov/sites/default/files/media/Why%20Local%20Food%20MattersThe%20Rising%20Importance%20of%20Locally%20Grown%20Food%20in%20the%20U.S.%20Food%20System.pdf.

USDA-AMS (Agricultural Marketing Service). 2016. "Farmers' Markets and Direct to Consumer Marketing." US Department of Agriculture. www.ams.usda.gov/services/local-regional/farmers-markets-and-direct-consumer-marketing.

WinklerPrins, Antoinette. 2017. "Defining and Theorizing Global Urban Agriculture." In *Global Urban Agriculture: Convergence of Theory and Practice between North and South*, edited by Antoinette WinklerPrins. Boston: CABI Publishers.

Is Alternative Food Exclusionary?

What kind of place are farmers' markets? Visit a farmers' market in your area. Observe how many vendors are present and what they sell. Take note of food variety and prices. How different is it from a typical supermarket? Then focus on the consumers: How do they behave? Do they interact with vendors and other shoppers? Do they rush through the market or take time to enjoy the scene? What do they typically purchase? Can you gather any socioeconomic information based on superficial observation? Who may feel out of place at the farmers' market, and why?

Farmers' markets and community gardens are at the forefront of "locavorism" and the so-called alternative food movement in the United States and elsewhere around the world. Yet, many argue that growing your own food or shopping at the local farmers' market is out of reach for those with the greatest needs.

The recipe provided here is for a kale salad. In many ways, kale has come to represent the alternative food movement. An almost forgotten vegetable from the cabbage family, it has been hailed as a superfood because of its concentration of vitamin C, vitamin A, vitamin K, and omega-3 fatty acids. In California, it is grown almost year-round in community gardens, and several varietals are sold at farmers' markets. Yet, the current ubiquity of kale on restaurant menus and in health-promotion materials has led to some backlash against "kale evangelism" (Godoy and Barclay 2013), raising questions about social exclusion in "alternative" and "local" food.

Local Kale Salad with Butternut Squash and Almonds

Ingredients

1 bunch locally grown kale, preferably Lacinato or Tuscan, purchased at a farmers' market, stems removed, cut into ½-inch-wide ribbons

1 medium butternut squash, peeled, seeded, and chopped in ½-inch cubes

¾ cup almonds, toasted and roughly chopped

8 tablespoons olive oil

3 tablespoons lemon juice (from about 1 lemon)

1 tablespoon honey

1 tablespoon Dijon mustard

1 small shallot, minced

salt and pepper, to taste

Parmesan cheese, shaved with a vegetable peeler (optional)

⅓ cup dried cherries or cranberries (optional)

Preparation

Preheat oven to 450 degrees Fahrenheit. Toss squash in 3 tablespoons of oil, salt, and pepper and spread evenly on a baking sheet. Roast in oven for 20 to 25 minutes, turning occasionally, until tender and golden. Meanwhile, prepare the dressing by whisking together the remaining 5 tablespoons of oil, lemon juice, honey, and Dijon mustard. Season with salt and pepper and add shallot. In a large salad bowl, toss the kale with the dressing and let it rest while the squash is roasting. Add slightly cooled squash, almonds, and cherries to the kale. Toss well. Top with shaved Parmesan.

Reference

Godoy, Maria, and Eliza Barclay. 2013. "Is It Time to Cool It on Kale Already?" *The Salt*. National Public Radio. www.npr.org/sections/thesalt/2013/10/02/228499704/is-it-time-to-cool-it-on-kale-already.

PART III

BODIES

CHAPTER 12

Food, Ethnicity, and Place

PRODUCING IDENTITY AND DIFFERENCE

Pascale Joassart-Marcelli, Zia Salim, and Vienne Vu

Textbox 12.1. Learning Objectives

- Recognize the relationship between food and ethnicity through the lens of place and mobility.
- Distinguish between the concepts of identity and difference.
- Critique fixed notions of national cuisines and investigate their social production.
- Explore the positive role of food in creating a sense of place, facilitating cultural encounters, and promoting the inclusion of ethnic minorities, refugees, and immigrants.
- Consider the power relations underlying the representation and appropriation of ethnic foods by others.
- Use a case study of food in the Vietnamese diaspora of Southern California to illustrate key themes developed in the chapter.

Identity and Difference

It is practically impossible to write a chapter on food and identity without quoting Brillat-Savarin's famous aphorism, "Tell me what you eat, I shall tell you what you are" (1825). Food is indeed an important marker of **identity**, including ethnic identity. For example, Italians are known for their pizzas, Japanese for their sushi, and Indians for their spicy curries—despite the sophistication and diversity of their cuisines. At the same time, ethnic groups are often described in derogatory ways by their foods: krauts for Germans, frogs for the French, beaners for Mexicans, and roast beef for the British. Interestingly, food is also used to describe the mixing of cultures and ethnicities, as in a melting pot, smorgasbord, stir-fry, curry, or gumbo. These examples suggest a strong relationship between food and identity, but also hint at the relational and negotiated aspects of this relationship on which this chapter focuses.

In a transnational context, where people, goods, and ideas are increasingly mobile, food is a particularly powerful cultural *symbol* that allows people to communicate who they are and where they come from. Conceptualizations of food as a symbol of self-identification dominate much of the older literature on ethnic food in which it is seen as a *reflection* of identity. For instance, anthropologist Lévi-Strauss (1968) wrote about food as a system of language that can reveal "significant knowledge of the unconscious attitudes of the society [. . .] under consideration" (87). Since then, numerous scholars have studied how food reflects traditions and social structures, embodies religious and cultural values, and preserves memories and identities. This line of work has been especially fruitful in ethnic and migration studies where food is associated with the **performance** of identities and cultures that are presumably threatened by migration and assimilation (Gabaccia 1998; Diner 2001). For example, researchers have shown how generations of Chinese, Italian, and Jewish immigrants to the United States have brought with them traditional recipes and food protocols that define their culture and maintain their heritage (Gabaccia 1998).

Yet, food is more than semiotics and self-identification. Similarly, **ethnicity** is more than a unified culture, identity, or set of values that can be revealed by studying food. Rather than reflecting a fixed and rigid identity embodied in a few classic dishes, ethnic foods may be better described as a set of *practices* and part of the *everyday*. As a result, more-recent understandings of ethnic food emphasize how it is socially constructed through interactions between places and people. Likewise, ethnic identities are multifaceted; they are shaped and negotiated through everyday food practices such as cooking, eating, shopping for food, sharing meals, watching food shows on television, or growing vegetables. Ethnic food is created and performed by members of particular ethnic groups as well as others who consume it. As such, ethnic food is not just about visible minorities, but should consider other groups and the hierarchies of power that underpin inter-ethnic relations. In that relational framework, the concept of **difference** may be more appropriate than identity in understanding the connections between food and ethnicity. While identity implies an essence that may need to be discovered or expressed (possibly through food), difference is based on relationships to others in which particular identities are produced, consumed, regulated, and represented. In short, difference is lived out in social relations and everyday practices.

Food, Ethnicity, and Place

In these different understandings of ethnic food, whether they emphasize symbols or practices and favor the concepts of identity or difference, **place** plays a central role in structuring the relationship between food and ethnicity. As a symbol, ethnic foods are linked to places of origin and to ethnic enclaves, often in nostalgic ways. Indeed, ethnicity itself has often been defined as "primordial attachment" or "belonging" to place (Banks 1996; Sanders 2002). Marcel Proust's famous madeleine in *Remembrance of Things Past* illustrates the profoundly nostalgic role of food and its ability to conjure places and feelings associated with the past. It is these associations with real and imagined places that give food meaning and authenticity. To enjoy a traditional dish, one must shop in specific stores, patronize certain restaurants, or ideally, go back "home." Similarly, to "discover" authentic food, outsiders must travel to remote and exotic places, reinforcing essentialist notions of race and ethnicity. In other words, the places where food is produced, prepared, and consumed give it value and significance.

As a set of practices, ethnic food is also connected to processes of **place-making** in immigrant communities. For instance, when Chinese immigrants open restaurants and food stores in what are described as Chinatowns, they invest in place. These investments are embedded in larger political, social, economic, and cultural dynamics affecting these groups and their position in society. A place perspective can therefore be helpful in understanding how immigrants and ethnic minorities relate to, use, and transform food. It will also shed light on processes of social inclusion and exclusion that occur around food and eating. Here, a dialectical or dynamic perspective that emphasizes relationships between places and people at multiple scales may be particularly useful. For example, the tensions between places of origin and destination, familiar and exotic, and local and global are likely to have a significant effect on food, ethnicity, identity, and difference.

In this chapter, we adopt a place perspective to highlight three significant areas of research on ethnic food that straddle the tension between identity and difference. First, we take a critical look at ideas of national cuisine and explore how they are socially constructed. Doing so, we emphasize the role of transnationalism and the interplay between global and local forces in producing particular foodways. Second, we consider the processes of cultural encounters and social inclusion that ethnic food may enable, paying particular attention to ethnic foodscapes, including restaurants and ethnic markets. In the last section, we question these transformative possibilities as we explore the appropriation of ethnic food by others and engage with critical race theory. We end the chapter with a case study of Vietnamese food in Southern California to illustrate these concepts.

National Cuisine

Food scholar Sidney Mintz (1996) argues that there is no such thing as a national American cuisine, which according to him consists of a series of ethnic and regional culinary traditions. Others, however, argue that it is this very diversity that makes American cuisine unique (Gabaccia 1998; Johnston, Baumann, and Cairns 2009). If you think about the typical "American" diet or quintessential "American" dishes, you will probably think about items associated primarily with white and Anglo-Saxon settlers, but ignore dishes linked to other, more-recent "ethnic" groups. For some, hot dogs, hamburgers, fried chicken, and macaroni and cheese are commonly associated with American food. For others, American food is "tasteless" and summed up by fast, highly processed, bland, fried, and super-sized food (Belasco 2008).

What is more or less "American" has changed over time as new food items are added to the mix. Pizza, still very much associated with Italy, has become one of the most common dishes consumed in the United States, from school cafeterias to casual restaurants to home kitchens. The Jewish bagel has become a ubiquitous and convenient breakfast. Tacos are now a classic Tuesday-night meal in many homes, yet it is unclear whether they have become "American." For Gabaccia (1998), Americans may not have a single **national cuisine**, but they have a common culinary culture. She writes: "What unites American eaters culturally is *how* we eat, not *what* we eat. As eaters, all Americans mingle the culinary traditions of many regions and cultures within ourselves. We are multi-ethnic eaters [. . .] Eating homogenous, processed, mass-produced foods is no more, or less, American than enjoying the multi-ethnic mixtures of particular regions" (225–26).

Many scholars reject this multicultural, cosmopolitan, and somewhat romanticized version of American national cuisine, as it hides hierarchies of power and posits an assimilation model in which all ethnic cuisines become part of the mainstream as groups assimilate in American society (Padoongpatt 2011; Pilcher 2014; Williams-Forson 2006)—a topic to which we return in the last section of this chapter. Nevertheless, this example illustrates how national cuisines are not fixed in the past but change as a result of mobility and influences from other places. It also raises questions about how national cuisines evolve, and hints at the influence of immigrant cooks, food marketers, government agencies, public health professionals, media, and consumers in constructing cuisines. This suggests that national and ethnic cuisine may be parts of larger projects linked to nation-building and immigrant integration.

To understand how ethnic cuisines are socially constructed, it may be useful to briefly consider how food scholars contrast various ethnic or regional **foodways**. Belasco (2008) summarizes this research in five elements: 1) main staples or basic foods (e.g., corn tortillas in southern Mexico—see chapter 3); 2) preparation techniques (e.g., mixing, marinating, drying, fermenting); 3) seasoning or flavor principles (e.g., herbs, soy sauce, ginger, garlic, spices, chilies, oils, citrus, vinegar); 4) set of socially accepted food behaviors (e.g., time and place of food preparation and consumption, use of utensils, table manners); and 5) food infrastructure which organizes food provision "from farm to fork."

For example, southern Italian cuisine is characterized by a heavy reliance on grains, pasta, fish, tomatoes, eggplants, olives, and peppers. Foods are often grilled and braised, and typically flavored with garlic, capers, olive oil, and herbs such as oregano and basil. They are typically sourced from local farms and markets, and constitute important features of social life (including daily meals, feasts, and holidays). There is a long tradition in folkloric studies of documenting particular dishes in specific settings: the lobster roll in New England (Lewis 1998), the chili in Cincinnati (Lloyd 1998), the crawfish étouffée in New Orleans (Gutierrez 2012), and the *cioppino* in San Francisco (Peters 2013). Until recently, this work has been mostly descriptive and rarely engaged with social theory and critical perspectives. Static (and often self-aggrandizing) depictions of ethnic, national, or regional foods ignore their evolution over time and space and their **embeddedness** into social and political-economic relations that span multiple scales.

In his classic study of Belizean food, Wilk (2002) shows how national cuisine emerged in a context where **globalization** would have predicted its disappearance under homogenizing pressures. He argues that Belizean foodways, like those of many nations or regions of the Global South, have historically been shaped by global connections through colonialism, trade, and immigration. Local identity and globalization are not in opposition to one another but depend upon each other. Contemporary Belizean food reflects legacies of colonialism in that the most valuable ingredients are packaged, preserved, and branded imports (similar to those imported by its British rulers), instead of plentiful local ingredients such as lobster, meats, fruits, and vegetables that were associated with "natives" and racialized as inferior. During the colonial era, cooks for affluent households struggled to re-create English food by hiding local ingredients in pastries and sauces, which remain important elements of Belizean cuisine today. Over time, the cuisine became **creolized** through a blending of ethnic influences: Meat dishes with European origins were marinated in Yucatecan spice mixes, ingredients from one country were substituted into dishes from another, and food items were mixed in new ways. In recent decades, tourism and immigration have continued to transform Belizean food, as foreign tourists expect an authentic and traditional experience, and immigrants living abroad use simplified and compressed versions of national dishes to make a living as restaurant owners, showcase their culture at public festivals, and maintain nostalgic connections to Belize. Eventually, these dishes circulate back into Belize through return migration and continue to influence what Belizean food means through transnational connections.

This classic example points to the difference between everyday, non-reflective, and unconscious food habits on the one hand and the performative, self-conscious, and political idea of national cuisine on the other. While national cuisine may emerge slowly over time and reflect changing circumstances, in some cases it is part of a much more conscious political project. For example, pad thai—the iconic wok-fried noodle dish—was originally created as a state strategy to develop "Thai-ness" and demonstrate the strength and unity of the Thai nation (Van Esterik 2000). Similarly, Mexican cuisine became more unified after independence, when mestizo dishes became a symbol of the nationalist ideology of modern Mexico and helped to legitimize postrevolutionary governments (Pilcher 1996). It was only reluctantly that the "wheat-eating European elite" accepted the food of indigenous "people of corn" in the popularization of creolized dishes like mole poblano. That such food gained notice in the United States also helped give it acceptability among Mexican elites. By presenting a unified cuisine and downplaying regional distinctions, the political project of nation-building via food further erased histories of racism and oppression of indigenous people in Mexico (Pilcher 1996). These examples are not unique. Research from India (Appadurai 1988), Italy (Helstosky 2003), and Israel (Baron 2016) illustrate how "national" cuisines and dishes have been deliberately constructed to bind groups together and artificially erase tensions.

Ethnic Foodscapes, Culinary Citizenship, and Cultural Encounters

Like national cuisine, ethnic foodways evolve over time and are shaped by insiders as well as outsiders. Rather than being linked to a particular nation or territory, ethnic cuisine is typically associated with immigrants and diasporas away from their homeland. From a place perspective, the mobility associated with the food of immigrants adds a degree of complexity that has fascinated researchers. In this section, we focus on how immigrants and ethnic minorities relate to food and use it in positive ways. In the following section, we turn our attention to how *others* have used ethnic foods in ways that reproduce difference.

As migrants prepare and consume traditional food in one place, they maintain material and cultural connections to another (home)place. For example, Portuguese immigrants in New Jersey stay connected to the motherland by eating *bacalhau*—the Portuguese national dish, consisting of dried, salted cod (Baptista 2009); Australians miss and seek out Vegemite—a salty, slightly meaty Australian food spread—while living overseas (Arvela 2013); and Bengali Americans in New York City consume a diet that is "more Bengali" than that of comparable families in Kolkata today (Ray 2004). These food practices are related to notions of attachment and belonging; food creates bonds to and between new and old places.

The tension between here and there, however, is not static; it evolves in a dialectic fashion, resulting in new foods, tastes, and ways of eating. These foodways are not just reflections of core identities tied to the lives left behind, but are active ways of becoming new subjects and creating new places. For example, Diner (2001) explains how Italian immigrants to New York began using more meat and developing new "traditional" dishes, such as spaghetti with meatballs, by adapting old recipes to new economic realities of food availability. Similarly, for East European Jewish immigrants, America became "the land of meat and cake and ice cream" (Diner 2001, 20). Because many of these early-twentieth-century immigrants had been food-deprived in their homeland, their experience of food in America was a sort of "revenge of the poor" and a great source of pride and pleasure.

Home kitchens, food gardens, restaurants, and ethnic food markets are important places where immigrants and members of particular ethnic groups enact and negotiate ethnicity and other intersecting identities such as gender, class, and race (see chapters 8, 11, and 15). While home relates to mostly unconscious and everyday food practices, restaurants are the public face of ethnic cuisine and tend to be more purposeful and self-conscious. Together, these different places constitute an ethnic **foodscape** that affects subjectivities and collective identities (see chapter 8 for a detailed discussion of this concept). These foodscapes are most noticeable in ethnic neighborhoods where environments (e.g., home kitchens, restaurants, street markets, gardens), people (e.g., cooks, chefs, immigrants, natives, tourists), as well as objects, ideas, and feelings (e.g., ingredients, smells, cookware, recipes, prepared dishes) interact to give the area particular meanings linking food, ethnicity, and place (see figure 12.1).

Home kitchens are often described as "escapes"—private places where immigrants and racialized minorities can retreat to gain emotional strength and experience a sense of **belonging** (see chapter 15). The smell of food alone, along with the acts of cooking and eating, can elicit feelings of attachment—being at home—while at the same time bringing back memories of a romanticized homeland. Mannur (2009), in her study of South Asian diasporic culture, equates this simultaneous process of place- and identity-making through food to "culinary citizenship—that which grants subjects the ability to claim and inhabit certain identitarian positions via their relationship to food" (Mannur 2009, 20). As she argues, however, this process of using food to create attachment

Figure 12.1. Urban ethnic foodscape
Chinatowns are home to numerous food stores and restaurants, which have historically provided immigrants with social, economic, and cultural opportunities. Here, a messenger delivers food to or from a restaurant in New York City's Chinatown.
Source: Carol Highsmith Archive, Library of Congress. Available at: www.loc .gov/pictures/item/2011631401/.

and strengthen political projects of nation-building is not without problems, as it rests on gendered ideals of domesticity, which place a disproportionate responsibility on women (see chapter 15). In many cases, the evolution of taste and the adoption of new foods are a source of tension within many home kitchens, including across generations.

This example from South Asian diasporic kitchens suggests that homes, far from being isolated locations, are instead transnational spaces. For example, immigrant cooks often invest time and resources to procure culturally relevant foods that are not available in the destination country. This includes the breads, moles, candies, and chilies that travelers transport from Mexico to Alaska (Komarnisky 2009) and the smuggling of Thai plants, fruits, and vegetables into the United States, where these ingredients are unavailable (Padoongpatt 2011). These practices connect cooks and kitchens globally.

Gardens have also been studied as important elements of the ethnic foodscape. Specifically, they tend to be seen as therapeutic places of healing and self-expression for immigrants and ethnic minorities. In *Paradise Transplanted*, Hondagneu-Sotello (2014, 4) writes: "Even when immigrants have occupied subordinate social positions and have found themselves excluded from legal citizenship, subjected to racism, and relegated to bad low-wage jobs, they have actively cultivated plants and gardens. In this regard, gardens can serve as minizones of autonomy, as sites and practices of transcendence and restoration. Gardens offer compensation for lost worlds, bringing moments of pleasure, tranquility, and beauty, and they articulate future possibilities." This suggests that gardens are also places of collective identity formation and resistance (see chapter 11).

Restaurants are often described in the literature as places of encounter, where immigrants can share their cultural practices with others. In addition, they provide many immigrants with a source of income in places where other economic opportunities may be limited (see figure 12.2). In his study of Chinese restaurants in the United States, Chen (2014) argues that it was not the government nor large food corporations that democratized and diversified American dining, but Chinese immigrants—"a politically disenfranchised, culturally despised, economically marginalized and numerically insignificant group of people" (p. 1). Through their labor, working long hours in restaurants, they expanded the culinary landscape of America with dishes like chow mein, chop suey, and egg foo young that became increasingly popular among American consumers in search of fast, cheap, and exotic food. Chinatowns, which were essentially "food towns" (p. 77), played an important role in facilitating this cultural encounter. At first these ethnic enclaves mostly served Chinese immigrants, providing them with a relatively safe place to live, work, and cook in a hostile land. According to Chen, Chinatowns also helped to preserve and shield Chinese cuisine. Over time, Chinatowns became exotic destinations for adventurous eaters and tourists. Eventually, Chinese restaurateurs ventured to other urban neighborhoods and settled in suburban strip malls, but they continued to hire labor and purchase ingredients from nearby Chinatowns.

Figure 12.2. Ethnic entrepreneurship and Americanization of immigrant food
Hot-dog stands are ubiquitous on the streets of New York City today, and hot dogs are typically considered a quintessential American food. This part of the city's foodscape emerged in the 1860s, when German immigrants began selling hot dogs (or "Dachshund sausages," in honor of the small and long German dog) in carts they would push around the city, as depicted in this image. Over time, hot dogs evolved to reflect American preferences.

Source: Detroit Publishing Company Collection, Library of Congress, 1906. Available at: www.loc.gov/pictures/item/det1994012110/PP.

There is an older and well-established literature on **ethnic enclaves** and ethnic economies that emphasizes the profound impact that the spatial concentration of ethnic businesses and residents has had on cities around the world (see Marcuse 1997). Many draw attention to the specific role of ethnic restaurants and food markets in revitalizing decaying urban neighborhoods, where new immigrant groups are often segregated. As Hum (2002, 27) puts it in his study of Latino and Asian immigrants in Sunset Park in Brooklyn, New York: "Immigrants' capital and sweat equity has pumped new life into a 'dying neighborhood' and, in the process, has transformed decaying urban spaces into vibrant marketplaces and streetscapes." Other illustrations of this abound, from Mexican entrepreneurs in Los Angeles who use food to "break into" economic and cultural systems that might have been closed off to them otherwise (Ferrero 2002) to the South Asian entrepreneurs in Birmingham (UK) who have capitalized on the growing demand for "Indian" food (Ram et al. 2002).

These stories tend to emphasize the positive effects of ethnic restaurants and retail businesses on neighborhood change, supportive social networks, economic opportunities, and upward mobility. As such, they illustrate an assimilationist framework that views these restaurants (and ethnic enclaves in general) as stepping-stones in a long-term trajectory of upward mobility. Many, however, have rejected "straight-line" assimilation theory as simplistic, no longer applicable to the realities of immigration in globalized postfordist economies, and oppressive to newer and mostly nonwhite immigrants in an increasingly transnational context (see Nagel 2009). There is also evidence challenging the positive impact of ethnic enclaves and suggesting that they reproduce residential and occupational segregation, foster exploitation of co-ethnics, and therefore limit upward mobility (Light and Gold 2000; Sanders and Nee 1987). For example, many ethnic restaurants rely on self-exploitation and unpaid labor from family members and co-ethnics to stay in business. In a study of Turkish immigrants in the kebab industry in Finland, Wahlbeck (2007) found that new immigrants accepted very low or deferred wages and poor working conditions in hopes of eventually starting their own kebab business. Furthermore, some argue that ethnic enclaves, particularly restaurants, are sites of spectacle and entertainment that cater to tourists and adventurous visitors rather than places of meaningful encounter. It is to this criticism and the broader issue of power relations involved in defining ethnic food that we turn in the following section.

Authenticity, Representation, and Appropriation

In *Taco USA*, Arellano (2012) shows "how Mexican food conquered America." This is evidenced by the billions of dollars made each year by Taco Bell and by the more-recent overnight success of gourmet taco trucks selling tortillas stuffed by celebrity chefs "with Korean barbecue, with Argentine sausage, with sautéed tofu and even jackfruit" (51). For Arellano (2012), it is the "chameleonic" qualities of Mexican food and the taco in particular that have helped to ensure its lasting success and give it a place in American cuisine (see recipe 8). Chen (2014), in his study of Chinese food in America, makes a similar argument when he argues that the popularity of Chinese food in the United

States owes much to the fact that it was adapted to appeal to non-Chinese tastes and eating preferences, providing Americans at the turn of the twentieth century with the equivalent of "the Big Mac [in] the pre-McDonald's era" (4).

There are numerous examples of the adaptation of ethnic food. As its name indicates, the California sushi roll has its origin in the United States, where chefs tried to reproduce the texture of raw fish and appease fears of Americans about such ingredients by using avocado instead. Similarly, some sushi restaurants in Brazil use beef and processed fish to cater to local tastes (Yang 2013). Thinking about these local adaptations on a wider scale, we can appreciate why Chinese food, for instance, may taste very different in France than it does in America or Australia, since each place adds its imprint on the food and makes it different.

These examples illustrate the fluidity of ethnic or national cuisine, as we discussed earlier in this chapter. In addition, it hints at the power relations underlying the meaning of ethnic cuisine and its status as authentic. The Korean barbecue taco described by Arellano (2012) and the chop suey inspiring Chen (2014) would probably not be recognizable to most people in Mexico and China, respectively. While some view these dishes as a form of creativity, a culinary improvement or a symbol of **multiculturalism** and assimilation, others see them as heresy and subjugation—abandoning one's roots for economic profit or social acceptance.

These tensions raise questions about food **authenticity**, which has animated popular writing on food and recent research in anthropology, geography, sociology, and history. Authenticity assumes the existence of a pure, genuine, real, and unaltered cuisine, typically grounded in the homeland. Paradoxically, authenticity can only be seen from the outside—from the viewpoints of immigrants, tourists, and consumers from different ethnic or national backgrounds in search of that essence. For people "at home," questions of authenticity rarely arise; food practices are part of the taken-for-granted everyday. As van den Bergh (1984, 395) puts it: "like ethnicity itself, ethnic cuisine only becomes a self-conscious, subjective reality when ethnic boundaries are crossed."

Thinking about authenticity as a place-based phenomenon linked to mobility raises questions of social inclusion and exclusion in defining what is authentic ethnic food. Specifically, it encourages us to think about **representation** and **cultural appropriation**. The former refers to ways in which ethnic food is described and depicted by members of that ethnic group, but more often by others. The latter is about the adoption of elements of an ethnic cuisine by others, typically for self-aggrandizing purposes, such as social distinction or economic profit. Both processes are shaped by power geometries that tend to construct minoritized groups as *exotic others* and usurp their ability to define their own foodways. Food (mis)appropriation by dominant society can either fix or ostensibly subvert and homogenize expressions of ethnic difference.

Authenticity is often contrasted to Americanization, assimilation, or adaptation, which presumably compromise the integrity of ethnic food. This idea—that changes in ethnic foodways reflect duplicity and dishonesty—is based on static notions that contradict the fluid and transnational character of food highlighted in the previous two sections. It also reflects a racialized and classed process in which immigrant and poor people's foods are not allowed to change and depart from tradition, while "white" food, especially haute cuisine, is viewed as enhanced by creativity and bor-rowing from other traditions. In that context, it is critical to ask who gets to define what is authentic, and for what purposes.

Krishnendu Ray's research on ethnic restaurants in the United States shows how cuisines are framed differently according to race and class. French and Japanese cuisines have both been framed as "foreign," while other cuisines (e.g., Mexican, Chinese, and Indian) tend to be considered "ethnic" (2016). *Foreign* food is code for "prestigious"—the artistic creation of chefs with extensive expertise. In contrast, *ethnic* translates as "basic"—the labor of cooks with minimal training, who produce "cheap," "oily," and "spicy" food with "strong smells." Indeed, one of the defining characteristics of "ethnic" food is its low cost, as highlighted by examples from Canada (Turgeon and Pastinelli 2002), the United States (Ray 2016), and the UK (Buettner 2012). **Class** is a key factor here, since low cost typically means low wages. In addition, **race** plays an important role; it is no surprise that ethnic food is typically prepared by visible minori-ties whose skin color, accent, and clothing easily distinguishes them.

Consumers (re)produce these hierarchies in their representations of ethnic foods, as observed in online restaurant reviews such as Zagat and Yelp that reflect whiteness and unconscious racial bias (Ray 2016; Zukin, Lindeman, and Hurson 2015). For instance, Zagat's list of "America's Top [100] Restaurants" includes 32 American, 19 French, 19 Italian, and 13 Japanese restaurants, but only 2 Mexican, 2 Thai, 1 Indian, 1 Chinese, and 1 Vietnamese restaurants (Ray 2016). There is a clear underrepresenta-tion of ethnic restaurants given the size of these populations and the very large number of restaurants within these ethnic categories. The 100 Best Restaurants in America list created by Open Table (2015), an online restaurant reservation and review network, is even less inclusive; it is dominated by American (49 percent), French (27 percent), Italian (9 percent), and Japanese (5 percent) restaurants. There are no Thai, Mexican, or Indian restaurants on the list, and the only restaurants with other ethnic affiliations are described as "international," "Asian," "fusion/eclectic," or "Middle Eastern"—broad categories that deny ethnic and place specificity.

Representations are also produced by chefs who try to position themselves in an increasingly competitive and aesthetically driven restaurant industry. To become accepted as haute cuisine, ethnic food must artfully balance the tensions between authenticity and creativity and be prepared by a chef, whose "postures and gestures [embody] professionalism" (Ray 2016, 158). Cookbooks illustrate this process when they create chef personas as part of a marketing strategy (see chapter 16). The avenues available for ethnic cooks to become chefs are limited. Often it entails positioning oneself as coming from humble origins, being respectful of traditions, and working hard—in other words, embodying the American dream (a central theme in food films, as illustrated in textbox 12.2). In contrast to the rigid set of expectations facing ethnic chefs, white restaurateurs have a much wider range of options, some of which include the appropriation of ethnic cuisine. For example, one of Chicago's most acclaimed restaurants is Topolobampo, the flagship establishment of white American chef Rick Bayless, described by Michelin (2016) as serving "original south-of-the-border fare with an upscale twist." The ability to appropriate Mexican cuisine and market it as authentic is a form of white privilege rarely questioned.

Textbox 12.2. The Immigrant Experience and the Production of Ethnicity in Food Films

Food films represent a new genre in mainstream media. Within this genre, there are numerous films telling stories about immigrant dreams through ethnic restaurateurs, illustrating ideas about assimilation and difference. Examples include *Big Night* (1996), *The Hundred-Foot Journey* (2014), *Today's Special* (2009), and several others. Watching these films with a critical perspective may shed some light on issues related to the production of difference in food.

All three films illustrate the tension that "ethnic chefs," whether Italian or Indian, face in adapting their cuisine to meet consumer demand in a "foreign" place. While they use nostalgia to portray chefs as working-class artisans, loyal to their roots and families, they also show-case the chefs' ability to transcend this narrowly defined space by incorporating ingredients and techniques from other cuisines (by interning for a world-renowned chef in France, for instance), perfecting one's own culinary heritage (by "going home" and rediscovering "authentic" recipes), rejecting industrialized and mass-produced food in favor of quality and tradition, embodying principles of personal responsibility and work ethic, and typically falling in love with a white woman who is instrumental in opening doors to multicultural encounters.

These films also tend to glamorize and fetishize ethnic food through highly aesthetic and colorful scenes meant to awe viewers and highlight the formidable skills of the ethnic chef, whose chopping, stirring, frying, and juggling of various ingredients and techniques put most cooking shows to shame.

The struggles of immigrants are not absent from these films, yet they are simplified and usually overcome by the main character's tenacity, the unconditional love of his family, and the discovery of his culinary genius by outsiders, who are often white and affluent consumers. By glossing over these struggles in favor of a happy ending, these films fail to reveal the larger social structures leading to migration, discrimination, poverty, and social exclusion. Similarly, they tend to essentialize particular ethnicities, as complex markers of difference are reduced or erased to produce stable, fixed, homogeneous, and marketable identities.

Other media, including food magazines, blogs, travelogues, and television shows, also contribute to representations of ethnic food that disempower participants. Often, this occurs by positing a romanticized or idealized context in which difference is flat-tened, complex histories are simplified, negative aspects are erased, and stereotypes are conveyed uncritically (Heldke 2003). Johnston, Baumann, and Cairns (2009) provide a number of illustrations of how food writing creates an ethnic "other" through repre-sentations of ethnic food that produce a counterpoint to white American food. Es-sentialized representations of ethnic food often reinforce other differences, such as class, race, and gender, as if only women, impoverished peasants, and people of color living in poor and isolated places have the ability to make real food.

These sorts of representations facilitate the **commodification** of ethnic food, which leads to cultural appropriation by consumers, producers, and marketers. When consumers seek authentic ethnic food as a source of pleasure and distinction, they engage in a form of appropriation, which bell hooks (1992) describes as "eating the other" and Heldke (2003) considers a form of "cultural colonialism." Although ethnic restaurants seem to provide opportunities for cross-cultural encounters and apprecia-tion, they do so by creating "fictitious lands that are static, immune to political strife, poverty, and any oppression due in part to the intervention of the so-called first world"

(Diamond 1995, 4). As a result, they present an overly simplified version of reality that is more likely to serve the needs of elite consumers in search of **exoticism** than to generate a truly meaningful encounter based on respect of difference.

Educated and affluent cosmopolitan consumers appear to be much more interested in learning about ethnic food and the distant and exotic places where it presumably originated than about the immigrants who prepare that food. A Pakistani taxi driver in New Zealand sums it up: "I wish they liked us as much as they like our curry" (Pearson and Kothari 2007, 53). Curry has indeed become embroiled in food politics (Jackson 2010). In 2001, British foreign secretary Robin Cook declared that chicken tikka masala was "a true British national dish," using it as a symbol of the multicultural agenda he wished to support (Jackson 2010). This claim, based on the great popularity of the dish and the rumor that it was invented in an Indian restaurant in Glasgow, is hotly contested by those who argue that it has been prepared in India for generations. The fact that Indian immigrants in England face significant economic discrimination and social exclusion on a daily basis suggests a very superficial and opportunistic appreciation of Indian culture.

Chefs often appropriate the food of others as a way to "spice up" their own cuisine. This happens in acclaimed independent restaurants (like Topolobampo), touristic establishments, corporate restaurant chains, and retailers, all of which need to sell food to make a profit and stay in business. Going back to the example of chicken tikka masala, its appropriation by various political and corporate actors has transformed it into a transnational cultural commodity. It is no longer just served in ethnic restaurants, where it is ordered by 65 percent of patrons, but it is offered in workplace and school cafeterias and department store cafes and sold as convenient frozen dinners in virtually every supermarket in the UK (Jackson 2010). It now inspires numerous products, including pizza, potato chips, and pasta sauce that are produced by large corporations and, somewhat ironically, exported to India.

In summary, authenticity is socially constructed through partial representations of culture that benefit certain groups, including consumers in search of unique experiences and opportunities to stand out, chefs looking for inspiration, and corporations seeking profits through new products. In a global era when both the material and the discursive circulate at heightened speed, the meaning of authenticity is constantly negotiated and transformed. Yet, elite consumers do not have full control of this process, as immigrants, ethnic restaurateurs, and minority chefs also play a role in shaping these culinary hierarchies. For Ray (2016), ethnic food is like fashion—a highly aestheticized and dynamic element of everyday life—and as such it is extremely malleable. As "hipster foodies" and "tourists from the metropole" search for the next fashionable food in remote destinations and urban ethnic enclaves, "ethnic entrepreneurs" push back and in turn influence taste and culture.

Case Study: Vietnamese Americans in Orange County, California

In the section below, we examine some of the ways in which Vietnamese cuisine and food practices have evolved in Southern California and illustrate some of the key concepts developed in the previous sections. It is based on research by Vu (2008) and Vu and Voeks (2012).

Vietnamese immigration to the United States began on a large scale in 1975 at the end of the Vietnam War, when many refugees fled the country. Today, Vietnamese represent the sixth-largest immigrant group in the United States, with 1.3 million immigrants, and more than 2 million reporting Vietnamese ancestry in 2014 (Zong and Batalova 2016). More-recent immigrants differ from the earlier wave of refugees in their English ability, socioeconomic status, and availability of governmental assistance, with many struggling with poverty, unemployment, social exclusion, and cultural pressures to fit the "desperate-turned-successful" model of assimilation (Espiritu 2006; Zhou and Xiong 2005).

Little Saigon in Orange County, California, arose out of the first wave of refugees. After a brief stay in the reception center set up at the Camp Pendleton military base (just sixty miles south), many first-wave refugees were channeled into predominantly white Orange County, after resettlement agencies in San Diego, Los Angeles, and San Francisco complained that their cities were already dealing with too many other immigrant groups. By the late 1970s, a handful of Vietnamese restaurants and grocery stores and a Vietnamese newspaper had been established. Today, this three-square-mile enclave is the largest "Little Saigon" in the United States; it is home to almost 200,000 Vietnamese Americans, and continues to attract new immigrants (see figure 12.3).

The food experiences of Vietnamese Americans in Little Saigon and its hinterlands reveal varying stages of connectedness to both the home and host country, and are shaped by their migration experience. Accordingly, they differ by period of arrival and across generational divides, reflecting different social processes of identity formation,

Figure 12.3. Little Saigon, Orange County, California
Little Saigon is home to the largest Vietnamese-American community in the United States. Hundreds of Vietnamese restaurants and food retailers are located within the area, attracting local residents and outsiders.
Source: Photo by Zia Salim.

attachment to place, economic opportunities, and social inclusion. For many first and "1.5" generation Vietnamese migrants, food helps to maintain a connection to the Old Country, and reveals new food preferences (Vu and Voeks 2012). The following experiences help to illustrate this.

Since arriving in the United States in 1975 at the age of twenty-eight, Yvonne, a first-generation refugee, has been avidly preparing Vietnamese fare for herself and her family. Always having lived within a twenty-minute drive of a Vietnamese market has helped her retain her food culture. She feels that she relates more to Vietnamese than American culture, and tells of her partiality to Vietnamese music, but also expresses her keen interest in Korean soap operas. She prefers Vietnamese food to all others. Even when dining out, her inclination is toward Vietnamese restaurants. She has, over the years, learned how to prepare a few non-Vietnamese dishes to accommodate the broadening palates of her children. Some of these include spaghetti, pizza, and lasagna. She also taught herself how to make burritos and enchiladas, which are common in the region given the large presence of Latinos. Now that her children are out of the house, she cooks Vietnamese food almost exclusively. During holidays and special occasions, she diversifies her cooking to please her daughters-in-law, who are Chinese-American and Mexican-American.

Another example comes from Ngoc, a 1.5 generation immigrant who arrived in the United States in 1992 at the age of five. Her early experiences with non-Asian dishes were negative and visceral ones. She recalls her encounter with cafeteria food in the California public school system:

> My sister and I used to go to elementary [school] when we first moved to America, and we used to be afraid of the school lunches because we thought they were trying to poison us because it was so weird looking, like mashed potatoes. They had, like, Mexican food, but it was really nasty Mexican food, it was, like, just beans and cheese, and when you ate it you felt really horrible, you felt really full or thick, so we really thought they were . . . it was a conspiracy or something.

Since then, she has limited her palate to include only foods from the eastern and southeastern regions of Asia. She occasionally prepares meals, but these are not Vietnamese. She prides herself on her Korean barbecue. She does not like the traditional Korean recipe, so she alters the ingredients to fit her own taste—she adds lemongrass, a common ingredient in North Vietnamese fare, soy sauce to neutralize the sweetness of traditional Korean barbecue sauce, and red peppers from her backyard. The finished product is a Korean-Vietnamese fusion barbecue. The second dish she commonly prepares is spaghetti, which she considers Chinese despite the incorporation of marinara sauce. In addition to store-bought marinara sauce, Ngoc adds Asian ingredients such as soy sauce or fish sauce, and eats the dish with chopsticks. She considers the way she prepares and consumes this dish "Asian."

In many instances, members of the 1.5 generation—especially those who arrived more recently—show an appreciation for a variety of cuisines, but feel that the dish is incomplete without the addition of Vietnamese ingredients. It is not uncommon to hear of *nuoc mam* (fish sauce) being added to entrees such as enchiladas, or even used to baste the Thanksgiving turkey. Exploring beyond Vietnamese cuisine usually equates to trying foods that might be labeled as "Asian." The first and 1.5 generations most commonly straddle the cultural boundary between home and host country, and the food practices of this group reveals as much.

Second-generation Vietnamese Americans have more exposure to the diverse food cultures of Southern California, beginning at school. Because they were born in the United States, many feel more American than Vietnamese. Yet, they remain exposed to Vietnamese culture at home and within their community. As a result, some feel caught between what may seem as contradictory cultures, leading to confusion and, at times, resistance. Given this sociocultural ambivalence, their tastes (and identities) are perhaps more flexible and ready to be shaped in different directions, reflecting their experiences as immigrants

Tamarrah belongs to the second generation. She is thirteen years old, and has attended schools where the majority of her classmates are white. She considers herself to be American. She can understand Vietnamese, but cannot speak it well. She indulges in the same entertainment and pop culture as her American schoolmates. The only Vietnamese traditions that she practices are eating Vietnamese food and celebrating *Tet* (Vietnamese New Year). At home, she enjoys the traditional Vietnamese dishes that her mother prepares. At school she dislikes the cafeteria food, so she usually eats the sandwiches that her mom packs for her. On occasion, her mother will include Vietnamese items in her lunch bag. It is during these times that she experiences feelings of being different.

> Whenever I take Vietnamese food to school, everybody thinks it's weird and gross because they've never seen it. And one time in elementary school I brought [Vietnamese] beef jerky, and it looked like beef jerky, it looked fine, but it smelled different and I guess it tasted different, so it seemed kinda odd. . . . It makes me not want to bring any more [Vietnamese food] because it makes me feel like an outsider.

Tamarrah's comments suggest that, at least among teenagers, food is used to reproduce ethnic difference and demarcate sociocultural hierarchies, whereby white cafeteria food is normalized as universal and Vietnamese food is seen as inferior and strange. Tamarrah's mother was quite surprised and alarmed to hear this statement coming from her daughter. To her, eating Vietnamese food is as natural as speaking English is to the daughter, and giving it up would symbolize a loss of identity.

Place is instrumental in changing foodways. As a refugee, ten-year-old Tam and her family were immediately exposed to Western culture when they were placed about fifty miles east of Sacramento in the small town of Scottsville, California. At the time, they were the only Asian family in Scottsville. She remembers feeling out of place because she looked different and did not speak the same language as her classmates. Her family was immediately exposed to new foods, as ingredients necessary for Vietnamese recipes were not available. A year later, they moved south to Orange County. Although they did not live in Little Saigon proper, they were immediately immersed in the company of other Vietnamese people and had access to markets that provided all of the spices and ingredients they needed for their traditional fare. From that point,

Tam went back to eating primarily Vietnamese meals. Now married and a mother of two, she prepares mainly Vietnamese food for her household, and when she goes out to eat, she prefers Vietnamese restaurants.

Despite being comfortable with Asian cuisines in general, or even experimenting with the hybridization of home and close-to-home dishes, the idea of others attempting to replicate traditional Vietnamese food is unappealing to some Vietnamese Americans. As Vietnamese cuisine grows in popularity, more and more non-Vietnamese restaurant owners are re-creating Vietnamese foods. In particular, pho—rice noodles in a fragrant broth, usually served with fresh herbs and meat—has become very popular in Southern California. Non-Vietnamese entrepreneurs, including mostly Korean and other Asians, have capitalized on the dish's popularity and opened restaurants specializing in this type of food. According to a recent news article by celebrity chef and television personality Rosengarten (2012), "the Vietnamese boomlet makes a great deal of sense, in these diet-conscious times—since Vietnamese cuisine is one of the lighter, fresher manifestations of Asian cooking, perfectly in key with our national taste of the moment." In other words, Vietnamese food is prime for cultural appropriation, as illustrated in textbox 12.3.

In some cases, chefs try to stay true to the original ingredients, but not infrequently, they take some liberties with the recipes and substitute ingredients. One Korean-American restaurant worker expressed his dismay when hearing the negative reactions of Vietnamese-American patrons, stating, "I don't understand why they don't like the food. We use all of the same ingredients that they use. What's the difference?" From the point of view of a first-generation Vietnamese immigrant, however, "the ingredients are not right. They're not the same, so it doesn't taste right . . . Actually, I've tried two places run by Korean people and they're not good." These sentiments are not uncommon within the Vietnamese community, with many being offended by the cultural appropriation of Vietnamese cuisine.

For example, in 2015, Vietnamese students and others at Oberlin College protested against the "Vietnamese" banh mi sandwiches served with incorrect ingredients. Similarly, a blogger, who self-identified as "Angry Asian Man" (2016), expressed strong feelings against a food truck named "White Girl Asian Food," which he described as a manifestation of white privilege. Finally, an outcry arose on social media recently when the white chef of an upscale "Southeast Asian" restaurant in Philadelphia explained how to eat pho in a video—including steps that Vietnamese readers considered inaccurate—prompting the magazine to retitle the article, remove the associated video from its website, and apologize (*Bon Appétit* 2016).

Some of these arguments imply that authentic Vietnamese food can only be prepared by Vietnamese people with deep roots in Vietnam. As noted above, this assumption tends to dominate popular food writing on authenticity, which is also linked to specific places like immigrant communities and ethnic enclaves. Indeed, the recent popularity of Vietnamese food has meant that a growing number of foodies seek to discover authentic Vietnamese restaurants and visit places that once served an exclusively Vietnamese clientele. According to Rosengarten (2012), "If you want the very best pho in America, you have to seek out the Vietnamese communities in those few American cities with very large Vietnamese populations"—of which Orange County's Little

Textbox 12.3. Sriracha and Cultural Appropriation

The immensely popular Sriracha chili sauce provides a perfect example of hybridization and cultural appropriation of ethnic food. The sauce is distinguishable by its rooster logo, its description written in Vietnamese and several other languages, and its green cap and transparent plastic bottle revealing its bright red content. The sauce was invented in the 1980s by Vietnamese-American refugee-turned-entrepreneur, David Tran, and is manufactured in southeast Los Angeles County, not far from Little Saigon. There is some controversy about the origin of the recipe, which some claim comes from the town of Sri Racha in Thailand. Tran himself is of Chinese-Vietnamese ancestry, suggesting perhaps a hybridization of pan-Asian cultures (Viet World Kitchen 2011).

Today, the hot sauce has become ubiquitous and is used to spice up many dishes, from fast-food hamburgers to potato chips and gourmet crispy Brussels sprouts. The idea that it is a traditional sauce found next to bowls of phó on every Vietnamese table has been challenged by many (Viet World Kitchen 2011), yet it has been a symbol of Vietnam for Vietnamese expatriates and others. It was first "discovered" by foodies in search of exotic flavors in the mid-2000s. Chefs like Jean-Georges Vongerichten in New York used it as a "sleeve trick" to flavor dishes like rice-cracker tuna with citrus sauce and asparagus with hollandaise sauce (Edge 2009). Korean-American chef Roy Choi of the now-famous Kogi BBQ trucks used it to flavor his kimchi-garnished Korean barbecue tacos. By the end of the decade, food writers and bloggers had taken notice: *Bon Appétit* (2009) named Sriracha one of the ingredients of the year; it was declared "A Chili Sauce to Crow About" in the respected weekly food section of the *New York Times* (Edge 2009); several best-selling cookbooks focused on Sriracha were published (Clemens 2001); and it appeared in a *Simpsons* foodie episode in 2011.

Unfortunately for Tran, because the name was never trademarked, it is now being used by many large food corporations, such as Heinz, Frito-Lay, P. F. Chang's, Subway, and Jack in the Box, which have developed their own versions of the sauce (Pierson 2015). Furthermore, Tran's company faced resistance from some residents of the southeast Los Angeles neighborhood where the manufacturing plant is located, partly because of the smell it generates. Some have interpreted these legal battles as forms of race-based NIMBYism (a "not-in-my-backyard" approach to land use).

As Sriracha makes its way into mass-produced mainstream dishes, it is slowly growing out of fashion and losing its authentic appeal among foodies, who have ordered it to "move over" and make room for the next thing: the Korean smoky chili condiment Gochujang (*Bon Appétit* 2015). Meanwhile, Vietnamese immigrants and subsequent generations of Vietnamese Americans will probably continue to use the sauce regularly to flavor phó and other dishes without much consideration of its symbolic value as a foodie cult ingredient or its possible lack of authenticity.

Saigon is the largest. By "discovering" Vietnamese food in those places, foodies give it a different meaning and commoditize it by turning it into a form of entertainment.

At the same time, Vietnamese restaurants are rarely considered places of haute cuisine, unless they adopt techniques, ingredients, and decor from more-respectable traditions. The connection with French cuisine is particularly relevant, given Vietnam's colonial past, and is often used as a way to valorize Vietnamese food. Yet, this tends to occur outside of Little Saigon, in white spaces where consumers are more likely to be charmed by this narrative. For instance, Beverly Hills was home to acclaimed "modernist Vietnamese" restaurant Red Medicine (now closed), where chef Jordan Kahn served "new-wave Vietnamese food" (Snyder 2014) that was "a little punk-rock" (Gold 2014) and "essentially New Nordic through the lens of Asian ingredients" (Eater Los Angeles 2014). A meal might include "peas, trout eggs and lemon curd served in a goldfish bowl capped with a thin sheet of frozen pea-pod purée, a salad of wild roots and stalks with crunchy dried cabbage and marbles of walnut marzipan, and a delicious if unexpected dish of baby potatoes cooked with butter and yeast" (Gold 2014). Kahn, a Georgia native, has trained under some of the nation's most acclaimed chefs, including Thomas Keller of French Laundry in Napa Valley and Grant Achatz of Alinea in Chicago. Yet, he has no apparent connections or experience with the Vietnamese community of Southern California. To make matters worse, the restaurant's original logo included an image of Ho Chi Minh, a rather unpopular figure in the local Vietnamese community, whose members had fled the communist regime he helped to create.

Because of the growing popularity of Vietnamese establishments, ingredients have been progressively altered to accommodate palates of a diverse clientele. This reflects a **hybridization** of Vietnamese cuisine, which some interpret as a "watering down" to suit the taste of non-ethnic patrons. Over time, Vietnamese consumers grow accustomed to, and even enjoy, these new flavors that represent a new hybrid culture associated with diasporic life. Yet, the evolution of Vietnamese cuisine in Little Saigon does not follow a linear path of hybridization and assimilation into mainstream culture. Similarly, Vietnamese refugees and immigrants do not integrate in American society in frictionless trajectories of Americanization. As some food traditions are abandoned, others are being reinforced and occasionally become forms of resistance or strategies for economic advancement. Some are also appropriated, raising questions within the Vietnamese community. Through these negotiations, new identities and subjectivities are being formed and expressed, often in contradictory ways. These changes do not happen in a vacuum, but are embedded in American society and its relationships to Vietnamese immigrants through food and place. Recognizing changes in food practices and attitudes may aid in understanding the immigration experience and shed light on the ways in which place, ethnicity, and food are intertwined.

Conclusion

Food, ethnicity, and place interact in complex ways that question essentialist and rigid notions of ethnic identity. As we have shown in this chapter, food is dynamic; it evolves over time and across space, as it is shaped by social relations, political agendas, and economic imperatives. So are identities—never fixed and always in flux. A place-based approach to ethnic food allows its social life to come to the surface, highlighting its functions in the maintenance of group identity, economic survival, and social inclusion. It also points to ways in which food is used, represented, and appropriated to create difference. Food, therefore, is simultaneously a symbol, an expression, and a producer of difference. As it connects people and places through complex relations of power, it is intensely social and geographic.

Key Terms

authenticity	foodways
belonging	globalization
class	home
commodification	hybridization
creolization	identity
cultural appropriation	multiculturalism
difference	national cuisine
embeddedness	performance
ethnic enclave	place
ethnicity	place-making
exoticism	race
foodscape	representation

Summary

- Food is an important marker and maker of identity; it is a symbol, a performance, and a constitutive practice of identity and difference.
- Identity is not a fixed notion, but a fluid idea of who we are that is influenced by our own everyday experiences and the way others view us.
- National cuisines are socially constructed; they evolve over time, embody multiple global and local influences, and tend to promote political projects of nation-building.
- The relationship between food and ethnicity is place-based. Ethnic foodscapes reflect the dynamic ways food and place interact to create a sense of belonging, provide economic opportunities, and foster cultural encounters.
- Understanding of ethnic foods and authenticity is shaped by power relations that often involve processes of othering and cultural appropriation, which restrict particular groups' ability to control how their foodways are represented and used.

Additional Resources

For scholarly work on national cuisine, see Appadurai (1988), Pilcher (1996), and Wilk (2002).

For critical work on race and food, see Heldke (2003), hooks (1992), and Williams-Forson (2006).

For popular writing on particular ethnic foods in the United States, see Arellano (2012) and Chen (2014).

Gabaccia (1998) and Diner (2001) provide rich historical accounts of the evolution of ethnic food in the United States and its relationship to assimilation.

Ray (2016) offers a particularly relevant analysis of ethnic restaurateurs and their roles in today's food culture.

A provocative discussion of cultural appropriation among foodies is provided at: http://everydayfeminism.com/2015/11/foodie-without-appropriation/.

In addition to the films mentioned in textboxes 12.2 and 12.3, you may consider *City of Gold* (2015), which explores Los Angeles's ethnic foodscapes through the eyes of one of its most notorious food critics. Anthony Bourdain's television shows, *No Reservations* (2005–2012) and *Parts Unknown* (2013–2016), provide nice overviews of ethnic cuisine, with an emphasis on place, and opportunities to critically explore issues of appropriation and representation.

References

Angry Asian Man. 2016. "There is a Food Truck Actually Called 'White Girl Asian Food.' " http://blog.angryasianman.com/2016/01/there-is-food-truck-actually-called.html.

Appadurai, Arjun. 1988. "How to Make a National Cuisine: Cookbooks in Contemporary India." *Comparative Studies in Society and History* 30(1): 3–24.

Arellano, Gustavo. 2012. *Taco USA: How Mexican Food Conquered America*. New York: Simon & Schuster.

Arvela, Paula. 2013. "Ethnic Food: The Other in Ourselves." In *Food: Expressions and Impressions*, edited by Don Sanderson and Mira Crouch, 45–56. Oxford: Inter-Disciplinary Press.

Banks, Marcus. 1996. *Ethnicity: Anthropological constructions*. London: Routledge.

Baptista, Lori D. B. 2009. "Peixe, Patria e Possibilidades Portuguesas: 'Fish, Homeland, and Portuguese Possibilities.' " *Text and Performance Quarterly* 29(1): 60–76.

Baron, Ilan Z. 2016. "Reading Cookbooks: Israeli Food and the International Relations of the Every Day." *Arts and International Affairs*. DOI: *10.18278/aia.1.1.4.*

Belasco, Warren. 2008. *Food: The Key Concepts*. New York: Berg.

Bon Appétit. 2009. Best Food of the Year. https://www.bonappetit.com/uncategorized/article/best-foods-of-the-year-from-bon-appetit

———. 2015. "Gochujang, the Hottest Hot Sauce on the Market." May 4. http://bonapp.it/1IG8VNX.

———. 2016. "About that Phó Video." Update #2. September 6. www.bonappetit.com/story/how-you-should-eating-pho.

Brillat-Savarin, Jean A. 1825. *The Physiology of Taste: Or Meditations on Transcendental Gastronomy*. New York: Knopf [2009].

Buettner, Elizabeth. 2012. "'Going for an Indian': South Asian Restaurants and the Limits of Multiculturalism in Britain." In *Curried Cultures: Globalization, Food, and South Asia*, edited by Krishnendu Ray and Tulasi Srinivas, 143–74. Berkeley: University of California Press.

Chen, Yong. 2014. *Chop Suey, USA: The Story of Chinese Food in America*. New York: Columbia University Press.

Clemens, Randy. 2011. *The Sriracha Cookbook*. New York: Ten Speed Press.

Diamond, Rena. 1995. "Become Spoiled Moroccan Royalty for an Evening: The Allure of Ethnic Eateries." *Bad Subjects* 19: 4–5. http://bad.eserver.org/issues/1995/19/diamond.html.

Diner, Hasia R. 2001. *Hungering for America: Italian, Irish, and Jewish Foodways in the Age of Migration*. Cambridge: Harvard University Press.

Eater Los Angeles. 2014. "Eater 38: The 38 Essential Los Angeles Restaurants July 2014." http://la.eater.com/maps/the-38-essential-los-angeles-restaurants-july-2014.

Edge, John. 2009. A Chili Sauce to Crow About. *New York Times*. Dining & Wine. May 19. http://www.nytimes.com/2009/05/20/dining/20united.html?pagewanted=all.

Espiritu, Yêên. 2006. "Toward a Critical Refugee Study: The Vietnamese Refugee Subject in US Scholarship." *Journal of Vietnamese Studies* 1(1-2): 410–33.

Ferrero, Sylvia. 2002. "Comida Sin par. Consumption of Mexican Food in Los Angeles: 'Foodscapes' in a Transnational Consumer Society." In *Food Nations: Selling Taste in Consumer Societies*, edited by Warren Belasco and Philip Scranton, 194–219. New York: Routledge.

Gabaccia, Donna R. 1998. *We Are What We Eat: Ethnic Food and the Making of Americans*. Cambridge: Harvard University Press.

Gold, Jonathan. 2014. "Review: Red Medicine, A Little Punk Rock and Splendid in its Own Way." *Los Angeles Times*. April 25. www.latimes.com/food/la-fo-gold-redmedicine-201404 26-story.html.

Gutierrez, C. Paige. 2012. *Cajun Foodways*. Jackson: University Press of Mississippi.

Heldke, Lisa. 2003. *Exotic Appetites: Ruminations of a Food Adventurer*. New York: Routledge.

Helstosky, Carol. 2003. "Recipe for the Nation: Reading Italian History through La Scienza in Cucina and La Cucina Futurista." *Food and Foodways* 11(2-3): 113–40.

Hondagneu-Sotelo, Pierrette. 2014. *Paradise Transplanted: Migration and the Making of California Gardens*. Berkeley: University of California Press.

hooks, bell. 1992. "Eating the Other: Desire and Resistance. In *Black Looks: Race and Representation*, edited by bell hooks, 21–39. Boston: South End Press.

Hum, Tarry. 2002. "Asian and Latino Immigration and the Revitalization of Sunset Park, Brooklyn." In *Contemporary Asian American Communities: Intersections and Divergences*, edited by Linda T. Võ and Rick Bonus, 27–44. Philadelphia: Temple University Press.

Jackson, Peter. 2010. "A Cultural Politics of Curry: The Transnational Spaces of Contemporary Commodity Culture." In *Hybrid Cultures, Nervous States: Britain and Germany in a (Post) Colonial World*, edited by Ulrike Lindner, Maren Möhring, Mark Stein, and Silke Stroh, 167–88. Amsterdam: Rodopi.

Johnston, Josée, Shyon Baumann, and Kate Cairns. 2009. "The National and the Cosmopolitan in Cuisine: Constructing America through Gourmet Food Writing." In *The Globalization of Food*, edited by David Inglis and Debra Gimlin, 161–83. New York: Berg.

Komarnisky, Sara. 2009. "Suitcases Full of Mole: Traveling Food and the Connections between Mexico and Alaska." *Alaska Journal of Anthropology* 7(1): 41–56.

Lévi-Strauss, Claude. 1968. *Structural Anthropology* (Vol. 1). New York: Basic Books.

Lewis, George H. 1998. "The Maine Lobster as Regional Icon: Competing Images over Time and Social Class." In *The Taste of American Place: A Reader on Regional and Ethnic Foods*, edited by Barbara G. Shortridge and James R. Shortridge, 65–84. Lanham, MD: Rowman and Littlefield.

Light, Ivan H., and Steven J. Gold. 2000. *Ethnic Economies*. San Diego, CA: Academic Press.

Lloyd, Timothy C. 1998. "The Cincinnati Chili Culinary Complex." In *The Taste of American Place: A Reader on Regional and Ethnic Foods*, edited by Barbara G. Shortridge and James R. Shortridge, 45–56. Lanham, MD: Rowman and Littlefield.

Mannur, Anita. 2009. *Culinary Fictions: Food in South Asian Diasporic Culture*. Philadelphia: Temple University Press.

Marcuse, Peter. 1997. "The Enclave, the Citadel, and the Ghetto: What Has Changed in the Post-Fordist US City." *Urban Affairs Review* 33(2): 228–64.

Michelin. 2016. "Topolobampo." *Michelin Guide*. www.viamichelin.com/web/Restaurant/ Chicago-60654-Topolobampo-269297-41102.

Mintz, Sidney W. 1996. *Tasting Food, Tasting Freedom: Excursions into Eating, Culture, and the Past*. Boston: Beacon Press.

Nagel, Caroline R. 2009. "Rethinking Geographies of Assimilation." *Professional Geographer* 61(3): 400–07.

Open Table. 2015. "100 Best Restaurants in America for 2015." www.opentable.com/m/best -restaurants-in-america-for-2015/.

Padoongpatt, Tanachai M. 2011. "Too Hot to Handle: Food, Empire, and Race in Thai Los Angeles." *Radical History Review* (110): 83–108.

Pearson, Sarina and Shuchi Kothari. 2007. "Menus for a Multicultural New Zealand." *Continuum* 21(1): 45–58.

Peters, Erica J. 2013. *San Francisco: A Food Biography*. Lanham, MD: Rowman and Littlefield.

Pierson, D. 2015. "With No Trademark, Sriracha Name Is Showing up Everywhere." February 10. *Los Angeles Times*. www.latimes.com/business/la-fi-sriracha-trademark-20150211-story.html.

Pilcher, Jeffrey M. 1996. "Tamales or Timbales: Cuisine and the Formation of Mexican National Identity, 1821–1911." *The Americas* 53(02): 193–216.

———. 2014. " 'Old Stock' Tamales and Migrant Tacos: Taste, Authenticity, and the Naturalization of Mexican Food." *Social Research: An International Quarterly* 81(2): 441–62.

Proust, M. 2009. *Remembrance of Things Past* (Vol. 1). Originally published in 1913. Hertfordshire: Wordsworth Editions.

Ram, Monder, Trevor Jones, Tahir Abbas, and Balihar Sanghera. 2002. "Ethnic Minority Enterprise in Its Urban Context: South Asian Restaurants in Birmingham." *International Journal of Urban and Regional Research* 26(1): 24–40.

Ray, Kreshnendu. 2004. *The Migrant's Table: Meals and Memories*. Philadelphia: Temple University Press.

———. 2016. *The Ethnic Restaurateur*. New York: Bloomsbury Publishing.

Rosengarten, David. 2012. "Vietnam's Great Culinary Gift to the US . . . and Where to Find the Best Bowl of It!" *The Blog. Huffington Post*. February 23. www.huffingtonpost.com/david-rosengarten/vietnamese-pho_b_1291487.html.

Sanders, Jimy M. 2002. "Ethnic Boundaries and Identity in Plural Societies." *Annual Review of Sociology* 28: 327–58.

Sanders, Jimy M., and Victor Nee. 1987. "Limits of Ethnic Solidarity in the Enclave Economy." *American Sociological Review* 52: 745–67.

Snyder, Garrett. 2014. "R.I.P. Red Medicine, Lindy & Grundy, Fifty Seven, and More." *Los Angeles Magazine*. September 25. www.lamag.com/digestblog/r-p-red-medicine-lindy-grundy-fifty-seven.

Turgeon, Laurier, and Madeleine Pastinelli. 2002. " 'Eat the World': Postcolonial Encounters in Quebec City's Ethnic Restaurants." *Journal of American Folklore* 115(456): 247–68.

van den Bergh, Pierre L. 1984. "Ethnic Cuisine: Culture in Nature." *Ethnic and Racial Studies* 7(3): 387–97.

Van Esterik, Penny. 2000. *Materializing Thailand*. New York: Berg.

Viet World Kitchen. 2011. "Tackling Sriracha Myths, Truths and Confusion." November 7. www.vietworldkitchen.com/blog/2011/11/sriracha-myths-truths-and-confusion.html.

Vu, Vienne. 2008. "The Changing Foodways of Vietnamese Americans in Orange County, California." Master's Thesis, California State University, Fullerton.

Vu, Vienne, and Robert Voeks. 2012. "Fish Sauce to French Fries: Changing Foodways of the Vietnamese Diaspora in Orange County, California." *The California Geographer* 52: 35–55.

Wahlbeck, Östen. 2007. "Work in the Kebab Economy: A Study of the Ethnic Economy of Turkish Immigrants in Finland." *Ethnicities* 7(4): 543–63.

Wilk, Richard. 2002. "Food and Nationalism: The Origins of 'Belizean Food.' " In *Food Nations: Selling Taste in Consumer Societies*, edited by Warren Belasco and Philip Scranton, 67–90. New York: Routledge.

Williams-Forson, Psyche A. 2006. *Building Houses Out of Chicken Legs: Black Women, Food, and Power*. Chapel Hill: University of North Carolina Press.

Yang, Wen. 2013. "The 'Authenticity' of Sushi: Modernizing and Transforming a Japanese Food." Master's Thesis. University of Arizona.

Zhou, Min, and Yang S. Xiong. 2005. "The Multifaceted American Experiences of the Children of Asian Immigrants: Lessons for Segmented Assimilation." *Ethnic and Racial Studies* 28(6): 1119–52.

Zong, Jie, and Jeanne Batalova. 2016. "Vietnamese Immigrants in the United States." *Migration Information Source. Migration Policy Institute*. www.migrationpolicy.org/article/vietnamese-immigrants-united-states.

Zukin, Sharon, Scarlett Lindeman, and Laurie Hurson. 2015. "The Omnivore's Neighborhood? Online Restaurant Reviews, Race, and Gentrification." *Journal of Consumer Culture* 0(0): 1–21.

FOOD FOR THOUGHT

Are We What We Eat?

Does your family have a recipe that has been passed from generation to generation and reflects your ancestry or ethnic identity? If not, is there a specific dish that has been meaningful to you, perhaps because you consumed it regularly as a child? Where did the dish originate? Do you know who brought it here? Has the dish evolved over time? Are you familiar with other versions of the dish (perhaps as packaged prepared food, served in restaurants, or cooked by other families)? What do you think about those variations of the dish? What is it that you particularly like about your family's dish? Does it set you apart from others or bring you closer to them? Do you feel that this dish speaks about your identity in a specific way, whether positive or negative?

Immigrants often adapt traditional recipes when they move to a new place. The desire to maintain tradition is challenged by the lack of availability of typical ingredients and the opportunity to use other ingredients, which might have been out of reach in the home country. For example, meat dishes like bò lúc lắc were reserved for special celebrations and holidays in Vietnam, but in the United States, this dish has become a standard in many Vietnamese restaurants. Bò lúc lắc is named for the way it is cooked—"shaken" in the pan.

This dish happens to be a family favorite of Vienne Vu, one of the authors of chapter 12. Her family orders it almost every time they visit a Vietnamese restaurant. Recently, in a Little Saigon restaurant, they were pleasantly surprised to find french fries (not a traditional Vietnamese ingredient) mixed in with the beef. The author's mother shares her recipe for her "modern immigrant" version of bò lúc lắc here. She rarely uses measuring instruments, and cooks "by feel," as many traditional Vietnamese home cooks do. Therefore, the measurements in this recipe are approximate and can be adjusted for taste.

Bò Lúc Lắc (Shaken Beef)

Ingredients (for four)

For the marinade:

1 teaspoon fish sauce
⅛ teaspoon salt
5 cloves crushed garlic
¼ teaspoon black pepper
½ teaspoon sugar
½ tablespoon vegetable oil
1 pound filet mignon (or choice cut of beef), cut into ¾-inch cubes
1 cup french fries, made from a large fresh potato cut into strips and fried in vegetable
　　oil (or from a frozen package prepared according to directions)
1 tablespoon vegetable oil
chopped green onions
1 tomato, sliced
leaves of 1 head of butter lettuce

Preparation

Combine beef and marinade in a large bowl and let it rest for at least 1 hour.

Prepare french fries while the beef marinates.

Heat vegetable oil in a large wok or skillet on high heat. Toss or "shake" the cubes of beef until seared on all sides. Cook until desired wellness is achieved. Toward the end of cooking, reduce heat and toss in the french fries until the excess juice from the meat is absorbed by the fries (about 3 minutes). To avoid overcooking the beef, you can remove it from the pan and set aside on a plate before tossing the fries in the cooking juices. Serve the beef and fries over the lettuce leaves. Top with chopped green onions and place tomato slices along the side of the dish. Accompany with rice.

CHAPTER 13

Critical Nutrition

CRITICAL AND FEMINIST PERSPECTIVES ON BODILY NOURISHMENT

Jessica Hayes-Conroy and Allison Hayes-Conroy

Textbox 13.1. Learning Objectives

- Become familiar with the emerging field of critical nutrition.
- Evaluate statements about obesity in relation to both rhetoric and scale.
- Recognize claims to healthy eating as historically and politically situated.
- Understand how social inequality and neoliberal capitalism play a role in determining nutritional health.
- Appreciate how the material/visceral body comes to matter in the complex processes of bodily nourishment.
- Identify and delineate helpful alternatives to mainstream nutrition intervention.

In this chapter, we explore the field of critical nutrition, a field that is emergent in numerous places at once—for example, among scholars in geography, anthropology, and sociology; in interdisciplinary programs like food studies, environmental studies, and women's studies; within certain food activist groups; and also among concerned nutrition practitioners (who often call this field *critical dietetics*). What unites the field is a central concern over the principles and practices of "mainstream nutrition"—the nutrition tenets that have been promoted widely within the United States and beyond. The concern is that mainstream nutrition often ignores issues of diversity, context, and hierarchy. Another way of saying this is that mainstream nutrition is not particularly place-based; instead, it is based on the idea that good nutrition can be defined universally, for anybody, anywhere. Critical nutrition, on the other hand, understands bodily nourishment as something that is deeply embedded in daily life struggles for power, resources, recognition, and meaning. Accordingly, critical nutrition paves the way for new discussion topics that were previously unfamiliar to nutrition—for example, questions of rhetoric and scale, attention to history and politics, concerns over inequality and economic process, and a focus on the complexity of human bodies.

In 2014, *Gastronomica: The Journal of Critical Food Studies* ran a special issue on critical nutrition called "Nutritional Deficiencies: Dietary Advice and Its Discontents." In the introduction, food scholar Julie Guthman is careful to explain that the critiques offered by critical nutrition are *not* directed at nutrition science alone, nor just at professional nutritionists. Rather, many people can and do advance "mainstream" nutrition. From educators, journalists, marketers, church leaders, government officials, parents, and peers to, yes, scientists and health professionals, many people have the power to pass along nutrition ideas and behaviors to others. Our critique here, too, is pointed toward mainstream nutrition at large.

Mainstream Nutrition

What is mainstream **nutrition**? While not monolithic, mainstream nutrition is often recognizable by a few common properties. As we argue in the introduction to our book, *Doing Nutrition Differently* (Hayes-Conroy and Hayes-Conroy 2013), mainstream nutrition tends to be: 1) standardized; 2) reductionist; 3) decontextualized; and 4) hierarchical.

Standardized nutrition is nutrition that assumes food-body relationships can be understood through universal systems of measurement. Calorie counting and the body mass index (BMI) are two common examples. Such standardization goes hand in hand with *reductionist* nutrition, which considers food to be best understood as the sum of its standard parts—nutrients. Nutrition labels are a good example; they communicate the idea that we know food through content measurements of calories, proteins, fats, and vitamins. Another example is the USDA's online "super tracker," which encourages counting and sorting foods into daily food group targets.

Decontextualized nutrition is nutrition that ignores context. A standardized, reductionist approach to nutrition ignores aspects of life specific to particular places or people because the generalizable logic of nutrients and calorie counts is thought to supersede those specificities (see chapter 12 on food and ethnicity). We see this when culturally specific recipes are "translated" into low-calorie versions, or when 100-calorie snack packs become the way to handle specific bodily cravings.

Finally, *hierarchical* nutrition is nutrition that emphasizes expert knowledge. Experts are positioned *hierarchically* above nonexperts (usually poor, disenfranchised persons), who are presumed to lack the specific knowledge that experts hold (see chapter 16 on celebrity chefs). Thus, most nutrition interventions, or strategies meant to bring about nutritional change, are aimed at educating the nonexperts on what they are presumed not to know. Importantly, what is missing here is that so-called nonexperts actually hold a great deal of contextual, place-based knowledge about how food-body relationships unfold in daily life.

Rethinking Obesity

One of the most common reasons for mainstream nutrition intervention is the oft-cited "obesity epidemic." Obesity has come to play a huge role in the way many people think about nutritional health. It is also an especially place-based concept in that it is frequently associated with particular places. In Europe, for example, Americans are often depicted as overeaters to suggest that obesity is connected to US food, culture, and values. Within the United States, this stereotype is narrowed to particular cities, like Memphis or Shreveport, made infamous as the fattest places in America (Bernardo 2016). And, even within cities, particular design choices are sometimes labeled "obeso-genic" when they fail to support individual behaviors that promote weight loss (Swin-burn et al. 1999 and Guthman, in chapter 9 of this volume). Beyond such labels, how-ever, there is much about obesity that is unknown, and much that is debated. What has caused the so-called obesity epidemic? And why do we associate obesity with ill health? These questions are just some of those that concern critical nutrition scholars.

THE RHETORIC OF OBESITY

One key task proposed by critical nutrition involves questioning the idea that **fat-ness** itself is inherently "unhealthy." Geographers Bethan Evans and Rachel Colls, for example, have critiqued the use of body mass index (BMI), arguing not only that BMI fails to capture the material realities of people's lives, but also that it has not proven to be effective as a scientific measure of health (Evans and Colls 2009). In their book *Body Respect* (2014), Linda Bacon and Lucy Aphramor take this critique into an account of the "health at every size" movement (HAES), which contends that it is possible to achieve good health at any weight. Unsurprisingly, this claim is not popular, not least because, as the authors explain, the negative stigma of obesity is so prevalent in Western society that people are quick to shun anything that "condones" fatness. People are primed to see HAES as a way to "give up" on health, rather than a way of redirecting attention away from variable features like body size, and onto factors known to have devastating health impacts, like social inequality and discrimi-nation (Bacon and Aphramor 2014).

Importantly, this focus on rhetoric is not at the expense of hard data or scientific facts; rhetoric matters in real, concrete ways. For example, measures like BMI not only obscure more-complex, scientific understandings of body weight, but they may also produce fear, stress, depression, and even disordered eating among those measured. In addition, size discrimination impacts people in ways that are deeply connected to health. Because fatness is typically associated with laziness, the stigma of obesity can influence one's job security, socioeconomic status, and access to quality health care. Size discrimination can also impact mental health (see textbox 13.2). When such size discrimination intersects with other modes of prejudice—sexism, racism, and hetero-sexism, for example—the impacts to bodily health are intensified.

SCALING UP

Another way to question obesity is to shift the **scale** at which we intervene. While most intervention strategies advocate individual solutions that focus on behavioral change, those interested in critical nutrition insist that we look beyond the individual. There are several reasons why this is important. First, an individual approach to obesity puts

Textbox 13.2.   Experiences of Size Discrimination

In the spring of 2016 we ran a participatory study on nutrition in a predominantly Latino neighborhood in Philadelphia, Pennsylvania. During our group discussion, the conversation turned to experiences with medical care:

> My husband, he went to the ear doctor. He had . . . a problem with his ear. So he went to the doctor, [and] he said the first thing [the doctor] said [was], "Well, you know, you're overweight." And my husband said, "He's gonna ask me about my weight? What the hell's that got to do with my ear?"

> Nobody likes to be judged, especially when weight is an issue. . . . I get on the scale once and it's 'cause my doctor forces me to. I literally look away.

> The doctors said my child is obese. . . . They should ask him how he feels. He feels bad, and I don't want him to feel bad. He exercises. He walks everywhere, he plays soccer; I don't like when he says, Mama, I don't want to eat nothing. . . . He didn't eat lunch for two weeks because the doctors told him he's obese. Doctors say you have to be this BMI and all you see is the numbers, but it's more than [that]; it's feeling and things like that.

As these quotations reveal, size discrimination, stigma, and cultural assumptions about weight can negatively impact doctor-patient relationships, leading to stressful health-care experiences. When combined with prejudice in other areas of life, these disadvantages can have devastating impacts on physical and mental health.

the blame on personal choices, furthering stigma. Second, an individual approach fails to consider the broader contexts in which personal choices take place. For example, women's studies scholar Tamara Beauboeuf-Lafontant argues that rather than ask about black women's particular eating choices, the question of why many American black women are obese should be reframed as a question about race and gender-based oppression. She asks, "What is it about being black and female in America . . . that is causing an increasing number of [black women] to carry more weight than [they] can handle?" (Weathers 2003 in Beauboeuf-Lafontant 2013, 42). This shift from the individual to the broader society opens the door to new paths of inquiry, and insists that attention to oppression becomes integral to the study of obesity.

In her book *Weighing In*, food scholar Julie Guthman (2011) also moves beyond the individual in analyzing obesity (see chapter 9). Among several key emphases, she focuses on the impact of endocrine-disrupting chemicals (EDCs) like Bisphenol-A (BPA). BPA is found in food wrappers, the lining of canned goods, and store receipts, and can have "epigenetic" effects that alter gene expression and impact metabolism. Importantly, a focus on BPA helps take the blame off the individual and shifts focus to other factors, like poverty, neoliberal capitalism, and the chemical industry (see chapter 9). When we teach about obesity, we often ask our students to create a mental map of everything that might impact obesity rates. The map usually ends up looking something like figure 13.1, illustrating both the complexity of obesity and many potential avenues for intervention. Unfortunately, most prevention strategies continue to emphasize individual behaviors, like caloric intake and physical activity (HSPH 2016), at the expense of this expanded view.

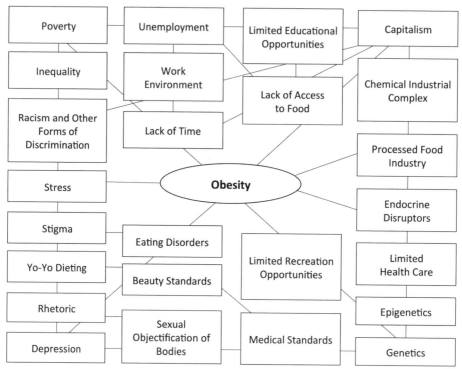

Figure 13.1. Mental map of impacts on obesity
Source: Authors.

Healthy Eating

One of our favorite recipe books is *Hunger's Table*, by Margaret Randall. In it, Randall shares a recipe for grape pie. The end of the recipe has the following instructions:

> But wait.
>
> Listen for the voices of César's people
> in the grape fields of California.
> If you hear them striking
> you must refuse to serve or eat this pie. (Randall 1997, 14)

As we write this, a strawberry boycott is ongoing, protesting the treatment of Driscoll farmworkers. And yet it is rare, in the myriad calls for eating fresh fruits and vegetables, to see strikes and boycotts mentioned in the same breath as "healthy." So, what counts as healthy? Work in critical nutrition reminds us that calls for healthy eating are never purely factual; instead, they are always based upon particular beliefs about what counts as good, and how to measure goodness. Healthy eating is defined differently across both time and place. Although many would argue that healthy eating is quite simple, we contend that it is anything but.

HISTORIES OF NOURISHMENT

One way to put healthy eating in context is to look at the history of nutrition science. In her book *Eating Right in America*, food scholar Charlotte Biltekoff demonstrates that nutrition in the United States has always been an ideology as much as a science. As the science of nutrition progressed, it often did so alongside calls for strong citizenship and nationhood. For example, during World War II, a nutritional booklet aimed at workers and their wives asked, "Are you Helping Uncle Sam? Then: Eat a hearty lunch . . . Drink plenty of milk . . . Learn about food values" (Biltekoff 2013, 72). In this case, eating well meant eating foods that would give workers stamina, and thus help win the war. To eat poorly meant, in contrast, to "help Hitler" (Biltekoff 2013, 71).

Communications scholar Jessica Mudry has looked similarly at the history of the calorie, revealing the relationships between calorie intake and social identity. In the early 1900s, eating well meant eating economically and knowing exactly how many calories different bodies needed, based on occupation, gender, age, and more. As the homemakers of America, women were encouraged to select and prepare foods in a measured manner that would "maximize health and . . . make [one's] home more American" (Mudry 2006, 59). To *not* engage in the science of home economics meant being a poor housewife and a lousy citizen (see chapter 15). The point here is, again, that healthy eating was tied to particular cultural beliefs and social identity—it was never a politically neutral science.

SCIENTIFIC UNCERTAINTY

Today, nutrition science might seem more advanced, but calls for healthy eating remain embedded in contemporary culture and politics. Countless recent studies offer insight into weight loss, longevity, or athletic performance—all predominant Western values. Of course, these studies are rarely reported with the same nuance and complexity in popular texts as they are in academic journals. Moreover, the production of scientific knowledge about nutrition is still heavily influenced by particular cultural beliefs, funding streams, lobbying advocates, and food industries (Nestle 2007). Yet, science scholar Gyorgy Scrinis explains, nutrition science has "generally been positioned as a trusted ally by academics, public health authorities and food activists," mostly managing to "escape critical scrutiny" (Scrinis 2013, 239). When scientific claims help to legitimize particular cultural beliefs as "facts" rather than viewpoints, they are easily accepted. Facts garner attention, and are highly marketable.

Nevertheless, there are critics who dare to question the scientific authority of nutrition. One ongoing area of debate is over the recommendation to eat a low-fat diet (Scrinis 2013). Recent reporting has countered the claim that low-fat is best, and instead suggested that low-fat is neither better for heart health nor for weight loss (O'Connor 2016; Press Association 2016; Agence France-Presse 2016). As Scrinis notes, these counterclaims are not new, but researchers have recently pushed back against the data itself, claiming the evidence supporting low-fat eating simply does not exist (Park 2015). This finding is potentially shattering to what most Westerners believe about healthy eating, and it has been met with backlash. Most broadly, the low-fat debate reveals that what counts as "healthy eating" is neither simple nor resolved, and it is undoubtedly embedded in context.

(Beyond) The Social Determinants of Health

According to the World Health Organization, the social determinants of health are "the conditions in which people are born, grow, live, work and age," which are shaped by "the distribution of money, power and resources" (WHO 2016). These conditions largely determine health disparities, including those associated with nutrition. As the social-determinants-of-health framework has come into acceptance in public health and nutrition scholarship, it has shaped the way that linkages between social/economic status and nutrition are understood. For example, "food desert" work, now promoted by the US Department of Agriculture (USDA), is premised on the notion that food access (economic and geographic) is an important consideration in the promotion of healthy bodies (see chapter 9).

However, critical nutrition scholars suggest that this framework has not done enough to bring matters of power within the purview of nutrition scholarship. In June of 2009, a group of practitioners and scholars published a declaration on critical dietetics in the Dieticians of Canada quarterly, *Practice: Exploring Members' Practice Issues.* In this declaration, the authors note that critical dietetics emerged from "long-awaited conversations regarding gender, race, class, ability, size, [and more]," while striving "to make visible our assumptions, give voice to the unspoken, embrace reflexivity, reveal and explore power relations, encourage public engagement and diverse forms of expression, and acknowledge that there are no value-free positions" (Critical Dietetics 2009, 1–2). The declaration reveals that these topics—power, reflexivity, and difference—are not yet fully engaged within mainstream nutrition scholarship.

REFLEXIVITY AND DIFFERENCE

One of the keys to exploring power, and recognizing power inequity, is to practice **reflexivity**. Reflexivity is, perhaps, the most crucial call in the above declaration. Reflexivity is a practice embedded in place; it means an awareness of how one's place in the world influences what they know and believe. For example, reflexivity tells us that our own definitions of "healthy eating" emerge from the socioeconomic positions, family traditions, cultural landscapes, and ecological terrains that we have called home. When reflexivity becomes a part of nutrition, we are forced to acknowledge that there are no value-free positions, not even within (nutrition) science.

Most nutrition intervention is premised on experts educating others, who are presumed to not know how to eat well. While "good eating" may appear as a value-free constant, rarely are the "facts" of "good eating" themselves questioned. Even more rarely do educators step back to ask: With whom does mainstream nutritional advice *not* resonate, and why? Data from our research projects in several diverse communities have suggested that it is not unusual for mainstream nutrition advice to be considered "white" in origin, meaning that many accepted "healthy eating" practices, like low-fat and vegetarian diets, are associated with white culture (Hayes-Conroy 2014). Meanwhile, the counter message is often that black food, or Latino food, is less healthy (see also chapter 8). These messages are not only upsetting, but they can be devastating to cultural reproduction, social legitimacy, and even self-confidence. Moreover, they advance rather than ameliorate discrepancies in social power.

Reflexivity allows researchers to investigate such differences in knowledge and power honestly, even if it means destabilizing what we have come to know as "true." Our students often ask us, "But if education isn't the solution, what are we to do?" One of our answers has been to look beyond food. If you want to ensure that people have the power to make healthy food decisions, focus on structural problems like job insecurity, housing discrimination, domestic violence, and intersectional oppression. (To learn how this discussion links to eating disorders, see Thompson 1992.)

NEOLIBERAL CAPITALISM

Today, it is not possible to understand how health and nutrition intersect with "the distribution of money, power and resources" (WHO 2016) without examining **neoliberal capitalism**—the predominant economic ideology and practice since the late 1970s, characterized by privatization, deregulation, and free trade. Recently, neoliberal capitalism has been blamed for greatly intensifying economic inequality around the globe (Udland 2016). The "Occupy" movement that emerged out of the 2008 economic crisis and housing market collapse was a challenge to the policies of neoliberal capitalism. Most students reading this chapter will have known no other economic system in their lifetime.

Social theorist Lauren Berlant contends that we should understand nutritional ill health as an effect of neoliberal capitalism. Berlant explains that eating is often a lot like "self-medicating," in that it offers a sense of resilience and (temporary) strength that allows people to cope with the harsh realities of everyday life, and especially with the demands of labor. She points out that much of what we think of as "healthy" actually means "energy to be more productive" within the capitalist system (Berlant 2010, 28). Her outlook on obesity and nutritional ill health is not pretty: "The bodies of US waged workers will be more fatigued, be in more pain, be less capable of ordinary breathing and working, and die earlier than the bodies of higher income workers, who are also getting fatter, but at a slower rate, and with relatively more opportunity to exercise" (Berlant 2010, 33). Importantly, Berlant also notes that African Americans and Latino/as "are especially bearing this bodily burden along with the symbolic negativity long attached to it" (32). In our own research on food activism, we found this burden to be true for many disadvantaged populations (see textbox 13.3). Fatefully, both Berlant and Guthman (2011) also point out that the capitalist system actually benefits from a rise in obesity and dietary disease, since market-based solutions profit from the never-ending cycle of consumption and dieting. This means that market-based solutions to nutritional problems are unlikely to create the kind of systemic change that we need.

Understanding Bodies

Imagine a food that makes you feel warm, calm, or comforted. Is the food something you grew up eating? Do you associate it with particular people or events? Do you seek it out when you are stressed? Many people have foods that they would call "comfort foods." Some stereotypically American comfort foods include things like chicken soup, macaroni and cheese, and ice cream. Whatever our own picks might be, comfort foods are an example of how our physical, material bodies play a role in our daily food lives. Our bodies' emotional states, physical sensations, sensory experiences, and, of course, our "**tastes**," can greatly influence the food experiences we have, and the food choices that we make.

What does it mean to study the material **body**? Biology and kinesiology are two fields that might quickly come to mind. And, indeed, these fields yield great insight into the workings of the human body. But for many who are interested in the production of tastes, or the experience of comfort or disgust (for example), the material body is more than just biological; it is also thoroughly social. A more precise way of saying this is that our bodies become what they are through **biosocial** processes. A food activist (see textbox 13.3) describes such a biosocial process when he discusses how taste develops within the context of social inequality. In his description, these tastes are neither purely biological (involving only taste buds), nor purely social (involving only social relationships), but rather, emerge as the physical body develops in response to a range of specific stimuli in one's daily life. Thus, studying the material body means

---

Textbox 13.3. Coping with Inequality through Food

During a research study in California, we sat down to talk with a Chicano food justice activist. At one point, our conversation turned to how people in his community use food to cope with social inequality:

> [I think] that we are filling voids—emotional, social, psychological voids—and we find that we do get the right chemicals moving when we eat certain junk. . . . It will fulfill feelings that our people are sometimes looking for in these unjust times. . . . Whether it's a sense of sweetness that we might not be feeling; it's easy to fill us up with other sweetness, [like] *pan dulce Mexicano*. . . . You really experience that sweetness and that rush in your blood and your whole chemistry changes, and for a moment you really feel good.

He continues later:

> We are not gravitating towards [junk foods] saying, "[These people are treating me badly], so I am going to go eat this to protect me from them," but there is a part of our intelligence that starts to realize, "Hey, I feel like this when I eat this, and either, I want to feel like that right now, or I might want that [food] in me before something like this." . . . It's our refuge at times . . . a quick, easy way to feel a way that we [desire]. (Hayes-Conroy and Hayes-Conroy 2010)

The sentiments displayed here mirror those of Berlant (2010) and Beauboeuf-Lafontant (2013), who note that this kind of food-based "coping" with the burdens of inequality happens more frequently within poor and nonwhite communities.

paying attention to the ways that social and biological processes commingle, and thus coproduce our lived experiences, including our experiences with food and nutrition.

VISCERAL MATTERS

When discussing matters of the material or "biosocial" body within food and nutrition studies, we often prefer to use the term "**visceral**." As feminist scholar Elspeth Probyn describes, *visceral* literally means " 'of the viscera,' the inner organs" (Probyn 2000, 14), and as she illustrates in her book *Carnal Appetites*, studying visceral or gut reactions can tell us a great deal about our sociocultural world—about what we find appealing, or gross, and why. Moreover, visceral reactions are important considerations in the practice of reflexivity; even researchers need to pay attention to what they find delicious or disgusting, since it is often through these feelings that ethnic and cultural differences become tangible, and that prejudice becomes lived. For example, strong smells and spices might be pleasant and familiar to some, while others might find them unusual and even unbearable (Longhurst et al. 2008).

There are many reasons why such a visceral approach matters to nutrition. For one, as we note above, a visceral approach can help us to practice reflexivity, and thus to remain aware of our own food-based judgments and prejudices. In addition, it can give us critical insight into what motivates people to make particular food decisions—what is important to them, what they struggle with, and what they desire. These insights can help scholars, practitioners, and activists to approach nutrition intervention with both empathy and respect. Beyond these reasons, there is also some evidence that visceral reactions to food might significantly impact metabolism—that feelings like comfort or disgust can influence a body's physical ability to be nourished by a particular food (Hallberg et al. 1977). Although more research is needed on this issue, the potential implications of these findings are game-changing for nutrition intervention, as it would mean that sociocultural differences are *viscerally* connected to nutritional health.

BODY LITERACY

Despite these important reasons to pay attention to the physical, material body, mainstream nutrition often advocates the opposite: tricking the body or otherwise resisting its cravings and desires (Bordo 1993). For example, the popular diet book *Skinny Bitch* demeans women for being weak and lazy if they heed their bodily hunger (Freedman and Barnouin 2005). And most, if not all, typical "comfort" foods are considered to be unhealthy, fattening, or otherwise bad for you. Indeed, rather than acknowledging and examining visceral reactions, we are often compelled to ignore them. We argue that, for many reasons, this strategy is both misguided and damaging to bodily health.

The term *body literacy* has been discussed in a variety of contexts, but most basically it just means paying attention to one's own material body. Jessica Mudry invokes a type of body literacy when she distinguishes between her intellectual understanding of "good eating," learned from formal education, and her embodied knowledge of taste preferences, derived from her own lived experiences (Mudry et al. 2014). Linda Bacon and Lucy Aphramor also advocate body literacy when they encourage "nonjudgmental attentiveness" and "attuned" movement and eating (2014, 82). We should be clear, however, that a call for body literacy does not mean that we believe self-knowledge to be an uncomplicated and straightforward endeavor. As products of numerous, ongoing biosocial processes, the bodies we seek to know are undoubtedly complex and ever-changing. Still, as Lauren Berlant's (2010) work on capitalism urges, it is worth asking why so many of us are persuaded to think of our bodily needs and desires as something to overcome, rather than something to learn from.

Doing Nutrition Differently

We want to end this chapter by discussing the possibility of "doing nutrition differently" (Hayes-Conroy 2013). Both in food activism and professional practice, there is a fair amount of response to the failures of mainstream nutrition. From this response, we see three core principles of critical nutrition developing: 1) radical nonjudgment; 2) happy contradiction; and 3) contextual nourishment. We offer these concepts below as a way of both summarizing our arguments and offering potential solutions.

Radical nonjudgment simply means letting go of the belief that there is one right way to eat well, and instead accepting that bodily nourishment is complex—scientifically, culturally, and socially. Whether investigating the causes of obesity, the meaning of healthy eating, the structural barriers to nourishment, or the workings of the biosocial body, critical nutrition is not about universal answers. While this doesn't mean that we should throw out everything we hold true, it does mean recognizing that our own definitions are incomplete and biased by our own experiences of eating in this world. One of the easiest ways to practice radical nonjudgment is to listen openly to the experiences of others, rather than attempting to "educate" them about nutrition standards. Reflexivity is also part of this process. We have seen radical nonjudgment practiced in many dialogues facilitated by critical dietetics advocates and conference-goers, and also by activists and professionals like Navina Khanna and Hank Herrera, whose food justice work is both critical and responsive (Alkon 2013).

Happy contradiction refers to the understanding that all ideas about food and nutrition are culturally specific, and can therefore sometimes be in contradiction. Importantly, contradiction does not mean that one idea must be proven correct and the other(s) wrong; in fact, such tensions can produce a more complex and nuanced understanding of what it actually takes to nourish a body. The easiest way to promote happy contradiction is by actively seeking out different ideas and perspectives. We see this work happening through the use of qualitative, participatory action research within nutrition intervention. One example is the work of the Food Action Research Centre in Nova Scotia, which encourages storytelling and knowledge sharing when gathering data on food security.

We have emphasized that nourishment always happens in particular contexts; it cannot be separated from place. Therefore, *contextual nourishment* means shifting our focus from the imagined (standardized and placeless) individual to the real, material contexts in which nourishment happens, including the body, community, economic networks, physical terrain, and broader sociocultural landscapes. One of the ways to accomplish this goal is to facilitate collective dialogue about these contexts, so that the specific desires, needs, and obstacles of community members can be heard and heeded. One example of this type of approach comes from nutrition projects aimed at dietary "decolonization," such as the work of Luz Calvo and Catriona R. Esquibel. Calvo and Esquibel have organized a blog and Facebook page (as well as a cookbook; 2015) that contextualize nourishment along historical, ethnic, and political lines, particularly among the US-born Latino/a community.

These are just some of the ways that we can already see critical nutrition practiced in real-world contexts. As an emergent and developing field, our hope is that critical nutrition will continue to grow as people engage with the topics and challenges that the field invites. Below we offer suggested readings and resources for those interested in exploring more. While these works may not refer to "critical nutrition" by name, we believe that they represent ideas and trajectories in line with the work that we have outlined here. As always, we invite further engagement and critique as this exciting field continues to expand in theory and in practice.

Key Terms

biosocial
body
fatness
neoliberal capitalism
nutrition

reflexivity
scale
taste
visceral

Summary

- Critical nutrition challenges mainstream nutrition science and advocates, seeing bodily nourishment instead as something that is embedded in daily life struggles for power, resources, recognition, and meaning.
- Bodily nourishment is complex, and there is not one right way to eat well. Ideas about food and nutrition are culturally specific. Instead of seeking universal answers, critical nutrition encourages reflexivity and listening to the experiences of others to overcome our own biased definitions about eating practices.
- Nourishment cannot be separated from place and it must be contextualized. It is crucial to pay attention to the different settings in which nourishment takes place, from the body to larger social and cultural landscapes.

Additional Resources

SUGGESTED READING

Body Respect: What Conventional Health Books Get Wrong, Leave Out, and Just Plain Fail to Understand about Weight by Linda Bacon and Lucy Aphramor (2014; BenBella Books)

Doing Nutrition Differently: Critical Approaches to Diet and Dietary Intervention edited by Allison and Jessica Hayes-Conroy (2013; Ashgate Press)

Eating Right in America: The Cultural Politics of Food and Health by Charlotte Biltekoff (2013; Duke University Press)

"Nutritional Deficiencies: Dietary Advice and Its Discontents," a special issue of *Gastronomica: The Journal of Critical Food Studies*, Vol. 14: No. 3 (Fall 2014)

Weighing In: Obesity, Food Justice, and the Limits of Capitalism by Julie Guthman (2011; University of California Press)

RECIPE BOOKS

Decolonize Your Diet: Plant-Based Mexican-American Recipes for Health and Healing by Luz Calvo and Catronia Rueda Esquibel (2015; Arsenal Pulp Press)

Hunger's Table: Women, Food and Politics by Margaret Randall (1997; Papier-Mache Press)

BLOGS AND SOCIAL MEDIA

Critical Dietetics: www.criticaldietetics.org
Decolonial Food for Thought: www.decolonialfoodforthought.com
Decolonize Your Diet: decolonizeyourdiet.org
Decolonizing Diet Project: decolonizingdietproject.blogspot.com
Environmental and Food Justice: ejfood.blogspot.com
Sistah Vegan: www.sistahvegan.com

References

Agence France-Presse. 2016. "Replacing Animal Fat in Diet May Not Reduce Heart Risk, Says Study," *Guardian*, April 12. www.theguardian.com/society/2016/apr/13/replacing-animal-fat-in-diet-may-not-reduce-heart-risk-says-study.

Alkon, Alison H. 2013. "Food Politics and Nutrition: A Conversation with Navina Khanna and Hank Herrera." In *Doing Nutrition Differently: Critical Approaches to Diet and Dietary Intervention*, edited by Allison Hayes-Conroy and Jessica Hayes-Conroy, 23–40. London: Routledge.

Bacon, Linda, and Lucy Aphramor. 2014. *Body Respect: What Conventional Health Books Get Wrong, Leave Out, and Just Plain Fail to Understand about Weight*. Dallas: BenBella Books, Inc.

Beauboeuf-Lafontant, Tamara. 2013. "Our Plates Are Full: Black Women and the Weight of Being Strong." In *Doing Nutrition Differently: Critical Approaches to Diet and Dietary*

Intervention, edited by Allison Hayes-Conroy and Jessica Hayes-Conroy, 41–60. London: Routledge.

Berlant, Lauren. 2010. "Risky Business: On Obesity, Eating, and the Ambiguity of Health." In *Against Health: How Health Became the New Morality*, edited by Jonathan M. Metzel and Anna Kirkland, 26–39. New York: New York University Press.

Bernardo, Richie. 2016. "2016's Fattest Cities in America." In WalletHub. https://wallethub .com/edu/fattest-cities-in-america/10532/.

Biltekoff, Charlotte. 2013. *Eating Right in America: The Cultural Politics of Food and Health.* Durham: Duke University Press.

Bordo, Susan. 1993. *Unbearable Weight: Feminism, Western Culture, and the Body.* Berkeley: University of California Press.

Calvo, Luz, and Catronia Rueda Esquibel. 2015. *Decolonize Your Diet: Plant-Based Mexican-American Recipes for Health and Healing.* Vancouver: Arsenal Pulp Press.

Critical Dietetics. 2009. "Declaration" in *Practice: Exploring Members' Practice Issues*, 1–2. Publication of the Dieticians of Canada.

Evans, Bethan, and Rachel Colls. 2009. "Measuring Fatness, Governing Bodies: The Spatialities of the Body Mass Index (BMI) in Anti-Obesity Politics." *Antipode* 41(5): 1051–83.

Freedman, Rory, and Kim Barnouin. 2005. *Skinny Bitch: A No-Nonsense, Tough-Love Guide for Savvy Girls Who Want to Stop Eating Crap and Start Looking Fabulous!* Philadelphia: Running Press.

Guthman, Julie. 2011. *Weighing In: Obesity, Food Justice, and the Limits of Capitalism.* Berkeley: University of California Press.

———. 2014. "Introducing Critical Nutrition: A Special Issue on Dietary Advice and Its Discontents." *Gastronomica: The Journal of Food and Culture* 14(3): 1–4.

Hallberg, Leif, E. Björn-Rasmussen, L. Rossander, and R. Suwanik. 1977. "Iron Absorption from Southeast Asian Diets. II. Role of Various Factors that Might Explain Low Absorption." *American Journal of Clinical Nutrition,* 30(4): 539–48.

Harvard School of Public Health (HSPH). 2016. "Obesity Prevention Strategies." www.hsph .harvard.edu/obesity-prevention-source/obesity-prevention/.

Hayes-Conroy, Allison, and Jessica Hayes-Conroy. 2010. "Visceral Difference: Variations in Feeling (Slow) Food." *Environment and Planning A* 42(12): 2956–71.

———, eds. 2013. *Doing Nutrition Differently: Critical Approaches to Diet and Dietary Intervention.* London: Routledge.

Hayes-Conroy, Jessica. 2014. *Savoring Alternative Food: School Gardens, Healthy Eating and Visceral Difference.* London: Routledge.

Longhurst, Robyn, Elsie Ho, and Lynda Johnston. 2008. "Using 'The Body' as an 'Instrument of Research': Kimch'i and Pavlova." *Area* 40(2): 208–17.

Mudry, Jessica. 2006. "Quantifying an American Eater: Early USDA Food Guidance, and a Language of Numbers." *Food, Culture & Society* 9(1): 49–67.

Mudry, Jessica, Jessica Hayes-Conroy, Nancy Chen, and Aya H. Kimura. 2014."Other Ways of Knowing Food." *Gastronomica: The Journal of Critical Food Studies* 14(3): 27–33.

Nestle, Marion. 2007. *Food Politics: How the Food Industry Influences Nutrition and Health.* Berkeley: University of California.

O'Connor, Anahad. 2016. "A Decades-Old Study, Rediscovered, Challenges Advice on Saturated Fat." *New York Times*, April 13. http://well.blogs.nytimes.com/2016/04/13/a-decades -old-study-rediscovered-challenges-advice-on-saturated-fat.

Park, Alice. 2015. "Where Dietary Fat Guidelines Went Wrong." *Time*, February 9. http://time .com/3702058/dietary-guidelines-fat-wrong/.

Press Association. 2016. "Official Advice on Low-Fat Diet and Cholesterol Is Wrong, Says Health Charity." *Guardian*, May 23. www.theguardian.com/society/2016/may/22/official-advice-to-eat-low-fat-diet-is-wrong-says-health-charity.

Probyn, Elspeth. 2000. *Carnal Appetites: FoodSexIdentities*. Hove, UK: Psychology Press.

Randall, Margaret. 1997. *Hunger's Table: Women, Food, Politics*. New York: Papier-Mache Press.

Scrinis, Gyorgy. 2013. "The Nutricentric Consumer." In *Doing Nutrition Differently: Critical Approaches to Diet and Dietary Intervention*, edited by Allison Hayes-Conroy and Jessica Hayes-Conroy, 239–48. London: Routledge.

Swinburn, Boyd, Garry Egger, and Fezeela Raza. 1999. "Dissecting Obesogenic Environments: The Development and Application of a Framework for Identifying and Prioritizing Environmental Interventions for Obesity." *Preventive Medicine* 29(6): 563–70.

Thompson, Becky Wangsgaard. 1992. "A Way Outa No Way": Eating Problems among African-American, Latina, and White Women." *Gender & Society* 6(4): 546–61.

Udland, Myles. 2016. "IMF: The Last Generation of Economic Policies May Have Been a Complete Failure." *Business Insider.* www.businessinsider.com/imf-neoliberalism-warnings-2016-5.

World Health Organization (WHO). 2016. "What Are the Social Determinants of Health?" www.who.int/social_determinants/sdh_definition/en/.

Is Healthy Food Turning You Off?

Search online or in a magazine for a healthy recipe you could make. Examples include Eating Well: www.eatingwell.com, Cooking Light: www.cookinglight.com, Shape: www .shape.com/healthy-eating/healthy-recipes, Health: www.health.com/food, and Clean Eating: www.cleaneatingmag.com. How do you feel as you look through images and think about preparing something healthy? Do you find it fun, or stressful? Is the thought of following one of those recipes a source of pleasure or anxiety? Why do you feel that way? Why do you think many people are intimidated or turned off by the idea of healthy food as presented in these magazines, while others embrace it? Is there a better way to do nutrition?

As food researchers who spend a lot of time thinking about the complexities and challenges of cooking—about the way that economic inequality, gender norms, daily schedules, taste preferences, and racial and ethnic diversity, among other factors, influence how and what one cooks—we have found recipes at times to be too static and inflexible for the realities of the modern-day cook. Therefore, we offer something different: a non-recipe, a flexible concept, something adaptable to a wide array of food items that you might find in your refrigerators and pantries. The idea is to experiment and learn what works best—for you—as you go. Enjoy!

Concept Cobbler (A Non-Recipe)

1. Begin with three handfuls of a quick-cooking grain/flour. We recommend rolled oats and/or some type of flour (wheat, almond, coconut, spelt, oat, rice, or whatever you have on hand.)
2. Add to the above a few spoonfuls or more of oil/fat; for example, butter, ghee, coconut oil, or palm oil are all fine choices.
3. Include some sweetener to taste; for example, raw sugar, granulated *panela*, or maple syrup, (be aware that liquid versus solid will change the consistency of the recipe!).
4. Add a few dashes of salt, as well—more, if you like salty-sweet tastes.
5. Mix all of the above ingredients and try to achieve a somewhat crumbly texture—but somewhat runny is okay, too. Don't be afraid to experiment.
6. Cut up fruit of your choice, enough to fill a pie pan: Apples, pears, peaches, and berries are traditional in cobblers, but tropical fruits work, too! You can use fresh or frozen fruits.
7. Add a sprinkle of water or juice to the bottom of the pie pan, under the fruits, so they don't dry out. This takes some experimentation, because drier fruits (apples, for example) typically need more liquid than berries or mango. Then cover them with the crumbly/runny flour mixture. This will not look like a perfect pie, but rather a haphazard heap of granola pressed on top of fruit. Don't worry; it'll still taste great!
8. Bake uncovered (or covered, if you prefer moisture over crispness) for about 25 to 35 minutes in a 350-degree oven. The cobbler is done when the juices around the fruits bubble and the topping looks lightly browned. Serve with a scoop of ice cream, or a dash of heavy cream, if desired.

CHAPTER 14

Food, Biopower, and the Child's Body as a Scale of Intervention

Sarah E. Dempsey and Kristina E. Gibson

Textbox 14.1. Learning Objectives

- Understand the body as a scale of political intervention.
- Appreciate the significance of biopolitics to food.
- Recognize how the child's body functions as a contested space.
- Apply the concept of biopolitics to the US National School Lunch Program.

Understanding how the body functions as a political space is essential to developing a nuanced perspective of food and place more generally. This chapter presents a critical perspective on food and bodily politics by introducing the concept of *biopower* and drawing examples from the US National School Lunch Program. Biopower describes power aimed at controlling and maintaining populations' health. The concept directs attention to how society intervenes in the health of its citizens, and the justifications used to authorize control over bodies (see also chapter 13). The concept of biopower allows us to see how the child's body and eating practices have become a contested site of policing, moralizing, and even public shaming. There is a long history of social control of child bodies. As future adult citizens, children are seen as valid and important sites of public health interventions. In Western contexts, socioeconomic disparities in childhood nutrition are increasingly subject to biopolitical modes of surveillance and control exerted at the scale of the body. Drawing on examples from the US school lunch system, our chapter places the so-called obesity epidemic within the bodily politics of children's eating and the social-economic landscape of childhood nutrition.

Children as Targets of Social Control

Children have long been seen as appropriate sites of intervention for reform because of their liminal status as future adult citizens. The State deems it important to have a healthy population of laborers and citizens for its growth and defense. As not-quite citizens, children are seen as ideal targets of social control and reform. Children are taught to manage risk in a wide variety of ways, including hygiene, physical activity, and food consumption. Law regulates some behavior, such as through age limits on smoking or alcohol consumption. Other practices, such as how to eat healthful food, are socially proscribed by family tradition, economic income, and geographic location. As such, children experience a socially and politically mediated form of citizenship (Valentine 2003). **Children's and childhood studies** have challenged the dominant conception that children lack agency and therefore must be controlled, disciplined, and surveilled. Across the centuries, reform movements targeting children illustrate how children's bodies become objects of concern in broader debates about food, eating, and even citizenship and belonging.

In the early twentieth century, amid increasing waves of immigration, new ideas about health and nutrition spurred the rise of social reform efforts aimed at addressing childhood malnutrition (Levine 2008). School feeding programs were only one of many major progressive social reforms addressing the state of children's bodies. Other interventions that began during the same time were physical and health education in schools, YMCAs, Boys and Girls Clubs, Scouting, children's camps (summer camps), and the development of the juvenile justice and foster care systems. Collectively, these institutions emphasized through their programming that the physical, social, and moral development of children would factor into the qualities of future adult citizenship. Citizenship itself is a highly contested category, implying membership, rights, and responsibilities.

In the early twentieth century, poor and immigrant children suffered from malnutrition, bad hygiene, high rates of childhood illness and mortality, and inequalities associated with poverty and discrimination. Child malnutrition manifested through vitamin deficiencies and stunted growth, caused in part by a lack of fats and insufficient calories. Poor nutrition often led to underdeveloped bones and bad vision. High levels of child labor in mills, mines, and factories created numerous injuries and developmental issues that further decreased the ability of children to grow into healthy adults. Such conditions gave rise to a concerted effort by progressive reformers, unions, and ultimately the State to place children in schools where their labor, education, and health could be more closely regulated (see Levenstein 2003; Levine 2008). Education, including instruction focused on food and eating, was seen as an effective tool for cultivating adherence to dominant formulations of national identity at a time of increasing immigration.

As detailed by sociologist Evelyn Nakano Glenn (2002), the category of citizenship has played a key role in creating and maintaining inequality in the United States. When linked to the idea of citizenship and nation, food and eating became both a measure and marker of good citizenship. Reform efforts targeting child malnutrition often dovetailed with efforts to assimilate new immigrant populations. Some social reformers drew upon eugenics and its assumptions about so-called white racial superiority to justify interventions into immigrant populations who were coded as nonwhite. Concerns over which groups might claim and be granted full citizenship rights combined with biases against immigrants in philanthropic and governmental efforts targeting the social and physical development of children. Settlement houses targeted young, immigrant mothers as recipients of cooking and nutrition instruction, while churches and schools increasingly added lunchroom and charity food programs for impoverished children.

In the contemporary context, malnutrition is more likely to stem from limited access to healthy and affordable proteins and vegetables. A globalized industrialized agricultural industry produces an overabundance of unhealthy fats and sugars. For those with the least income in the United States, the cheapest foods contain large amounts of fats, sugars, and salts. Consequently, childhood health and nutrition reform efforts have shifted toward the problem of rising childhood obesity. While early interventions into malnutrition contained ethnocentric biases that characterized immigrant eating behaviors as morally inferior, contemporary debates show a similarity in stigmatizing inner-city schools as sites of unhealthy eating, or linking poor diets with race and poverty. Importantly, the framing of obesity as an individual moral failure playing out at the scale of the body minimizes the broader structural inequalities of the industrial food system causing hunger and food insecurity. The concept of biopower, discussed next, is helpful for further understanding the connections between food, power, and the child's body.

Biopower

Biopower is a theory put forth by French sociologist Michel Foucault addressing how the State intervenes in the social and physical health of its citizens. The concept of *biopower* helps us see how the child's body functions as a highly contested scale of intervention into food and eating practices. In the modern, Western world, children's lives are highly regulated and surveilled by adults (Pike 2008; Valentine 2003). Because of this, children's eating habits and food choices are intertwined with the complex and dynamic power relations of childhood (Massey 1999), and in this case, the school. These "power-geometries" are deeply structured by income, race, and gender, as well as age. Despite connections between childhood obesity and limited access to healthy and affordable food, popular discourses persist in blaming children and families for making unhealthy choices (Gibson and Dempsey 2014). In reality, children's food choices involve complex negotiations with parents and other adults over what, when, and how to eat (Pike 2008, 2010). Typically, adults adjudicate and provide for children's food wants and needs. Because of children's position as future adult citizens and subjects of social control and regulation, they are often the key sites of biopolitical interventions.

Biopower describes forms of power aimed at controlling life itself through the management and administration of populations' health (Foucault 2003; Rose 2009. Biopower is best understood through the synthesis of three interlinked mechanisms (Rabinow and Rose 2006). First, biopower involves truth **discourses** about the "vital" character of living beings. *Truth discourses* involve arguments about what makes people healthy or unhealthy, and even frame the boundaries of health itself. Certain groups, such as doctors or scientists, gain the status of experts. These designated experts create and reinforce truth discourses. They also discredit and silence other perspectives as "non-truth." For example, most people in the United States would agree that milk is an essential component to a healthy diet for children. The US School Lunch Act mandates that milk be available for children at every meal. However, this assumption belies decades of marketing and promotion by both the US Department of Agriculture and the dairy industry to promote the sale of milk. The vitamins and nutrients in milk can be found in a variety of foods that have far less ecological and economic impact than the dairy industry (DuPuis 2002).

Second, **biopolitics** involves *collective interventions*. Examples of collective interventions include public hygiene campaigns and widespread childhood immunization. Notions of the common social good and the health of the nation provide rhetorical justifications for these collective interventions. Reformers draw on these notions to make arguments about how to correctly diagnose and solve problems related to children's eating.

Third, biopower involves modes of *subjectification*, which includes training individuals to **discipline** themselves in the name of individual and collective health (Rasmussen 2011; Welch et al. 2012). *Self-discipline* involves individuals exercising control over their own personal behavior. Taken together, these techniques of biopower fortify the authority of the State to control, maintain, and oversee populations' health in the name of state security and social stability.

The movement from direct forms of power to modes of self-regulation has meant that power and control become untethered from their specific sources of origin (Costea, Crump, and Amiridis 2008). This seemingly hands-off form of state control is often called *governmentality*. In top-down forms of direct control, the exercise of power is much more transparent. So, too, are the targets of **resistance**. However, resistance becomes uncertain within biopower, as populations are taught to regulate their own individual behavior, such as by making "better" eating choices.

Public health interventions like school lunch programs, antismoking campaigns, and age limits on alcohol consumption are important examples of biopower at work. It is important to understand the body as a political space. By pushing the individual to self-regulate their own health, the State hopes to mitigate both social and economic costs associated with weight and health. As discussed, an important element in biopower includes the use of expert knowledge to convince individuals to change their own individual behavior. By labeling obesity an "epidemic," the State invokes the language of medicine, science, and crisis to justify and focus interventions.

However, labeling the fat body as a problem of individual behavior has led to social stigma and shaming of what is a complex intersection of behavioral, social, and economic factors. In Western society, low-income populations have less access to healthy, affordable food and suffer from higher rates of obesity and health-related problems. However, the rhetoric of health and nutrition often involves modes of personal shaming for those who do not self-discipline (see chapters 9 and 13). These types of interventions guide individual behavior in the name of a larger public "good"—having a healthy citizenship. By marshaling the power of professional and expert knowledge surrounding both good and poor health practices, the State is able to put forth mechanisms and practices that affect how people see their own health, and thereby change behaviors. A key element of biopower is the regulation of behavior "from within" as individuals are convinced to control their own actions and thus mitigate risk to a wider society. A particularly compelling example of how biopolitical processes intersect with children and health exists in the public school food system. In the United States, the National School Lunch Program has served as a biopolitical intervention to ensure the development of future citizens able to serve the nation in times of war.

History of School Food Biopolitics

The US school food system has undergone significant transformations since its inception at the beginning of the twentieth century. Its development over time clearly illustrates biopower mechanisms in action. In the school lunch program, *truth discourses* promoted by experts, social reformers, and child advocates justify *collective interventions* into the eating practices of children. Through the school lunch program, children are taught to *self-discipline* by emulating lunchroom eating norms and social practices in the space of the school. A short history of the school food program (see textbox 14.2) illustrates how the justifications for collective interventions into children's eating have differed, along with changing expert discourses of health and nutrition.

When widespread public schooling began in the United States in the late 1800s, children brought food from home or purchased cheap food from street vendors. Many children were undernourished, having little or no food to bring to school. The earliest attempts to create school lunch programs originated from individual philanthropic efforts and local charitable groups (Poppendieck 2010). In the early twentieth century, penny lunches became the solution to what food reformers called the problem of child malnutrition. Societies and associations such as the Red Cross and the New York Association for Improving the Condition of the Poor served three-cent hot lunches in public schools (Levenstein 2003). In addition, a patchwork of female volunteer "mother's helpers" prepared meals in some schools. In smaller school districts, girls themselves would make food for their classmates during class (Caton 1990). School food was not considered the purview of the federal government, and few schools had dedicated lunchrooms. The idea that schools should provide lunch was a new one.

Things changed during the Progressive Era (from 1890 until World War I), when what was dubbed the "New Nutrition" movement created awareness about malnutrition and associated childhood diseases. Evaluations of malnutrition were linked to the current knowledge about food and eating. Children became increasingly linked with notions of the health of the nation as the United States faced what historians refer to as the "Great Malnutrition Scare" in the years 1907 to 1921 (Levenstein 2003). Rising food prices and industrial recessions combined to increase food scarcity, with food riots breaking out in New York, Boston, and Philadelphia in 1917. The creation of nutrition experts and professionals, along with the rise of the New Nutrition movement, spurred new truth discourses about food and eating in a time of social and economic upheaval. New Nutrition began to be taught to children in schools, and these new ideas about "good" and "bad" food fueled the development of early school lunch programs targeting immigrant and poor children. Advocates of the New Nutrition approach attempted to persuade immigrants and the poor and working classes to focus on the quality rather than the quantity of the food they consumed. This approach drew upon expert knowledge, counseling eaters to consume less meat and to eat more

Text Box 14.2. School Lunch Menus over Time

School lunches have changed in the past century. The following are a sample of typical weekly lunch menus from different eras:

1914 SCHOOL LUNCH MENU

In New York City, philanthropic organizations created "3-penny" lunches by 1914 (*Christian Science Monitor*, August 29, 1914):

> *Monday: Rice, tomato soup, and bread*
> *Tuesday: Mashed potatoes, meat gravy, and bread*
> *Wednesday: Pea soup and bread*
> *Thursday: Lentils, rice, and bread*
> *Friday: Potato soup, croutons, and bread*

In general, school lunches were made from basic staples that were filling and could be cooked in large quantities to save on cost. Food leaned heavily on starches and carbohydrates but often lacked sufficient and healthy proteins. In Philadelphia schools, hot cocoa was often available because school lunch officials believed it to be a good source of protein (Caton 1990).

A la carte items already existed by 1914. Students could, for a penny more, buy baked sweet potatoes, rice pudding, a jam sandwich, hot sausage, a banana, figs, oranges, pretzels, and cake, to name but a few.

1950 SCHOOL LUNCH MENU

By the 1950s, school lunches reflected the mechanization of the agriculture industry. A typical school lunch might look like this: canned corn, canned fruit mix, a small carton of milk, and lasagna (made from canned tomatoes and dried pasta).

However, many items would have still been made from scratch, such as meatloaf, casseroles, stews, and breads. A dish such as beef macaroni casserole was a staple of school lunchrooms across the country. A typical recipe for small lunchrooms would read something like this:

> Mix 5 pounds of ground beef with salt and pepper; cook through. Cook 3 pounds of macaroni and drain. Sauté 1 cup of chopped onion and green pepper. Mix meat, pasta, onion/pepper, and a can of diced tomatoes. Sprinkle with cheese and bake for forty minutes at 350 degrees.

Many schools were investing in mechanized cooking equipment and large freezers during this era. The cost of food was increasing, so buying food that was packaged, dried, or frozen in larger quantities was one way to reduce cost (Caton 1990). Rural and low-income urban schools could rarely afford these investments, however.

1971 SCHOOL LUNCH MENU

By the 1970s, the modern school lunch of processed, high-fat, high-sugar, low-nutrient foods had evolved. A newspaper in Pennsylvania published the school lunch option for a typical October day as follows (*Daily Courier*, Connellsville, Pennsylvania, October 8, 1971):

Pizza   Applesauce
Tossed salad with Italian dressing   Brownies
Green beans with butter   Milk

By the late 1960s, private food management companies were allowed to operate school food programs. Schools were encouraged to centralize and privatize their food service operations in order to save on costs (Levine 2008). By 1970, the USDA mandated that school lunch programs had to be made available to all children as part of a broader poverty program (Caton 1990). It was during this time that school food began to acquire a "fast-food," more-consumer-driven look. Students were opting out of school lunches, and cafeterias struggled to balance underfunded budgets.

2016 SCHOOL LUNCH MENU

A typical week of lunches in an upstate New York elementary school in 2016 looks like this:

Monday: Whole-grain chicken nuggets, seasoned brown rice, green beans, mixed fruit, fresh fruit, milk
Tuesday: Hot dog on a whole wheat bun, baked beans, baked french fries, peaches, fresh fruit, milk
Wednesday: Hot meatball sub, spinach and white beans, green beans, applesauce, fresh fruit, milk
Thursday: Ham and cheese on a whole-grain bagel, broccoli florets, cucumber coins, pears, fresh fruit, milk
Friday: Whole-grain cheese pizza, garden salad, veggie sticks, applesauce, fresh fruit, milk

While there is an effort to add in whole grains and provide more fresh fruit, modern school lunch menus still fail to strike a balance between healthy proteins, fats, and carbohydrates. School lunch programs struggle to create appetizing, healthy, affordable, and culturally appropriate menus that children will eat.

carbohydrates. As Hayes-Conroy and Hayes-Conroy discuss in chapter 13, nutritional advice (and understandings of health more generally) reflect power relations, with "mainstream nutrition typically ignoring issues of diversity, context, and hierarchy."

Private clinics arose to teach New Nutrition principles, such as the New England Kitchen. The New England Kitchen was a commercial operation providing "nutritionally sound" meals for low prices to schoolchildren. Although many of the private-enterprise attempts to change poor, immigrant, and working-class eating behaviors were unsuccessful, schoolchildren came to be seen as an ideal population to target for a *collective intervention* into the broader nation's eating habits (Levenstein 2003). Early advocates for a public school food system drew inspiration from the New England Kitchen model that was guided by New Nutrition truth discourses.

During World War I, the problem of widespread malnutrition gained increased governmental focus. The Great Depression of the 1930s brought massive unemployment and intensified food scarcity. During the 1930s, child malnutrition was rampant, with some schools reporting as high as 75 percent of their children suffering from poor nutrition (Levine 2008). Two important changes at the federal level would shape the school food program for decades to come. First, Congress included a provision in the 1936 amendments to the Agricultural Adjustment Act, addressing the need to distribute surplus agricultural goods. The provision opened the door to pinning excess farm surpluses to feeding impoverished schoolchildren. As school food became tied to federal farm subsidies, the US Department of Agriculture (USDA) became the administrative mechanism for collective interventions into children's eating practices. Second, 1935 also saw the creation of the Works Progress Administration (WPA), which provided relief for unemployed workers (Poppendieck 2010). By 1935, the WPA employed several thousands of women in school lunch programs, while the National Youth Administration employed 16,000 youth in lunchrooms (Levine 2008; Poppendieck 2010) (see figure 14.1). The WPA created school lunch jobs because other jobs—such as construction— were deemed inappropriate for women, and it was assumed that women already possessed cooking skills (see figure 14.2). In 1945, the federal government became involved, founding the National

Figure 14.1. Works Progress Administration poster advertising school lunch program

Source: Library of Congress Collection. Available at: www .clker.com/clipart-a-good-lunch-one-hot-dish-meat -vegetables-sandwich-fruit-milk-wpa-school-lunch-.html.

School Lunch (NSL) Program. During both world wars, a significant number of draftees were considered ineligible for service due to long-term malnutrition (Levine 2008). Thus, the State deemed it vital to its future security to start school lunch programs—a classic biopolitical intervention.

From the beginning, school lunch programs provided a subsidy for the agricultural sector alongside functioning as a nutrition program for children. After the Great Depression and World War II, the US government took a renewed interest in stabilizing and regulating the food commodities market. Significant investments

Figure 14.2. Randolph Henry High School cafeteria, Keysville, Virginia
A typical fifteen-cent lunch at the time included candied yams, macaroni and cheese, fruit salad, deviled eggs, dessert, and milk. Many students brought produce from their family's farm instead of money to pay for lunch. Thousands of women were hired by the WPA to prepare nutritious lunches with available food items.
Source: Philipp Bonn (1943) for the Federal Security Administration. Library of Congress. Public domain. Available at: www.loc.gov/pictures/item/owi2001032202/PP/.

and interventions were made in the dairy, beef, and corn markets. The food provided to school lunch programs was unpredictable, contingent on which foods needed to have their surpluses bought or prices stabilized (Poppendieck 2010). For instance, one school might receive only ground beef, while another too much canned corn or tomatoes. Food supplies came in large amounts designed to last for significant lengths of time. Especially in poorer schools and schools with no kitchens, school lunch workers were forced by necessity to use low-cost, pre-prepared, and heavily processed foods (Levine 2008).

In 1946, the National School Lunch Act formalized a federal-level feeding program for schoolchildren. The program continued to couple children's eating practices with broader concerns about the health and economic security of the nation. The School Lunch Act is a key example of how collective interventions operate within biopolitics. Upon signing, President Truman observed, "no nation is any healthier than its children or more prosperous than its farmers" (quoted in Poppendieck 2010, 52). The National School Lunch Act of 1946 declared:

> as a measure of national security, to safeguard the health and well-being of the nation's children and to encourage the domestic consumption of nutritious agricultural commodities and other food, by assisting the States, through grants-in-aid and other means, in providing an adequate supply of food and other facilities for the establishment, maintenance, operation and expansion of nonprofit school lunch programs. (quoted in Poppendieck 2010, 51)

Despite its federal aspirations, the early school lunch program failed to reach many low-income children. By 1950, the program only reached about one-third of school-aged children. Because schools had to match or exceed federal funds to produce free meals for poor children, school lunch programs were nearly bankrupted from their beginning. Schools receiving federal school lunch funds and food subsidies were required to hire professional lunchroom staff rather than depend on volunteer efforts. Many schools couldn't afford to join the original federal school lunch program at all. By 1968, 6.5 million low-income children still did not have access to free lunches (see especially Levine 2008, 128; Poppendieck 2010), with middle-class children more likely to be able to take advantage of the program.

By the early 1970s, school lunches transitioned from agricultural subsidies to a poverty program; however, the regulation and supply of food remained under the control of the USDA. In many schools, cafeteria lunch became stigmatized as a program for poor children. Ironically, the poorest schools were the least able to offer free meals and accept federal aid. The number of children eligible for free meals increased while paying youth declined. The quality of school lunches suffered. Food was often high in sugar and fats, all by-products of the subsidized agricultural sector.

By the mid-1970s, weight issues in youth gained increasing recognition as a widespread and politicized social problem. School lunches became an object of criticism for promoting poor eating habits. This continued into the end of the twentieth century, as schools resorted to vending machines, fast food, and high-calorie, high-fat, a la carte snack options such as chips as a way to fund free lunch programs and make up for gaps in government funding (Levine 2008). Poorer schools had a larger percentage of children eligible for free lunch, far fewer paying students, and therefore more incentive to privatize food service. Modern-day school-lunch staples of pizza, chicken nuggets, and french fries reflect both agricultural subsidies and the privatization of school food systems (see textbox 10.3 in chapter 10).

By the beginning of the twenty-first century, many school lunchrooms looked more like fast-food joints, especially in low-income communities of color where inviting private vendors into public schools was seen as the only way to fund free lunches (see textbox 14.2 above). Federal policies of fiscal devaluation, such as failing to fully fund school food programs, reproduce health inequalities. Recurring budget gaps in low-income school districts create uneven geographies of high-calorie, low-nutrient food for poor and minority students (Levine 2008). As discussed in chapter 8, food environments, and in this case, the National School Lunch Program, are actively produced by political, economic, social, and cultural factors that reflect class and racial inequalities.

From One Kind of Malnutrition to Another: The Discovery of the "Obesity Crisis"

In earlier eras, malnutrition typically resulted from food scarcity and vitamin and mineral deficiencies. However, the rise of the industrial agriculture era has ushered in a different type of malnutrition. Changes in the industrial food system, along with shifts in work and lifestyle practices, has brought a new kind of health crisis reflected in rising levels of heart disease, diabetes, obesity-related illnesses, and rates of childhood obesity. The global industrial food system is characterized by massive quantities of highly processed, high-calorie, high-fat cheap food, such as that served by fast-food restaurants.

The meanings associated with fat have likewise changed. In earlier times, obesity served as a marker of wealth. However, as cultural critics have noted, fatness is increasingly stigmatized as obesity has become associated with cheap food (Guthman 2011). Obesity is now a marker of poverty in the United States. However, the economic underpinning of obesity has been obscured by social stigmatization of individual fat people. As Kathleen Lebesco (2003) argues, fatness and obesity are increasingly seen as fundamentally violating core American values such as moral character, hard work, and self-discipline (see also chapters 9 and 13). Here, fatness signals not a lack of healthy food tied to economic status, but rather only a lack of individual self-control, and thereby a failure of citizenship.

The National School Lunch Program as a site of biopolitics increasingly became subject to collective scrutiny in the broader cultural "war on obesity." The discovery of the "obesity crisis" in the late 1980s led to increased concern over the child's body size, and the space of the school as a failed *biopolitical* intervention. Changes in price supports and farm technologies created a massive glut in government inventory of cheese, butter, dairy products, and beef. The increasing surplus of these products came as schools were struggling under federal budget cuts (Levine 2008; Poppendieck 2010). It is not surprising, then, that cheeseburgers and other foods high in saturated fat became standard items featured both on school lunch trays and outside of school as well.

The content of school food lunches quickly came to be seen as symptomatic of broader eating trends negatively affecting Americans' health. During the late 1980s, the consumer advocacy watchdog organization Public Voice for Food and Health Policy played a key role in publicizing a series of high-profile reports and annual school lunch report cards critical of the high-fat, -calorie, and -sodium content of school food. Other groups, such as the Center for Science in the Public Interest increasingly called for restrictions on fat, sugar, and sodium in school meals. An early-1990s federal study did little to assuage fears that school food was suspect, finding that on average, 38 percent of the calories in school lunches came from fats, with 15 percent from saturated fats (Poppendieck 2010). The Healthy Meals for Healthy Americans Act of 1994 in part created new dietary guidelines for schools. The extent to which these and more-contemporary attempts to increase the quality and nutrition of school food have been successful is the subject of debate. But as was the case in the 1990s, school lunch continues to be caught between the contradictory aims of social welfare, maintaining favorable agricultural commodity subsidies, and balancing constricting state and federal budgets (Levine 2008). At the same time, the school lunch program functions as a major anti-hunger social welfare program, feeding millions of children who would otherwise go hungry. Attacks focused on the health qualities of school lunch occur within a broader context of attempts to dismantle social programs in the name of budget austerity. When debates over school food center narrowly on healthiness, fixating on the making of better individual choices, the broader social and economic

Textbox 14.3. The Black Panther Party's Radical Anti-Hunger Feeding Programs

Contemporary school feeding programs originated in part from black revolutionary anti-hunger and antipoverty social praxis, such as illustrated by the Black Panther Party's Free Breakfast for Children Program. The Black Panther Party (BPP) created its visionary Free Breakfast Program in 1968. It would go on to become both the impetus and model for the federally funded school breakfast program in the United States authorized by Congress in 1975 (Heynen 2009). The Free Breakfast Program reflected the BPP's critique of the state-sponsored violence of hunger, poverty, and police brutality against black communities. It flowed out of the BPP's focus on radical self-determination of black communities through grassroots organizing, community-based survival programs, and mutual aid programs.

In addition to their Free Breakfast Program, the BPP created more than sixty Serve the People programs, including, for example, community health clinics, community food pantries, and teen programs (Nelson 2011). At its peak, the BPP and its volunteers were serving free breakfasts to approximately twenty thousand children in at least nineteen cities across forty-five chapters in the United States, with funding for the program coming from local stores, churches, grocery stores, and personal donations. As the BPP gained in popularity and local influence, it quickly became the target of surveillance, infiltration, and violent suppression by the FBI's COINTELPRO program in an attempt to impede the efforts of black radicals. Ultimately, as Heynen (2009) argues, the BPP was able to reshape anti-hunger politics in the short term through their Free Breakfast Program, as well as in the longer term by "essentially forcing the United States to do a better job of feeding hungry children because it saw the revolutionary power of radical anti-hunger and antipoverty politics" (p. 419). The legacy of the BPP's Free Breakfast Program, with its focus on ensuring the most basic bodily need of food, can be seen in contemporary school breakfast feeding programs that provide critical emergency food aid for the millions of schoolchildren across the United States who are living in poverty.

context of hunger and food insecurity are ignored. The struggles of fighting hunger, which have animated many grassroots and radical groups in recent history, become depoliticized (see textbox 14.3).

School Lunch as a Biopolitical Intervention in Children's Obesity

In broader debates about health and obesity, the child's body functions as a potent symbol of futurity and therefore a powerful scale of intervention. From its origins in concerns about citizenship and belonging, national defense, and a productive labor force, school lunch has remained a consistent site of biopolitics in action. The 2010 publication, "Too Fat to Fight: Retired Military Leaders Want Junk Food Out of American Schools," compiled by retired senior military leaders who joined forces in a group called Mission: Readiness, makes the links between school food, the child's body, and the health of the nation's military explicit. In the report, Gen. John M. Shalikashvili, former chairman of the Joint Chiefs of Staff, states:

Every month hundreds of otherwise excellent candidates for military service are turned away by recruiters because of weight problems. Since 1995, the proportion of recruits who failed their physical exams because they were overweight has risen by nearly 70 percent. We need to reverse this trend, and an excellent place to start is by improving the quality of food served in our schools. (Mission: Readiness 2010, 2)

Obesity is also increasingly seen as a national threat because of rising health-care costs to taxpayers.

From First Lady Michelle Obama's national campaign to fight child obesity, to the rise of the **school food reform** movement, the child's body has become subject to increased surveillance around food and eating. The school food reform movement has emerged at a critical time in which concerns over children's health and obesity have achieved the status of a moral panic (Guthman 2011; Wright and Harwood 2009). Child obesity thus has become a contested site of national anxieties about military readiness, labor productivity, and growing health costs. The school food reform movement encompasses loosely connected efforts aimed at creating change within the public school food system. Participants include parents' groups, school administrators and cafeteria workers, public health and nutrition advocates, farmers and agriculturalists, and professional chefs.

Reform discourses and practices converge around three connected claims about the inauthenticity of school food, the need for fresh, local, high-quality foods, and the benefits of involving schoolchildren in food education and production. As discussed in chapter 16, chefs and food celebrities like Jamie Oliver and Alice Waters have become involved in this movement and increased its public visibility (see also Gibson and Dempsey 2013). Within the contemporary school food reform movement, truth discourses spark collective interventions justified by references to state and nation. In a classic form of biopolitics, as the problem of the child's body becomes understood in terms of obesity, and as obesity has shifted to serve as a cultural marker of moral failure, children are increasingly encouraged to self-discipline. Individualized exercise programs, popular advice centered on making good choices in the space of the school, and the rise of digital dieting apps combine to urge children to take individual control over their bodies and their eating practices in the name of the broader social good. In the case of young children, this sort of self-discipline also affects parents, especially mothers, who experience great stress in feeding their children healthy diets (see chapter 15). In short, the discourses and interventions surrounding the so-called obesity epidemic have coalesced around children, but also impact mothers and minorities, who are seen as morally inferior and in need of being surveilled and controlled.

Key Terms

biopolitics

children's and childhood studies

discipline

discourse

resistance

school food reform

Summary

- When it comes to food politics, the body is also a political space.
- The concept of biopower is helpful to describe society's attempts to intervene in the health of its citizens and control their bodies.
- In Western societies, children's bodies have been the target of different forms of biopower and surveillance through public health interventions targeting either malnutrition or obesity.
- From a geographic perspective, a criticism of the emphasis on the obese or undernourished body as an individual or family moral failure is the lack of attention to the broader geographical structural inequalities caused by the industrial food system.
- The history of the National School Lunch Program in the United States is a good example to illustrate how food assistance and public health programs can be used as biopolitical interventions.

Additional Resources

The following websites provide useful information regarding school lunches in the United States and reform efforts:

Edible Schoolyard Project (http://edibleschoolyard.org/)
Parents, Educators, & Advocates Connection for Healthy School Food (http://peachsf .org/)
School Nutrition Association (http://schoolnutrition.org/)
US Department of Agriculture Food and Nutrition Service (www.fns.usda.gov/)

References

Caton, Jay. 1990. *The History of the American School Food Service Association: A Pinch of Love.* Alexandria, VA: American School Food Service Association.

Costea, Bogdan, Norman Crump, and Kostas Amiridis. 2008. "Managerialism, the Therapeutic Habitus and the Self in Contemporary Organizing." *Human Relations* 61: 661–85.

DuPuis, E. Melanie. 2002. *Nature's Perfect Food: How Milk Became America's Drink.* New York: NYU Press.

Foucault, Michel. 2003. *Society Must Be Defended: Lectures at the College de France, 1975–1976,* trans. D. MacRose. New York: Picador.

———. 2008. *Birth of Biopolitics: Lectures at the College de France 1975–1976,* trans. G. Burchell. London: Palgrave Macmillan.

Gibson, Kristina E., and Sarah E. Dempsey, S.E. 2013. "Make Good Choices, Kid: Biopolitics of Children's Bodies and School Lunch Reform in Jamie Oliver's Food Revolution." *Children's Geographies* 13(1): 44–58.

Glenn, E. Nakano. 2002. *Unequal Freedom: How Race and Gender Shaped American Citizenship and Labor.* Harvard University Press, Cambridge.

Guthman, Julie. 2011. *Weighing In: Obesity, Food Justice, and the Limits of Capitalism*. Berkeley: University of California Press.

Heynen, Nik. 2009. "Bending the Bars of Empire from Every Ghetto for Survival: The Black Panther Party's Radical Antihunger Politics of Social Reproduction and Scale." *Annals of the Association of American Geographers* 99: 406–22.

Lebesco, Kathleen A. 2003. *Revolting Bodies? The Struggle to Redefine Fat Identity*. Boston: University of Massachusetts Press.

Levenstein, Harvey A. 2003. *Revolution at the Table: The Transformation of the American Diet*. Berkeley: University of California Press.

Levine, Susan. 2008. *School Lunch Politics: The Surprising History of America's Favorite Welfare Program*. Princeton, NJ: Princeton University Press.

Massey, Doreen. 1999. *Power-Geometries and the Politics of Space-Time*. Heidelberg: University of Heidelberg.

Mission: Readiness. 2010. *Too Fat to Fight: Retired Military Leaders Want Junk Food Out of American Schools*. A Report by Mission: Readiness: Military Leaders for Kids. Washington, DC.

Nelson, Alondra. 2011. *Body and Soul: The Black Panther Party and the Fight Against Medical Discrimination*. Minneapolis: University of Minnesota Press.

Pike, Jo. 2008. "Foucault, Space and Primary School Dining Rooms." *Children's Geographies* 6(4): 413–22.

———. 2010. " 'I Don't Have to Listen to You! You're Just a Dinner Lady!': Power and Resistance at Lunchtimes in Primary Schools." *Children's Geographies* 8(3): 275–87.

Poppendieck, Janet. 2010. *Free for All: Fixing School Food in America*. Berkeley: University of California Press.

Rabinow, Paul, and Nikolas Rose. 2006. "Biopower Today." *BioSocieties* 1(2): 195–217.

Rasmussen, C. 2011. *The Autonomous Animal: Self-Governance and the Modern Subject*. Minneapolis, MN: University of Minnesota Press.

Rose, Nikolas. 1999. *Powers of Freedom: Reframing Political Thought*. Cambridge, UK: Cambridge University Press.

———. 2009 *The Politics of Life Itself: Biomedicine, Power, and Subjectivity in the Twenty-first Century*. Princeton, NJ: Princeton University Press.

Valentine, Gill. 2003. "Boundary Crossing: Transitions from Childhood to Adulthood." *Children's Geographies* 1(1): 37–52.

Welch, R., S. McMahon, and J. Wright. 2012. "The Medicalization of Food Pedagogies in Primary Schools and Popular Culture: A Case for Awakening Subjugated Knowledges." *Discourse: Studies in the Cultural Politics of Education* iFirst article: 1–16.

Wright, Jan, and Valerie Harwood. 2009. *Biopolitics and the "Obesity Epidemic": Governing Bodies*. New York: Routledge.

Is Food a Way to Control People?

What kind of rules apply to food consumption? Are there restrictions on what, where, how, and how much you eat? Who enforces these "rules": parents, teachers, doctors, governments, friends, media, or yourself? Do you ever feel that others use food in an attempt to control you or define who you are?

Many societal norms influence the way we think about food. This is especially true of children's food, making it a target of intervention to promote health, assimilation, discipline, and various moral values. Fears about children's nutrition are not new, and often intersect with classed and raced notions of healthy behavior. In the early 1900s, at the height of immigration from Eastern Europe, many in the New York school system were concerned about the health of immigrant children. Social reformists and advocates of the school lunch programs were particularly concerned about pickles, which immigrant children purchased for a penny from pushcart vendors in Jewish neighborhoods like the Lower East Side (Ziegelman 2011). These children, who could not go home for a proper lunch because their mothers were working, were left on their own to eat. Many feared that the popularity of pickles reflected a form of addiction to stimulants that would eventually turn to alcoholism. Homogenizing school food was part of an effort to Americanize and discipline immigrant children. Today, pickles are once again popular and ironically praised for the nutritional content, including vitamins, minerals, antioxidants, and probiotics, which promote digestive health.

Dill Pickles

Ingredients

2 pounds small pickling cucumbers (or Persian), cut lengthwise into four spears
3½ cups water
1¼ cups white vinegar
1 tablespoon sugar
1 tablespoon sea salt
2 cloves garlic, peeled and smashed
1 bunch fresh dill

Preparation

Put water, vinegar, sugar, and salt in a saucepan on medium heat and bring to a boil. Remove from heat. Place the cucumber spears, fresh dill, and garlic in a large glass container. Pour cooled vinegar mixture over and seal container with lid. Refrigerate for at least two days, and up to three weeks.

Reference

Ziegelman, Jane. 2011. "Immigrant Identities, Preserved in Vinegar?" *New York Times.* Opinion Pages. August 3. www.nytimes.com/2011/08/04/opinion/immigrant-identities-preserved-in-vinegar.html.

CHAPTER 15

Cooking at Home

GENDER, CLASS, RACE, AND SOCIAL REPRODUCTION

Pascale Joassart-Marcelli and Enrico Marcelli

Textbox 15.1. Learning Objectives

- Consider food-preparation activities as both performances influenced by gender roles and social expectations, as well as everyday practices that reshape these social norms of domesticity.
- Conceptualize the home and the kitchen as places where social relations are embedded and negotiated.
- Explore the tensions between cooking for leisure and cooking as a chore, and examine how race, class, and gender interact to shape these experiences.
- Describe the economic, social, and cultural challenges of feeding families.

In an effort to curb obesity and save the planet, we are being increasingly encouraged to cook at home. Home-cooked meals have become a panacea to many contemporary societal ills (Sifton 2011). In addition to making us healthier, home-cooked meals—especially those prepared with locally grown, organic, and whole foods—arguably minimize environmental impacts and nurture social and emotional cohesion. According to Pollan (2013), "taking back control of cooking may be the single most important step anyone can take to help make the American food system healthier and more sustainable. Reclaiming cooking as an act of enjoyment and self-reliance, learning to perform the magic of these everyday transformations, opens the door to a more nourishing life." These encouragements to "get back in the kitchen" occasionally turn to fear and reprimand, when we blame the disappearance of family meals for children's poor school performances, teenage pregnancy, low self-esteem, obesity, depression, eating disorders, drug abuse, and other problems (see chapter 14).

In that context, public policy and social advocacy are increasingly focused on promoting cooking at home and encouraging families to eat together. For instance, efforts are being made to increase access to fresh foods, including fruits and vegetables, and promote their consumption—especially among low-income populations. Several states have also recently added restrictions to the types of foods that can be bought under the Supplemental Nutrition Assistance Program (SNAP, or "Food Stamps"). These highly controversial—some would argue punitive—limitations are meant to increase the preparation and consumption of wholesome and healthy meals at home. Many public health programs focus on teaching people how to cook—"going back to the basics," which have presumably been forgotten. Organizations such as the Family Dinner Project (2016), housed at Harvard University, provide the public with tips on scheduling dinner, preparing simple "one-pot" meals, and playing "dinner games" that stimulate meaningful conversation, in order to fully realize the alleged benefits of family meals.

These calls for home cooking, however, rarely take into account the numerous barriers to feeding families, which are deeply entangled with meanings of home. While food is often romanticized for bringing families together and creating homes, the work involved in doing so is typically devalued or ignored. Indeed, in many homes, food preparation and mealtimes are sources of tension, which often revolve around gender and parent-child relations, and involve family expectations.

In this chapter, we explore the work involved in cooking and the obstacles families face in putting food on the table. We pay particular attention to the role of gender, class, and race in structuring social reproduction activities associated with food. Our argument builds on a geographic understanding of home as a place that is socially produced and embodies broader social, economic, and political dynamics.

We begin with a theoretical discussion of the home, emphasizing its social construction. We then examine three interrelated issues that underlie home-making, focusing specifically on cooking for families. First, we consider the gender division of labor that influences expectations about and negotiations of men and women's roles in the kitchen. Second, we explore how class helps to shape cooking practices, including the tension between cooking as a chore and cooking for leisure, and its relationship to employment and earnings outside the home. Finally, we turn to race and investigate how it intersects with class and gender in influencing the relationship between home and food.

"Home is Where the Heart/Hearth Is"

There is no doubt that food is intimately related to understandings of **home** and domestic life. For many of us, cooking for others, sitting together and sharing a meal, or simply smelling the aroma of food conjures feelings of belonging, comfort, and safety often associated with home. This is echoed in Yi-Fu Tuan's definition of home as "the place that offers security, familiarity and nurture" (2004, 164), suggesting that home is more than a physical place or a building, but is comprised of social and emotional relations that give it meaning and "stretch beyond it" (Massey 1992, 14). It is everyday activities, such as preparing food and sharing meals, which structure domestic life and create a sense of home. Sandra Dudley's (2011) research demonstrates this point when she shows the contribution of bodily actions, like cooking and eating, in bringing about a sense of being "at home" among "homeless" Burmese refugees involuntarily displaced to camps along the Thai border.

Recently, geographers and other scholars in the humanities and social sciences have begun "to open the door and look at what's happening inside" (Domosh 1998), focusing on the contradictions and tensions that are often part of the home. Blunt and Varley (2004, 3) describe home "as a space of belonging and alienation, intimacy and violence, desire and fear, [. . .] invested with meanings, emotions, experiences and relationships that lie at the heart of human life." Likewise, Rapport and Dawson (1998, 4) suggest that "home brings together memory and longing, the ideational, the affective and the physical, the spatial and the temporal, the local and the global, the positively evaluated and the negatively." The everyday practices that constitute home life, such as cooking or eating together, reflect similar tensions to the extent that they can be experienced as pleasurable activities, remembrance of things past, as well as drudgery and sources of anxieties or domestic conflict.

Another important and related theme in this literature is that of **embeddedness**: the idea that the home is not a private space, isolated from the public sphere, but instead is embedded in a set of social, political, economic, and cultural relations constructed at different scales, ranging from the body to the global. The literature on **social reproduction** emphasizes this reciprocal relationship between what takes place at home and what goes on in other spaces, including neighborhood, work, community, and nation. According to Laslett and Brenner (1989, 382), "social reproduction [refers to] the activities, attitudes, behaviors and emotions, responsibilities and relationships directly involved in the maintenance of life on a daily basis and intergenerationally." That includes among other things the provision of food, clothing, and shelter, and the care of children, the sick, and the elderly. Much of this work, which is essential for the economy and the state to continue functioning relatively smoothly, is performed within the home. When David Harvey (1989, 19) writes that "unlike other commodities, [. . .] labor power has to go home every night," he underscores the political-economic importance of the home as the place where the labor force can rest, eat, and gain the strength needed to go back to work the next day.

The social significance of the home as a site of nourishment and restoration, as well as its capacity to facilitate these tasks, are influenced by economic conditions, public policies, ideologies about family, intimacy, and privacy, and social relations of class, gender, and race. For example, Geraldine Pratt's (2012) research on Filipino immigrant child-care workers in Vancouver, Canada, highlights the complexity and sociopolitical embeddedness of home-making. Affluent and primarily white households often purchase services on the market or hire domestic help to perform tasks needed to maintain their home and family (e.g., child care, cooking, cleaning, medical care). Many depend on immigrants and people of color, who are themselves often unable to care for their own home because they are too poor, too tired, or too far away to do so. The Filipino immigrant women in Pratt's study have families on the other side of the globe with whom they share remittances, but not the everyday activities that define the meaning of home. This transnational regime of social reproduction has been facilitated by the dismantling of the welfare state ushered by neoliberal policies and an increase in international migration linked to globalization and economic restructuring in the Global South. Moreover, it is affected by gendered and raced assumptions about care work and personal responsibility. In short, the home is a porous space, permeable to political, economic, social, and cultural forces unfolding across diverse scales.

A few scholars have adopted a similar perspective, which draws attention to the relationality of place, to analyze the kitchen—a place often described as the symbolic heart or the hub of the home (see Floyd 2004). Historians, for example, have studied how the kitchen space evolved over time in ways that reflect changing norms of **domesticity**. Specifically, the Industrial Revolution brought about changes in employment and family structures, technological innovation such as piped water, the gas stove, and the refrigerator, and a bourgeois ideology of privacy that turned the modern kitchen into a closed space and managed almost exclusively by women—either servants or middle-class housewives (Johnson 2006; Meah 2016).

In the Global South, especially in rural and peri-urban areas, kitchens have remained physically and socially open, often being located outdoors and used by extended family, kin, and neighbors. This phenomenon is well documented in Maria Christie's ethnographic research (2008) in Central Mexico of what she calls "kitchenspaces"—a combination of indoor and outdoor food-preparation spaces that are meaningful sites of gendered social and cultural reproduction. Despite their significance, however, open and collective kitchens are slowly disappearing as a result of urbanization and changing lifestyles. Today, in the Global North, the kitchen is no longer a "dirty place" relegated to the back of the dwelling, as it was during most of the nineteenth and the early twentieth century. Instead, open floor plans have removed physical and cultural walls and placed the kitchen at the center of the home and family life. Could this physical transformation reflect changes in values and practices underlying the way we cook?

"A Woman's Place Is in the Kitchen"

We began this chapter with concerns about "the end of cooking"—the idea that people no longer cook for themselves and their families, but instead consume fast food, takeout, and highly processed ready-made meals. While there are many potential reasons for this putative trend, most explanations invariably turn to women and raise questions about **gender**. Many blame second-wave feminists for encouraging women in the 1960s to reject domestic life, get out of the home, and compete with men in the workplace (see textbox 15.2 for a brief discussion of the three waves of **feminism** as it relates to cooking). For example, in *The Feminine Mystique*, Betty Friedan (1963) argues that women were "trapped" in their suburban homes, struggling "as [they] made the beds, shopped for groceries, matched slipcover material, ate peanut-butter sandwiches with [their] children, chauffeured Cub Scouts and Brownies, lay beside [their] husband at night—[. . .] afraid to ask even [themselves] the silent question—'Is that all?' " (15). The suburban home, with its modern kitchen and amenities, was a site of isolation, discontent, and oppression. Rejecting domestic life was seen as a path toward greater gender equity. Then and today, women continue to be blamed for having reneged on their duties as wives and mothers as they join(ed) the labor force, regardless of whether they did or do so for economic necessity or individual fulfillment.

For others, women have been duped by new technologies and products that have contributed to the deskilling of their labor. As McFeely (2001, 97) argues, "the productive housewife [. . .] was replaced in the 1950s by a woman pushing a supermarket cart,

Textbox 15.2. Cooking and the Three Waves of Feminism

Feminism is very broad and often misunderstood. It represents philosophies, ideologies, and social movements that, in the United States, began in the early 1800s and centered on understanding and promoting both slaves' and women's rights (Zinn 2015). However, scholars have described its chronological evolution in terms of three "waves." The first wave of feminism (in the late nineteenth and early twentieth century) focused on women's political rights, including the right to vote and own property. Little attention was given to what was perceived as the private lives of women, and few challenged feminine ideas of domesticity, including women's responsibility for social reproduction. The relatively privileged socioeconomic status of suffragettes (who were mostly white, middle-class, and educated) and their ability to rely on servants and domestic workers might explain why their advocacy centered on the public realm and ignored gender inequalities at home.

The second wave of feminism (beginning in the early 1960s) argued for reproductive rights and equality at home and in the workplace. In the eyes of Betty Friedan and most feminists writing at that time, cooking was viewed as oppressive; it kept women at home, curtailed their opportunities to compete in the labor market, and reproduced their dependence on men. The women's liberation movement demanded that cooking be rejected, or at least shared equally within households. It was premised on that idea that "the personal is political"—in other words, what is going on at home or at work is part of a larger system of patriarchy that must be challenged.

In the 1990s, third-wave feminism emphasized the diversity of women's experiences and identities, paying attention to the interaction between gender and other social categories (like class, race, and sexuality), and challenging universal definitions of femininity. Judith Butler (2011) was influential in reframing feminist theory by recognizing that essentialist, rigid, and dualist identities were oppressive to all who were socially constructed as different and therefore expected to behave in certain ways. This perspective promoted the notion that women could take pleasure in cooking as a form of agency and self-expression that did not automatically reproduce oppressive gender identities. A similar and somewhat controversial argument was made regarding sex work, which until then had been unequivocally associated with the exploitation of women, and now was being reenvisioned as a potentially empowering activity. In other words, women could wear makeup, be fashionable, cook, and still be feminists—an idea reflected in "girlie" or "babe" feminism (Munford 2007). Some criticize third-wave feminism for taking for granted the freedoms achieved through the first and second waves and rejecting a movement in favor of individual self-expression and lifestyle choices, suggesting a sort of "postfeminism."

bending over a freezer, or peering into a refrigerator." In addition to devaluing the labor involved in food preparation, technology turned these activities into a form of consumption associated with the commercialization of kitchen culture (Hollows 2016). Advertising, and the media in general, including celebrity chefs (see chapter 16), have played a key role in turning the home kitchen into a space full of new appliances (e.g., microwaves, blenders, food processors, espresso makers) and increasingly processed food products (see textbox 15.3). Although these new technologies are assumed to be "labor saving," studies show that having a pasta maker, a juicer, or a food processor raises expectations for homemade linguini, juice, and cupcakes (Cowan 1983).

Textbox 15.3. Producing Gender in the Modern Kitchen

Beginning in the 1940s, advertising for modern kitchen appliances such as refrigerators and dishwashers almost exclusively targeted women. When men were shown or mentioned in ads, it was usually as white-collar breadwinners, earning income to support their families and "give" their stay-at-home wives modern appliances that would presumably make their lives easier. In most ads, men were shown sitting down or relaxing, while women were busy cooking or serving food. The ads in figure 15.1 reflect numerous gender norms about women: the importance of physical attractiveness, the duty to cook for their husbands, the enjoyment they get out of cooking and serving others, as well as their submissive, yet manipulative and emotional nature. These representations contribute to what Inness (2001) calls a "kitchen culture"—the taken-for-granted idea that women belong in the kitchen.

Figure 15.1. Representation of women in food-related advertising

Source: (a) Pieces of the Past via Flickr. Available at: www.flickr.com/photos/100392997@N08/13939807803.

(continued)

Box 15.3. *Continued*

Figure 15.1. Representation of women in food-related advertising (*continued*)

Sources: (b) Imgur. Available at: http://imgur.com/EI25bVp.
(c) Sally Edelstein via Flickr. Available at: www.flickr.com/photos/retro-arama/6220646733/.

Figure 15.1. Representation of women in food-related advertising (*continued*)

Source: (d) Methodshop via Flickr. Available at: www.flickr.com/photos/methodshop/7599550944.

In many accounts, there is a tendency to romanticize the traditional role of the housewife. For instance, in her 2008 book documenting her family's yearlong efforts to grow and eat their own food, Barbara Kingsolver writes:

> When we traded homemaking for careers, we were implicitly promised economic independence and worldly influence. But a devil of a bargain it has turned out to be in terms of daily life. We gave up the aroma of warm bread rising, the measured pace of nurturing routines, the creative task of molding our families' tastes and zest for life; we received in exchange the minivan and the Lunchable. (2008, p. 126)

In other words, women have been fooled into giving up cooking—a fulfilling and creative task that allows them to show their love for family and friends. According to Sherrie Inness (2001), this ideology of cooking as a duty, a natural skill, and a universal source of pleasure for women is so pervasive, that in most households women continue to perform the majority of food preparation regardless of their employment status.

The American Time Use Survey (Bureau of Labor Statistics 2015) is the best source of data to analyze how people in the United States spend time on various activities such working and sleeping, as well as shopping and preparing food. In

2015, the average American spent thirty-six minutes per day on food preparation and cleanup. While that is slightly more than the half-hour we spent a decade ago, it is less than half the amount of time used in the 1960s. A closer look at the data also reveals significant variation between men and women. While 70 percent of women participate in domestic food preparation and cleanup, only 43 percent of men do. In addition, among those who cook, women spend a daily average of seventy-one minutes doing so, compared to forty-nine minutes for men. The gender gap is significantly wider among heterosexual married couples with children under eighteen, reflecting the importance of gender roles associated with being a mother and a wife. In fact, married mothers who are employed full-time work more than three times longer preparing food than married fathers with the same employment status. Unemployed married fathers spend less time cooking than mothers who are employed full-time—a fact that Marjorie DeVault (2008) attributes to the desire by men who do not meet the "breadwinner" social expectation to reassert their masculinity by not engaging in domestic chores viewed as feminine.

Hochschild (1989) used the phrase "second shift" to describe the socially reproductive labor that many employed women do when they come home and make dinner, do laundry, clean bathrooms, and help with homework. Her research was among the first to show the detrimental effect of the second shift on women's opportunities for employment and advancement in the labor market. This creates a vicious cycle by keeping women's wages lower than men's, and in turn justifying women's disproportionate responsibility for domestic labor.

In 1965, women spent seventy-five minutes per day on food preparation—over 1,000 percent more than men's daily average of six minutes. Although women today still spend more time on daily food preparation than men, the gender gap has been consistently narrowing. If trends continue at the same rate, men and women will reach "equality" in about 2050, when the same proportion of men and women would be involved in food preparation and both would spend similar amounts of time doing so. The increase in men's cooking has often been described in the media in gendered terms, with men being applauded for doing something seen as unusual and almost heroic (Swarns 2014). Cooking is typically redefined as a masculine activity that "is not for sissies," by appealing to the "hunter and provider" instinct and emphasizing a "manly-man approach to cooking" that involves "bacon, burgers and brews" (Premack 2016). Celebrity chefs and **food media** have played an important role in (re)producing these gendered approaches to cooking (see chapter 16). In that context, for the men who have picked up cooking in the past decade, preparing food tends to be a form of leisure—a project that they perform on their own terms, usually on weekends or for special occasions. This contrasts with the experience of women as the "default cook," primarily responsible for everyday cooking—a chore that includes rushed weeknight dinners when everybody is hungry and the fridge seems invariably empty.

In spite of these changes in men's participation, cooking remains highly gendered and a significant source of tension in many households—including same-sex households where divisions of labor also prevail (see Oerton 1997). As a social and symbolic object, food can express care and affection, but also control and power (Punch, McIntosh, and Emond 2010). Therefore, family meals may be experienced as a site of domestic conflict as well as a celebration of family life. In her ethnographic research on married couples' household routines, Marjorie DeVault (2008) relates these tensions to gendered expectations that connect cooking with being a wife and a mother. While some men may expect to be served home-cooked meals, occasionally resulting in domestic abuse or violence, in most households these expectations are rarely voiced directly. Instead, women themselves have taken for granted men's entitlement to "good food," especially after a long day of hard work. This manifests itself in women's deference to men—a process in which women experience feelings of guilt and inadequacy when they are unable to meet socially produced but unspoken expectations. Current fears about childhood obesity, food safety, and environmental degradation have exacerbated the pressures and anxieties that many women experience about feeding their families. Meanwhile, the labor involved in cooking continues to be ignored or devalued by the enduring perception bolstered by advertising that it is "quick, fun, and easy."

Class and race are likely to shape the negotiation of masculinities and femininities that take place in the kitchen and at the dinner table. We turn to these topics in the next sections.

Class

Engagement with cooking is most visible among "**foodies**" who publicize their activities on Instagram, Facebook, and an ever-growing number of blogs dedicated to this topic. *Foodie* is a term that was recently added to the dictionary to describe "a person who enjoys and cares about food very much," as well as "a person having an avid interest in the latest food fads" (Merriam-Webster 2016). More importantly, foodies tend to be people who have the financial, temporal, and other resources that allow them to "play with food" and use it as a means of distinction (see chapter 8). For example, cooking a whole pig "from snout to tail" is not just a fun endeavor, but a way to signify ethical values and cultural superiority. Needless to say, most people do not embark on this sort of cooking project for a variety of reasons, including limitations linked to income, access to food stores, availability of ingredients, space for storing and cooking food, lack of appliances and utensils, as well as confidence and familiarity with cooking techniques. For the majority, especially for low- and middle-class families, food preparation is a form of labor (i.e., production) rather than a leisure activity (i.e., consumption).

Two factors are particularly relevant to **class**: income and time. In the past, middle-class families would trade off time and income, forgoing a second income in order to allow one adult (typically the wife/mother) to stay home and perform domestic tasks such as cooking. Low-income women often did not have that option and instead needed to seek employment outside the home. Many worked as cooks and maids in affluent households that bought time by hiring outside help. Since the 1970s, growing economic inequality has eroded the middle class, creating a bifurcated distribution of income, with many adults at the bottom feeling the pinch of economic anxiety, and those in top income groups enjoying more security, more flexibility, and the ability to buy time. Studies also indicate that people today are finding it increasingly difficult to juggle work with other aspects of life, and feel more time-pressured than in the past—suggesting a potential cause for the decline in cooking and change in eating patterns (Jabs and Devine 2006). Coping strategies, however, differ significantly according to income.

The assumption that low-income people should have more time to cook at home because their marginal cost of labor is lower rests on obsolete assumptions regarding the labor market and the welfare state. In a context of increased job insecurity, tighter restrictions on social assistance, and the absence of family-friendly policies, the poor often have to prioritize employment over social reproduction. Working multiple jobs, overtime, and inconsistent shifts leaves little time or energy for food work. For instance, among single parents, 75 percent of mothers and 85 percent of fathers work. Although households across all income groups have reduced food preparation at home, cut family meals, and increased the consumption of convenience or ready-made foods, low-income households have adopted these strategies at a slightly faster pace (Smith et al. 2013). While higher-income households eat out in restaurants or purchase take-out food more frequently, low-income families turn to convenience foods that require little preparation and are more affordable.

This points to the role of the food system in shaping eating and cooking practices. It is now well documented that the global industrial food system favors the production of energy-dense and highly processed foods over fresh and perishable whole foods like fruits and vegetables. In the United States in particular, agricultural policy has long subsidized large-scale production of wheat and corn, which generates a large surplus that makes its way into a multitude of products (like soda, breakfast cereals, and frozen meals) and keeps the cost of those foods relatively low (Nestle 2002; Pollan 2006). It is therefore not surprising that people in poverty or with limited income turn to convenience foods to feed themselves and their families.

This divergence in food preparation and eating practices between low- and high-income households has been accompanied by a cultural **food politics** that produces new subjectivities and reinforces class distinctions. As discussed in several chapters in this volume (especially chapters 6, 13, and 14), food is increasingly infused with morality; ethical consumers control their food intake, cook at home from scratch, shop at the farmers' market, buy organic and unprocessed food, and patronize restaurants that serve authentic food. Those who don't partake in these activities are perceived as uneducated, lazy, careless, and immoral. For instance, mothers feeding their babies store-bought jarred food may be viewed as irresponsible; those who care about their children—and the Earth—would prepare their own baby food with home-grown or locally purchased organic produce. Foodies' obsession not only with cooking, but also with growing, pickling, canning, and curing food, has shaped the dialogue around food preparation. On the one hand, it has reconfigured feminist thought about cooking by acknowledging that women (and men) can find pleasure in the kitchen without feeling oppressed or abiding to a singular and fixed idea of the housewife (De Solier 2013). On the other hand, foodies have increased the pressure that many women experience in managing their everyday life. The "supermoms" who are able to meet these new expectations contribute to the mantra that "you can do it all"—an ideal often reflected in representations of French women (see textbox 15.4). Others either experience guilt, prejudice, or other negative feelings that render cooking unpleasant, or resist these social pressures by rejecting it altogether.

Textbox 15.4. The Sophisticated French Home Cook and the Supermom

When it comes to food, Americans and much of the Western world tend to put the French on a pedestal—admiring their seemingly effortless, yet sophisticated, approach to shopping, cooking, and eating. This admiration goes well beyond taste and technique; it focuses on an often imaginary easygoing lifestyle. For a large number of popular writers, the French seem to do it right: taking the time to cook at home and eat long dinners together is keeping traditions alive, farmers and artisans in business, waistlines trim, children well-mannered, and families intact. Indeed, cooking advice based on observations of French women is often conflated with guidance on marriage, sex, and/or parenting (see, for example, Druckerman's *Bringing Up Bébé: One American Mother Discovers the Wisdom of French Parenting* [2014]). Much of this is owed to French women's superior attitude toward cooking. For instance, Giard (1998), in her classic ethnographic research, shows that the majority of French women view cooking as an "agreeable obligation"—a responsibility they embrace because it provides them with pleasure, self-discovery, and creative expression of identity.

In her popular book *In a French Kitchen,* American writer Loomis exemplifies this perspective by asking "How does the French cook do it?" (2015, 1). To her rhetorical question "Why does the French cook always look so good?" she answers: "Sophie is my favorite example. She gets home from a long day at the office, drops off her briefcase, goes into the kitchen. In an hour, dinner is almost ready; she has the appetizers on the table and her husband, Jean, has poured the wine. She is still wearing heels, her hair looks great, and before she takes a sip she puts on lipstick. It's a simple habit with Sophie, and most of the [French] women I know [. . .] they just show up looking great and stay that way all day" (p. 16). Numerous gendered and classed assumptions are implicit in both her question and the answer she provides.

What Loomis (and other authors who embrace similarly romanticized perspectives on the French home cook) fails to mention is the importance of the State in supporting social reproduction. In *Perfect Madness: Motherhood in an Age of Anxiety*, Judith Warner (2006) contrasts the experiences of mothers in France and the United States. She argues that in France the State plays a key role in supporting families (via subsidized parental leaves, child care, school lunches, etc.), relieving mothers of their traditional gender roles as caretakers and allowing them to engage in cooking (and other aspects of social reproduction) as a form of leisure. In contrast, women in the United States, who enjoy unprecedented freedoms, experience intense stress and social pressure to do it all and behave like "supermoms" without much State assistance or supportive social culture.

The ideal of the French home cook has captivated Americans since Julia Child's *Mastering the Art of French Cooking* (1961). In the past five decades, many have followed her steps in learning the French ways with food, as exemplified in Julie Powell's blog and the film it inspired, *Julie and Julia*. Julie's decision to replicate the 524 recipes of Julia Child's aforementioned book within a year reflects a privileged class position (in spite of her limited budget and small kitchen in her Queens apartment). Her passion for cooking aligns with the imagined lifestyle and individual ethos of foodies who "know" and "choose" "good food." While her quest embodies certain ideas of femininity (i.e., women as caretakers), like Child before her, she rejects the traditional model of the housewife by envisioning cooking as an antidote to the drudgery of the everyday (Hollows 2016). It is worth noting that this attitude is enabled by her class position.

Race

There are two dominant narratives surrounding **race** and cooking, both of which intersect with class and gender. Of course, these also relate to ethnicity, nativity, and immigration status, which critical race theorists view as related to race to the extent that they reinforce processes of racialization by which immigrants, visible minorities, and brown bodies are constructed as different. The first narrative pertains to cooking as an exploitative form of labor—a characteristic linked to the fact that it is often performed by racialized minorities, including immigrants who may be white but are viewed as "ethnic others." The second emphasizes the importance of everyday practices, like cooking, in sustaining individual and collective **identities** among marginalized groups. In these different perspectives, the kitchen is the site where race relations and identities are produced.

In the United States, paid food-preparation jobs from fast-food workers to dishwashers, line cooks, meat packers, and factory food processors are almost entirely filled by people of color and immigrants—similar to farming (see chapter 5). In the home, where labor is typically unpaid, things may be different. Nevertheless, when households hire outside help for food-related activities, they often rely on the same demographic groups: women of color, immigrant women, and poor women who have engaged in paid domestic work for decades (Duffy 2007). Similarly, in other parts of the world, affluent households often hire cooks with racial identities different from their own. For example, in Singapore, domestic cooks are often Chinese, Thai, or Malaysian. In the Arab Gulf states, they come primarily from India, Indonesia, Sri Lanka, and the Philippines. In France, many are from francophone North African countries and Eastern Europe. And in Latin America, most are of indigenous origins. Recent research by the International Labor Organization (2013) reports that globally, 83 percent of domestic workers are women. One in thirteen employed women is a domestic worker, with the ratio increasing up to one in four in Latin America and the Caribbean, and almost one in three in the Middle East. In some countries, girls as young as five years old perform domestic tasks, like food preparation, in someone else's home.

Cooks have a liminal position in the households where they work; they are both insiders and outsiders. Because of the caring and intimate nature of cooking for others, cooks are emotionally connected to their employers' families. Even when described as cherished "family members," cooks are often invisible or asked to be so, eating leftovers alone in the kitchen while family members sit together in the dining room. The spatial isolation of the servants' kitchen, usually in the back of the house, reinforces the distinction between the cook and her employer. This ambivalence regarding the cook's position within the physical and emotional space of the home is often reflected in traditional representations of the female cook. The character of Aunt Jemima, or the black mammy in general, best illustrates this vision of a loving and caring person whose identity is fully defined by her job and constricted by the kitchen where she works (see figure 15.2). These narratives appease the fears of white employers by portraying black mammies as completely committed to serving their white families, naturally caring, always smiling, full of wisdom about food and life, yet seemingly free of any domestic responsibilities outside of the home where she works and devoid of

Figure 15.2. Race in the kitchen

The "help"—as black cooks were often called in the US South—is an enduring image that illustrates the role of race in systematically devaluing domestic labor and producing a sort of fetish used to sell all sorts of food-related products. In this particular ad, the "good old Down South eating like we have on the old plantation" is praised. Aunt Jemima's portrayal as a simple, uneducated, cheerful, and loving woman is racist and dehumanizing.

Source: *Woman's Day*, October 1, 1940. Available at: http://gogd.tjs-labs.com/show-picture?id=1188047251.

aspirations and desires (Tipton-Martin 2014). Deck (2001) argues that popular depictions of the black mammy, in films, advertising, television sitcoms, and novels, create a type of fetish—an idealized (and racialized) image of the domestic cook that hides oppression and exploitation.

Despite the exploitation and hardship associated with cooking for others, scholars envision the kitchen as a space of **resistance** where servants and slaves exercise power and creativity. For example, Davis (1999) argues that, in the oppressive space of the plantation kitchen, African-American women established Southern cookery and challenged their perceived cultural inferiority, reclaimed their humanity through rituals of hospitality in the face of hatred, and engaged in self-definition by resisting essentialist images of the mammy. For Davis, this "kitchen legacy"—the ability of black women to transcend oppressive locations—can serve as a model of resistance in other spaces of oppression.

Stories of marginalized women's cooking in their own homes usually present visions of escape, relief, and resistance. Writing about her mother and other black women in the US South, Wade-Gayles (2005) states:

> I am certain that gender definitions or responsibilities placed them in the
> kitchen rather than men, but I believe most of them converted what might
> have been a demand into a desire, a responsibility into a joy, a task into a
> talent. (96–97)
>
> Like other women in her community, she saw the kitchen as hers, a
> place she breathed into existence, a place in which she experienced balance,
> achievement, recognition and influence. Her language, like that of her
> peers, said as much: "Don't step on *my* kitchen floor. It's not dry." Or "I
> need some new curtains for *my* kitchen windows." (99)

Throughout her work, bell hooks also writes extensively about the importance of a
"homeplace" for black women. Drawing attention to the intersectionality of race, class,
and gender, she argues that black women, who experience racist oppression outside the
home, attach different meanings to their home and kitchen than white women do. The
"homeplace" is a space for resistance, "renewal, self-recovery, heal[ing] and becom[ing]
whole" (2015, 49). Recalling childhood memories, she writes: "Houses belonged to
women, were their special domain, not as property, but as places where all that truly
mattered in life took place—the warmth and comfort of shelter, the feeding of our
bodies, the nurturing of our souls" (2015, 41).

Narratives of resistance in the kitchen transpire in popular films such as *Like Water
for Chocolate* (1992), *Babette's Feast* (1987), *Fried Green Tomatoes* (1991), and *Woman
on Top* (2003), where lead female characters find refuge in their kitchens and escape
various forms of oppression by reclaiming cooking as a form of creative expression.
These stories illustrate the ambivalence of women's role in the kitchen, describing
cooking as both liberating and exploitative, and acknowledging women's agency amid
severe constraints. For many feminists, however, there is a danger in narratives that
reproduce nostalgic notions of cooking and essentialist ideas about family, home, and
race. For instance, Latino families are often portrayed in research and popular media
as both family- and food-centered. Working in the kitchen is seen as a way to bring
generations of women together. Similarly, family meals are represented as social and
cultural glue. This has the effect of raising expectations about women's cooking beyond
feeding their families to include sustaining familial and social networks and reproducing cultural heritage. The ideology that a women's love for family and culture is expressed through food is obvious in Mexican-American actor and activist Eva Longoria's
cookbook, aptly titled *Eva's Kitchen: Cooking with Love for Family and Friends* (2011).
Inspired by her mother's ability to have a career, take care of six children, and have
dinner ready for her husband every night at six p.m., she writes:

> I cannot count the number of times that I've found myself in a Gucci dress
> and heels—with full hair and makeup, about to run out to an event—pull-
> ing a roasted chicken out of the oven in order to make sure my family is fed
> before leaving the house to face a hundred photographers on a red carpet (9).
>
> Ultimately, there are few places I'd rather be than my kitchen. I am rarely
> alone there: my kitchen is the go-to place for family and friends. It is a place
> to which I benevolently [. . .] single-handedly run. (Unless, of course, we
> are making enchiladas, which go much faster with many hands—most often
> my sisters', aunts' and mom's). (11)

The positive role of food in keeping memories alive for immigrant and diasporic communities has been the focus of numerous fictional and nonfictional works. Few authors, however, question the burden this imposes on women, who are mostly responsible for preparing and transmitting "traditional" and "ethnic" recipes. For many, the desire to re-create a fondly remembered home through cooking practices conflicts with the new meanings of gender, family, and food that emerge in the processes of migrating and settling in new places. Given the precarious economic situations of immigrants and refugees, it is equally challenged by a lack of resources. For instance, Mexican immigrant women often struggle in feeding their families for a variety of interrelated reasons (see textbox 15.5).

Textbox 15.5. Home Cooking among Immigrants: Stress and Changing Food Practices

Most immigrants come from communities where women are primarily responsible for food preparation, with cooking and eating done in the home. As a result, immigrant women often experience cooking and eating at home as a way of staying connected with their place of origin in a very visceral way (Longhurst, Johnston, and Ho 2009). Yet, mobility tends to destabilize and put into question traditional norms and behaviors, including those linked to gender and domestic responsibilities. In addition, the economic vulnerability of many immigrants, especially those from the Global South, means that they often struggle to find time and resources for everyday activities like shopping for food, cooking, and sharing meals.

Evidence from two surveys—the 2007 Boston Metropolitan Immigrant Health and Legal Status Survey (BM-IHLSS) and the 2012 Los Angeles County Immigrant Health and Legal Status Survey (LAC-MIHLSS), for example, suggests that the longer Brazilian, Dominican, and Mexican immigrants reside in the United States, the fewer fruits and vegetables from home-cooked meals their diets include, and the more they rely on convenience and processed foods. For instance, the percentage of adult Brazilian immigrants who consumed USDA-recommended fruit and vegetable intake (FVI) levels of two servings of fruit and three servings of vegetables daily upon arrival (32 percent) is estimated to have fallen to that of the US adult population (11 percent) over a period of about two decades (Marcelli and Serra 2012; Marcelli 2014).

This trend provides a potential explanation for the so-called Latino health paradox—the assertion that the health of Latin-American immigrants worsens with acculturation. While some are quick to blame women (and the fact that they spend less time cooking after years in the United States than they did in their country of origin, or just after migrating), it is important to note that this shift is linked to changes in employment, increased demands on time, and the availability of relatively affordable convenience foods. In fact, many women who migrated from Brazil, the Dominican Republic, and Mexico report experiencing stress in several domains of life, including marriage, family, work, and home. Although there is insufficient space to report this here, some of our work finds that stress at home is positively correlated to stress at work, as well as to the time spent preparing meals. However, it is negatively correlated to the sharing of domestic tasks with one's spouse or partner. Not surprisingly, women's satisfaction with home life increases with a more equal domestic division of labor.

Conclusion

Suggesting that we need to reclaim cooking as a pleasurable and self-fulfilling activity ignores the complexity of factors that shape the multiple meanings of this seemingly mundane and essential activity. In this chapter, we have shown how gender, class, and race influence the experience of cooking at home. By focusing on the kitchen and the home as discursive and material places of social reproduction, we have shown that cooking is embedded in social, political, economic, and cultural relations. Food preparation is not just a matter of having the time to plan a meal and cook it, having the right ingredients and the necessary skills, but it also involves emotional labor—even when reinvented as a form of leisure. What, how, and for whom we cook reflects, reveals, and/or fashions who we are. While cooking can be drudgery, routine, or oppression, it can also be love, care, self-expression, and creativity. The boundaries between these different meanings are shifting and at times overlapping. Encouraging people to cook at home more regularly requires that we consider and challenge these boundaries through a radical reimagining of social reproduction and the home.

Key Terms

class   food politics
domesticity   home
embeddedness   identity
feminism   race
foodie   resistance
food media   social reproduction
gender

Summary

- Food preparation is a central component of social reproduction and is deeply ingrained in socially constructed and gendered understandings of home and domesticity.
- Today, women continue to be primarily responsible for food preparation. While some enjoy cooking as a form of leisure and self-expression, many view it as a chore. These different experiences of food preparation are shaped by the intersection of gender, class, and race.
- As a place, the kitchen is embedded in social processes unfolding at larger scales. Although it is often described as a place of isolation and oppression, it can be reclaimed as a place of resistance.

Additional Resources

A geographic perspective on the home (and social reproduction in general) is provided by Domosh (1998), Blunt and Varley (2004), Blunt and Dowling (2006), and contributors to a 1997 special issue of *Women's Studies International Forum* on "Concepts of Home."

Classic studies of gender in food preparation include Inness (2001), DeVault (2008), McFeely (2001).

For a portrait of family meals in the United States, see the *New York Times Magazine*, Food Issue (2011): www.nytimes.com/interactive/2011/10/02/magazine/02 -families.html#16.

Several fictional films provide a window through which the relationships of gender, race, and class to cooking can be explored. They include *Babette's Feast, Like Water for Chocolate*, and *Fried Green Tomatoes*.

References

Blunt, Alison, and Robyn Dowling. 2006: *Home (Key Ideas in Geography)*. Abingdon, UK: Routledge.

Blunt, Alison, and Ann Varley. 2004. "Geographies of Home: Introduction." *Cultural Geographies* 11: 3–6.

Bureau of Labor Statistics. 2015. *American Time Use Survey*. Washington, DC: US Department of Labor. www.bls.gov/tus/home.htm.

Butler, Judith. 2011. *Gender Trouble: Feminism and the Subversion of Identity*. New York: Routledge.

Child, Julia. 1961. *Mastering the Art of French Cooking*. With Louisette Bertholle and Simone Beck. New York: Knopf.

Christie, Maria E. 2008. *Kitchenspace: Women, Fiestas, and Everyday Life in Central Mexico*. Austin: University of Texas Press.

Cowan, Ruth S. 1983. *More Work for Mother: The Ironies of Household Technology from the Open Hearth to the Microwave*. New York: Basic Books.

Davis, Olga I. 1999. "In the Kitchen: Transforming the Academy through Safe Spaces of Resistance." *Western Journal of Communication* 63(3): 364–81.

Deck, Alice A. 2001. " 'Now Then—Who Said Biscuits?' The Black Woman Cook as Fetish in American Advertising, 1905–1953." In *Kitchen Culture in America: Popular Representations of Food, Gender, and Race*, edited by Sherrie Inness, 69–94. Philadelphia: University of Pennsylvania Press.

De Solier, Isabelle. 2013. *Food and the Self: Consumption, Production and Material Culture*. London: Bloomsbury.

DeVault, Marjorie. 2008. "Conflict and Deference." In *Food and Culture: A Reader*, 2nd ed., edited by Carole Counihan and Penny Van Esterik. New York: Routledge.

Domosh, Mona. 1998. "Geography and Gender: Home, Again?" *Progress in Human Geography* 22: 276–82.

Druckerman, Pamela. 2014. *Bringing Up Bébé: One American Mother Discovers the Wisdom of French Parenting*. New York: Penguin.

Dudley, Sandra. 2011. "Feeling at Home: Producing and Consuming Things in Karenni Refugee Camps on the Thai-Burma Border." *Population, Space and Place* 17(6): 742–55.

Duffy, Mignon. 2007. "Doing the Dirty Work: Gender, Race, and Reproductive Labor in Historical Perspective." *Gender & Society* 21(3): 313–36.

Family Dinner Project. 2016. http://thefamilydinnerproject.org/fun/dinner-games/.

Floyd, Janet. 2004. "Coming Out of the Kitchen: Texts, Contexts and Debates." *Cultural Geographies* 11(1): 61–73.

Friedan, Betty. 1963. *The Feminine Mystique*. New York: Dell Publishing.

Giard, Luce. 1998. "Doing-Cooking." In *The Practice of Everyday Life. Volume 2: Living and Cooking*, edited by Michel De Certeau, Luce Giard, and Pierre Mayol, translated by Timothy J. Tomasik, 149–248. Minneapolis: University of Minnesota Press.

Harvey, David. 1989. *The Urban Experience*. Oxford: Blackwell.

Hochschild, Arlie R. 1989. *The Second Shift: Working Parents and the Revolution at Home*. New York: Avon Books.

Hollows, Joanne. 2016. "The Feminist and the Cook: Julia Child, Betty Friedan and Domestic Femininity." In *Gender and Consumption: Domestic Cultures and the Commercialization of Everyday Life*, edited by Emma Casey and Lydia Martens, 33–48. New York: Routledge.

hooks, bell. 2015. *Yearning: Race, Gender and Cultural Politics*. New York: Routledge.

Inness, Sherrie A., ed. 2001. *Kitchen Culture in America: Popular Representations of Food, Gender, and Race*. Philadelphia: University of Pennsylvania Press.

International Labor Organization. 2013. *Domestic Workers Across the World: Global and Regional Statistics and the Extent of Legal Protection*. Geneva: International Labor Office.

Jabs, Jennifer, and Carol M. Devine. 2006. "Time Scarcity and Food Choices: An Overview." *Appetite* 47(2): 196–204.

Johnson, Louise C. 2006. "Browsing the Modern Kitchen: A Feast of Gender, Place and Culture (Part 1)." *Gender, Place & Culture* 13: 123–32.

Kingsolver, Barbara. 2008. *Animal, Vegetable, Mineral: A Year of Food Life*. With Camille Kingsolver and Steven L. Hopp. New York: Harper Perennial.

Laslett, Barbara, and Johanna Brenner. 1989. "Gender and Social Reproduction: Historical Perspectives." *Annual Review of Sociology* 15(1): 381–404.

Longhurst, Robyn, Lynda Johnston, and Elsie Ho. 2009. "A Visceral Approach: Cooking 'at Home' with Migrant Women in Hamilton, New Zealand." *Transactions of the Institute of British Geographers* 34(3): 333–45.

Longoria, Eva. 2011. *Eva's Kitchen: Cooking with Love for Family and Friends*. New York: Clarkson Potter Publishers.

Loomis, Susan H. 2015. *In a French Kitchen: Tales and Traditions of Everyday Home Cooking in France*. New York: Avery.

Marcelli, Enrico A. 2014. "The Community-Based Migrant Household Probability Sample Survey." In *Migration and Health: A Research Methods Handbook*, edited by Marc B. Schenker, Xóchitl Casteñada, and Alfonso Rodriguez-Lainz, 111–40. Berkeley: University of California Press.

Marcelli, Enrico A., and Rosemary Serra. 2012. "Dietary Behavior of Legal and Unauthorized Brazilian Migrants in the Boston Metropolitan Area." Paper presented at the annual meeting of the Pacific Sociological Association, San Diego, California.

Massey, Doreen. 1992. "A Place Called Home." *New Formations* 7: 3–15.

McFeely, Mary D. 2001. *Can She Bake a Cherry Pie? American Women and the Kitchen in the Twentieth Century*. Boston: University of Massachusetts Press.

Meah, Angela. 2016. "Extending the Contested Spaces of the Modern Kitchen." *Geography Compass* 10(2): 41–55.

Merriam-Webster. 2016. "Foodie." In *Merriam-Webster's Learner Dictionary*. www.merriam -webster.com/dictionary/foodie.

Munford, Rebecca. 2007. "Wake Up and Smell the Lipgloss." In *Third Wave Feminism: A Critical Exploration*, edited by Stacy Gillis, Gillian Howie, and Rebecca Munford, 266–79. New York: Palgrave Macmillan.

Nestle, Marion. 2002. *Food Politics*. Berkeley: University of California Press.

Oerton, Sarah. 1997. " 'Queer Housewives?' Some Problems in Theorizing the Division of Domestic Labor in Lesbian and Gay Households." *Women's Studies International Forum* 20(3): 421–30.

Pollan, Michael. 2006. *The Omnivore's Dilemma: A Natural History of Four Meals*. New York: Penguin.

———. 2013. *Cooked: A Natural History of Transformation*. New York: Penguin Books.

Pratt, Geraldine. 2012. *Families Apart: Migrant Mothers and the Conflicts of Labor and Love*. Minnesota: University of Minnesota Press.

Premack, Rachel. 2016. "Why So Many Men Are Cooking." *Washington Post*. July 19. www.washingtonpost.com/news/wonk/wp/2016/07/19/why-so-many-millennial-men-are-cooking/?utm_term=.1e270830da4a.

Punch, Samantha, Ian McIntosh, and Ruth Emond. 2010. "Children's Food Practices in Families and Institutions." *Children's Geographies* 8(3): 227–32.

Rapport, Nigel, and Andrew Dawson. 1998. *Migrants of Identity: Perceptions of Home in a World of Movement*. Oxford: Berg.

Sifton, Sam. 2011. "Why Does It Matter that Families Eat Together?" *New York Times Magazine*: The Food Issue. September 30.

Smith, Lindsey P., Shu W. Ng, and Barry M. Popkin. 2013. "Trends in US Home Food Preparation and Consumption: Analysis of National Nutrition Surveys and Time Use Studies from 1965–1966 to 2007–2008." *Nutrition Journal* 12(1): 1–10.

Swarns, Rachel. 2014. "When Their Workday Ends, More Fathers Are Heading Into the Kitchen." *New York Times*. The Working Life. November 23. https://mobile.nytimes.com/2014/11/24/nyregion/when-the-workday-ends-more-fathers-are-heading-to-the-kitchen.html?referer=&_r=0.

Tipton-Martin, Toni. 2014. "Breaking the Jemima Code: The Legacy of African-American Cookbooks." *Ecotone* 10(1): 116–20.

Tuan, Yi-Fu. 2004. "Home." In *Patterned Ground: The Entanglements of Nature and Culture*, edited by Stephan Harrison, Steve Pile, and Nigel J. Thrift, 164–65. London: Reaktion Books.

Wade-Gayles, Gloria. 2005. " 'Laying on Hands' through Cooking: Black Women's Majesty and Mystery in their Own Kitchen." In *Through the Kitchen Window: Women Explore the Intimate Meanings of Food and Cooking*, edited by Arlene V. Avakian. New York: Berg.

Warner, Judith. 2006. *Perfect Madness: Motherhood in the Age of Anxiety*. New York: Riverhead Books.

Zinn, Howard. 2015. *A People's History of the United States*. New York: Harper Collins Publishers.

Is Home Cooking a Form of Oppression?

Think about a recent memorable meal in a home setting—perhaps a holiday, a family celebration, or a gathering with friends. Who did most of the cooking? Did the cooking seem stressful or enjoyable? Was there a gendered division of labor? Why or why not?

Women have traditionally been responsible for cooking at home and preserving culture through food and domesticity. Among Italian Americans, Sunday dinners are an important way to sustain family ties and cultural roots (Cinotto 2013). For generations, women have prepared meat and tomato sauce—simply known as gravy or sauce—for this weekly ritual. Occasionally, men would get involved in making the gravy, turning it into a big show, as in the famous scene from Francis Ford Coppola's *The Godfather*, where Clemenza teaches Michael Corleone how to make Sunday sauce. But mostly, they would stay out of the kitchen.

The time-consuming dish, which takes all day to prepare, illustrates the role of food in the social construction of home, family, and identity, as well as gendered expectations of domesticity. Today, few Italian-American families make sauce on a weekly basis, but many have fond memories of their grandmothers and mothers in the kitchen. This recipe is from Nanny (Louise) Marcelli, the grandmother of one of the authors of chapter 15. Be warned: To this day, no one has been able to make it exactly the way she did!

Sunday Dinner "Gravy"

Ingredients (for twelve)

For the sauce:

¼ cup olive oil
3 cloves garlic, peeled and minced
1 sweet onion, peeled and finely chopped
1 tablespoon dried oregano
2 (6-ounce) cans of tomato paste
4 (28-ounce) cans of crushed tomatoes, preferably San Marzano
2 bay leaves
4 tablespoons sugar
1 tablespoon sea salt
1 teaspoon pepper

For the meat:

2 tablespoons olive oil
2 pounds Italian sausages
2 pounds pork ribs
2 pounds ground beef, such as chuck (approximately 20 percent fat)
½ cup breadcrumbs
¼ cup grated Parmesan cheese
1 egg, beaten
1 clove garlic, minced
2 tablespoons fresh chopped Italian parsley
salt and pepper to taste

Preparation

Warm olive oil on medium heat in a very large pot (preferably cast-iron, or one with a heavy bottom). Add onion, garlic, and oregano and stir until softened. Add the tomato paste and stir, adding 1 can of water. Add crushed tomatoes, sugar, bay leaves, salt, and pepper. Cover the pot, turn the heat to low, and cook for 4 hours, turning occasionally and adding water (up to 2 cups) to keep the sauce from getting too thick.

Meanwhile, prepare the meatballs. Mix the ground beef, breadcrumbs, egg, garlic, Parmesan, and parsley together with your hands and season with salt and pepper. Mix well until all the ingredients are incorporated and stick together. Form small meatballs of about 1½ inches in diameter. Heat olive oil in a large cast-iron skillet and cook the meatballs, using a wooden spoon to brown on all sides. Add to the sauce, which should have been cooking for about 4 hours by then.

Using the same skillet, cook the sausages. Cut in two or three segments and add to the sauce. Finally, cook the pork chops and add to the sauce as well. Stir very gently with a wooden spoon to make sure that the meat is covered in the sauce. Add a little water if necessary and simmer gently on very low heat for at least another 2 hours, but preferably 4.

To serve, take the meat out of the sauce and assemble on a large dish. Pour the remaining sauce in a separate serving bowl. Serve with your favorite shape of pasta, such as rigatoni, spaghetti, or penne. Sprinkle with freshly grated Parmesan.

Reference

Cinotto, Simone. 2013. *The Italian American Table: Food, Family, and Community in New York City*. Chicago: University of Illinois Press.

CHAPTER 16

Chefs

CELEBRITIES, EXPERTS, OR ADVOCATES?

Blaire O'Neal and Pascale Joassart-Marcelli

Textbox 16.1. Learning Objectives

- Contextualize the rise of chefs to celebrity status in contemporary cultural politics and food anxieties.
- Use a place perspective to think about professional kitchens and consider their relationship to other food spaces.
- Explore who celebrity chefs are, taking into account the role of class, race, and gender.
- Focus on three areas where chefs have had a significant impact in changing the way we eat, including sustainability, health, and authenticity.
- Critically evaluate the role of celebrity chefs in promoting food justice.

Chefs have become celebrities, and as such play an influential role in shaping what, where, and how we eat. Today, eight in ten adults in the United States and Britain watch chefs on television, and many own their cookbooks, purchase products they endorse, read their blogs or posts on social media, search for their recipes online, and aspire to eat at their restaurants. **Food media**, especially television, has facilitated chefs' movement into our everyday lives, opening up the space of professional kitchens and allowing consumers to peer inside. At the same time, chefs are taking on advocacy roles and venturing into new places, including schools, farms, and political organizations. While some view this cultural shift as a sign of improvement in our food system, stimulating growing interest in better and healthier food, others have begun to question the broader implications of the unprecedented attention drawn by a handful of chefs, such as Jamie Oliver and Alice Waters.

In this chapter, we explore who these celebrity chefs are and the ways they influence our relationship to food in a context of growing food anxieties, including fears of obesity, toxicity, environmental degradation, and cultural loss. We focus specifically on the role of class, gender, and race in shaping chefs' influence on the way we eat and the broader food system. We provide several examples to illustrate our arguments, emphasizing the impact of celebrity chefs on health, sustainability, and cultural authenticity.

The Rise of the Celebrity Chef

The rise of chefs to a celebrity-status level is a relatively new phenomenon, occurring only in the past twenty years. **Celebrity chefs**' fame emerged in a social and cultural context where the role of class and race were being downplayed and replaced instead with a different form of **identity politics**, based on personal experience. This shift coincides with a restructuring of the economy toward postfordism. As industrial mass production, exemplified by Henry Ford's assembly line, was replaced by flexible manufacturing and services, culture became an increasingly important source of profit. A **cultural economy** emerged favoring consumerism and the creation of economic value through branding, **commodification** of lifestyles, and repositioning of seemingly basic products as luxury commodities. Eating became an "act of distinction," and food, a "sign" that symbolized personal character, values, status, and **taste**. Under these new circumstances, chefs became celebrities and replaced intellectuals and experts as the source of public knowledge through a combination of spectacle and ordinariness that endeared them to viewers, readers, and consumers (Lewis 2010). Chefs' cultural authority was built on a wide range of media projects, from food television to blogs and trade publications, which enabled them to create or reinforce food trends and harness tremendous social and economic power. Chefs, and the food media in general, played an instrumental role in elevating the status of simple foods.

For example, dishes like hamburgers and macaroni and cheese became gourmet by using high-quality ingredients, adding unique flavors, and using sophisticated techniques. Searching for the most exquisite aged balsamic vinegar, heirloom grains, unpasteurized cheeses, and rare smoked chilies became a hobby for home cooks who were increasingly inspired by celebrity chefs. These items' historical portrayal as simple peasant foods allowed consumers to use exotic ingredients to distinguish themselves without appearing elitist. Johnston and Baumann (2014) argue that this "cosmopolitan omnivorousness"—the rejection of "haute cuisine" and the seeming willingness to eat anything—is central to the **foodie** identity. It resolves the uncomfortable tension between "an inclusionary ideology of democratic cultural consumption on the one hand, and an exclusionary ideology of taste and distinction on the other" (p. 165). The celebrity chef also embodies this ambivalence, being "at once an artist (gifted producer of 'original' work); an artisan (producer of handmade products to be consumed); a laborer who sweats in the dirt; and a manager, a cracker of whips, a capitalist" (Hyman 2008). As such, chefs participate in multiple and often contradictory narratives about who they are.

This process has been a geographic one: It began in professional kitchens, but continues to expand to other geographies. Professional kitchens—in restaurants, on television sets, or in the glossy pages of magazines—have been the principal space where the celebritization of chefs and the valorization of food took place. This space, reserved for those trained in the best culinary schools and strong enough to withstand its physically and emotionally taxing conditions (as portrayed in Anthony Bourdain's *Kitchen Confidential*), granted chefs the authority to sensationalize ordinary food, making it out of bounds for common cooks working in their home kitchens. As professional kitchens overshadowed home kitchens, cooking became less about nutrition and more about performance. Starting in the 1990s, the booming food television industry, under the facade of democratization, reinforced this process. Using stylistic representations of dishes that are practically impossible to reproduce, except by the most devoted home cooks with the time and resources to acquire quality ingredients, specialized utensils, and expensive appliances (see chapter 15), the industry widened the gap between the tangible and the sensational. This trend has been controversially described by numerous critics as "food porn"—a term that emphasizes the unattainable characteristics and excitement that these depictions of food generate (McBride 2010).

To be sure, programs featuring high-status chefs and their sensationalized food have been accompanied by the expansion of more-democratic shows designed for the home cook. Along with Emeril Lagasse, Bobby Flay, Mario Batali, Tom Colicchio, Gordon Ramsay, Jamie Oliver, and other (mostly male) professional chefs, another group of (mostly female) food celebrities, such as Martha Stewart, Rachael Ray, Nigella Lawson, Paula Deen, and Ina Garten gained popularity on the small screen and in the press. The latter have puzzled feminists who often describe them as "corporate housewives" who reinforce **gender** stereotypes by emphasizing home cooking (Hollows 2008). Their cooking shows are typically set in what looks like a home kitchen— a private and much more gentle environment than the hypermasculine and cutthroat environment of the restaurant kitchen (Nathanson 2009). As a result, many view these women as "cooks," setting them apart from the more-respected male "chefs." Socially constructed ideas about what makes a "great" chef put the title out of the reach of women, who must exaggerate their femininity to participate in popular **food culture** by becoming either sexualized or motherly figures. The few who are granted access to "real" professional kitchens must erase their gender and adopt a sexless demeanor to blend into this largely masculine world (see textbox 16.2).

In addition to gender, **race** also appears to be an important factor in determining chefs' status, with most celebrity chefs being white and "classically" trained within the well-respected traditions of French and Italian cuisine. Although food has become increasingly cosmopolitan, chefs working with other culinary repertoires (e.g., Mexican, Thai, Indian) continue to be seen as "cooks" who merely follow traditional "ethnic" recipes (Ray 2016). Their kitchens are often devalued as dirty, noisy, and unsafe places (see chapter 12). These examples make it clear that despite the pretense of democratization, class, race, and gender continue to shape the way we eat in subtle ways, with chefs at the core of this cultural realm.

More recently, food has become a major source of social anxieties related to environmental sustainability, health, and a loss of cultural identity. Given chefs' expert status, it is not surprising that so many people have turned to them for answers. This added pressure has complicated the role of chefs, many of whom have joined the so-called food movement and become advocates for an alternative food system (see chapter 5). These new activist chefs are increasingly engaged outside of the professional kitchen, being seen in places such as school cafeterias, urban farms, and government offices, expanding their geographies even further. For some, these **food advocacy** activities are taking them to distant and exotic locations in search of different ways to grow, prepare, and enjoy food. Indeed, just as the 1990s brought the professional kitchen into the home via the television set, the new millennium has further magni-

Textbox 16.2. A Social Hierarchy of Culinary Personas

In their analysis of celebrity chefs' cookbooks, Johnston, Rodney, and Chong (2014) point to the difference between personality and persona. The former refers to the individual, while the latter is a socially constructed public identity that seeks to appeal to audiences. Celebrity chefs gain authority and legitimacy through the cultural production of their personas, which may be entirely different from their personalities. These representations are based on existing cultural norms and tend to reproduce understandings of race, class, and gender by reinforcing stereotypes.

Johnston et al. (2014) identifies seven personas by coding almost one hundred cookbooks. For instance, statements such as "Rachael Ray is not a chef. She is a cook schooled in a home kitchen run by her mother" help to categorize her in the "homebody" category. A number of women (e.g., Nigella Lawson, Padma Lakshmi) fall in the "pinup" category due to the emphasis on sensual pleasures and the author's sexualized physical appearance. Yet, like most women food celebrities, their focus remains on daily meal preparation.

In contrast, culinary masculinities are linked to personas like the "chef-artisan," the "maverick," the "gastrosexual," and the "self-made man"—all of which presume a professional in control of the kitchen. The chef-artisan persona, for example, relies on abstract and artistic photography, thick pages, and unusual book formats to create a representation of chefs inspired by art and originality (e.g., Emeril Lagasse, Gordon Ramsay, Marco Pierre White). The gastrosexual persona, while embracing feminized aspects of cooking and caring, is clearly positioned as professional and heterosexual. Jamie Oliver, for example, champions home-cooking and gardening, but asserts his masculinity by bringing professional standards to the home kitchen, joking about his nights of drinking with pals, and bragging about his sex life with his "missus." The different culinary personas are not neutral; they underscore a hierarchy of status and prestige, with white men having the highest status, and women and minorities being pigeonholed into less-respected social constructs (Johnston et al. 2014, 20). As such, these representations tend to reproduce stereotypes and limit opportunities for women and people of color by restricting the number of acceptable categories they can occupy as food professionals.

fied the reach of chefs into additional spaces of everyday life, increasing their power in influencing our relationship to food.

Yet, their particular role in our "food-obsessed" society (Adema 2000) remains poorly understood. Are chefs challenging established food norms and structures, or are they capitalizing on our current cravings and willingness to pay a premium for local, organic, healthy, sustainable, and authentic food? The central role of chefs in selling food and lifestyle goes well beyond the meals served at their restaurants, including processed food, kitchen utensils, tableware, and cookbooks carrying their names. Their sponsorship of these products potentially contradicts their desires to overhaul the food system, particularly in regard to food justice.

Examining chefs' influence on **food justice** is central to this chapter. A vast and growing literature reveals deep inequalities in our food system. Although there are variations in the definition of food justice, it typically entails the rights of people to access affordable, healthful, and culturally appropriate food (i.e., food security) that is produced in an ecologically sound way (i.e., food sustainability), and to participate in the decision-making process that shapes their food system (i.e., food sovereignty). In this chapter, we critically explore three areas where chefs have been actively involved, including health, environmental sustainability, and cultural diversity, and assess the impact of their activities on transforming the food system and promoting food justice.

Chefs and the Obesity "Crisis"

During the past decade, fears regarding "obesity epidemics" have grown in the United States and elsewhere. The emotionally charged term suggests a widespread and uncontrollable phenomenon, which has led to a flurry of one-sided explanations that justify various interventions typically targeting a single cause (Guthman and DuPuis 2006). While there are valid reasons to be concerned about expanding waistlines, the hype surrounding the "war on obesity" is contributing to a new type of **body politics** that normalizes thinness and leads to the stigmatization of fat bodies as morally inferior (see chapter 13).

Given the dominance of the "energy-balance" explanation for obesity (see chapter 9), specifically the emphasis on how much people eat, "eating right" carries a new kind of power that distinguishes individuals who presumably have the education, resources, and will to control their appetite from others who seemingly lack those virtues. In the current cultural context, no one is better positioned to show people how to eat right than chefs, whose celebrity status makes them expert in anything related to food, including health.

Encouraging healthy behavior has become the mantra of several famous chefs, including Rachael Ray, Alice Waters, Jamie Oliver, and others (see figure 16.1). Some have even formed or joined nonprofit organizations to carry on their outreach activities, focusing mostly on children and education. Common among these actors is the idea that exposure to fresh, wholesome, quality ingredients, along with basic cooking skills, are central to promoting a healthy diet (see chapters 9 and 15). Yet, even the most health-conscious celebrity chefs may have a limited impact on health for three primary reasons.

First, because of the profit-driven nature of their professional activities, celebrity chefs occupy an ambivalent position as advocates in the war on obesity, resulting in contradictory messages. The dominant discourse of "eat more" and "don't be afraid to indulge" sits uncomfortably with advice to reduce caloric intake. Although people overwhelmingly trust that celebrity chefs' recipes are healthy, studies have provided evidence that the majority fall short of government recommendations for healthy eating, with excessive amounts of total fat, saturated fat, sodium, and sugars (Jones et al. 2013). Furthermore, the average portion sizes displayed in food media are usually much larger than recommended. Therefore, "cooking like a pro" may not be the most effective pathway to healthy eating, and may encourage overconsumption. This is likely exacerbated by advertising, which accompanies most television shows and food publications and promotes low-nutrient, high-energy snacks and processed food. Indeed, Adema (2000) argues that "food television offers a vicarious experience of cooking and serves mostly to promote the consumption of unhealthy ready-to-eat products."

Figure 16.1. Celebrity chefs in action
In the top photo, Jamie Oliver is shown interacting with children at The Stop Community Food Centre's Green Barn in Toronto. In the bottom photo, Alice Waters is speaking at a "We Garden" public event at the California State Capitol in Sacramento.
Sources: Top: GoodFoodRevolution (2010); bottom: Kelly Huston (2009).

This ambivalent message is also embedded in the outreach activities of many chefs who encourage consumption while preaching austerity. For instance, Paula Deen—notorious for her fried food and generous use of butter—gave a number of presentations in schools to teach children how to cook and eat healthy food in connection with the promotion of her book, *Paula Deen's Cookbook for the Lunch-Box Set*. While the book includes notes about manners, it does not mention health, and contains numerous recipes that would irritate nutritionists.

Second, the types of outreach activity in which chefs participate tend to reproduce a **neoliberal** model of governance in which communities are responsible for addressing their social ills (see chapter 5). For example, Alice Waters (see figure 16.1), the chef-owner of Chez Panisse—a highly ranked restaurant famous for its farm-to-table cuisine—has been a leader of the "farm-to-school" movement through organizations like the Edible Schoolyard Project, the Chez Panisse Foundation, and the Waters Advocacy Coalition. Their activities have been criticized, however, for privileging localism over health. The emphasis on consuming a variety of local products contributes to confusion about healthy diets and to the idea that eating healthy is reserved for high-income individuals. It also reinforces the devolution of responsibility for providing healthy food away from the federal government into local and private entities. As a result, only select schools or districts benefit from these highly mediatized, top-down, chef-led projects, while others are left to struggle on their own out of the public eye (Allen and Guthman 2006).

A third concern with chef-led health advocacy is the emphasis on healthy choices, which reinforces a personal responsibility narrative that blames individuals for their weight and leaves structural factors associated with obesity unchanged. For example, Jamie Oliver's television shows have been criticized for reinforcing behavioral and individualistic approaches to health promotion by focusing primarily on teaching adults and children how to cook. Those who do not respond positively, mostly women and economically disadvantaged people, are portrayed as irrational and ignorant, without any consideration of their everyday lives and the structural forces that shape them (see textbox 16.3). In general, advocacy efforts by celebrity chefs have been interpreted with

---

Textbox 16.3. Jamie Oliver's "Food Revolution" and "Ministry of Food"

Jamie Oliver's reality television shows aim at teaching people, including children and working-class men, how to cook so they can "make good choices." The overarching assumption is that individuals can unlearn the bad habits they have been taught by their mothers, teachers, and school cafeteria workers through a combination of exposure to "good" food and fearmongering about "bad" food. As a young, affluent, white man descending on economically disadvantaged towns like Rotherham in South Yorkshire (England) and Huntington in West Virginia (USA), Jamie Oliver resorts to fear and shaming as a way to convince people to make what he deems rational choices that will save them from the threat of the "obesity epidemic."

This approach is common on other popular lifestyle shows, like *The Biggest Loser*, *Fat Camp*, *Huge*, and *My 600-Lb. Life*. As Warin (2011) points out, however, Jamie's shows focus on entire communities, which are portrayed as dysfunctional, justifying the judging and monitoring of their residents' private lives by millions of spectators. In that negative setting, carefully selected individuals show viewers that it is possible to learn how to cook and eat differently, as dramatically symbolized in the emotional burial of a deep fryer and discarding of frozen chicken nuggets. By positioning these few individuals as responsible and morally superior compared to the majority of the population, these shows re-create classed and gendered perceptions about fat bodies as weak, lazy, and morally inferior. While this may encourage some to "choose health," it also generates significant resistance from those who feel disparaged and patronized by this dominant narrative, doing little to reduce obesity concerns.

ambivalence, with some lauding their efforts at addressing pressing health concerns, and others interpreting them as counterproductive top-down food policing (see chapter 14).

Chefs and Environmental Sustainability

Celebrity chefs are not only amateur nutritionists, but also environmental stewards. Environmental **sustainability**, defined as the environment's ability to meet today's demand without reducing its capacity to allow people to live well in the future, is central to many chefs' palates, and dishes are now often served with a side of environmental ethics. In the past decades, evidence has continued to surface linking the conventional food system to climate change, aquatic dead zones, deforestation, and the loss of critical pollinator species, biodiversity, and global fisheries. These rising environmental anxieties have inspired a new lifestyle celebrity persona: the "sustainable chef," whose influential power is used to promote sustainable eating. Such practices have been granted **culinary capital** in a context where ethical consumption and market-based ecological citizenship has become a marker of identity (see chapter 6 for a critical analysis of ethical food consumerism). Choosing organic or local food conveys health, status, and social responsibility. Sustainable chefs sell these virtues, infusing popular media with manifestos on the future of sustainable cuisine.

Chefs encourage sustainability primarily by promoting the consumption of local, organic, and seasonal ingredients and discouraging the consumption of ecologically taxing foods, such as meat and endangered fish species. Recently, chefs have also drawn attention to the negative impact of food waste, using discarded food and less-desirable parts of ingredients to create gourmet dishes. Although their advocacy has generated much positive publicity and prompted many in the food service industry to revamp their menus and products, its impact on the food system may be constrained by a number of factors, including the **fetishization** and exclusivity of the foods they champion.

First, chefs tend to fetishize and reify certain foods for their ecological properties, without questioning the social relations of production or considering the implications of meeting the growing demand that typically follows the popularization of such food. Chef Alice Waters, a figurehead of sustainable eating, illustrates this point well. With roots in the 1960s alternative food movement, she became vice president of Slow Food International in 2002—an organization that originated in Italy in the late 1980s to preserve local culinary and agricultural traditions and encourage organic farming of local plants and livestock. In her popular cookbook, *The Art of Simple Food: Notes, Lessons, and Recipes from a Delicious Revolution*, Alice Waters encourages readers to "eat locally and sustainably; eat seasonally; shop at farmers' markets; plant a garden; eat and cook together." Her recipes showcase fresh produce such as persimmons, kumquats, quince, huckleberries, kohlrabi, kale, and puntarelle, which she presumably purchased at the local farmers' market. This "simple" food dominates the expensive menu at her Berkeley restaurant, Chez Panisse, which was established in 1971, and is credited with putting California cuisine on the map.

Throughout her work, it is simply assumed that organic and local foods reflect an "alternative" food system that is better for the environment. Yet, it is unclear how it departs from the profit-driven capitalist model. As consumer demand for organic foods continues to rise, production is becoming increasingly centralized and industrialized, generating massive quantities of organically labeled food and huge profits, while leaving working conditions, capital and land ownership structures, and distribution chains untouched (Guthman 2004). This fetishization of local and organic foods hides these considerations and ultimately does little to change the relations of production or alleviate larger food justice issues.

Recently, a few chefs have attempted to defetishize sustainable food by drawing attention to the farming process itself. Chef Dan Barber's sustainability platform is decidedly research-based and educational. In his *New York Times* bestseller, *The Third Plate* (2014), he criticizes the farm-to-table movement for "cherry-picking items that are often ecologically demanding and expensive to grow" (p. 15), and calls for a "whole system" approach in which "good farming" and "good food" are intimately connected. He argues that the local environment and the bounties of the soil should dictate what is on the menu, not the other way around. Yet, his attention to seed breeders, geese farmers, and other renegade cultivators tends to reify the farm. We must still question whether the food system Barber promotes will necessarily be a just one. The thoughtful sustainable menu he proposes for the year 2050 is full of heritage and underutilized ingredients. However, he offers little in the way of how plates like "trout with phytoplankton" can penetrate the homes of people who are struggling to meet their basic needs.

This example brings up a second important criticism of chef-led sustainability initiatives: their exclusivity and **class** bias. Arguably, Alice Waters, Dan Barber, and other chefs are trying to change people's relationship to food by advocating a turn away from the established meat-centric plate toward a vegetable-centric plate based on the rhythms of nature. Yet, it is doubtful that low-income people will embrace their recommendations with the same enthusiasm as privileged, higher-income consumers. Despite claims to the contrary, organic and local foods are currently a luxury limited to those who can afford to purchase such foods and have convenient access to them at nearby stores or farmers' markets. This is partly caused by agricultural policies that subsidize the production of corn, soy, and wheat, whose by-products are used to manufacture conventional processed food, but provide little support for organic field and tree crops. Chefs are regularly photographed at farmers' markets, purchasing fresh food for their restaurants and encouraging us to do the same. Yet, scholars have described them as spaces of whiteness (see Slocum 2007), where the food practices of primarily white and affluent shoppers are normalized as healthy and sustainable, in contrast to those of others who shop at conventional stores. This sort of market-based ecological citizenship reinforces a process of "**othering**" and social exclusion (see chapter 11 for an analysis of alternative food practices).

Despite these limitations, chefs are currently the most visible faces of a sustainability movement that is best summed up by the phrase "delicious is the new environmentalism" (Seaver 2011). Chefs have taken a leadership role on sustainability issues from the land to the sea (see textbox 16.4), working to influence food production, markets, and personal tastes while continuing to promote delicious food. Chefs' efforts have led to the creation of new organizations like Chefs Collaborative

---

Textbox 16.4. Sustainable Seafood

Sustaining fisheries is an important platform for celebrity chefs turned environmental activists. Overfishing and commercial fish farming have put considerable stress on marine ecosystems; over 70 percent of fisheries are exploited, overexploited, or have already collapsed. This evidence has prompted chefs to change their menus and create new tastes. Whether it's advising consumers how to shop for sustainable seafood at the grocery store, inspiring curiosity through underutilized sea products, advocating for alternative meal staples, or creating markets for successfully conserved fisheries, chefs have a significant impact on the sustainable seafood movement.

For instance, Alice Waters and Dan Barber both advocate for sustainable seafood. Waters encourages her cookbook readers to eat ocean-friendly dishes, directing them to the Seafood Watch website for help in selecting seafood, while Barber dedicates a whole portion of his book to promoting ecological aquaculture systems. Barton Seaver, a chef at multiple restaurants in Washington, DC, and elsewhere, is another particularly salient voice for sustainable seafood. Seaver calls for "restorative seafood" consumption that would replenish fisheries by abstaining from endangered seafood (e.g., shark and swordfish) and orienting diets toward well-managed fisheries (e.g., mussels, sardines, and Atlantic mackerel) and vegetables. His aptly titled book *For Cod and Country* (2011) argues that this abstinence is a form of patriotism that will allow communities, like those built on the cod fisheries of the New England coast, to continue living from the sea in the future.

Seaver stands out not only in his more striking approach to seafood, but in his consideration of economic concerns: "We must continue to eat the best seafood possible, if at all, but we also must eat it with a ton of vegetables. The best part about restorative seafood, though, is that it comes . . . in a five-ounce portion of tilapia breaded with Dijon mustard and crispy broiled breadcrumbs, and a steaming pile of pecan quinoa pilaf with crunchy, grilled broccoli . . . and the best part is all of those ingredients are available to every family at the neighborhood Walmart" (Seaver 2010). This again may seem contradictory, and reflective of the ambivalence surrounding chef advocacy: In his consideration, he condones a corporation that has been a symbol of what is wrong with our industrial global food system.

(est. 2007), which in its own words helps "the greater culinary community [become] a catalyst for positive change by creating a market for good food and helping preserve local farming and fishing communities" (Chefs Collaborative 2016). This motive to sell and encourage the consumption of "good" food remains one of the biggest obstacles to chef-led sustainability initiatives that rely almost entirely on individual consumption as an agent of change, leading some to characterize their work as "**hollow advocacy**" (Hudson and Hudson 2003).

Chefs and Authentic Food

Globalization has had a profound impact on what we eat, both expanding our culinary repertoires with additional ingredients available year-round and constricting them through homogenization. Chefs have played a key role in this process, exposing consumers to "exotic" foods and educating them about their "**authenticity**." Although this phenomenon is not typically seen as advocacy or activism, since chefs here do not campaign for a specific cause or policy (e.g., hunger, obesity, sustainability), it nevertheless addresses one of our fears about the contemporary global food system: the loss of culture and tradition. As cultural producers, several chefs have taken it upon themselves to preserve regional foodways. For example, Italian food is no longer just Italian; it is Neapolitan pizza, Bolognese Ragù, or Venetian prawns. In the United States, where it has been notoriously challenging to define national food, geographic variations in cuisine are also frequently highlighted, from Texas barbecue to Maine lobster rolls. This quest also expands to the Global South where regional variations in "ethnic" foods are increasingly noted. A number of popular cookbooks and television shows focus on unfamiliar foods and exotic places (e.g., Anthony Bourdain's *A Cook's Tour, No Reservations,* and *Parts Unknown*).

Yet, this search for authenticity remains primarily motivated by a desire to create value. By constantly repositioning products as new, different, and better, these foods become markers of knowledge and distinction that allow consumers to enhance their culinary cultural capital. Heldke (2003) argues that authenticity rarely represents what insiders to that culture view as genuine or traditional, but instead relates to outsiders' expectations and desires. Paramount to this process is the creation of an exotic "Other" that is used to produce authenticity (see chapter 12). While local restaurateurs, farmers, and artisans are often celebrated in the media for producing authentic foods, the chefs who "discovered" their food (and presumably improved it) typically control the discourse, marketing, and financial benefits of such discoveries. This process is particularly visible in the discursive construction of "ethnic food," which depends on an exoticized, racialized, and classed alterity. Producers of authentic food rarely reach the chef status; instead they are cooks or homemakers who embody expectations of charm, docility, simplicity, and tradition.

For example, when food celebrity Anthony Bourdain writes "the Ecuadorian, Mexican, Dominican and Salvadorian *cooks* I've worked with over the years make most CIA-educated white boys look like clumsy, sniveling little punks," he (perhaps unconsciously) uses race as a proxy for certain desirable labor characteristics. In contrast to ethnic cooks, celebrity chefs like Jean-Georges Vongerichten (who is executive chef at a number of French-Asian restaurants in New York, Las Vegas, Paris, Shanghai, and Tokyo) and Rick Bayless (who owns a series of Mexican restaurants in Chicago) are perceived as elevating ethnic cuisine with their creativity, technique, and expertise. To become noticed or successful, minoritized chefs have two options. First, they can adopt a white persona and prove their credentials by training at the best schools, apprenticing under white celebrity chefs (preferably in France), competing on television, earning Michelin stars, and serving food in an elegant and contemporary setting. Second, they can embrace an essentialized, ethnic Other—such as the Japanese sushi master with impeccable knife skills (Hirose and Pih 2011) or the naturally caring black Aunt Jemima figure (see chapter 15)—that is constructed to entertain and meet the expectations of elite consumers. In short, although celebrity chefs can be instrumental in preserving traditional foodways and exposing consumers to unfamiliar foods in an era of McDonaldization, they do so by decontextualizing "authentic" food and repackaging it in ways that negate the historical context in which it emerged.

Conclusion

As chef Dan Barber notes, "we [chefs] now have the power to quickly popularize certain products and ingredients . . . but also possess the potential to get people to rethink their eating habits" (2014, p. 11). Contemporary cultural dynamics have turned chefs into celebrities and experts—not just on food, but also on health, sustainability, and culture. This expertise is legitimized by classed, gendered, and racialized chef personas that constrain who can achieve celebrity status and ultimately influence how we eat. Chefs are typically not nutritionists, yet they are trusted to advise the public on healthy food choices. They are not ecologists or environmental scientists, but they inform public perception on environmentally sound farming. And while these celebrity chefs are primarily white, they are still granted the privilege to educate on the authenticity of food cultures that are not their own. Indeed, in the past two decades, chefs have ventured out of the professional kitchen—first, to the private space of homes via the television set, and more recently to the public space of food advocacy through a wider range of media, giving greater visibility to the causes they choose to join.

Their advocacy, however, has been characterized as "hollow," raising doubts about its transformative potential. The fact that chefs are in the business of selling food, experience, and lifestyle limits their ability to challenge the market system on which they depend. Instead, they typically focus their activism on a single popular issue that contributes to their distinct brand (e.g., healthy school lunch, farm-to-table, sustainable seafood, authentic cuisine). Despite this narrow focus, broad claims are often made regarding "food justice," conflating "good" food with "just" food. Educating the public about food prepared with fresh, minimally processed, organic, local, and native ingredients may be useful in nudging consumers to make healthier choices, but it is hardly counter-hegemonic. Although it encourages new forms of consumption, it does not challenge the economic structure and cultural discourse that underlie deep inequalities within the food system.

Key Terms

authenticity
body politics
celebrity chef
class
commodification
culinary capital
cultural economy
fetishization
food advocacy
food culture
foodie

food justice
food media
gender
hollow advocacy
identity politics
neoliberalism
othering
race
sustainability
taste

Summary

- Chefs have become celebrities and have gained unprecedented power in shaping what and how we eat. This rising social power is the result of changing cultural politics, where identities have become more fluid and are increasingly tied to consumption.
- Celebrity chefs create media personas to market themselves and the products they endorse. These personas embody social hierarchies and typically reinforce gender, race, and class stereotypes.
- Chefs have stepped out of their professional kitchen and ventured into other places, including farms, schools, and communities, expanding the scope of their influence on our relationship to food. Their outreach efforts tend to focus on issues of health, environmental sustainability, and cultural authenticity.
- Because chefs are partly motivated by profit, their food advocacy is ambivalent and often hollow: It seeks to change the food system while encouraging consumption and supporting a market economy. As such, it excludes those who cannot afford to participate or are otherwise socially excluded. Therefore, it falls short of creating food justice.

Additional Resources

For a discussion of the central place of celebrities in today's society, see Lewis (2010), Hyman (2008), and Rousseau (2012).

The role of race in shaping representations of chefs is featured in Hirose and Pih (2011), Ray (2016), and Tipton-Martin (2014). The role of gender is addressed in Druckman (2010), Hollows (2008), and Johnston, Rodney, and Chong (2014).

A critical perspective on various forms of food activism, in which chefs have been involved, is provided by Allen and Guthman (2006), Guthman (2003), and Hudson and Hudson (2003).

There are a number of recent documentary films that focus on chefs, including *Spinning Plates*, *A Matter of Taste*, *Three Stars*, *Jiro Dream of Sushi*, and the *Chef's Table* series.

References

Adema, Paulina. 2000. "Vicarious Consumption: Food, Television, and the Ambiguity of Modernity." *Journal of American Culture* 23, No. 3 (2000): 113–23.

Allen, Patricia, and Julie Guthman. 2006. "From 'Old School' to 'Farm-to-School': Neoliberalization from the Ground Up." *Agriculture and Human Values* 23: 401–15.

Barber, Dan. 2015. *The Third Plate: Field Notes on the Future of Food.* New York: Penguin.

Chefs Collaborative. 2016. *About Us.* www.chefscollaborative.org/about/.

Druckman, Charlotte. 2010. "Why Are There No Great Women Chefs?" *Gastronomica* 10(1): 24–31.

Guthman, Julie. 2003. "Fast Food / Organic Food: Reflexive Tastes and the Making of 'Yuppie Chow.' " *Social and Cultural Geography* 4(1): 45–58.

———. 2004. "The Trouble with 'Organic Lite' in California: A Rejoinder to the 'Conventionalisation' Debate." *Sociologia Ruralis* 44(3): 301–16.

Guthman, Julie, and Melanie DuPuis. 2006. "Embodying Neoliberalism: Economy, Culture, and the Politics of Fat." *Environment and Planning D: Society and Space* 24(3): 427–48.

Flanagan, Caitlin. 2010. "Cultivating Failure: How School Gardens Are Cheating Our Most Vulnerable Students." *The Atlantic*. January/February Issue. www.theatlantic.com/magazine/archive/2010/01/cultivating-failure/307819/.

Heldke, Lisa. 2003. *Exotic Appetites: Ruminations of a Food Adventurer*. New York: Routledge.

Hirose, Akihiko, and Kay K. H. Pih. 2011. "'No Asians Working Here': Racialized Otherness and Authenticity in Gastronomical Orientalism." *Ethnic and Racial Studies* 34(9): 1482–1501.

Hollows, Joanne. 2008. "Feeling Like a Domestic Goddess: Postfeminism and Cooking." In *Feminist Television Criticism. A Reader*, 2nd ed., edited by Charlotte Brunsdon and Lynn Spigel, 154–73. New York: Open University Press.

Hudson, Ian, and Mark Hudson. 2003. "Removing the Veil? Commodity Fetishism, Fair Trade, and the Environment." *Organization and Environment* 16(4): 413–30.

Hyman, Gwen. 2008. "The Taste of Fame: Chefs, Diners, Celebrity, Class." *Gastronomica* 8(3): 43–52.

Johnston, Josée, and Shyon Baumann. 2014. *Foodies: Democracy and Distinction in the Gourmet Foodscape*. New York: Routledge.

Johnston, Josée, Alexandra Rodney, and Philippa Chong. 2014. "Making Change in the Kitchen? A Study of Celebrity Cookbooks, Culinary Personas, and Inequality." *Poetics* 47: 1–22.

Jones, Megan, Emily Freeth, Kathleen Hennessy-Priest, and Ricardo Costa. 2013. "A Systematic Cross-Sectional Analysis of British-Based Celebrity Chefs' Recipes: Is There a Cause for Public Health Concern?" *Food and Public Health* 3(2): 100–10.

Lewis, Tania. 2010. "Branding, Celebritization and the Lifestyle Expert." *Cultural Studies* 24(4): 580–98.

Lindenfeld, Laura. 2010. "On the Ethics of Food Television: Does Rachael Ray Really Promote Healthy Eating?" In *Whose Weight Is It Anyway? Essays on Ethics and Eating*, edited by Sofie Vandamme, Suzanne van de Vathorst, and Inez de Beaufort, 161–74. Leuven: Acco Academic.

McBride, Anne E. 2010. "Food Porn." *Gastronomica* 10(1): 38–46.

Naccarato, Peter, and Kathleen LeBesco. 2013. *Culinary Capital*. New York: Berg.

Nathanson, Elizabeth. 2009. "As Easy as Pie: Cooking Shows, Domestic Efficiency, and Postfeminist Temporality." *Television & New Media* 10(4): 311–30.

Ray, Kreshnendu. 2016. *The Ethnic Restaurateur*. New York: Bloomsbury.

Rousseau, Signe. 2012. *Food Media: Celebrity Chefs and the Politics of Everyday Interference*. New York: Bloomsbury Publishing.

Seaver, Barton. 2011. *For Cod and Country: Simple Delicious Sustainable Cooking*. New York: Sterling Publishing.

Slocum, Rachel. 2007. "Whiteness, Space and Alternative Food Practice." *Geoforum* 38(3): 520–33.

Tipton-Martin, Toni. 2014. "Breaking the Jemima Code: The Legacy of African American Cookbooks." *Ecotone* 10(1): 116–20.

Warin, Megan. 2011. "Foucault's Progeny: Jamie Oliver and the Art of Governing Obesity." *Social Theory and Health* 9(1): 24–40.

Could We Promote Food Justice One Meal at a Time?

As this volume shows, there are many ways to resist the global industrial food regime. What do you plan to do? Is there a specific action that you could commit to take? What type of activism does your plan fall into: ethical consumerism, grassroots community organizing, global resistance, educational outreach? How do you hope it will impact you? How will it make the food system more socially just, both locally and globally? What would it take for your efforts to be most impactful?

Sustainable seafood has been on the agenda of a growing number of celebrity chefs. By drawing attention to the unsustainability of industrial fishing practices and educating consumers about less-damaging types of seafood and simple ways to prepare them, chefs hope to have a positive impact on the environment. This recipe uses mussels, which is considered one of the most sustainable proteins. Indeed, farmed mussels require no feed, since they simply filter nutrients from the water. In addition, their shells absorb atmospheric carbon dioxide, potentially reducing greenhouse gas effects. This recipe is inspired by one provided by chef Barton Seaver on the Monterey Aquarium Seafood Watch's Sustainable Recipes website (www.seafoodwatch.org/consumers/sustainable-recipes/mussels-saint-ex).

Mussels in Spicy Broth

Ingredients (for four entree-size portions)

2 tablespoons olive oil
1 shallot, peeled and finely chopped
4 garlic cloves, peeled and thinly sliced
1 tablespoon sweet smoked paprika
2 teaspoons ground coriander
4 ounces Spanish chorizo (or any other dried spicy salami), sliced and cut into matchsticks
¾ cup white wine
4 pounds mussels, cleaned (scrub the outside, remove any of the "beard" hanging, and
  discard open ones)
sea salt and pepper to taste
¼ cup chopped fresh Italian parsley
1 large tomato, cubed

Preparation

Warm olive oil in very large pot on low to medium heat. Add chorizo and stir for a couple of minutes. Add shallots, garlic, and spices and stir until spices are fragrant and shallot softens. Add the wine and turn the heat to high. When wine begins to boil, add mussels and cook until their shells open, about 4 minutes. Season with salt and pepper, and add parsley and tomatoes. Toss well. Serve in four soup bowls with toasted crusty bread to sop up the juices.

Glossary

Agency (ch. 14) is the capacity of individuals to act independently and make their own choices. It is influenced by one's position in society, including **class**, **race**, **gender**, **ethnicity**, and age. Oppressed and marginalized people are often assumed to lack agency. Such notions have been challenged by new conceptualizations of agency that emphasize small and ordinary ways in which people exert agency and **resistance**.

Alternative food practices (ch. 11) loosely describe a set of practices that challenges the dominant capitalist, industrial, and global food system. It includes efforts to localize food production and consumption through farmers' markets, **urban agriculture**, community gardens, homesteading, and community-supported agriculture, which together support an **alternative food system**. **Alternative food networks** is a term often used to describe the same set of practices while emphasizing the accountability, transparency, and interpersonal proximity characterizing the connections between producers and consumers. Some scholars argue that these practices have become mainstream (and therefore no longer alternative), since they fail to challenge the structural roots of our food system's problems, which lie in capitalism and inequality.

Authenticity (ch. 12, 16) refers to the original or traditional nature of a product, practice, or **place**. It is a problematic concept because it presumes the existence of a singular, deep, and essential **culture** and fails to acknowledge that tradition is a socially constructed and contested concept.

Belonging (ch. 5, 12) refers to social attachment to a group or community as well as spatial attachment to a place. The latter describes a sense of comfort and inclusion experienced in particular places, such as homeland, cities, neighborhoods, and public spaces. Oppressive social norms, combined with surveillance and policing of space, curtail marginalized people's sense of belonging.

Biopolitics (ch. 14) refers to the politics surrounding questions of biological life. For Michel Foucault, a prominent scholar of biopolitics, it includes the **disciplining** and regulation of bodies by society, directly through intervention, as well as indirectly through **discourse** and **surveillance**. The related concept of **biopower** (and **governmentality** in general) describes the power aimed at controlling and maintaining population health, including knowledge and technologies that influence individual behavior.

Biosocial (ch. 13) describes processes in which biological and social elements interact. The **body**, for instance, is seen as shaped by interrelated biological and social factors.

Body (ch. 2, 13) is an increasingly important **scale** in critical food studies, where it is seen as the place where biological and social processes commingle. **Class, race, gender**, and other social categories of **difference** are inscribed onto the body and influence its anatomy. Similarly, historically and geographically specific cultural norms define bodies as healthy, beautiful, or fat.

Body politics (ch. 2, 16) refers to social attempts to regulate the human body and the struggles to control one's own body. Regulation may occur directly, through government policies (e.g., antiabortion laws), and indirectly, through social norms (e.g., classed, raced, and gendered understandings of health), in which case it often becomes internalized and self-imposed. Social responses and attitudes toward **obesity** and **fatness** illustrate complex body politics.

Bracero Program (ch. 5) was a "guestworker" program designed by the US government to import seasonal workers from Mexico to the United States, mostly to work in agriculture and fill wartime labor shortages. The program was in place from 1942 to 1964 and brought five million workers to the United States.

CAFO: See **Concentrated animal feeding operation**.

Capitalism (ch. 2, 4, 6, 13) is the dominant economic system today. It describes an economy in which capitalists, typically organized as corporations, invest capital (i.e., money) in a variety of activities with the purpose of making a profit. Capital grants power to its owners, who are able to extract value out of workers in order to make a profit and accumulate more capital, defining **class** relations. This profit motive is a key aspect of capitalism and drives its expansion into new products and markets. The reliance on markets is another key characteristic that implies that decisions regarding what, where, and how to produce are driven by the interactions of producers and consumers. Political economists, including Karl Marx, view capitalism as inherently unstable and prone to crises, and argue that capitalism requires state intervention and institutions (such as private property) in order to function. **Neoliberalism** is typically associated with capitalism, as it represents an institutional and policy framework designed to support the expansion of markets and capitalism.

Celebrity chef (ch. 16) is a chef who has reached notoriety and stardom though the media, including television shows, cookbooks, and magazines. It is a relatively recent social phenomenon in which "ordinary" people are given authority to influence our behavior and consumption patterns with potentially large monetary benefits. Many criticize this movement for **fetishizing** chefs and their food and devaluing everyday cooking and food knowledge.

Children's and childhood studies (ch. 14) is an interdisciplinary field dedicated to understanding the meanings and experiences of childhood. It argues that **childhood** is a socially constructed concept that is contingent upon place and time and deeply influenced by adults' perspectives that have historically devalued children and their views. It emphasizes the **agency** of children in shaping their lives and communities and supports their engagement in research and policy.

Circular migration (ch. 5) is a pattern of temporary or short-term labor migration in which the migrant maintains a "home base" and family in the community of origin.

Civil society (ch. 10) is a fluid and dynamic category that includes all nongovernmental institutions representing the interests of citizens. It consists primarily of **nonprofit** and community organizations, but also includes families and informal groups involved in serving the needs of, and advocating for, their members.

Class (ch. 8, 9, 12, 15, 16) is a hierarchical categorization system in which individuals or groups are divided according to their social status based on economic and cultural factors such as wealth, income, occupation, and prestige. For Marx, class is the principal organizing factor of social and economic relations under **capitalism**. The capitalist class (which owns the means of production or capital) has power over the working class (which is forced to sell its labor power) and uses this power to maintain its class position through exploitation and control of the state, leading to inherent tensions and conflicts.

Commoditization/commodification (ch. 6, 8, 12, 16) refers to the transformation of a good or service into a commodity that can be exchanged for a monetary value. This process expands the reach of the market, as illustrated by the commodification of **culture**, natural resources, ethics, and care, which may not have been previously traded. Commoditization is criticized for reducing everything to money and leading to **commodity fetishism**.

Commodity chains and **commodity production networks** (ch. 3) refer to networks of processes, relationships, materials, people, and animals, through which commodities are produced and distributed. These networks include nodes of activity and flows of product; they are located in specific places, and also connect places together. The idea of chain suggests a linear process of commodity production, in contrast to network, which consists of multidirectional and circular relations.

Commodity fetishism (ch. 6) reduces goods and services to an abstract commodity defined by its monetary exchange value. In Marxist theory, commodity fetishism serves to hide the relational processes of production and consumption, including labor exploitation, environmental degradation, and **cultural appropriation**, and instead focuses attention on the price paid and the satisfaction obtained. It allows consumers to distance themselves from troublesome aspects of production.

Community (ch. 11) refers to a group of people having a common interest or cause. Although members of a community typically live in the same **place**, information technologies and social networks have permitted the creation of virtual communities of interests across space. As some have pointed out, several problematic assumptions apply to the idea of community, including the romantic notion that communities are inclusive, homogenous, and benevolent.

Concentrated animal feeding operation (CAFO) (ch. 3): A feeding operation that confines large numbers of animals in a small area. Exact definitions for size thresholds depend upon species. Animals are fed grain or forage that is imported into the system, rather than being fed on pasture.

Cosmopolitanism (ch. 8) is an ideology based on the belief that all humans belong to the same universe (cosmos). It reflects a positive attitude toward cultural difference and a desire to build global alliances. Cosmopolitanism is somewhat ambiguous because of the tension that exists between respecting local differences and advocating for global values. It has been criticized for embracing superficial, decontextualized, and **commodified** notions of **difference** that ignore power relations underlying cultural hierarchies.

Creative city (ch. 8) is a concept put forth by Richard Florida that emphasizes the role of creative industries and people, including artists, designers, researchers, and programmers, in shaping contemporary cities. It must be understood in the context of **postfordism** and **neoliberalism**, where it justifies a new approach to **urban governance** and planning in which state and local governments focus their energy and resources on branding the city and attracting private investors and the creative class that would contribute to that brand. These policies have been criticized for promoting **gentrification** and inflating the role of the creative class at the expense of other urban residents.

Creolization (ch. 12) typically refers to the mixture of indigenous, African, and European people in the context of colonization, particularly in the Caribbean region. More generally, however, it involves a process of cultural exchange that produces new cultures, underlying the fluidity and **hybridity** of identities and cultural practices. This concept has become especially relevant in a globalized economy where local cultures are continuously reshaped by global influences.

Critical nutrition (ch. 13): See **Nutrition**.

Critical perspective (ch. 1) in the social sciences usually implies generating knowledge that informs theoretical understandings of various forms of oppression and inequality. This includes questioning the numerous biases that shape the assumptions, objects and scales of inquiry, and methods of analysis. For many, a critical approach also involves participation in efforts to challenge and resist the deleterious effects of food on bodies, subjectivities, communities, economies, and environments, as exemplified in participatory research and activist scholarship to promote **food justice**. An important aspect of a critical approach is **reflexivity**.

Cuisine (ch. 2, 12) is characterized by a set of ingredients and dishes and a particular style and technique of food preparation. It is typically associated with specific geographies, cultures, or social classes. Examples include French cuisine, Southern cuisine in the United States, and haute cuisine.

Culinary capital (ch. 16) describes the possession of culinary knowledge that may confirm social status or economic benefits. LeBesco and Naccarato argue that, in a world where we are exposed to an expanding array of food and restaurants and rapidly changing food knowledge disseminated by **celebrity chefs**, **nutrition** experts, travel bloggers, and others through a variety of media, the acquisition of culinary capital has become a significant way to distinguish oneself. This idea is closely related to Bourdieu's concepts of **taste** and social capital.

Cultural appropriation (ch. 12) is the adoption of elements of a **culture**, including food, by others, typically for self-aggrandizing purposes such as social distinction or economic profit. This process is shaped by power geometries that usurp minoritized groups' ability to define their own culture and determine how it is to be used. Cultural appropriation subverts and homogenizes expressions of **difference**. For example, ethnic cuisine is often appropriated by chefs who "discover" and "improve" it, with great personal rewards.

Cultural economy (ch. 8, 16) is an economy based on entertainment, art, and other lifestyle amenities in which food figures prominently. It is associated with the aestheticization of consumption and the valorization of cultural commodities. **Postfordism**, **neoliberalism**, and **postmodernism** are related to the rise of the cultural economy, which also fuels **creative cities**.

Cultural imperialism (ch. 3) is the process by which the dominant culture is imposed upon others, devaluing and potentially destroying cultures deemed inferior. This was a common feature of colonialism under which indigenous and native cultures were portrayed as backward and forcibly replaced by Western ideas and practices. Many argue that **globalization** is a form of cultural imperialism to the extent that it homogenizes consumption around the world.

Cultural landscape (ch. 5, 8): See **Landscape**.

Culture (ch. 2) traditionally refers to the beliefs and behaviors that distinguish one group from another and are transmitted from one generation to the next through language, rituals, objects, arts, and institutions. There are important differences in the way scholars understand culture, however, with a strong distinction between those who view culture as a rigid set of inherited beliefs and values and those who conceptualize it more dynamically and experientially as a way of seeing and being in the world. While the former perspective often seeks to understand culture through its various **representations**, the latter tends to focus on **performances**.

Devolution (ch. 10) is a spatial and fiscal shift of responsibility and resources from higher levels of government to lower tiers, including local governments, community organizations, and families. It typically reflects a neoliberal ideology that believes in small government, states' rights, and individual responsibility, and seeks to dismantle the welfare state.

Difference (ch. 2, 8, 12) refers to socially produced categories such as **race**, **gender**, age, sexuality, religion, **class**, and others, which distinguish people and underlie the production of **identities**. Scholars who use the term *difference* tend to view identities as caused by a variety of intersecting processes of differentiation and avoid privileging one social category (such as class) over others.

Discipline (ch. 5, 14) is the practice of training people to follow rules and behave in socially acceptable or desirable ways. It typically relies on punishment to prevent disobedience and promote certain behaviors. As Michel Foucault argues, in contemporary society, such punishment does not need to involve physical force, but instead is a form of self-imposed control based on internalized social norms and fear generated by social **surveillance**.

Discourse (ch. 14) is the communication of ideas, meanings, and values in society. It refers to the story or narrative we tell about particular issues and reflects the social context in which it emerges. Discourse cannot be separated from the social relations of power, which give it credibility and visibility, including the media, politics, and science.

Domesticity (ch. 15) refers to life inside the **home**. Because the domestic sphere has typically been associated with feminine work and responsibilities, it is a highly gendered concept. Challenging norms of domesticity that equate femininity with taking care of the home has been an important aspect of **feminism**.

Embeddedness (ch. 2, 11, 12, 15) is a theoretical concept that describes how social phenomena are shaped by the context in which they take place, including social relations, political institutions, economic structure, and culture.

Embodiment (ch. 2) is the phenomenon of external social factors shaping and marking physical bodies. It can be a material process in which structural inequalities, like poverty, racism, and social exclusion, are internalized by bodies that experience disproportionate exposure to environmental hazard and limited access to amenities. It may also refer to a discursive process in which someone's class or race is linked to particular physical features or body types, as when obese bodies are associated with lower socioeconomic status.

Energy-balance model (ch. 9) explains obesity by an excess of calories absorbed in food consumption relative to calories burned in physical activity. While caloric imbalances are undoubtedly related to weight, the dominance of this theoretical model precludes researchers from investigating other causes of obesity, including environmental factors not related to caloric intake.

Entitlements (ch. 7), as formulated by Amartya Sen, refers to the set of alternative commodity bundles that a person can command in a society using the totality of rights and opportunities that he or she faces. Sen argued that famines are not caused by a lack of food, but by a lack of entitlements that limits people's ability to obtain food. Entitlements are influenced by one's position in society and the functioning of global, national, and local institutions. **Class**, **gender**, **race**, and other **differences** influence the availability and security of entitlements. Institutional factors, including property rights and the functioning of markets, also exercise a significant impact on entitlements.

Epigenetics (ch. 9) is a relatively new field that considers the interface of gene-environment interactions and focuses on changes in gene expression that occur without modifying the DNA sequence. Within that framework, researchers have begun studying the effects of various environmental factors and adverse conditions, including exposure to stress or certain chemicals, on gene expression or regulation. It has important applications in the study of **obesity**, where such processes have been linked to individual susceptibility to gain or lose weight.

Ethical consumerism (ch. 6) is a form of activism based on the notion that consumers can influence production through their consumption choices and spending behavior. It relies on the market economy and the belief that reducing the demand for (or boycotting) unethical products will force producers to adopt a morally superior approach to production in order to remain profitable. Similarly, increased demand for ethical products will provide financial incentives for producers of goods labeled as **fair trade**, **organic**, conflict-free, and/or **sustainable**.

Ethnic enclaves (ch. 12) are neighborhoods where members of a given ethnic group live and work. Many ethnic enclaves, such as Chinatowns, emerged as a result of discrimination and spatial exclusion. Yet, enclaves have been shown to enhance social networks, maintain cultural heritage, and provide economic opportunities to their residents.

Ethnicity (ch. 12) identifies people who share a common ancestry, language, and culture. It often overlaps with national origin, religion, and **race**. Like other categories of **difference**, ethnicity is often used in **othering** people.

Exoticism (ch. 12, 16) refers to the attractiveness and desirability associated with being different and coming from distant places. Instead of showing respect and understanding of foreign cultures, exoticism tends to value a superficial and biased view of exotic people, practices, and places, reflecting **commodification** and **othering**.

Extensive production system (ch. 3) is a farming system with lower productivity that requires few inputs other than pasture, grazing land, or other food sources, such as waste from human food systems.

Fair trade (ch. 6) is a mechanism in which products are fairly traded, meaning that a premium is paid by consumers to ensure that producers receive a fair price for their products, which presumably allows them to earn a living wage. It has become the dominant form of **ethical consumption**, particularly in the market for coffee, chocolate, and bananas.

Famine (ch. 7) is systemic and chronic **undernutrition** at the population scale. It is a catastrophic disruption of society in which the cumulative failure of political and economic systems of production, distribution, and consumption reduces **entitlements**, increases **vulnerability**, and weakens **resilience**.

Fatness (ch. 13) is a term that describes the condition of being fat or overweight. In contrast to the medical term of **obesity**, fatness also attends to the social experience and representation of fat bodies. For example, feminist scholars of fatness question the assumed relationship between fatness and ill health, and argue that the negative stigma associated with fat bodies is itself unhealthy and damaging.

Feminism (ch. 15) represents philosophies, ideologies, and social movements that center on understanding and promoting women's rights. It is often a poorly understood and vilified movement that can take many contradictory forms, as illustrated in its three distinct waves. While first-wave feminism focused on women's right to vote, second-wave feminism fought for reproductive rights and equality at home and in the workplace, and third-wave feminism turned its attention toward identity politics, challenging essentialist ideals of femininity and exploring the intersection of **gender**, sexuality, **race**, and other forms of **difference**. Feminist approaches to research are informed by these struggles as they seek to generate a new understanding of gender and inequality.

Fetishization (ch. 16) is about being irrationally devoted to something. This process involves stereotyping, objectifying, **exoticizing**, sexualizing, and generally **othering** people, places, or products. This distorted relation negates the ability of those being fetishized to represent themselves and their experiences in producing particular goods and services for the benefit of the fetishizer.

Food (ch. 1) includes all of the substances, mostly from plants or animals, which are ingested by an organism for nutritional purposes. It is necessary to sustain life and produce energy. What is considered food is socially constructed and varies over time and space.

Food advocacy (ch. 16) refers to a set of activities aimed at influencing what, where, and how we eat. Traditionally, food advocacy was done by community-based organizations and interest groups to draw attention to and gain support for the needs of those they represented or served, including the hungry and malnourished. Today, as discontentment with our industrial food system has grown, food advocacy has taken new forms and expanded its focus to a wider range of issues, including health, taste, social justice, and environmental sustainability. New actors, including **celebrity chefs** and **ethical consumers**, are now engaged in food advocacy, with the media playing a key role.

Food banks (ch. 10) are large food warehouses that collect, systematize, and deliver food to communities. They are the central node of networks connecting farmers, food producers, and retailers to a large number of local food organizations, such as pantries, homeless shelters, churches, and community centers.

Food culture (ch. 8, 16) refers to the practices, ideologies, and institutions surrounding the production, distribution, and consumption of food. Food cultures are time- and place-specific, and are an important aspect of **culture**.

Food desert (ch. 9) is a food environment where access to nutritious and affordable food is limited. It is typically identified by the absence of supermarkets within a short distance, coupled with a high proportion of low-income households. Food deserts are considered **obesogenic environments** because the lack of supermarkets leads residents to make poor food choices. Some have criticized the food desert concept for failing to take into account other sources of food, including smaller grocery stores, ethnic markets, and community gardens, and stigmatizing low-income communities of color.

Food environment (ch. 9) describes the material context in which people obtain food. It includes different types of retailers (food stores and restaurants), alternative food sources (e.g., farmers' markets, community gardens), and community resources (e.g., pantry). The **obesogenic environment** thesis posits that the food environment influences individual behavior and obesity.

Foodie (ch. 8, 15, 16) is a person who enjoys food in broad and diverse ways, such as gaining and sharing knowledge about food and dining, participating in food-related hobbies (e.g., gardening, shopping, traveling), preparing and consuming food, and/ or caring about food-related issues. Foodies are often criticized for being elitist and uncritically embracing consumerism.

Food justice (ch. 2, 11, 16) has become a popular term that is often used loosely and inconsistently. Generally, it implies that material resources and power are shared equitably so that people and communities can meet their food needs and lead secure food-based livelihoods with dignity, now and into the future. Food justice is more demanding than food access or **food security**; it also requires equal opportunity, freedom from oppression and exploitation, and environmental **sustainability**. It is related to ideas of **spatial justice**.

Food landscape/foodscape (ch. 2, 8, 12) draws attention to the places where people grow food, purchase food, prepare food, discuss food, or gather information about food. The idea of **landscape** emphasizes human relationships to the built and natural environments, including the way we shape, view, and represent them.

Food media (ch. 15, 16) is the wide range of outlets where food is discussed and represented, including television, cookbooks, printed news, magazines, and ever-expanding online sources, such as videos, blogs, and social media. The growth of food television and online food media has contributed to the rise of the **celebrity chef**, the **commodification** and **fetishization** of food, and the significance of food as a marker of **taste** and distinction.

Food politics (ch. 15) refers to the political regulation of food production, distribution, and consumption, and the debates surrounding those issues. It includes ideological and ethical negotiations regarding animal well-being, health, corporate power, agro-food technology, labor, environmental sustainability, genetically modified organisms, etc.

Food regime (ch. 2, 4, 7) is a concept that describes the social organization of food production and distribution. It has its theoretical roots in **political economy** and draws attention to the social, political, and economic arrangements that underlie the production and distribution of food on a world scale. In that framework, food regimes are understood as products of historical processes of capital accumulation and state regulation. Scholars focus on the relations of dependency that exist between the Global South and North since colonialism, and how they have evolved through the developmental era and the unfolding of **neoliberalism**.

Foodscape. See **Food landscape/foodscape**.

Food security/insecurity (ch. 2, 7, 10): At the local level, food security is defined as having physical access to affordable, nutritious, and culturally appropriate food. Globally, food security refers to the planet's ability to feed the world population.

Food sovereignty (ch. 2, 4, 7) is "the right of peoples to healthy and culturally appropriate food produced through ecologically sound and sustainable methods, and their right to define their own food and agriculture systems." This definition is outlined in the Declaration of Nyéléni (2007), which was signed in Mali by more than five hundred representatives of landless peasants, indigenous people, urban farmers, and fishing communities, mostly from the Global South. It is related to the idea of **food justice**, but emphasizes the right of people to make independent decisions, which it views as severely undermined by the global capitalist **food regime**.

Food system (ch. 2) includes all the activities, institutions, places, actors, and networks involved in the production and distribution of food. It can be conceptualized at various **scales**, from local to global food systems. It includes growing, harvesting, processing, packaging, transporting, marketing, storing, preparing, consuming, metabolizing, and disposing of food and food-related items. Numerous networks span the globe to connect the various and increasingly complex stages of food provision. Many have raised questions regarding the **sustainability** of our contemporary food system.

Foodways (ch. 2, 12) refers to the practices and ideologies related to human nourishment. It describes how particular groups grow, purchase, prepare, share, consume, and dispose of food. It is broader than diet (the kinds of food a person typically eats) and **cuisine** (the style or method of cooking food), because it includes what people eat, but also the way they obtain and prepare food, the utensils they use, their table manners, and the patterning of meals. Foodways have been a central theme in anthropological and archaeological research, where food has provided a window through which to study **culture**.

Gender (ch. 7, 15, 16) refers to traits that characterize and differentiate what it means to be a woman or a man. While sex is biologically defined, gender is socially constructed; it reflects social understandings of femininity and masculinity as expressed in gender roles and identities.

Genetically modified organisms (GMOs) (ch. 4) are the products of recombinant DNA techniques that use organisms, their parts, or their processes to modify or create new living organisms with particular traits. These genetically engineered organisms include plants whose genomes contain inserted DNA material from other plants or species. Common examples are Bt corn that express the bacterial toxin *Bacillus thuringiensis*, making it poisonous to certain insects, and Ht corn, which is herbicide-tolerant and ready to withstand applications of chemicals such as Monsanto's Roundup. Conventional plant breeding and farming practices also produce new gene characteristics in plants, but they do so by working at the level of the whole plant, using techniques such as seed selection, cross-pollination, and hybridization.

Gentrification (ch. 8, 11) refers to the influx of white and affluent residents and investors in previously neglected areas, usually in low-income urban neighborhoods where property is undervalued by the market. It results in a **class** remake of the urban **landscape**, as low-income and minority residents can no longer afford to live in the revitalized neighborhoods and are displaced. This displacement is a central tenet of the concept of gentrification.

Geographic determinism (ch. 9) is the belief that the physical environment shapes societies and determines their fate. Despite criticism that environmental determinism negates the role of human **agency** and the possibility of other explanations, such as historical political and economic relations, it became a central feature of behavioral geography, a field that emerged in the mid-twentieth century, built on the notion that human behaviors are determined by environmental stimuli.

Geographical imaginaries (ch. 2, 6) refer to unconscious or unreflective mental images we have of the world and specific places. It is similar to the idea of political-ecological imaginaries. These sorts of images may perpetuate biased views of people and places. When applied to distant places, it relates to the concept of **exoticism** and **fetishization**.

Global commodity chains (ch. 6) refers to the worldwide network structure that connects the different actors involved in producing, transporting, distributing, and selling a particular product. Identifying these chains is an important step in documenting the relationship between producers and consumers. The concept of **global value chain** is similar, but emphasizes the distribution of value-added across the various stages of production and distribution. Studies show that producers in the Global South typically receive a much smaller share of income than processors and retailers in the Global North, who are more capital-intensive and control the end product. **Fair trade** represents an effort to modify global supply chains in order to redistribute value to producers.

Globalization (ch. 1, 2, 3, 4, 5, 6, 12) describes the growing extent, depth, and speed of economic, political, and social connections between people and places around the world. While globalization began in the fifteenth century with colonialism, it has been reinvigorated and transformed by modern transportation and information technologies.

Governance (ch. 3) refers to the structure and mechanisms of making political decisions—or governing. It includes laws, political institutions, and social norms. It emphasizes the ways various actors participate in the decision-making process. The term is often used to describe the manner in which a city, company, or global production network manages itself.

Governmentality (ch. 6) is a concept that describes social regulation. It refers to the government's ability to coerce and manipulate people without actually imposing rules, but by promoting self-**discipline**. Governmentality emphasizes the power of knowledge and ideas in controlling people and creating moral categories that divide people between "good" and "bad" citizens.

Hidden hunger (ch. 7) is a chronic lack of micronutrients, which may not lead to starvation or easily observable physiological consequences (such as growth stunting), but nevertheless impacts overall health, well-being, and productivity. Hidden hunger is closely related to **malnutrition**.

Hollow advocacy (ch. 16) refers to advocacy that is limited to rhetorical claims and is not accompanied by actions and commitment to change.

Home (ch. 12, 15) is not only the physical space of a house, but also a site where everyday lived experiences, including cooking and eating, come together to create domestic life. In this sense, the home is not a private space isolated from the public sphere, but rather a **place** that is embedded in a set of social, political, economic, and cultural relations constructed at different geographic **scales**, ranging from the **body** to the global.

Hunger (ch. 7, 10) is the painful and uncomfortable condition caused by a lack of necessary nutrients. It has deleterious long-term effects on physiological and psychological health. Because hunger is such an emotional and **visceral** concept, many researchers prefer to use the term **food security**, which can be more easily quantified.

Hybridization (ch. 12) is a term borrowed from biology, where hybridization signifies the mixing of organisms of different species to generate a new breed. In cultural studies, hybridity characterizes cultures that embody various cultural influences and yet are unique. It is an important concept in postcolonial studies, which focus on how indigenous and colonial cultures interact. The concept of hybridity relates to **multiculturalism** as it embraces fluid and anti-essentialist notions of culture.

Identity (ch. 12, 15) refers to the ways in which we understand who we are. Much like some definitions of **space**, the concept of identity is **relational** because it is defined in relation to difference, to the Other, or to what we are not. In contemporary human geography, **gender**, **race**, or **ethnicity**-based identities (among several others) are understood to be socially constructed, rather than natural or biological. In addition, there is recognition that people simultaneously espouse several identities at once (e.g., we are classed, raced, gendered, and so on), and that the way in which we understand these identities is both historically and geographically contingent.

Identity politics (ch. 16) refers to debates about the ways in which different identities are formed, maintained, and contested, and about how such processes are connected to different forms of oppression and **resistance**. In human geography, particular attention is paid as to how identity politics are mediated by **place** and **space**.

Industrial farmwork (ch. 5) is a labor regime that responds to the needs of industrial agriculture. It is characterized by discipline as well as spatial and temporal flexibility, which are reinforced through hierarchies of race/ethnicity, class, gender, and/or legal status.

Intensive production system (ch. 3) is a highly productive farming system that requires high concentrations of animals in small spaces, with feed transported in and wastes transported out. These concentrations purportedly allow for economies of scale and other efficiencies in production, although they also create significant problems for the environment and for the animals.

Landscape (ch. 2, 5, 8) refers to the "shape of the land." For cultural geographers, landscapes hold clues about local cultures and social relations, which can be "read" through careful examination of the spatial arrangement of buildings, signs, and symbols. Geographer Don Mitchell argues that the imprint of humans on the land is shaped by economic imperatives and unequal relations of power, suggesting that landscapes are purposely created to maintain capital accumulation. As a result, landscapes are uneven, segmented, and exclusionary. The idea of **cultural landscape** brings together the material and the cultural, which are deeply intertwined.

Livelihood (ch. 4, 5, 7) refers to a person's means of securing the basic necessities of life. In many contemporary societies, it is about the ability to earn an income. However, livelihoods have traditionally involved various ways of procuring food, water, shelter, and clothing, typically by relying on local natural resources and social connections. Globalization and the spread of capitalism are often said to destroy traditional livelihoods.

Local food organizations (LFOs) (ch. 10) consist of the range of formalized, professionalized, and resource-rich nongovernmental organizations; informal, basic-needs, and resource-poor community-based organizations; and social movements focused on transforming **food systems**.

Localization (ch. 11) refers to practices designed to position people closer to their food sources (e.g., **urban agriculture** and farmers' markets). The emphasis on the local scale is seen as one way to create a more-transparent and accountable **food system**, with shorter distances between producers and consumers and shorter supply chains, fostering more-sustainable production.

Malnutrition (ch. 7, 10) is an umbrella term that describes poor **nutrition**. It may consist of **undernutrition** (inadequate consumption or absorption of nutrients) or **overnutrition** (excess consumption of nutrients). While both forms of malnutrition traditionally have been seen as mutually exclusive, recent research shows that undernutrition is often accompanied by overnutrition, providing an explanation for why people who suffer from **hunger** may also experience **obesity**.

Malthusian theory (ch. 7) is based on the ideas of Thomas Malthus (1766–1834), who argued that population tends to grow faster than food production. Malthusian theory calls on checks on population growth to avoid famine and other calamities, since it maintains that population increases at a geometric rate (e.g., 1, 2, 4, 8, 16, and so on), while food production increases at an arithmetic rate (e.g., 1, 2, 3, 4, 5, 6, and so on). The theory has been challenged by historical evidence and arguments regarding technological change and the capacity of humans to find new ways to meet the demands of a growing world population.

Multiculturalism (ch. 8, 11, 12) refers to a social state and a political philosophy. Multicultural societies are characterized by the mixing of multiple cultures, including various ethnicities associated with global migration. Multiculturalism also represents an ideology that values diversity and recognizes different **identities**. It has been criticized for ignoring the unique circumstances, struggles, and histories of diverse groups and privileging an apolitical and consensus-oriented vision of diversity.

National cuisine (ch. 12) describes a set of dishes, ingredients, and cooking techniques that symbolize a nation. It is influenced by climate, natural resources, culture, and history. Food scholars have pointed out that national cuisines are not fixed in time and place, but are socially constructed to produce a sense of **identity** and demarcate a particular **culture** for political and economic purposes.

Neoliberal capitalism (ch. 13) describes the contemporary economic system created by neoliberal policies and ideologies, highlighting the intimate ties between **capitalism** as an economic structure and **neoliberalism** as the political framework that supports it.

Neoliberalism (ch. 2, 4, 6, 8, 10, 11, 16) is a political system supporting the privatization, decentralization, **devolution**, and dismantling of state responsibilities and a concomitant shift of power to private actors. It is based on an ideology that favors free markets as a form of social organization and values individual responsibility. It is associated with a decline of the welfare state, liberalization of trade and finance, reduction of taxes and subsidies, deregulation of economic activity, and privatization of public services.

Networks of resistance (ch. 3, 4) suggest that activism against any given form of oppression (or resistance) relies on the circulation of ideas and the participation of political actors involved in similar or related fights elsewhere. Many successful social movements rely on transnational networks.

Nonprofits (ch. 6, 10) are nongovernmental organizations (NGOs) formed to pursue a common goal that is not primarily motivated by profit. It includes charities and philanthropic and faith-based organizations working in areas such as education, health, social services, the arts, and the environment. Because these organizations are neither businesses nor governments, they are often described as the third sector. Nonprofits have become increasingly important actors under **neoliberalism** and state **devolution**.

Nutrition (ch. 13) is the intake of food. The term *nutrition*, however, typically refers to an adequate and balanced intake of nutrients—what some would call "good nutrition." Mainstream nutrition rests on hegemonic scientific and cultural understandings of what healthy food means and tends to marginalize other food practices and knowledges. **Critical nutrition** seeks to reaffirm these different perspectives and challenge universal and decontextualized understandings of healthy food.

Obesity (ch. 9) is the condition of having "too much" body fat (or adipose tissue), as commonly identified by a body mass index (BMI) over 30. A person's BMI is obtained by dividing her weight in kilograms by her height in meters squared. A high BMI has been associated with health problems, including type 2 diabetes, cardiovascular disease, and certain types of cancer. This seemingly straightforward and objective measure of obesity ignores waist circumference and muscle mass, which may have a significant impact on health, and lends support to studies emphasizing individual characteristics associated with obesity. Yet, obesity and associated concerns of obesity epidemics have recently become part of a socially constructed discourse in which fatness is a symbol of social and moral inferiority, which reinforces social inequality.

Obesogenic environments (ch. 9) are environments that promote high energy intake and low energy expenditure. They are characterized by an essentially unlimited supply of convenient, relatively inexpensive, highly palatable, and energy-dense foods, coupled with a lack of opportunities for walking or engaging in physical exercise. The obesogenic environment thesis posits that these environmental characteristics have caused the rise in obesity observed among racial minorities and low-income people who are more likely to live in so-called **food deserts**. Some argue that this thesis is poorly supported by evidence, rests on flawed behavioral models of obesogenesis, and fails to acknowledge the social, political, and economic nature and dynamism of people–place interactions on health.

Organic food (ch. 4, 6, 11) is food grown according to methods that respect ecological balance and biodiversity. What that entails varies depending on the country and certification agency in charge of determining and labeling organic products. It usually implies no (or limited) use of chemical inputs (e.g., fertilizers, pesticides, synthetic additives, growth hormones, and antibiotics), minimal processing, and restrictions on genetically modified organisms.

Othering (ch. 2, 7, 12, 16) is the process by which individuals or groups are perceived or portrayed as being different. Doing so typically helps a dominant group establish its **identity** in opposition to the othered. This concept has been used in postcolonial, feminist, race, and sexuality studies to describe the ways women, nonwhites, indigenous, and queer people have been constructed as primitive, uncivilized, deviant, immoral, and Other. By attributing essential characteristics to entire groups, identities, or cultures, othering denies the Other his/her own voice in representing him or herself.

Overnutrition (ch. 7) refers to the excess consumption of nutrients, including foods with high caloric value and low nutritious quality, such as sugar. Although this problem has been prevalent in the Global North, where food is generally more abundant, it is becoming increasingly common around the world, where industrial and highly processed foods are replacing whole foods and traditional diets.

Performance (ch. 12, 15) in critical theory is the acting of social and cultural norms. It emphasizes the way **identities** and norms are expressed in behavior and practices. For instance, women may perform traditional gender norms when they take on most of the cooking in their household. Researchers' focus on performance marks a departure from studying culture through **representations**, such as objects, artifacts, and symbols.

Place (ch. 1, 2, 3, 4, 9, 12) is often described as "inhabited **space**"—a geographic area which is made meaningful by the people who inhabit it or interact with it. Over time, theoretical understandings of place have evolved from a bounded locale (such as a city or a neighborhood) to a more-fluid concept reflecting the social and emotional connections that constitute it.

Place-making (ch. 1, 12) is the process of inhabiting a space and giving it social and cultural meaning and emotional value. It can also be associated with branding and marketing a place for economic and political purposes.

Political ecology (ch. 6) is a field of study that approaches environmental issues from a political and economic perspective and emphasizes power in shaping society–nature relationships, including the uneven distribution of natural resources and exposure to environmental hazards.

Postfordism (ch. 8) describes a phase of **capitalism** that began in the late twentieth century. It distinguishes itself from the large-scale production and mass consumption of the Fordist era, as exemplified by Henry Ford's assembly lines and consumer campaigns. Instead, it consists of just-in-time, flexible, and small production units and increasingly specialized consumer markets, connected through a series of local and global networks. Postfordism also reflects a shift from manufacturing to service industries. Many associate postfordism with **neoliberalism**, the weakening of labor unions, and the rise of the **cultural economy**.

Postmodernism (ch. 8) refers to a set of ideas and methods that are skeptical of grand, totalizing theories and privileged vantage points for conducting research. Instead, postmodernism points to the decentering of the subject away from universal and rigid categories of **race**, **class**, **gender**, and sexuality in favor of individual experiences and lifestyles. It also can refer to both a style (of architecture or art) and even an entire epoch (the end of the twentieth century), which are characterized by some elements of advanced **capitalism**, including an emphasis on consumption and superficiality.

Problem closure (ch. 9) was identified by Maarten Hajer as occurring when a specific definition of a problem is used to frame subsequent study of the problem's causes and consequences in ways that preclude alternative conceptualizations of the problem and support socially acceptable solutions. It emphasizes the role of power relations in producing **discourse** and dominant storylines regarding the causes of problems and their solutions.

Race (ch. 5, 8, 9, 11, 12, 15, 16) is a way to distinguish people based on their skin color. However, many scholars argue that race is not a biological or natural construct, but instead a category created socially and historically in ways that seek to deny racialized groups dignity, rights, and power. Particular groups are said to be racialized when presumably unique racial traits are being ascribed to them, typically in contrast to unspoken and universalized white norms—a process described as **racialization**, and related to **othering**.

Reflexivity (ch. 13) is the process by which we acknowledge and question our assumptions and explore the power relations that shape what we do and know. It is an essential component of a critical perspective, which fosters openness to and engagement with other viewpoints.

Representation (ch. 2, 7, 12), in critical studies, refers to the way people, practices, and places are being described and portrayed both in scientific and popular accounts, including the media. By definition, representation implies simplification and value judgment, since only part of reality can be shown or conveyed. This issue is particularly important when self-representation is denied and outsiders, including researchers, determine what traits to emphasize.

Resguardos (ch. 4) are indigenous territories based on communal landholdings in Colombia. Under the Colombian Constitution of 1991, indigenous peoples were given the right to manage the political and administrative affairs of their territories. There are currently 710 legally recognized *resguardos* located in 27 departments and 228 municipalities in the country. Similar systems of communal land ownership exist in other Latin American countries, including *ejidos* in Mexico. Communal land ownership is typically an outcome of postcolonial land reforms aimed at redistributing land to peasants.

Resilience (ch. 7) refers to the ability of a system, which could be a country, region, city, social group, household, or individual, to withstand stress. Although the concept was initially used in the context of natural disasters, it is increasingly used to describe adaptation to situations caused by systematic inequalities and political-economic decisions. Some warn that using resilience in those man-made contexts might encourage resignation and subservience, favoring individual and community adaptation over structural change.

Resistance (ch. 2, 3, 4, 14, 15) consists of ordinary and everyday acts of rejection or opposition. Unlike mass mobilization and protests, which are highly visible, resistance tends to be less organized and less defiant. It includes the small, subtle, and often hidden ways in which individuals and groups reject their circumstances, resist various forms of oppression, and exert **agency**.

Scale (ch. 2, 11, 12) refers to the spatial extent or reach of a process or phenomenon, and can range from the global to the microscopic. Cultural geographers argue that scales are social and discursive constructs devised to make sense of the world and warn against the tendency to privilege any particular scale, insisting that most social phenomena are multi-scalar.

School food reform (ch. 14): As early as the late nineteenth century, various groups in the United States have attempted to influence and transform school lunches for social goals, targeting children's bodies as a site of intervention and control. Some of the most significant reforms include the New Nutritionist movement of the Progressive Era, the National School Lunch Program first implemented in 1946, and various subsequent efforts to adapt it, including the 2010 Healthy Hunger-Free Kids Act promoted by First Lady Michelle Obama.

Social reproduction (ch. 5, 15) includes the daily activities and spaces outside of work that are nevertheless essential to the functioning of the economy, as well as to life and well-being. Social reproduction is highly gendered, since it consists of domestic activities that have typically been assigned to women, including cooking, cleaning, and taking care of children, the elderly, and the sick. Despite the importance of social reproduction, it is often ignored because it typically occurs outside of the formal labor market and the monetized economy (except in the case of paid care and domestic workers).

Space (ch. 2) is one of the fundamental concepts in geography and is often understood in three different ways. *Absolute space* is empirical, geometric, and measurable space, often associated with geography as spatial science (e.g., space as physical distance, or space as a container of objects or things). *Relative space* points to processes, and it is seen as the result of relations between two or more entities or objects (e.g., the property of distance only emerges if there are two objects that help to define it). *Relational space* also points to processes, but it is seen as the product of networks of social relations and objects that are often shifting (e.g., spaces emerge out of the interactions of both human and nonhuman objects, and they are not fixed or measurable but rather dynamic).

Spatial justice (ch. 2, 11) draws attention to the spatial aspects of social justice. To the extent that space is socially organized in ways that reflect and reproduce social inequality, justice requires the reorganization or reclaiming of space. In particular, spatial justice calls for an equitable distribution of resources and opportunities across space.

Structural adjustment programs (ch. 5, 6, 7) are a set of policies designed to restructure an economy. These sorts of programs are typically imposed by international organizations, such as the World Bank and the International Monetary Fund, in the context of lending to heavily indebted countries. As a condition for loans or debt restructuring, the borrowing countries must embark on a series of **neoliberal** reforms to liberalize trade, stimulate exports, reduce government spending and subsidies, privatize national assets, and deregulate the economy to attract investors.

Structural violence (ch. 7), as conceptualized by Paul Farmer, is a form of violence or slow death imposed on the powerless by structural inequalities and uneven development. This includes hunger and preventable diseases, which primarily affect the poor. Culpability for this type of violence cannot easily be attributed to specific individuals or corporations because they result from systemic forces, such as gender inequality, racism, and poverty.

Surveillance (ch. 5, 8, 14), as conceptualized by French philosopher Michel Foucault, refers to different forms of institutionalized monitoring of events and actions, both through technology and other means, that lead to a disciplining of the self and of society in general (e.g., the modern "disciplinary society").

Sustainability (ch. 6, 11, 16) is typically defined as the ability to meet the needs of the present without compromising the ability of future generations to meet their own needs. It implies the conservation of finite natural resources and the maintenance of ecological systems. Sustainability is said to have environmental, economic, and social components, because creating the conditions under which nature and humans can exist in productive harmony also requires the social and political will and resources to do so.

Taste (ch. 6, 8, 12, 13, 15, 16) in relation to food has both physical (e.g., sweet, sour, salty) and social meanings—the latest often derived from culturally constructed preferences for particular ingredients and dishes. According to Pierre Bourdieu, class and identity distinctions among social groups are made out of their different tastes for food and other commodities.

Undernutrition (ch. 7) refers to inadequate ingestion or absorption of nutrients over at least one year. It may be caused by lack of food, diseases that prevent the absorption of food (e.g., diarrhea), or anorexia.

Urban agriculture (ch. 11) refers to the production, processing, and marketing of food in urban and peri-urban areas; it is one of the most widespread alternative food practices that attempt to reconnect people to their food sources at the local scale. It is also an umbrella term that covers a variety of activities, including growing food in many different settings, from homes to institutional settings (like schools and hospitals) to small-scale farms.

Urban governance (ch. 8, 10, 11) describes the ways cities and everyday urban life are governed by a variety of actors. Many argue that cities are increasingly shaped and managed by multisector collaborations among public, private, and nongovernmental institutions. This shift reflects a devolution of state responsibilities to private agencies, including for-profit and nonprofit organizations, and communities. Scholars have suggested that this shift has impacted urban citizenship to the extent that it underlies social and spatial exclusion.

Visceral (ch. 2, 13) relates to a gut response (of the viscera), suggesting an instinctive and deep feeling. This idea has been particularly useful in conceptualizing how food and eating connects our bodies to space. It draws attention to the interactions between the emotional and the biological in understanding how external factors and conditions become **embodied** or inscribed into the **body**.

Vulnerability (ch. 7) is linked to a lack of **entitlements**, which limits an individual or group's capacity to mitigate or manage potential social or environmental stresses and weakens their **resilience** to recover from or cope with negative events. For example, certain groups or regions are more vulnerable to famine due to factors such as conflict, corruption, social exclusion, and climate change, which underscore their lack of resources and rights.

Index

anthropometrics, 109, 110. *See also* BMI

antismoking campaigns, 256. *See also* public health

anxieties: environmental 299; food 8, 265, 279, 292; social 272, 294

AOC/AOP, 4

Appadurai, Arjun, 8, 20, 215, 230

appropriation: culinary, 10, 211, 213, 220–23; cultural, 129, 211, 213, 220–23, 227–28, 231, 311, 312; of traditional knowledge, 55. *See also* colonialism; imperialism

aquaculture, 190, 301

Argentina, 15, 52, 56–58, 59, 63, 134–35, 190. *See also* cuisine; Buenos Aires; Mendoza

Arizona, 41, 43

art, 16, 20, 129, 131–32, 138, 140, 157, 199, 221, 293, 295, 299. *See also* aesthetic

artisan, 201, 222, 281, 293, 295, 302. *See also* craft

artisanal food, 55, 119, 133, 136. *See also* craft

Asia: food crops/exports from, 18, 91; hunger in, 112–13, 124, 166, 177–80. *See also* Cambodia; East Asia; India; Japan; Korea; Malaysia; Pakistan; Philippines; South Asia; Southeast Asia; Thailand; Vietnam

Asian cuisine. *See* cuisine

Asian diet, 37, 50. *See also* cuisine

assemblage, 22

assimilation, 212, 214, 219, 220, 222, 224, 229, 268. *See also* acculturation; Americanization

atmosphere, 130, 139, 201

Aunt Jemima, 282–283, 302

Austin, Texas, 132, 134

Australia, 39, 98, 216, 220

authenticity, 132–33, 136, 137, 139, 141, 212, 215, 219–23, 227, 228, 280, 292, 301–3

avocados, 12, 145–46, 220

baby food, 280

bacalhau. *See* cod

bagel, 213, 259

bakery, 6

bananas, 89, 258

barbecue/BBQ: Korean 134, 219, 220, 225, 228; Texan 302

Barber, Dan, 300–301, 303

Barcelona, Spain, 138

bar, 134, 140

Barthes, Roland, 16

Batali, Mario, 294

basil, 86, 214

Bayless, Rick, 221

beans, 56–58, 67, 225, 259. *See also* soy

beef: dishes, 12, 37, 50–51, 131, 134, 165, 211, 220, 226, 234–35, 258, 261, 291; livestock, 35–44, 46, 56; price 263. *See also* dairy; livestock

beekeeping, 190

beer, 12, 139

beets, 136

behavior: eating, 10, 16, 46, 93, 139, 148, 155, 214, 254–56, 259; health, 24, 148, 151, 154–55, 157, 237–39, 256, 266, 296–98. *See also* food practices

behavioral science, 155, 160, 237

Belize, 214–15

belonging, 6, 10, 15, 22, 70, 78, 82–84, 212, 216, 230, 254, 264, 271–72. *See also* place; inclusion

Bengali, 216

Berlin, Germany, 132, 140

berries, 70, 73, 79, 252, 299. *See also* strawberries

beverages, 108, 201. *See also* soda; milk; rum

biases: class-related, 139, 300; in policy, 99, 101, 246, 254–55; race-related, 221, 254–55; in research, 8, 246, 221, 254, 255; weight-related, 156. *See also* reflexivity; discrimination

biodiversity, 36, 55, 115, 124, 299, 322

biology, 81, 244

biomass, 35

biopiracy, 55

biopolitics, 10, 253–66. *See also* biopower; biosocial; body

biopower, 255–57, 266

biosocial, 244–46

biotechnology, 16, 52–64. *See also* GMO

biphenyls, 158

bisphenol-A (BPA), 158, 239

About the Contributors

Fernando J. Bosco is a professor of geography and a graduate advisor for the doctoral program in geography at San Diego State University. He received his PhD in geography from Ohio State University. He works in the areas of urban, political, and social geography. His research interests include the geographic dimensions of social movements and collective action, social and political geographies of children and families, geographies of food in urban contexts, emotional geographies, geographic thought and theory, and qualitative research methods.

Alida Cantor is an assistant professor of geography at Portland State University. Her research interests include water law and policy, political ecology, and environmental justice and sustainability of food, water, and energy systems.

Sarah E. Dempsey is an associate professor in the department of communication at the University of North Carolina, Chapel Hill. Her research has appeared in *Communication and Critical/Cultural Studies*, *Communication Monographs*, *Management Communication Quarterly*, and *Organization*. She is currently at work on a book project on the politics of US food service labor.

Jody Emel is a professor of geography at Clark University in Worcester, Massachusetts. Her research focuses on animal geographies, particularly those within the global production networks of industrial livestock. Other scholarly interests include Native Americans and natural resources, and the intersection of social, environmental, and animal justice.

Hannah Evans is a lecturer in women's studies at San Diego State University, where she teaches a course on gender, science, and technology. She holds a master's degree in geography from SDSU. Her thesis was entitled *Sustainable Sugar? Commodity Chains, Ethical Consumption, and the Violent Geographies of Sugar Production in Nicaragua*.

Daniel Ervin is a PhD candidate in the geography department at the University of California, Santa Barbara. He received a BA in psychology from George Washington

University, after which he worked in the nonprofit and public health sector for a number of years before returning to school to earn his MA in geography from the University of Wyoming. He is currently a graduate associate of the Broom Center for Demography. He conducts research on the relationship between agriculture, the environment, and demographic processes, the effects of migration on diet and diet-related health, the Nutrition Transition, and the Latino Mortality Paradox. He is also interested in the application of stable isotope ratio analysis as a tool for public health and social science research.

Elizabeth Fitting is an anthropologist who researches rural livelihoods, migration, and seed politics in Latin America. She is an associate professor in the department of sociology and social anthropology at Dalhousie University in Halifax, Canada.

Kristina E. Gibson is an author, photographer, and the owner of Magpie Bookshop in Catskill, New York. She is the author of *Street Kids: Homeless Youth, Outreach and Policing New York's Streets* (NYU Press, 2011).

Julie Guthman is a professor in the community studies department at the University of California, Santa Cruz. She is the author of *Agrarian Dreams: The Paradox of Organic Farming in California* (2004), *Weighing In: Obesity, Food Justice, and the Limits of Capitalism* (2011), and numerous articles.

Allison Hayes-Conroy is an assistant professor of geography and urban studies at Temple University. She has published widely on the food-body relationship and the role of bodies in food and community activism. She is co-editor of *Doing Nutrition Differently: Critical Approaches to Diet and Dietary Intervention*. Allison was awarded a National Science Foundation (NSF) CAREER grant for her project in Colombia, examining the role of bodies, sensation, and body movement in youth-based creative activity and community engagement. That project also engages students in course-based research on similar themes in Philadelphia, Pennsylvania, and complements another course-based project on critical nutrition. Allison's work on the body as a bridge between social and life sciences in STEM higher education has also been funded by the NSF.

Jessica Hayes-Conroy is an assistant professor of women's studies at Hobart and William Smith Colleges in Geneva, New York, where she teaches classes on health politics, food and environmental justice, and corporeal feminism. She holds a dual PhD in geography and women's studies from Penn State University. Jessica is the author of *Savoring Alternative Food: School Gardens, Healthy Eating, and Visceral Difference*, and co-editor of *Doing Nutrition Differently: Critical Approaches to Diet and Dietary Intervention*. She has also researched and published work on the Fukushima nuclear disaster from a feminist political-ecology perspective. Jessica currently studies, writes about, and advocates for critical and community-based approaches to nutrition intervention.

Pascale Joassart-Marcelli is a professor of geography and director of the urban studies program at San Diego State University, where she teaches Geography of Food, Food Justice, and Geography of Cities, among other courses. She earned a PhD in political economy and public policy from the University of Southern California. Her research focuses on the relationships between food, ethnicity, and place. She is interested in the role of food in structuring everyday life in immigrant and low-income urban neighborhoods, and has received funding from the National Science Foundation (NSF) to pursue research on this topic (with Fernando J. Bosco).

David López-Carr is a professor of geography at the University of California, Santa Barbara; director of the Human-Environment Dynamics Lab (HED); and head of the population, health, and environment research group for the Broom Center for Demography. His research focuses on links among population, health, rural development, agriculture, and marine and forest resource use and conservation through ongoing projects in Latin America, Africa, and Asia. He has authored more than 130 scientific publications, and along with colleagues and students has secured several millions of dollars in funding from more than fifty fellowships, grants, and awards from NASA, NSF, NIH, the Mellon and Fulbright Foundations, and numerous other sources.

Enrico Marcelli is an associate professor of sociology at San Diego State University. He is a demographer with a PhD in political economy and public policy (USC) and postdoctoral training in substance abuse (UCLA) and social epidemiology (Harvard). He currently teaches courses in quantitative research methods, immigration, and population health. His research focuses on estimating the number, effects, and integration of legal and undocumented immigrants in the United States, and on questions regarding the social and geographic sources of health.

Lise Nelson is an associate professor of women's, gender, and sexuality studies and geography at Pennsylvania State University. Her research examines labor, identity, and citizenship in the context of neoliberal globalization. Of particular interest is how globalization impacts, and is contested by, less-powerful groups whose experiences and opportunities are shaped by gender, race, class, and/or illegality (real or perceived legal status). Her recent work examines rural gentrification, immigrant labor regimes, and geographies of social reproduction. She is committed to fine-grained, historically situated qualitative analysis that strategically links processes of everyday life and "local" change with global transformations and power dynamics.

Harvey Neo is an associate professor in the department of geography at National University of Singapore. His research interests include animal geographies, ethical consumption, and the politics of nature and society.

Blaire O'Neal is a PhD student in the joint doctoral program in geography at San Diego State University and the University of California, Santa Barbara. Her dissertation research focuses on urban agriculture in Southern California, and investigates the role of process-based, technological innovation in achieving food justice.

Zia Salim is an assistant professor in the department of geography at California State University, Fullerton. His research examines topics in urban and social geography, with particular interest in transnational migration and cultural landscapes in Southern California and the Middle East. Some of his publications have appeared in *Urban Geography*, *Urban Studies*, *City*, *The Yearbook of the Association of Pacific Coast Geographers*, and *The California Geographer*.

Cascade Tuholske is a PhD student in the department of geography at the University of California, Santa Barbara. Funded through the US Borlaug Fellows in Global Food Security program, his dissertation focuses on understanding urban food security and nutritional challenges within sub-Saharan cities. He received a master's degree in geography from UCSB in 2016, and a bachelor's degree from George Washington University's Elliott School of International Affairs in 2010.

Vienne Vu received her master's degree in geography at California State University, Fullerton, where she researched the changing foodways of Vietnamese refugees and immigrants in Orange County, California. She is a second-generation Vietnamese American, and has spent most of her life in Southern California.

Daniel N. Warshawsky is an assistant professor in the department of urban affairs and geography at Wright State University, where he teaches courses in geography and conducts his research on urban food systems. Daniel earned his BA from the University of Illinois at Urbana-Champaign (2003), his MS from the University of Wisconsin at Madison (2006), and his PhD from the University of Southern California (2011). In his research, Daniel utilizes multiple methods to analyze urban food systems in North America and Africa. The results of these studies have been published in several academic outlets, including *The Professional Geographer*, *Urban Geography*, *Geoforum*, *Social and Cultural Geography*, among others. In addition to his academic work, Daniel has worked or volunteered at urban food banks and other local food organizations in the United States and South Africa.